THE WORLD-FAMOUS
ALASKA HIGHWAY

THE WORLD-FAMOUS ALASKA HIGHWAY

A GUIDE TO THE ALCAN
& OTHER WILDERNESS ROADS OF THE NORTH

4th Edition
TRICIA BROWN

FULCRUM
GOLDEN, COLORADO

For Mom, who drove Walsh's Wandering Wagon and fostered our love for camping

Library of Congress Cataloging-in-Publication Data

Brown, Tricia.
  The world-famous Alaska Highway : a guide to the Alcan & other wilderness roads of the North / Tricia Brown. -- 4th ed.
     p. cm.
  Includes bibliographical references and index.
  ISBN 978-1-55591-749-4 (pbk.)
  1. Alaska Highway--Guidebooks. 2. Automobile travel--Northwest, Canadian--Guidebooks. 3. Automobile travel--Alaska--Guidebooks. 4. Wilderness areas--Northwest, Canadian--Guidebooks. 5. Wilderness areas--Alaska--Guidebooks. 6. Northwest, Canadian--Guidebooks. 7. Alaska--Guidebooks. I. Title.
  F1060.92.B79 2011
  917.9804'52--dc22

                          2010040140

Printed in China
0 9 8 7 6 5 4 3 2 1

Design by Jack Lenzo
Cartography by Gray Mouse Graphics
Cover images: Sign courtesy of Will Elmore | Wikimedia Commons; Army trucks courtesy of Library of Congress, (LC-USW33-000949-2C); Train, bear, landscape, and bear sign © Tricia Brown

"Breaking Trail on the Military Highway" excerpted with author's permission from Chester L. Russell, author and publisher of *Tales of a Catskinner: A Personal Account of Building the Alcan Highway, The Winter Trail, and Canol Pipeline Road in 1942–43*.

"One Woman, Eight Tons of Trailer, and a Crude Highway" excerpted with publisher's permission from *The Road North: One Woman's Adventure Driving the Alaska Highway, 1947–1948*, by Iris Woolcock, edited by Edward Bovy, Greatland Graphics, 1990.

"Jack McQuesten's Sourdough Thermometer," © 2003 by Cecil Munsey, PhD, excerpted with author's permission from "Yukon Jack, Part I," *Bottles and Extras*, Summer 2004.

Fulcrum Publishing
4690 Table Mountain Drive, Suite 100
Golden, Colorado 80403
800-992-2908 • 303-277-1623
www.fulcrumbooks.com

CONTENTS

ACKNOWLEDGMENTS

As always, thank you to my husband, Perry, who trails up and down the Alaska Highway with me when he could be fishing. Thanks also to the folks at Fulcrum Publishing for agreeing that travelers need a book like this one, a personal voice with uncomplicated travel directions and friendly advice. I'm thankful to my editor, Carolyn Sobczak, for her discerning eye and editorial instincts, and to designer Jack Lenzo for creating such a beautiful package.

I really appreciate those who gave permission to retell their stories or share their photos: Chester Russell, Ed Bovy for Iris Woolcock, Liz Twan, Dr. Cecil Munsey, and the Anchorage Museum at Rasmuson Center archives.

For so many motorists, this trip is a once-in-a-lifetime experience, and it's been a pleasure to meet fellow travelers and the individuals in the travel industry who serve us. Thank you, one and all.

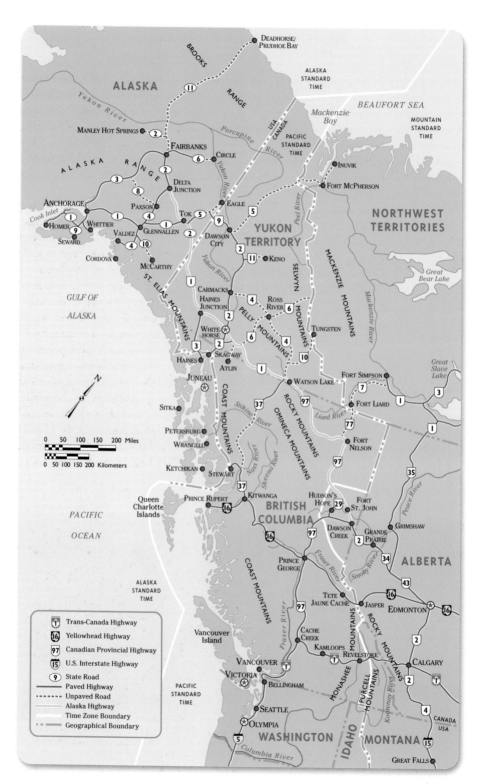

NORTH TO ALASKA

After decades of lobbying for statehood, the Territory of Alaska finally entered the Union in 1959, the same year that Johnny Horton cut his classic tune "North to Alaska." And as wonderfully corny as the song is, it continues to stir the hearts of people who live in the Last Frontier—and those who've always yearned to see it. So what if the song is about the Nome gold rush of 1901? The very title is an invitation. Come north. Take in the beauty of untrammeled places, watch cat-sized ravens play in the updrafts, pull a dime-bright salmon from a wild river, and marvel at a sun that doesn't rest. These are things you've only seen in videos. Time to see it for yourself.

Driving to and around Alaska is by far the best way to experience the 49th state, and the adventure begins for most at Mile 0 of the Alaska Highway, at Dawson Creek, British Columbia. Even 70 years after its construction, this remains the primary route into mainland Alaska, where you'll explore a state highway system that, measured to scale against this landscape, is nothing more than a dozen pieces of thread thrown against a fabulous, multicolored king-sized quilt. Our earth is old, but this place still feels so new.

North America's famous wilderness road was coined "the Alcan" during its construction through Canada and Alaska's backcountry. It began as a hastily built World War II supply line linking the continental United States to its far-off territory, where strategic military posts were poised to fend off enemy aggression. By 1948, however, when the road opened to the public, the civilian world learned what the military already knew: the thing was a beast, known for its twists, miry

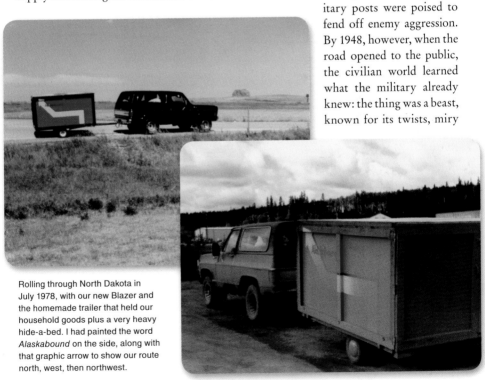

Rolling through North Dakota in July 1978, with our new Blazer and the homemade trailer that held our household goods plus a very heavy hide-a-bed. I had painted the word *Alaskabound* on the side, along with that graphic arrow to show our route north, west, then northwest.

Our shiny new rig and trailer took a beating on the unpaved road in 1978. By Fort Nelson, we had already replaced several tiny tires, plus the trailer's axle and tongue.

stretches, and burdensome length, and yet the road wound through extraordinary scenery that dared you to take your eyes off the road. It was a love-hate relationship.

The first civilians to tackle the road were true road warriors, driving tanklike vehicles that were burdened with extra tires, gas tanks, provisions, and lots of emergency gear. Many drivers today prepare for the Alaska Highway in much the same way. The good news is, you don't have to anymore.

After decades of improvements, the route has matured into a destination unto itself, and those who travel its length never forget the journey. Now approaching its 70s, the Alaska Highway has been surveyed, straightened, graded, rerouted, paved, and populated in places, and yet it's still something of a wild thing. Adventure seekers are just as drawn to this route that winds through some of the most uncivilized parts of the continent. For some, it's not the getting to Alaska that matters anymore—although Alaska is a lifetime dream for many—it's having traveled the road. That's why the souvenirs sell so well—just driving the highway places you in the "I did it!" club.

My first trip up the Alaska Highway was in 1978, when most of the Alcan was still unpaved and crooked beyond description, and my father's letters beckoned, "Come on up! There's money lying all over the place!" His letters arrived during the years when the Trans-Alaska Pipeline was under construction and money, indeed, was flowing just as the oil would. I remember a cousin calling from a pipeline construction camp in 1976, his voice echoing in the satellite connection. He told me he was making $1,200 a week picking up garbage. My hourly wage that year was under $2.50. So in July 1978, my young family of four moved from northern Illinois to Fairbanks to join nearly a dozen other family members who had already migrated up, one after another, like caribou crossing a stream. Some had arrived in time for the construction boom. We arrived on its heels, one year to the month after the pipeline first flowed oil. The last in my family to leave Illinois, I was a 23-year-old secretary with a husband and two preschool daughters.

My then husband and I had gone deep into debt that year and bought a new 1978 Chevy Blazer. He made modifications for our trip, removing the backseats and building a plywood platform. Our two little ones just rode back there on the foam bed (that's right, a DWI—driving while ignorant—we had no seat belts or safety concerns whatsoever). Beneath the platform bed was a storage compartment for our luggage and camp kitchen. On our 4,000-mile trek up the highway, we camped most nights. First order of business was to duct tape mosquito netting to the open windows, and then three of us crawled up on the platform bed, while the four-year-old had a cozy little nest on the floor. In tow was a supremely heavy homemade trailer that held our worldly goods. The tires regularly exploded into thin air, twelve times, in fact. And the trailer also suffered a broken tongue and, in a separate, equally inconvenient place, a broken axle.

The road we encountered then seemed to hate us and bucked like a wild mustang. The surface was either fine dust, squishy mud, or never-ending miles of gravel that made a deafening roar. As we neared a city and crossed onto pavement, the first moments of gravel-free silence were always startling. And oh, the road did wind and rise and fall, yet it had already seen vast improvements since wartime days, when it was hurriedly built around or over every obstacle. Back then, a young army sergeant named Troy Hise scrawled a few lines about the Alcan that have since appeared on countless T-shirts, postcards, and place mats, many times giving credit only to "Anonymous":

Winding in and winding out
Leaves my mind in serious doubt
As to whether the lout who built this route
Was going to hell or coming out.

Now a senior citizen, Hise and his wife can still be found traveling the highway, marketing products that bear his memorable poem.

Going to hell or coming out? Looking back to 1978, I remember asking myself the same question. The answer was several years in coming. Alaska was neither heaven nor hell, but was a rare and beautiful combination, a memorable place to spend the next 21 years.

During my time in Alaska, I drove every highway on its limited state road system. I've picnicked above the Arctic Circle, trundled down the sole road into Denali National Park, and often retraced the pioneering route of the Valdez–Fairbanks Trail, now the Richardson Highway. In one 10-year span, I put nearly 200,000 miles on my vehicle—all of them Alaska miles. But I never drove the Alaska Highway again. Over the years, friends and relatives made the trip without incident, arriving with glowing reports of moose and bear sightings, serene lakeside campgrounds, and awesome scenery. "The road's great!" they proclaimed. "It's almost completely paved now. You wouldn't recognize it." But I had vowed long ago, when I came off that first trip, "I'll never drive that road again!" That's why I laughed when Fulcrum Publishing asked me to write this book, and found I had to break my self-righteous promise. It was time to get back on the road and see it firsthand once more.

Maybe it's the same urge for you—to see it for yourself. Then it's time to get to it. We drive the highway from the Pacific Northwest every couple of years now. We own a fifth-wheel trailer but prefer to leave it at home and travel in a one-way RV rental, driving up and flying back or flying up and driving back. Each time, we've enlarged our experiences and watched the road further evolve into the remarkably safe and comfortable route that it is today.

In this book, I'll introduce you to roadside history, geography, Native cultures, and recreational opportunities in Alberta, British Columbia, the Yukon, and Alaska, covering miles well beyond the Alaska Highway itself. I've included details about attractions, restaurants, hotels, and campgrounds. You'll also meet some of the people who make the Northland so memorable. I hope this guide enhances your travels. We've had a great time, and I know you will, too.

Remember this, though: the Alcan, with all of its history, romance, and wonder, is not just about driving. It's a gateway to places you've only seen in pictures: the stomping grounds of the gold rush stampeders and pioneers. Land that's steeped in centuries of Native culture. Crystalline streams, jade-colored lakes, wild animals, snowy mountain peaks, and dark green forests. You'll meet new friends who are on the same journey and those who live along the way. Back at home, the images will linger in your mind and you'll wrestle to find descriptors better than *beautiful, incredible, big,* and *amazing.* You'll tell others that until they've experienced the Alaska Highway themselves, words seem inadequate. And you'll know as I do that before long, you'll be talking about the next trip.

You can't take it all, this exhibit at the Williams Lake Tourism Discovery Centre in BC reminds us. Packing efficiently is an art.

CHAPTER 1

PLANNING AND PACKING

Nearly every trip begins with the words, "How do I pack?" but the question becomes all the more important when you're driving into the unknown. That's why I'm here to help. For clothing, a little bit of everything is the best rule—you'll be passing through several microclimates, from the heat of the badlands to the cooler Rockies to the ever-changeable temperatures of Alaska's Interior, where people joke that the four seasons are "almost winter, winter, still winter, and construction season." Actually, early summer in Fairbanks is sweet and warm—routinely in the 80s—while nearly 400 miles south, in Anchorage, the coastal influence creates a cooler and often more rainy summertime.

Any experienced traveler knows the importance of researching a place before embarking on a trip. This chapter outlines in detail how to get ready for weeks on the road.

Some travelers arrive on the road with a trim, preplanned itinerary; others like to play it by ear, jumping from town to town and relying on word of mouth for where to go and what to see.

Your Travel Timeline

Time is the issue that separates the two types of highway travelers: those who just want to get to a place, and those who know that the journey can be as enjoyable as the destination. Canada's really a nice place. Slow down and look at it.

The first and best rule of thumb is to take your time. This is not a race. Stop for ice cream. Read the historical signs. Try not to think about making good time. Most of all, be mindful that posted speed limits are not suggestions, but law.

The laws of physics aren't flexible either. Some Alaskans (mostly male, for some reason) claim special bragging rights to having made their personal best time in covering the Alaska Highway. "Why, we went from Seattle to Fairbanks in 72 hours. 'Course, we never stopped. We traded off on driving." This is no great achievement, but rather an exercise in recklessness, not only for themselves and their passengers, but also for others on the road. The Alaska Highway as yet is no superhighway.

What to Pack

The old joke you've probably heard in your own hometown is true here as well: if you don't like this weather, just wait a few minutes. That's particularly true in the Northland during the summer months. So be ready with a little of everything, and if it turns chilly, put it all on!

The length of the Alaska Highway crosses several climate zones through Canada, with microclimates within them. In Alaska, it's no different. It can be 55°F at Mt. McKinley while it's 80°F in Fairbanks, just two hours away.

Beauty salons or barbershops are easy to find in most towns. Make an appointment, or walk in. Usually it's not a problem. Pharmacies likewise are not difficult to find.

The benefits of the midnight sun are many, including the growth of unnaturally large cabbages and squash and excessive energy in human beings. But for those who have trouble getting to sleep in the daylight, bring along a sleep mask.

Following is a packing checklist to help you get started. You decide how many of each item to bring, remembering that there will be no shortage of self-service laundries, so less is better.

Clothing

Several T-shirts

Short-sleeved shirts

Long-sleeved shirts

Pants for chilly weather

Hooded sweatshirt or sweater

Windbreaker

Raincoat

Swimsuit

Knit hat or baseball cap

Jacket with zip-in lining for extra warmth

Comfortable walking shoes (soft soles for
    grip in slippery places)

Lightweight pants or shorts

Dress clothes (one set, just in case)

Dress shoes

Socks and stockings

Slippers

Lightweight gloves

Other Items

Passport

Toiletries

Hair dryer

Curling iron

Prescription drugs and refill prescriptions

Mosquito repellent

Driver's license

Emergency medical information

Contact numbers

First-aid kit

Sunglasses

Zip-closure plastic bags

Extra memory card or film and batteries
    for your cameras, plus the recharger

Bottled water

Your pet's health certificate (for border
    crossings)

Cash (Canadian and US)

Bank card/ATM card

What Not to Bring

Although I'm suggesting one set of "nice" clothes might be a good idea—in the "just in case" department—leave your fanciest clothes and jewelry at home. Alaska and the Canadian North are places where informality reigns. Yes, you can dress up for a night on the town if you like, but at any given event or restaurant, you'll find people in all kinds of clothes, from cocktail dresses to jeans. Men, pack a jacket and tie if you plan to dine at a four-star restaurant in Calgary, Edmonton, or Anchorage. Ladies, a simple dress will do.

Don't bring guns. Unless you're headed into the backcountry on your own, you won't need one, and unless you know how to use it, you're probably more dangerous to yourself than that charging grizzly bear is. Hire a guide to take you backcountry hiking or fishing; he or she likely will carry a protective weapon. Canada is explicit and firm about the transport of firearms and bear spray across its borders (see the section on Guns/Ammo in Chapter 2, What You Need to Know A to Z).

Don't bring extra luggage for bulky or weighty souvenirs. You can have anything shipped home, from a chainsaw sculpture of a brown bear to a new parka, a hunk of jade, a piece of etched baleen, even your children's book collection—one for every child and grandchild in the family! Don't weigh yourself down. Insure the expensive stuff and ship it. I vote for mailing home all the paper you pick up at visitor centers, too—brochures, travel magazines, postcards, note cards, everything. It's so much better to travel light. This is especially true if you're making a one-way drive with a flight home.

And don't bring your radar detector or jammer into Yukon Territory, where its use is illegal. It will be confiscated whether or not it's turned on.

Preparing Your Vehicle

Make sure your vehicle is at its best before you leave home. If you're not mechanically oriented, take it to your mechanic for a once-over, or use this checklist to ensure that you don't overlook any of the automotive essentials:

Tires in good condition	Belts/seals/hoses
Full-size spare tire, fully inflated	Brakes/bearings
Jack, and knowledge of how to use it	Exhaust system
Tune-up	Windshield wipers
Oil change	Air-conditioning (yes, it may be needed)
Fluids	Radiator

Also, carry the following with you:

First-aid kit	Pencil and paper
Tow cable	Bottles of drinking water
Toolbox	Paper towels
Road flares/reflectors	Nylon rope
Flashlight and fresh batteries	Squeegee (for muddy windows)
Jumper cables	Spare headlight
Matches in a sealed container,	Gas can
like a film canister	Cell phone (even though it may not
Candles	work in some remote regions)

If you're a US resident, check with your insurance company before you travel. Ask about claims from within Canada and what will be provided for you in case you need assistance. Read your policy and understand it well, then ride on that security. Don't worry. Accidents are not commonplace. If you're a member of an auto club, familiarize yourself with their procedures in case of an emergency. Keep your membership number handy.

Including sections of the route that are under repair or realignment, 99.9 percent of the road is paved. Still, windshields are sometimes nicked or chipped by flying gravel. If you're concerned about your windshield, headlights, or paint job, consider attaching a screen to your vehicle's front end for extra protection.

There was a day when long-distance travelers carried many gallons of extra gas. That's really not necessary anymore, unless you're on Alaska's Dalton Highway or one of Canada's more remote unpaved roads that have not yet developed routine roadside services. (And if you're renting a vehicle, you've probably already agreed, by contract, to stay off certain unpaved highways.) Throughout the length of the Alcan and along most of Alaska's state highways, you'll find gas stations at regular intervals. An informal rule of thumb: never let the tank get below the halfway mark. Top it off before you leave a community.

Traveling by RV

Anyone who has ever spent a weekend or more in an RV knows the practice of living in a moving motel has its pluses and minuses. It's wonderful to have everything in its place, to unpack only one time, to fix a meal when you're hungry, and to slip between familiar sheets at night. But other matters must be considered, such as: Who is driving and who is navigating? Can he/she be trusted with the task? Did you remember to put the stairs up? Could you at least get your feet out of the way when I'm setting the table? Like naughty children thrown together in a room to have it out and then get along, traveling companions usually work these things out, and comfortable patterns emerge.

A squeaky-clean RV coming toward you is a good sign: that means the road ahead is paved and dry.

If you're already a regular RV traveler, you'll have shortcuts and camping methods of your own and likely have traded ideas with others in campgrounds across the country. That's another great thing about RV travel—making new friends and comparing notes about travel experiences and opportunities.

We learned that some people lighten their load by keeping the freshwater tank empty. They bring bottled water for cooking and drinking, and they hook up only occasionally for dishwashing and showers (or use the shower house). Others believe that carrying the extra weight is less of a problem than finding a campsite with full hookups.

RV campgrounds with full hookups are not always available without advance reservations, especially in the prime summer travel weeks, so empty your gray water and sewer tanks every day or two, and keep the freshwater topped off in case you decide to switch to the generator and take hot showers. Often, just electricity is available. Hot showers commonly are available at campgrounds that don't offer full hookups. Pull-throughs, those campsites that allow RVers to pull in at one end and go out the other, may be at a premium late in the day, so consider settling in before dinner.

"Dry camping" is a common option, and not a bad one if there's a shortage of space. That can be the case in June, July, and early August. The more spontaneous types don't mind driving into the unknown of "Where shall we stay tonight?" Others prefer a smartly choreographed itinerary with reservations in place, from one end of the country to the other, before leaving home. That doesn't leave much room for the winds of chance, but offers a lot of security. You'll find lists of campgrounds, some of which accept reservations, in the chapters that follow. And don't forget that, even in Alaska, superstores like Walmart have an open parking lot policy for wandering folks like you. This is not recommended for the best camping experience, but it sure works for a middle-of-the-night, sleepy-driver situation—not to mention that you can stock up before you head out again.

One-way or Round-trip?

Driving up *and* driving back? Perhaps you'd rather not put so many miles on your vehicle, or you just don't have the time. You may consider a drive-ship-fly option. You can drive to Anchorage and have your vehicle shipped to Seattle while you rent a car and spend the extra days seeing more of Alaska. In five to seven days, you fly down and pick up your car or RV from the shipper in Seattle or Tacoma. Check out Totem Ocean Express Transportation at www.totemocean.com. Toll-free in Alaska, call 800-234-8683. In the Lower 48, call the Tacoma office at 800-426-0074. Alaska Auto Transport will move your vehicle to, from, or within Alaska. They have offices in Anchorage and Seattle. See www.alaskaautotransport.biz or call 888-328-8649.

Campgrounds vary from basic to luxury level. Most, we found, had clean showers and restrooms and offered at least power and water. This is Brookside Campsite in Cache Creek, BC.

Yet another option is to drive to Haines or Skagway, where you and your vehicle can board a ferry on the Alaska Marine Highway, sailing southbound on the Inside Passage to Bellingham, Washington. You will not be allowed to sleep in your RV when it is in the ship's hold but will need to book a stateroom. For more on the Alaska Marine Highway, see Chapter 9.

Own or Rent?

Packing the RV is dependent upon your travel timeline and on whether you own the RV or are renting. Owners normally keep a second set of everything in their campers, road-trip ready. RV renters can arrange one-way or round-trip packages. Towels, bedding, and everything you need for the kitchen are available for an extra fee. Or, one-way travelers can bring along the basics with an eye toward throwing it in an extra suitcase or duffel for the homeward flight.

If you fly into Anchorage, you may choose to rent a motor home and tool around Alaska before flying back home. Here are some options:

- Cruise America, 800-327-7799; www.cruiseamerica.com
- Great Alaskan Holidays Motorhome Rentals, 888-2ALASKA; www.greatalaskanholidays.com

- ABC Motorhome Rentals, 800-421-7456; www.abcmotorhome.com
- Alaska Motorhome Rentals, 800-323-5757: www.BestofAlaskaTravel.com
- Clippership Motorhomes, Inc., 800-421-3456; www.clippershiprv.com

The rental company will provide all of the kitchen, bath, and bedroom items you need to be comfortable. You'll just need to stock up on groceries, be ready to refill the gas and propane as needed, and learn how to use a sani-dump. (Two words: rubber gloves.) As renters, you'll need to pay close attention or even take notes when the rental company representative or dealership is explaining how everything works—this is extremely important.

If you're renting an RV for the longer trip from the Lower 48 or Canada, you can rent the serviceware, cookware, and bedding for an extra fee, or stock it yourself. Here's my recommended housekeeping packing for the extralight, one-way RV traveler: think paper and plastic. Buy paper plates, but pack a few plastic mugs and glasses, and bring a selection of inexpensive "real" silverware. (Personally, I'd rather wash silverware than use the plastic variety.) For the kitchen, buy some small containers with lids for leftovers and a travel-sized bottle for liquid soap. Buy disposable salt and pepper containers and your other favorite spices. Bring two sizes of cooking pots and lids, one skillet and lid, a spatula, a large plastic spoon, a slotted spoon, a ladle, a couple of steak knives, and a manual can opener. Storage is at a premium, so think small, think sparse.

Bring along a small broom and dustpan. I throw in a sample-size piece of leftover carpet as a doormat, which I can toss at the end of our one-way trip—you really do need

This pair of German bicyclists were pedaling into Alaska when we met. They had begun their trip two years earlier in Argentina, and in a few days, their journey was about to end. Reentry was going to be tough, they admitted.

one, so buy one if you have to. Buy chemicals for the toilet; bring soap, shampoo, and other basic toiletries.

Also, I put several single load's worth of laundry soap into sandwich bags so I don't have to fiddle with collecting the right Canadian coins for dispensers that may or may not work. For each person, allow two bath towels, a washcloth, and a hand towel. Other linens for a couple should include one set of sheets, two blankets and pillows, and two dishtowels and dishcloths. Don't pay a baggage fee to haul it back. You can donate all that stuff to a thrift shop or charity at the end of the trip.

The RV life really does feel like playing in a dollhouse. Within a day or two, it's easy to make a meal, wash the dishes, sweep up, and be ready to roll in record time. The routine takes on its own familiarity even though you are far from home.

If you're like us, at the end of each day you will be road weary and yearning for a quiet place, so keep a wary eye out for the location of a busy road or railroad tracks before you choose a campsite. We've gotten in the habit of cruising the campgrounds to check for noisier sites before picking the one farthest away. In most cases, however, people are extremely respectful of each other, and the noise level goes down at 10 PM. Parents with children likewise are understanding of those who are not accustomed to noisy play, and they make sure the kids are in tow by evening.

At campgrounds, we walk, read, and play cards. We visit our neighbors, study maps, and review all the literature we picked up. I create a travel journal and keep track of our daily mileage, too. I encourage you to do the same, for all of those great memories will fade quickly unless you write down impressions and information about the photographs you took that day.

All in all, traveling by RV is extremely satisfying—it allows the security of familiar surroundings as we enter the larger picture of a world to explore together.

Bears are plentiful at roadside during a late spring trip, as they feed on fresh shoots of grass. So stay in your vehicle and use your zoom feature to get the photos you want.

Going by Car

RV life not your cup of tea? Then fear not. When you budget in the cost of gassing up a big rig, you might find hotel-hopping just as affordable, especially for a couple. Sure, there's the ordeal of moving your luggage in and out of the car. Then again, the clean sheets, a "real" mattress, and ease of parking may outweigh the comforts of a home on wheels. Many travelers carry a spacious cooler along and fill it with lunch fixings, snacks, and beverages, then enjoy a nice dinner on the town. Other families fill up the SUV with kids and camping gear and hit the road. Big-city hotels, in particular, are more family friendly than ever. In Canada, you'll find indoor water parks under the same roof as the hotel. Check the hotel listings at the end of each section for more details; I've included business websites and 800-numbers to help you plan.

Whether you choose to drive a car and stay in hotels, bring your own motor home, or rent an RV for the big trip, it's all about personal style. You be the judge.

Cameras

You already know how it feels to miss an important shot. We've all done it—the battery has failed, the memory card is full. So don't let it happen to you when a full-curl stone sheep is 20 feet away from the driver's door. Keep an extra memory card on hand, and pack extra camera batteries or the rechargeable kind. It's wise to bring a battery recharger that plugs into your vehicle's cigarette lighter or power outlet, so you don't have to wait until evening and power at the campground.

More and more folks are bringing their laptops and downloading photos from digital cameras on a daily basis. File management is a job unto itself, isn't it? Just naming and organizing your photos can fill hours. But taking care of it as you go rather than waiting until you get home may prove the smartest, most efficient way to deal with all of those images. Think in terms of the digital slide show—all ready to run—when you get home.

Driving on unpaved roads poses a dust concern, so you might keep electronics in their tote bags when they're not in use.

A few shooting tips: first and foremost, don't harass the wildlife. In most cases, that means stay in your vehicle. Don't creep up too close for their comfort and your safety. The best wildlife photographers choose a spot and wait for their shot. If you don't have time for that, then buy a bigger lens, or risk a ticket from a wildlife protection officer... or a charge from an animal you shouldn't have crossed.

Secondly, watch for groups of vehicles that have pulled over. That's a sure sign that something big and hairy, or feathery or furry, is near the edge of the road and will be the subject of many vacation photographs. Pull off the road completely and stop your vehicle before you begin shooting. Alaskans have seen it a million times—people standing in the middle of the road with their cameras stuck to their faces and no clue that an oncoming Winnebago is about to make a significant impact on their lives.

Videographers, remember to spend a few seconds shooting footage of identifying signs to help establish where you are. Or while you're running the camera, have your traveling companion read from a travel guide, brochure, or informational sign as you capture the scene. It's better than relying on memory later.

And one more tip for good measure: don't forget the people on your trip. Shots of beautiful scenery and wildlife are important vacation remembrances, but 10 or 20 years from now, or more, it will be the photos of the people with you, and the people you meet along the way, that will cause you to ooh and aah.

Strategy for Medical Needs

The greatest disruption on a vacation is illness or accident. Canada's national healthcare program does not cover visitors from other countries, so check with your own health insurance company to nail down exactly what would be covered should you become ill or injured while traveling in Canada. And you may want to purchase travel insurance to make up for any gaps. Keep your information cards handy in case of an emergency.

As for everyday health issues, bring along the basic medications for sniffles and headaches, and make sure your prescription medications have been filled just before you leave. Ask for a refill slip from your doctor if you expect to be gone for long.

Make a see-through zipper bag your first-aid kit. For its contents, buy travel-size containers to keep it from becoming unwieldy. Drop in your vitamins, adhesive bandages of various sizes, first-aid ointment, aspirin or other pain reliever, alcohol swabs, hydrogen peroxide, an Ace bandage, muscle ache ointment, cotton balls, a few safety pins, hand sanitizer, cold-medicine tablets, chewable tablets for indigestion, and throat lozenges, along with prescription drugs that you don't normally carry with you. You might keep your written prescriptions for refills in the first-aid kit, too.

In your purse or wallet, along with your identification and insurance card, carry a written statement of any medical conditions, allergies or other health alerts, and medicines that you're currently taking. List the name and number of your family doctor and the person to call in case of an emergency.

If you're traveling within Yukon Territory, you can get answers to your health questions by calling 811—the Yukon HealthLine, with its Ask a Nurse service. A healthcare professional can answer questions or direct you to nearby help.

Driving in Winter

Winter driving is not only possible, but some people actually prefer it, claiming that the road is better with fewer vehicles in front of them and a good layer of compacted snow under them. But extra care must be taken to pack smart. I remember the winter my father and brother slid off the road on a lonely stretch near the Alaska-Canada border. It was −40°F. They bundled up, then Dad built a fire and climbed back up to the road to flag down help, which happily did arrive before either of them suffered frostbite. They had packed emergency gear such as extra warm clothes, sleeping bags, and matches. Even though the car was totaled, in the end they were merely banged up, but it easily could have gone another way had they not been prepared.

It's a good idea to equip your vehicle with these extras:

Studded snow tires or chains	Blanket or sleeping bag
Ice scraper/brush	Extra parka, snow pants, warm boots,
Nonperishable snack foods	mitts, knit hat
Heavy-duty extension cord	Chemical-pack hand-warmers
Sandbag or kitty litter, for extra traction	Cell phone or CB radio (if you want an
should you become stuck	extra measure of security)
Shovel	

The farther north you drive, the colder it gets. So before you leave home, ask your mechanic to use 5-30W motor oil in your car. And have the shop install an engine-block heater or, at the least, an oil-pan heater, so the oil will not become so thick that you can't turn the engine over. With either heater under the hood, you will end up with a short three-pronged electric cord sticking out of the grill. Buy a 15- to 20-foot heavy-duty extension cord so you can access power when you turn the car off for two or more hours, or when you park it for the night. Many hard-core northerners loosely loop this extension cord from their side mirrors so it's always handy.

In the Far North, outdoor electric outlets are common; in Fairbanks or Dawson City, you'll see them at the heads of parking spaces in public lots. Ask about where to plug in when you check in at your motel. If you haven't plugged in all night, do so an hour or so before you plan to leave. Plugging in at 10°F or colder is a good idea. It means less wear and tear on your engine and less drain on your battery, not to mention a reassuring sound when the engine turns over effortlessly. And the sooner the engine heats up, the sooner you'll have warm air coming out of your interior blower.

Another trick among winter drivers of the North has to do with a quick and cheap addition to your front end: a large piece of corrugated cardboard. Wedge the flattened piece between your grill and radiator to prevent supercold air from passing through the radiator. The engine will get warm much faster—and stay warm—and in the end, your interior heater will be much more effective.

Winter travelers in RVs must pay more attention to protecting their water and sewer systems from freezing. You'll likely just plan to drain the lines and not worry about the problem. Rental companies will hold you responsible should the RV sustain damage from freezing.

Remember that winter days in the North are extremely short. You'll be driving in dim light or darkness, even if you limit your driving to daytime, so working headlights are especially important. Snowstorms can surprise you, too, so check your radio dial and ask the locals about the forecast when you stop, or request a number to call for recorded messages on road conditions.

Sharing the road with tractor-trailers can be a challenge because they tend to kick up a blinding snow shower, so back off rather than pass them. Vision is critical, so make sure your windshield wipers are in good shape. Use common sense for safe snow driving: bring down your speed a notch, never jam on the brakes, and as your driver's ed teacher told you, steer in the direction of the slide.

And, at the risk of nagging, I'll say it again: take your time.

CHAPTER 2

WHAT YOU NEED TO KNOW, A TO Z

Alaska-speak

English is spoken in Canada and the United States, but occasionally a regional term can trip you up. Here's a quick list of words in the Alaskan vocabulary:

Outside. Anywhere not in Alaska
Lower 48. The 48 continental states to the south
Cheechako. A greenhorn, a newcomer
Wanigan. Lean-to, usually in add-a-room-style attached to a cabin
Carhartts. Brand of warm, durable clothing commonly worn in winter; the Alaska tuxedo
Bunny boots. Large, usually white rubber boots with a built-in vapor barrier for extra insulation; boomed in use during construction of the Trans-Alaska Pipeline during the 1970s and still very popular
Breakup. Spring season when ice breaks up and moves out from the rivers
Termination dust. First snow that dusts the mountaintops; signals the termination of summer
Kuspuk. Brightly colored cotton tunic with flounce worn by some Alaska Native women
Alaska Native. Person of ancient heritage—Eskimo, Indian, or Aleut descent
Native Alaskan. Person of any race who was born and raised in Alaska
Sitka sneakers. Rubber boots commonly seen on commercial fishermen
Sourdough. An old-timer, a pioneer Alaskan
Snowmachine. A snowmobile
Rondy. Anchorage Fur Rendezvous, the biggest winter carnival in the country
PFD check. Portion of interest dividends and capital gains on the state's oil revenues; annual payment mailed by the state to every eligible resident. In 2009, the amount was $1,305 per person.

Alaska State Troopers

Not every town on the Alaska road system has its own police force. Alaska State Troopers enforce the law along the miles and miles of highway. Dialing 911 remains the universal call for help throughout the state, and trooper posts may be found in the following highway communities: Anchorage, Anchor Point, Cantwell, Coldfoot, Cordova, Cooper Landing, Delta Junction, Fairbanks, Girdwood, Glennallen, Haines, Healy, Homer, Nenana, Ninilchik, Northway, Palmer, Seward, Soldotna, Talkeetna, Tok, and Valdez.

The Municipality of Anchorage extends from the Knik River Bridge on the Glenn Highway to the town of Girdwood on the Seward Highway, and a host of police officers patrols the highways in this vast area, with support from the Alaska State Troopers.

Other road-system cities with their own police force include Fairbanks, Homer, Kenai, North Pole, Palmer, Seward, Soldotna, Wasilla, Whittier, and Valdez. In remote, off-road villages, local law enforcement often is handled by a VPSO, a Village Public Safety Officer. State Troopers fly into villages when a VPSO needs assistance.

Alaska Wildlife Troopers serve in a special branch of the Department of Public Safety. Even though they focus their efforts on enforcing fish and game laws, they can and will issue traffic tickets and pursue other criminal activity.

Alaska has no counties, so there are no sheriffs or deputies.

Alcoholic Beverages

Alcohol is not sold in grocery stores in Alaska, and liquor stores will not sell to individuals younger than 21. Drinking-and-driving laws are tough, so stop for the night

before you crack open that beer. Some Alaska villages are dry; some are damp. Just to be sure, don't fly into a village with alcohol in your suitcase.

US citizens who are 19 or older may transport duty-free alcoholic beverages over the US-Canada border in these quantities: 1.5 liters (about 51 ounces) of wine, 1.14 liters (about 38 ounces) of liquor, or 24 cans or bottles of beer.

Passports are now required to cross the border between the US and Canada.

A picturesque campsite, absolutely free, along a beautiful Yukon river named Aishihik.

Border Crossings

Current regulations require valid passports or passport cards (pass cards) for anyone crossing the US and Canada borders by land. US citizens should apply up to six months in advance, to allow plenty of time for processing. For more information, see www.cbsa-asfc.gc.ca. Have your vehicle registration or rental documents available, too, along with your pet's health certificate.

If you are traveling with a child for whom you share custody, be prepared to show custodial paperwork. A letter with specific travel dates and the signature of the other parent is a good idea, too, along with a phone number in case officials want to make a quick call. Likewise, grandparents traveling with grandchildren should carry a parental permission letter with contact information.

For visitors from the United States who are not US-born, Canadian authorities will ask for a Certificate of Naturalization, a green card, and perhaps a visa, depending on one's country of citizenship. No photocopies will be accepted.

US travelers with a criminal record must consult with a Canadian consulate or embassy several weeks before traveling to obtain a "waiver of exclusion." Contact the Canadian Embassy in Washington, DC, at 202-682-1740 for more information.

Most crossings are fairly routine. You will be asked a dozen or more questions and then be allowed to continue on your journey. Sometimes there's a waiting line, so allow time in your schedule for some stop-and-go traffic.

Occasionally, officials ask permission to look around inside a car or camper. Every so often, even after answering all questions honestly, a driver may be detained further as officials make a more thorough inspection of the vehicle or its contents. (Also see the following entries in this chapter: Alcoholic Beverages; Duty-free Shopping; Guns/Ammo; Pets; Plants.)

Campgrounds

Among those who love to camp, you'll find a spectrum of tastes and comfort zones. Some folks take their home with them on vacation in the form of a recreational vehicle—and their rolling accommodations include power, water, microwave, stove, refrigerator, toilet, shower, stereo, and VCR. At the other end of the scale are the tent campers, who sleep with a thin layer of waterproof material separating them from raw nature. No matter what the style, great numbers of mobile travelers have discovered the joys of camping.

As you travel throughout the North, you'll find plentiful options among campgrounds and good signage to help direct you. In the chapters that follow, I've included directions and contact information for campgrounds along the way. Operated privately or by government agencies, campground offerings range from a simple opening in the forest with a picnic table and fire ring to places equipped with extras such as cable, a swimming pool, golf course, horseshoe pits, playgrounds, swimming beach, boat dock, and, almost as important as hot showers to some campers, wireless service.

RV travelers will be most interested in whether a campground offers full hookups, meaning power, water, and sewer service. In a partial hookup, power and water are usually available, but sewer service is not. In most cases, however, a dump station (or sani-station, as it's often called in Canada) is available for emptying gray water and sewage. Also note that campgrounds in Canada will refer to sites as serviced or unserviced, indicating whether hookups are available.

In Alaska, it is legal to park for the night on a road wayside where the parking area is fully off the road. Nowhere in Alaska or Canada is it legal to dump sewage or gray water anywhere except in designated dump stations.

For provincial parks, you can pay in person at the campground fee station after you've chosen your site. If you're out of Canadian currency or don't have the exact amount, it's okay to put a check in the payment envelope.

For details, contact these sources:

Alaska: State campgrounds are operated on a first-come, first-served basis; however, reservations must be made for public-use cabins. Annual camping passes are no longer available. Visit Alaska State Parks online at http://dnr.alaska.gov/parks. Charge cards are accepted in most privately owned campgrounds. Checks are rarely accepted. Visit the Alaska Campground Owner's Association online at www.alaskacampgrounds.net. For more on camping in Alaska's state or national parklands, see www.travelalaska.com/regions/stateparks.aspx.

Alberta: To find a campsite or make a reservation in a provincial park, see www.albertaparks.ca. Reservations may be made up to 90 days in advance. Five of Canada's 19 national parks are found in Alberta. For detailed travel information and campground information, visit Parks Canada at www.pc.gc.ca.

British Columbia: For information or provincial campground reservations, call 800-689-9025, or visit www.discovercamping.ca. Overseas callers should dial 519-826-6850.

Reservations may be made 90 day in advance. Also, seven national parks lie within British Columbia. For more on visiting the parks, visit Parks Canada at www.pc.gc.ca.

Yukon Territory: The Yukon government operates 41 campgrounds along the territory's roads. Travelers may pay on site ($12 per night), or prepay for a campground permit at retail outlets along the highway, visitor reception centers, lodges, and fuel stations. There are no RV dump stations in the territorial parks, but you can get a list of dump stations from the Department of Environment at 867-667-5658 or on the territory's website at http://environmentyukon.gov.yk.ca/camping. To reserve a campsite in one of the Yukon's three national parks, visit Parks Canada at www.pc.gc.ca.

Canada-speak

Almost all western Canadians speak English as their first language, and until an unusual treatment of a familiar word pops up, US-centric travelers could forget they're guests in a foreign country: "I find it's a difficult PRO-cess," "My SHED-yule won't allow it," or "Tell me a-BOOT your problem." Here are some terms to aid interpretation:

At par. If you offer US dollars instead of Canadian currency for a purchase, the person at the register may say this, meaning that they won't calculate the exchange rate. It's an agreement to pay dollar for dollar.

Eh? A nonword that peppers the ends of many sentences. It is not a question, but rather a charming way to end a statement with an invitation for the other person to speak next…or it's just a regional speech pattern that means nothing whatsoever, similar to the use of *like* or *you know.*

First Nations people. Descendants of the ancient Native groups who first made this region their home

Gold dredges. Floating gold PRO-cessing ships that sorted out nuggets from rock and soil before depositing the tailings back on the ground

Licensed. Indicates that a business may legally serve wine, beer, and spirits.

Loonie. The $1 coin, imprinted with the image of a loon

Mounties. Royal Canadian Mounted Police, or RCMP

Pumpjack. Slow-moving oil pumps that draw oil out of the ground and into a pipeline or storage tank; often seen in rolling fields

Stampede. The "rush" in gold rushes of a century ago, when men and women stampeded from one gold discovery to the next; or, the term for a regional rodeo event, as in the Calgary Stampede

The Yukon. Use the territory's name without the *the* and you've just revealed that you're not from around these parts. That, and you keep getting your quarters mixed up with Loonies.

Toonie. The $2 coin, worth two Loonies

YOOP. Yukon Order of Pioneers

Cell Phone Service

Heading north into Canada, as you enter more mountainous or less populated regions, the less likely you'll have cell phone service, although areas surrounding major urban centers usually pose no problem. The best advice is to mentally prepare yourself for that reality, and don't let the number of bars on your phone dictate whether you're going to have a good day. Get out a credit card, calling card, or a mound of change and use a pay phone. We found that campgrounds with wireless made up for the lack of communication with cell service—you can usually reach the outside world.

On January 1, 2010, British Columbia passed a new law that forbids chatting or texting on cell phones or any other electronic device while driving.

Daylight Hours

In summer, the higher the latitude, the more daylight you will encounter, especially during the days surrounding June 20 or 21, the summer solstice. Fairbanks basks in 22 hours of daylight during its Solstice Celebration, which includes the Midnight Sun Baseball Game, which begins at 10:30 PM, without artificial lights. Farther south, in Anchorage, the longest day provides a mere 19.5 hours of daylight, enough to make bedtimes a challenge for adults and children alike.

Throughout the Yukon, northern British Columbia, northern Alberta, and Alaska, short growing seasons are supplemented by these long, long hours of sunlight, resulting in exceptional floral displays, grain crops, and certain vegetables that grow to gigantic proportions. Look for giant cabbages mixed in with border plants in many northern gardens.

On the other side of the calendar, December 20 or 21 is winter solstice, when darkness is at its peak after eating away at hours of daylight for months. In Fairbanks, the sun may rise and set before office workers get a chance to look out the window, rising at about 11 AM and setting just three hours later. In Dawson City, YT, daylight on winter solstice is 4.5 hours; in Whitehorse, YT, the shortest day is 5.5 hours.

Duty-free Shopping

If the value of your purchases does not exceed $400, residents of the United States who travel in Canada for more than 48 hours and less than 30 days may bring home personal or household merchandise without paying US duty and tax. The $400 figure applies for each member in your party. To avoid delays at the border crossing, keep receipts and purchases handy.

Fishing

A fishing license is required in all provinces and in Alaska, but it is easy to obtain one through sporting goods stores, other businesses, or even online.

Alberta. The province is home to 18 species of fish that are preferred for sportfishing and food, among them pike, walleye, bull trout, sturgeon, and arctic grayling. A 2004 regulation requires anglers to use barbless hooks. Sportfishing licenses are available at Alberta Sustainable Resource Development offices, most tackle shops and sporting goods stores, campgrounds, and many department stores. No license is required for youths age 15 and younger. You may pick up the current "Alberta Guide to Sportfishing Regulations" when you purchase your license. Fees for anglers who are not residents of Canada are $26.63 for one day; $47.63 for five days; $70.90 for the year. For more information, see www.mywildalberta.com, or contact Alberta Sustainable Resource Development, Fish and Wildlife: www.srd.alberta.ca or 780-944-0313.

British Columbia. You'll have to buy separate licenses for saltwater and freshwater fishing in British Columbia. You can pick them up at government agency offices, sporting goods stores, and many other retailers. Or, buy a license online at www.fishing.gov .bc.ca. Certain specific licenses are required in all national parks and may be obtained

Sunday Stinson of Anchorage hauled in her first king salmon, weighing 53 pounds, from the waters off Kodiak Island. Photo by Nikkia Atkins

at park headquarters. For inquiries, call 877-855-3222, Monday through Friday, 8:30 AM to 4:30 PM Pacific time. Freshwater fishing regulations and licensing information can be found online at the Ministry of Environment at www.env.gov.bc.ca/fw/fish. For tidal water or saltwater regulations, consult Fisheries and Oceans Canada at www.pac.dfo-mpo.gc.ca.

Yukon Territory. Licenses are valid from April 1 to March 31 and available at most sporting goods stores, highway lodges, or convenience stories. Youths under 16 are free. Nonresidents of Canada pay $10 for a day, $20 for six days, or $35 for the season. Salmon fishing is permitted throughout the territory, with restrictions. Pick up the "Recreational Fishing Regulations Summary" when you obtain your license, but be aware that short-notice closures can occur. Barbless hooks are recommended for angling in all Yukon waters and required in certain waters. Before you go fishing, check the regulations online at www.environmentyukon.gov.yk.ca or call Environment Yukon in Whitehorse at 867-667-5652.

For salmon fishing, you must have both the Yukon Angling License and a Salmon Conservation Catch Card. As soon as you catch a salmon, record necessary details on your catch card. You will be mailing or faxing the card to Fisheries and Oceans Canada no later than November 30, the end of the salmon season, or recording your catch (or lack of it) online. If you are fishing in Kluane, Ivvavik, or Vuntut national parks, a separate National Park Fishing License is required. Call 867-634-7250.

The territory has a good-neighbor policy with their neighbors in Alaska. Residents of the state may fish in the Yukon for the same $15 annual fee that territory residents pay.

Alaska. Sportfishing licenses are required for visitors 16 and older in fresh- and salt waters. A separate fee will be charged for a king salmon stamp. Licenses and fishing regulations are available at most sporting goods stores, grocery stores, or online. To arrange a license by mail, or for more information, write the Alaska Department of Fish and Game, Division of Sport Fish headquarters at PO Box 25526, Juneau, AK 99802-5526. Call 907-465-4180 or visit the website at www.adfg.state.ak.us. To speed up the process, you may apply for your license and purchase your king salmon stamp online at www.admin.adfg.state.ak.us/license.

Fuel

In Canada, gasoline is measured by the liter, which equals about a quarter of a US gallon, so there are roughly 4 liters per gallon. However, to convert exactly, multiply the number of liters by 0.2642 to find the number of US gallons. (See the section on Metric Conversion in this chapter.)

You may see an unusual fuel pump at some stations: propane-powered vehicles are becoming more common in western Canada.

We recommend you gas up in the US before crossing into Canada; typically, Canadian gas costs more.

Guns/Ammo

Canada has strict regulations regarding entry of firearms into the country. The Canadian Firearms Act requires individuals to obtain licenses to possess or purchase either guns or ammo. The law applies equally to residents and aliens on Canadian soil.

At the border, you'll be asked to declare any firearms and sign necessary paperwork. Ordinary rifles or shotguns used for hunting are categorized as "unrestricted." As long as they are broken down and stored properly, and you're at least 18 years old, you'll be permitted to take them into Canada. Of course the same firearm(s), and no new ones, must be accounted for upon return to the US. "Restricted" firearms are mostly handguns, but also include pepper spray and Mace.

In advance of your travel, you'll need to fill out a Non-Resident Firearm Declaration in triplicate, but leave it unsigned. You will sign it before the customs officer at the border and pay $50 Canadian. You can download Form CAFC-909 at www.rcmp-grc .gc.ca/cfp-pcaf/information/visit/index-eng.htm. To get a form in the mail, call 800-731-4000 in the US and Canada, or 506-624-5380 outside of the US and Canada. The forms are also available at any Canada Border Services Agency office. The approved Authorization to Transport forms are your temporary license and registration and are good for 60 days, should you cross the border again with the same firearms.

For more details, call the Canadian Firearms Program, operated by the Royal Canadian Mounted Police, at 800-731-4000 or visit their website at www.rcmp-grc.gc.ca/cfp-pcaf.

What is not allowed into Canada? Fully automatic rifles and machine guns, handguns with a barrel length of 105 mm (about 4 inches) or less, .25- or .32-caliber handguns, sawed-off shotguns, and converted automatics. Replicas count, too. Other handguns fall under the category of "restricted."

Headlights

Law officers suggest that you drive with your headlights on, day or night, and always when their use is posted, as on the Seward Highway in Alaska. Yukon Territory law requires having headlights on at all times; in British Columbia and Alberta, watch for signs.

Hunting

Licenses and permits are required in individual provinces, the Yukon, and in Alaska. No hunting is allowed in national parks.

Alberta. The province requires any adult (or young first-time hunters) to complete the Alberta Conservation and Hunter Education Course if they have not previously held a hunting license in Alberta. You must be 12 to obtain a license. All hunters must first obtain a Wildlife Identification Number, then apply for a hunting (or fishing) license. Licensing and permits are dependent upon the species, season, location, and other variables. Hunting regulations may be found online at www.albertaregulations .ca. Call 888-944-5494 with questions. Also see www.mywildaberta.com.

British Columbia. A hunting license as well as a species license is required for all resident and nonresident hunters. For Ministry of Environment hunting regulations or license information, contact the Fish and Wildlife Branch in Victoria at 250-387-9771. A synopsis of the hunting and trapping regulations is available online at www.env.gov .bc.ca/fw/wildlife/hunting/regulations.

Yukon Territory. To hunt for big game in the Yukon, you are required to arrange for a licensed guide. A waiting period is required for licensing, so plan ahead. For more information on local guides, browse www.yukonoutfitters.net. Hunting regulations may be found on that website as well, or call the Environment Yukon in Whitehorse at 867-667-5721, or visit www.environmentyukon.gov.yk.ca. Hunters should consult Client Services at 867-667-5652.

Alaska. Licenses for sportfishing or hunting may be purchased online or by mail. US citizens who are not residents of Alaska may obtain a nonresident big-game hunting license for $85 US, or a combination hunting/seven-day sportfishing license for $140. Either is good for the calendar year in which it is purchased. Nonresident aliens will pay $300 for a big-game license.

Additional fees will be charged for a tag, dependent upon the species that you're hunting. Licensed nonresident hunters seeking a brown/grizzly bear, Dall sheep, or mountain goat must hunt with a licensed guide or with a resident family member who is 19 or older. A federal migratory bird-hunting stamp must be obtained for duck hunting. For more details on fees, seasons, and management units, contact the Alaska Department of Fish and Game, PO Box 115526, Juneau, AK 99811 or call 907-465-4190. You may purchase your license and big-game tags online at www.admin.adfg.state.ak.us/ license. The same website holds information on special permits and lotteries.

Insurance

Health insurance. All legal residents of Canada are part of a national healthcare system that's paid for through taxes and administered by each province and territory. US citizens who need to see a doctor or visit a clinic while traveling in Canada should expect to pay for services up front. Keep all your receipts, as you'll have to file for reimbursement from your insurer later. Check with your insurer regarding extended coverage while you travel and what kind of help is available in case of an emergency that requires an ambulance or medevac services, which may not be covered on your regular policy.

Vehicle insurance. Check with your insurance agent before you leave home. You may need supplemental insurance for the trip. Make sure you understand how to file a claim if an accident occurs while you are driving in Canada. Carry proof of coverage with you at all times.

Lodging

Noncampers love the daily comfort of a clean, spacious bed, a hot shower, and cable television—and, if they're feeling especially wild, room service. In the following chapters, a list of hotels, motels, and lodges, along with contact information, follows each community profile. The amenities listed for each property will help you estimate the price range and whether the lodging is suitable for your party. More than ever, people are traveling with pets, and more hotels and motels can accommodate them today, so be sure to ask when making a reservation.

As you travel north, fewer places advertise that they are air-conditioned, and more advertise their "winter plug-ins," parking places where winter travelers can plug in a vehicle that's equipped with an engine-block heater. Contact numbers for local bed-and-breakfast associations also are included in some listings.

Certain hotels in the United States and Canada display their Diamond Rating, awarded by the American Automobile Association or the Canadian Automobile Association. Ratings go from One Diamond for an establishment considered good to Five Diamonds for a top-ranking luxury property with outstanding amenities. Also look for those businesses that have received a star rating in the Canada Select program, which rates cleanliness and maintenance standards, from one star for "good" to five stars for "exceptional."

Reservations are not always necessary, but it's best to call at least a day or two ahead anyway. Note that in some cases, toll-free numbers are operational only within the province or state, or only within Canada. If you hear that annoying message "Your call cannot be completed as dialed," it means you are outside the toll-free service area that was purchased by that business. Websites are included where available.

Metric Conversion

Canada uses the metric system of measurement, while the US system prevails on the other side of the border. A Canadian speed limit of 90 kilometers per hour is roughly equivalent to 55 miles per hour. Most speedometers are equipped with a dual scale. After several days in Canada, Americans usually become accustomed to the unfamiliar and make the conversion to kilometers easily.

Here's a tip: use your speedometer as a scale to translate distances accurately. A kilometer is roughly six-tenths (.6) of a mile; a mile is roughly 1.6 kilometers. Here are a few sample conversions, all approximate:

US/Metric Conversion

Kilometers		Miles
1	=	.6
100	=	60
150	=	90
200	=	120
300	=	180

To convert precisely between US and metric measurements, use the following chart:

From	Multiply by	To get
miles	1.6093	kilometers
kilometers	.6214	miles
feet	.3048	meters
meters	3.2808	feet
US gallons	3.7853	liters
liters	.2642	US gallons
imperial gallons	4.5460	liters
liters	.2201	imperial gallons
pounds	.4536	kilograms
kilograms	2.2046	pounds

Money

Call your credit card companies before you leave to inform them of your travel plans. They may otherwise assume that your credit card has been stolen, and you may encounter an embarrassing or upsetting delay while the situation is checked out. Best to call in advance.

Visit your bank before you leave home to exchange some US dollars into Canadian dollars. Pocket change is handy for snacks, phone calls, souvenirs, etc. Your bank will inform you of the latest exchange rate, which fluctuates almost daily. These days you'll get only slightly more bang for the US buck in Canada.

Traveler's checks (or *cheques* in Canada) are always a safe way to go, but you'll get the change in Canadian and may end up with odd dollars and cents in your pocket when you reenter the United States. If you don't want to carry around large quantities of Canadian cash, use your credit card for purchases and meals. Your bank will make the conversion to US dollars on your billing statement, including a small fee. ATMs, or cash machines, may be found in most towns, and likewise your bank will make the conversion in your account. Be prepared to pay an ATM fee.

Also, get ready to carry your dollars in a coin purse or pocket. Canada's favorite nonpaper currency is the loonie, a $1 coin imprinted with a loon. The $2 coin, worth two loonies, is a toonie. We found it easy to go through them faster than through paper bills, for some reason, and it was harder to keep track of how much change we were carrying, not unlike problems associated with the Susan B. Anthony dollar versus the 25-cent piece in the United States. Just a heads-up!

In Alaska most businesses accept Canadian coins, except for the loonie or toonie. Visit the bank or currency exchange to trade the Canadian dollar coins and currency.

Mosquitoes

Alaskans like to joke that the mosquito is the Alaska state bird. After you see their unusually large size, you may stop laughing and start running. Their cousins in Canada are just as big and persistent. They won't kill you, but they can make your outdoor experience an unhappy one.

Many a sourdough can recount stories of caribou herds incited to stampede because of mosquitoes, or backcountry hikers who jumped in a lake to escape. In fact, the term *gone caribou* often applies to people who, lacking spray-on repellent, begin hollering, waving their arms, and running to get away. Bring mosquito repellent and use it liberally. Anglers should not touch their fishing line with repellent on their hands, however. The chemicals will damage and weaken the line.

Sporting goods stores and websites offer hats equipped with mosquito netting to cover your face and neck. Or look for clothing that's been pretreated with repellent—that means fewer chemicals on your skin.

The gnat-size biting insects known as no-see-ums are a greater concern than mosquitoes for backcountry travelers, as they can creep under cuffs and into tight places. Sometimes, swarms of no-see-ums can become so thick that, without a head net, you cannot avoid breathing them in.

Pets

Take your dog or cat to a licensed veterinarian a week or less before you leave home, and obtain a signed health certificate with the declaration that the animal has received a rabies vaccination within the last 36 months. Keep its health certificate handy for international border crossings. The collar tag will not be enough proof. You may travel with a maximum of two puppies or kittens, along with a veterinarian's certificate stating that they are too young to vaccinate.

Make sure that your pet's prescription drugs are adequate for the number of days you'll be gone. Keep your hometown veterinarian's number close by in case an advisory call is needed.

The most important piece of luggage for your pet is a leash. Bring it along and make a habit of using it. Campgrounds are pet friendly, as are some hotels and motels (call ahead), but all of them require pet owners to keep their "fur persons" on a leash when they are outdoors.

Nearly all rest stops have pet areas. Bring a rubber glove or plastic bags and pick up after your pet's daily constitutional. Plastic newspaper wrappers work well.

Plants

If you're an RV traveler who likes the homey look of houseplants, best go with silk or plastic, just to make your crossing at the US-Canada border a breeze. Due to agriculture officials' concerns about native plant health, certain plants may not be allowed entry without an import permit. Fresh fruits or vegetables that cannot be grown in Canada are not problematic, only those that can be grown there. Check with an office of the US Department of Agriculture for more information.

Postage

If you are traveling in Canada and sending mail to a US address, expect to pay $1 Canadian for a stamp on mail weighing up to 30 grams (about an ounce), and $1.22 for postage on 30–50 grams. If your postcard or letter weighs up to 30 grams and is going to an international address, it will need $1.70 Canadian in postage.

Restaurants

The restaurant listings in the chapters that follow include a mix of casual family dining establishments, take-out or fast-food restaurants, ethnic dining choices, and fine dining restaurants.

Because chefs of the Northland pride themselves on their regional foods, we suggest you take advantage of northern specialties on the menu. In British Columbia, the Yukon, and Alaska, you may sample seafood entrées such as wild Pacific salmon (far superior in flavor and texture to farmed fish), king crab, shrimp, or scallops. Or, try reindeer or buffalo for the first time.

In Canada, certain ethnic restaurants may also offer what they call a Western menu. You might think of it as an American menu—one for those who are in the mood for chicken or a hamburger.

Road Manners

When you're driving the Alaska Highway, or any of the highways in this guide, give the other guy the benefit of the doubt, and don't drive like you're on the Beltway in rush hour. Please don't ride his bumper; do not pass in anger, or on a double yellow; and remember that RV drivers go only as fast as safety will allow. They know their vehicle's limits.

Especially important for RV drivers: Alaska law states that if you are driving under the speed limit and there are at least five vehicles behind you, you must pull over at the

Even though the Alaska Hwy. and all of its feeder routes are officially complete, as they say in the North there are two seasons: winter and construction. Expect one or two delays.

next available opportunity or you may be ticketed.

Should you pass by a wild animal on or near the road, flash your headlights to warn oncoming drivers to be on alert.

Keep your headlights on. Use your turn signals. Pass on the left. Smile and wave to the flagger. Just remember, this is supposed to be a vacation, not a commute.

Royal Canadian Mounted Police

Originally established in 1873 as the North West Mounted Police, the officers of the RCMP, or Mounties, bear the burden of the romantic image created in movies and books about their daring deeds. During the 1898 gold rush to the Canadian Klondike, the North West Mounted Police brought order to Dawson City and to the border crossings at the Chilkoot and White passes, demanding that stampeders carry a year's worth of supplies with them.

The Mounties are easily recognized in their dress uniforms of classic red tunics, sharply creased hats, and leather boots. Their daily work uniforms are much more mundane, as is the nature of most of their work. Like law enforcement everywhere, it's not all that romantic.

While Mounties do not patrol on horseback anymore (the official practice was discontinued in the late 1930s), the historical image remains popular. Don't miss an opportunity to watch a performance of the famed Musical Ride in Fort Macleod, Alberta, in which riders and their horses perform complex drill routines to music. Also in Alberta, officers of the K Division, along with other members of the Edmonton community, have formed the nonprofit RCMP Regimental Pipes and Drums corps, with the goal of using Celtic music to promote good relations between the RCMP and the public.

Time Zones

Most of Alaska is in the Alaska time zone, one hour behind Yukon Territory and British Columbia (Pacific time), which is one hour behind Alberta (mountain time). So if it is noon in Anchorage, Alaska, it is 1 PM in Whitehorse, Yukon; also 1 PM in Prince George, British Columbia; and 2 PM in Calgary, Alberta. Daylight saving time applies to all of these time zones. They "spring ahead" one hour in March to daylight saving time, then "fall behind" one hour in November to standard time.

Weather

The following chart provides a range of temperature and precipitation information for Alaska, the Yukon, Alberta, and British Columbia. In Canada, temperature is measured on the Celsius scale, and precipitation is measured in millimeters. Values in the Weather Chart below have been converted to Fahrenheit and inches.

To convert between US and Canadian measurements, use these formulas:
- Fahrenheit to Celsius: Subtract 32 from the Fahrenheit temperature. Multiply by 5 and divide by 9.
- Celsius to Fahrenheit: Multiply Celsius temperature by 9. Divide by 5. Add 32.
- 1 mm = .0394 inch   1 inch = 25.38 mm

Weather Chart Temperatures °F

Community	January Mean Low	July Mean High	Annual Precip./Inches
ALASKA			
Anchorage	6	65	15
Denali Park	−8	43	15
Eagle	−13	73	11
Fairbanks	−21	72	10
Haines	18	67	47
Homer	15	61	24
Juneau	16	64	52
Ketchikan	29	65	156
Prudhoe Bay	−22	45	5
Seward	18	63	66
Skagway	19	67	28
YUKON TERRITORY			
Burwash Landing	−9.2	54.5	11
Dawson City	−30.5	72	12
Watson Lake	−12.3	58.8	16
Whitehorse	−1.7	57.2	11
ALBERTA			
Calgary	14.7	61.5	16
Edmonton	6.4	60.8	18
Grande Prairie	4.3	60.8	18
Lethbridge	16.9	65.1	16
BRITISH COLUMBIA			
Abbotsford	36	62.8	62
Dawson Creek	5.2	59.2	19
Fort Nelson	−7.6	62.1	18
Lytton	27.9	70.5	17
Prince George	14.2	59.5	24

Wheelchair Access

Never before have so many travel opportunities opened for vacationers who rely on wheelchairs for mobility or for seniors who need a little extra help as they travel. Throughout Alaska and western Canada, you will find many hotels and motels equipped with access ramps, nonslip flooring, grab bars in the tub and shower, bath boards, and easy-open doors. Visitors with vision loss will be pleased to find large-print information cards and phones with extra-large numbers; those with hearing loss may reserve a room with a phone that amplifies sound.

Throughout western Canada, watch for the Access Guide Canada logo in hotel and motel windows. These member businesses have geared a number of their rooms with physical access in mind. For more information on Access Guide Canada and which businesses are participating, browse www.abilities.ca/agc.

In Alaska, businesses are tuning in to the needs of visitors who require wheelchair access. State parks and recreation areas are often equipped with wheelchair-accessible restrooms, plus wide, paved surfaces for trails into the woods. Certain tour coaches are equipped with wheelchair lifts, and some excellent fishing holes have been reserved for anglers in wheelchairs. Questions may be directed to the Alaska Travel Industry Association via e-mail at atia@alaskatia.org or call 907-929-2842. Also, as you plan your vacation, you may want to contact Access Alaska at 907-248-4777 or Challenge Alaska at 907-344-7399 for more information.

Wildlife

Every so often, the path of a plodding moose intersects the highway, and the person in the navigator's seat scrambles to grab the camera as you slow the vehicle and pull over in haste. The panic stop will happen again for a band of stone sheep, a caribou, a fox, a

Moose often walk through Anchorage neighborhoods. Motorists as well as pedestrians keep an eye out. This is a young bull moose, photographed in early summer.

ptarmigan. In early spring, we see dozens of bears (really) between the roadside and the edge of the forest. It's hard to think clearly when the adrenaline is rushing through your veins, but stay aware of any other traffic ahead and behind you, and pull completely onto the shoulder before you stop.

What a rare and thrilling opportunity to observe a world that remains so unchanged in the 21st century. But please be mindful of a few basic rules:

Don't feed the wildlife. Keep a respectful distance, knowing that powerful creatures such as bison or moose may panic and harm you. In the Far North, animal life is plentiful, and there are no protective bars between you and the wild things.

Years ago, a local woman driving near Fairbanks came car hood to kneecaps with a bull moose standing in the middle of the road. She had slowed and stopped, but the moose didn't appear to be in a hurry. He stayed put. She honked her horn. He snorted. She honked again. He lowered his head and did significant damage to her car's front end before he shuffled off in a huff. The moral of the story is don't harass the animals. For roadside wildlife sightings—and you're likely to experience several—it's best to stay in the car. But don't creep closer, honk, or yell. From the comfort of your vehicle, enjoy the vision before you, up close and in focus, with your binoculars or camera equipped with a telephoto lens.

If you are involved in an accident with a big animal, call 911. A safety official will investigate an accident, and, if possible, a local charity will be contacted right away to field dress the moose, caribou, or bison. The salvageable meat then will be donated to needy families.

As for sea life, full-day or half-day cruises on the ocean afford the opportunity to see marine mammals in spectacular settings. They are well worth the cost and often include lunch. Several day-cruise

Wildlife watching is a major attraction. Sometimes it's so exciting that you can forget you're on a highway. Do pull onto the shoulder if you see something wonderful—be it an animal or an amazing view.

operators have ticket offices in downtown Anchorage, and some provide shuttle transportation to their vessels in a community south of the city such as Seward, Whittier, or Homer. If you spend any time along the Inside Passage, you'll be treated to views of otters, eagles, plentiful bird life, and occasionally a whale.

A LONE ROAD THROUGH THE WILDERNESS

Alaska Highway Construction Facts

Length of historic route to Fairbanks: 1,523 miles (2,451 km)

US enlisted troops used in construction: 11,000

Civilian workers hired: 16,000

Heavy equipment used: 2,374 trucks; 374 graders; 2,790 dump trucks

Bridges constructed: 233

Culverts installed: 8,000-plus

Highest mountain pass: Summit Pass, 4,250 feet (1,295 m), at Historic Mile 392

Cost: $135 million (US wartime dollars; today, about $1.7 billion)

Construction authorized by President Franklin D. Roosevelt: February 11, 1942

Began: March 8, 1942

Completed: October 29, 1942

Officially opened: November 20, 1942, at Soldiers Summit, Mile 1061

Time: 8 months, 12 days

Opened to the public: 1948

Beginning: Dawson Creek, British Columbia, Mile 0

Official end: Delta Junction, Alaska, Mile 1422

Unofficial end: Fairbanks, Alaska, Historic Mile 1523

During 70 years of road improvements, the road was shortened by 35 miles.

Road builders created temporary bridges and corduroy roads out of log. In some of the worst sections, when protective overgrowth was stripped away, frozen pockets in the soil melted.

CHAPTER 3
HISTORY OF THE ALCAN:
THE SOLDIERS' ROAD

Protecting America's northernmost borders was a matter of national security in the early 1940s, and the task became especially critical after the Japanese bombed Pearl Harbor in December 1941. Without a land route between the Lower 48 states and Alaska, the US military outposts in Fairbanks, Anchorage, and elsewhere in the territory were virtually stranded, dependent on supply deliveries by water and air, and vulnerable to attack.

Ladd Airfield, in Fairbanks, was especially important to the Allies' defense plan. Ladd was the final US destination for warplanes that were flown along the Northwest Staging Route, which Canada and the United States built beginning in 1940. The route linked the continental United States with Fairbanks via Edmonton and other airfields along the way, such as those at Grande Prairie, Fort St. John, Fort Nelson, Watson Lake, and Whitehorse, constituting a dot-to-dot route through the Canadian wilderness. Along this line of airstrips, Lend-Lease program pilots—many of them women, who were not allowed to fly in combat—ferried aircraft for delivery to Russian pilots waiting in Fairbanks. These pilots then continued the journey over the Bering Sea to Russia. All told, nearly 8,000 fighters, bombers, and cargo planes were flown along the Northwest Staging Route.

Clearly a road was needed, and in fact it had been considered as early as 1905, when Major Charles Constantine of the North West Mounted Police was charged to build a road to the Klondike but was later recalled from that effort. In the late 1920s and early 1930s, other proposed routes were examined and debated. In February 1942, President Franklin D. Roosevelt approved the road construction, and Canada and the United States quickly came to terms on building the pioneer road then known as the Alaska-Canada Military Highway, or Alcan. Canada allowed rights-of-way, waived duties and taxes, and suspended immigration law temporarily, and it provided construction materials, while the United States provided the military equipment and manpower and paid civilian wages. Under the international agreement, the Canadian portion of the road would be turned over to Canada six months after the war's end.

When troop trains began pulling into Dawson Creek, British Columbia, the quiet hamlet boomed from a population of less than 600 to more than 10,000 by late March 1942, an invasion in its own right. Another 6,000 civilian contractors also arrived on the scene. The little farm town would never be the same.

Diaries recorded by the men who built the road portray an existence just as life threatening as it might have been in battle. In the preliminary stage, the heaviest equipment simply plowed through the forest that had been blazed by surveyors. Following and flanking, a team of other bulldozers widened the path, pushing over trees while still more heavy-equipment operators scraped debris to the sides and smoothed the new surface. Workers used felled trees to create corduroy road (a driving surface made by laying logs side by side) over the miry places and built temporary bridges that floated on pontoons. At Charlie Lake, a dozen American soldiers drowned while crossing the lake on a pontoon barge.

That winter, piercing cold was the enemy, along with the crude, temporary accommodations, bad food, and backbreaking seven-days-a-week labor. Heavy equipment

In spring 1942, flooding submerged several pieces of heavy equipment and the water then refroze in the drastically fluctuating temperatures. US Army Corps of Engineers photo

was sucked into the muddy shoulders and sometimes abandoned. In below-zero temperatures, the big machines were kept running 24 hours a day, as they might not start again if allowed to cool. Trucks and bulldozers were pulled out of seemingly bottomless mud holes, and troop morale sagged with little contact from the outside world. In the summer, mosquitoes, no-see-ums, and black flies tortured the work crews.

Just as the American military had feared, Japan attacked and landed troops on US soil in June 1942, briefly invading Alaska's Aleutian Islands at Kiska and Attu and further heightening the sense of need for the road's completion. In an ensuing battle at Kiska, soldiers on both sides were killed before Japanese troops retreated under cover of fog. Several Alaska Natives were taken from Attu to Japan as prisoners of war.

On September 25, 1942, the 35th Regiment of the US Army Corps of Engineers, working from the south, met the soldiers of the 340th Regiment, working from the north, at a place named by the soldiers themselves: Contact Creek. The final link occurred a month later, in Beaver Creek, Yukon Territory, when members of the 97th Engineers met the 18th Engineers and opened the road for military convoys to pass.

BREAKING TRAIL ON THE MILITARY HIGHWAY

Our assignment, that is A Company's, was to clear a right-of-way 75 feet wide. B Company's job was to knock down the trees. The ground was frozen and the trees were tall. Not having any cabs on the Cats to protect the operators, it was downright dangerous. They finally got some angle iron to make the frame for a cab and cut up oil drums to put over the top for protection from the falling limbs. That helped quite a bit. C Company's task was to put the finishing touches on the road. The other Companies just did whatever else had to be done.

A Company of the 648th Engineer Topographic Battalion, nicknamed the Topog Trail Blazers because they surveyed the trail for us to clear, was attached to the 35th Engineer Combat Regiment at Fort Nelson.

In our company, we had four fellows who were our trail blazers. They would go out and notch the trees of the centerline ahead of the Cats so that it would be easier for us to know which trees to bull-doze. Well, the first day they went out, it was getting late, and they still hadn't showed up back at camp. We were afraid they had gotten lost. What had happened was that they had chopped only one notch on a tree as they proceeded through the dense brush and trees. Everything had been going without difficulty, and they were well ahead of us when they decided to stop blazing for that day. When they turned around to come back, surprise! With their marks on only one side of the trees, they quickly lost their own trail. They quickly learned to notch on both sides of the trees to find their way back to camp.

Our first problem with D-8 Number 16 occurred when its power faded and it started to smoke. Gabe told me, "I don't think the Cat is getting enough air." We stopped and he took the oil bath off of the air cleaner. It looked good. Then he felt around in the air cleaner and touched some wing nuts, which he took off, but it didn't improve things. Then we discovered that everything was frozen. About this time our mechanic, Sergeant King, came up to see what was wrong, and we showed him. He went back to his truck and got his thawing torch. We still had the Cat running when he lit his torch, and boy, did we have a fire. It wasn't long until parts started falling out. Come to find out, we didn't know that we were supposed to periodically clean the screen that was in there. You might say we learned a thing or two during this project.

—Chester L. Russell, excerpted with permission from *Tales of a Catskinner: A Personal Account of Building the Alcan Highway, the Winter Trail, and Canol Pipeline Road in 1942–43*

Russell wrote his memoir at age 80 to correct misinformation that he'd read about the road's construction. Here, on the left, is a 35th Engineers D-8 along-side one of the new D-8 Cats (identified by its factory cab and bars to protect the operator) from the 340th Engineers work-ing toward the meeting point from Whitehorse, YT. The mood is high as the two roads have now become one (Sept. 24, 1942). (From *Tales of a Catskin-ner*, photo gift to Russell from Charles Flambo)

Some supplies for building the Alcan were transported by stern-wheeler. Photo courtesy of Library of Congress, (LC-USW33-000931-ZC)

A photograph from that day shows two nose-to-nose bulldozers and two weary soldiers—one African American, one white—shaking hands and smiling broadly for the camera. The official opening, along with a formal ribbon-cutting ceremony, came on a bitterly cold day—November 20, 1942—at what is now called Soldiers Summit at Kluane Lake, Mile 1061. Members of the Royal Canadian Mounted Police suffered in their dress uniforms at −35°F.

The Alcan would not be opened to civilian traffic until 1948, well after the war, and it remained a difficult journey suitable only for jeeps and specially equipped vehicles for many years.

The Canadian Army took over jurisdiction of the Canadian portion of the road in 1946 and continued maintenance until 1964, when that responsibility was handed to the Federal Department of Public Works. Since 1971, the Yukon Department of Highways and Public Works has been in charge of the portion that passes through the Yukon Territory.

Haines Junction, YT, presents an opportunity to take a spur road to the US border and onward to Haines, AK, on the Panhandle. Keep an eye out for signs that direct Alaska Hwy. motorists to take a right turn.

With the 50th anniversary celebration of the Alaska Highway in 1992, commemorative license plates were issued for those who drove the route. In preparation for the anniversary year, paved but damaged sections of the highway were repaired, and unpaved stretches were widened and improved. In the years that followed, road crews have continued to upgrade targeted sections, and today the only unpaved stretches are those that are undergoing another round of stripping and repaving or widening. Vestiges of the older road are occasionally visible, especially where engineers have abandoned the wildly curvy route and blasted a straighter line through rocky barriers that confounded the hurried road builders of the 1940s.

For the 50th anniversary, tourism associations on both sides of the border joined forces to erect historic mileposts—most of which are no longer standing, and in most cases would not match current milepost or kilometerpost numbers. That's because the highway is now shorter than it used to be, thanks to all of the straightening and rerouting improvements of the last seven decades.

Significant historic sites include construction camps, airstrips of the Northwest Staging Route, the memorably steep Suicide Hill, memorial sites for those who lost their lives, and boundary lines marking responsibility of various contractors.

For you history buffs who want more on the beginnings of the highway, there are several options:

- At Dawson Creek's Northern Alberta Railway Park (site of the World-Famous Alaska Highway sign at Mile 0), the Dawson Creek Station Museum within the visitor center offers an hour-long video on the road's construction, along with local natural history and archaeological displays.
- Also in Dawson Creek, you'll be taking your photo at the Mile 0 milepost sign in the middle of the intersection of 102nd Ave. and 10th St. One corner is home to a must-see minimuseum called the Alaska Highway House. Donations accepted.
- The Alaska Highway Interpretive Centre, at Watson Lake, YT, at Mile 613, offers free exhibits on the building of the Alcan, which include historic documents, photos, and displays of life in the work camps.

On September 28, 1996, the American Society of Civil Engineers recognized the wartime road that was built with remarkable speed. Meeting in Dawson Creek, the organization announced that the Alaska Highway had been designated the 16th International Historic Civil Engineering Landmark. With that, the Alcan joined the Eiffel Tower and the Panama Canal as rare examples of the world's construction marvels.

Nearly every motorist on the highway stops for a photo at the Northern Alberta Railway Park in Dawson Creek, BC, Mile 0.

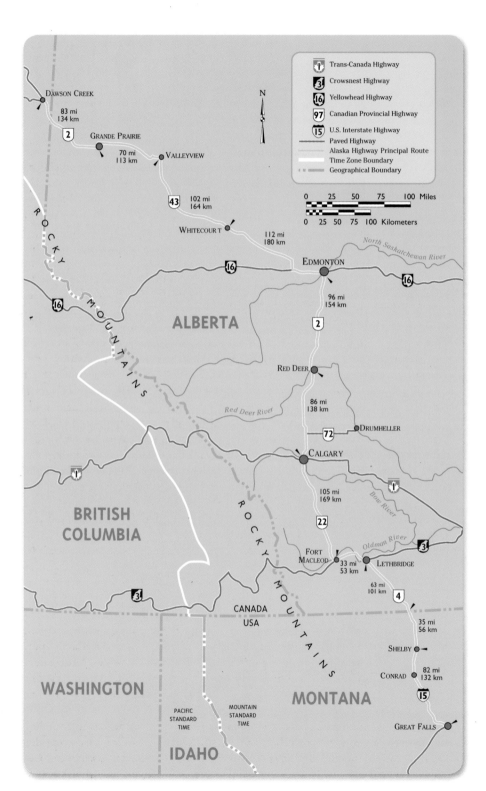

DAWSON CREEK
83 mi
134 km

GRANDE PRAIRIE
70 mi
113 km
VALLEYVIEW

43
102 mi
164 km
WHITECOURT
112 mi
180 km

ALBERTA

EDMONTON
North Saskatchewan River

16
16

96 mi
154 km

2

RED DEER
86 mi
138 km
Red Deer River

72
DRUMHELLER

CALGARY

105 mi
169 km
Bow River

22

BRITISH
COLUMBIA

ROCKY MOUNTAINS

FORT MACLEOD
33 mi
53 km
Oldman River
LETHBRIDGE

63 mi
101 km
4

3

CANADA
USA

35 mi
56 km

SHELBY

82 mi
132 km
CONRAD

15

WASHINGTON

MONTANA

PACIFIC
STANDARD
TIME

MOUNTAIN
STANDARD
TIME

GREAT FALLS

IDAHO

ROCKY MOUNTAINS

N

Legend:
1 Trans-Canada Highway
3 Crowsnest Highway
16 Yellowhead Highway
97 Canadian Provincial Highway
15 U.S. Interstate Highway
— Paved Highway
Alaska Highway Principal Route
Time Zone Boundary
Geographical Boundary

0 25 50 75 100 Miles
0 25 50 75 100 Kilometers

CHAPTER 4

THE EASTERN ROUTE:
THROUGH ALBERTA TO DAWSON CREEK, BC, AND MILE 0

Drivers headed for Alaska from the East Coast, the Deep South, and the Midwest make a land cruise across the country on a customized trek that eventually leads them to Montana, from Great Falls to Sweetgrass on I-15, then onward into Alberta. The passage through northern Montana and into southern Alberta is settling to the soul—farms and fields, horses and cattle, and well-used barns. Look out the side window and your gaze may be met by a cow looking back. Fertile farmland rolls away in gentle, undulating waves beneath a bright sky. In late August, farmers may be seen baling hay, and huge, golden rolls are strewn about the fields in broad symmetry. In small towns, grain elevators are clustered next to the railroad tracks. The pace is nice and easy.

And yet this corridor into Alberta no more represents the entire province than the Inside Passage represents all of Alaska. Depending on where you spend most of your time, your definition of Alberta may be drawn from the stark badlands surrounding Drumheller, from the stunning mountain vistas of Waterton Lakes National Park, from the cityscapes of Edmonton and Calgary, or from the raw, mountainous wilderness of the northern regions of the province.

Within the past 200 years, across the desertlike landscape of southern Alberta, the Plains Indians roamed freely and hunted wild game such as buffalo, pronghorn antelope, and coyote for food and furs. Here and farther north, these people of the First Nations lived an untrammeled existence until the arrival of explorers, traders, cowboys, law officers, and government representatives bearing treaties. The stories of the aboriginal peoples—or at least a portion of them—are told today in culturally important places such as Head-Smashed-In Buffalo Jump, Fort Whoop-Up, Indian Battle Park, Calgary's Heritage Park, and in smaller interpretive sites throughout the province. In western Canada, as in other regions of North America, aboriginal people are reawakening to some of their lost practices and celebrating with dance, song, storytelling, and art. And they are sharing it through cultural tourism.

More recent settlers of southern and central Alberta came to farm, work in the forests, or draw oil and natural gas from beneath the ground. Today, farming is flourishing with the aid of modern irrigation practices, and oil, timber, and tourism also feed the province's healthy economy. As you motor through, you'll see livestock sharing some fields with working oil pumpjacks. In "fields" of their own, dense forests are grown for the purpose of cutting, just like wheat and hay—but harvest seasons are decades, not months, apart. Roadside signs show the date when a particular forest was last logged and replanted. In mill towns, visitors are invited in to see the latest manufacturing processes.

Tourism is a burgeoning industry as well, growing in leaps after the Alaska Hwy. was opened, when travelers were more apt to discover the attractions of Alberta during their long-distance journey. Its diverse wildlife, topography, and climate make this province more than just a place to pass through, but rather a place to count among your travel destinations.

For raw backcountry experiences, go northeast to the northern woods surrounding Lesser Slave Lake, or to the top of the province, where much of the wilderness remains untouched. To thrill to the province's prehistory, go east to Drumheller, where the one-time presence of dinosaurs is now a tourist attraction. If outdoor recreation is part of

ALBERTA AT A GLANCE

Size: 255,541 square miles, or 661,848 square km

Population in 2009: 3.7 million

Capital: Edmonton

Tourism and lodging: Travel Alberta, 800-ALBERTA (toll-free in the US or Canada); www.travel
aberta.com

Fishing and hunting: Alberta Sustainable Resources, 877-944-0313 (toll-free) or 780-944-0313;
www.srd.gov.ab.ca

Canada border information: 204-983-3500 (outside Canada); www.cbsa-asfc.gc.ca

Road reports: Alberta Motor Association, 877-AMA-HWYS (877-262-4997); www.ama.ab.ca

your vacation, throughout Alberta you'll find plenty of opportunity for camping, fishing, boating, swimming, and the like.

To learn more about what to see and do in Alberta, travel information is available at 800-ALBERTA (in Canada or the US) or at www.travelalberta.com. And if you're interested in staying in bed-and-breakfast accommodations, visit the Alberta Bed & Breakfast Association online at www.bbalberta.com. Those traveling with a pet should inquire if the B&B or hotel is pet friendly. Many operations do allow pets for a small additional fee.

MONTANA-ALBERTA BORDER

To Lethbridge, AB: 63 miles (101.5 km)
To Dawson Creek, BC: 753 miles (1,212 km)

I-15 is the northbound highway from Great Falls, Montana, to the Canada border. Little more than an hour north of Great Falls, stop at the little town of Shelby to top off the fuel tank. The price there will be lower than any other you'll encounter throughout western Canada. As you drive north, the terrain will be familiar in Alberta. Like northern Montana, it is virtually treeless, with grain fields sweeping away from the roadsides. The road is generally straight and wide, with little change except the occasional rise and fall. Oil pumpjacks are sometimes visible here, too, where a minor oil field lies beneath the farmland.

On the Montana side of the international border, the speed limit is 75 mph (110 kmh). Once you cross the border and start up Alberta Hwy. 4, no place will be higher than 110 kmh—more often it's 100. If you encounter a stretch of road construction, the speed limit may drop to between 50 and 80 kmh (30 to 50 mph).

The border crossing is a cluster of buildings in the middle of nowhere and open 24 hours a day. On the Montana side, the place-name is Sweetgrass, a name it shares with the Sweetgrass Hills, a low mountain range on the eastern horizon. Coutts is the Canadian border town. Northbound travelers will stop at US Customs and Border Protection to answer a few questions, then continue to Canadian Customs and Immigration. Between them, you'll see a duty-free shop. The shop may be more attractive to southbound US citizens as the place for "last chance" shopping. Here you can purchase Canadian goods with Canadian funds on Canadian soil, with savings on liquor, tobacco, perfume, souvenirs, toys, T-shirts, and caps. (See the section on Border Crossings in Chapter 2, What You Need to Know, A to Z.)

Road Notes

Like northern Montana, southern Alberta enjoys a semiarid climate, with so much sunshine that farmers rely heavily on irrigation. Above the more level farmland, the foothills are wrinkled and dimpled, treeless except for occasional clusters in the distance.

A gigantic marauding dinosaur is the first face to greet you at the Milk River Visitor Information Centre, just north of the Montana-Alberta border.

At the Milk River Travel Information Centre, 12 miles (19 km) north of the border, you'll find clean bathrooms, a picnic area, and information about the area's attractions, its history, and prehistory. A giant dinosaur sculpture is there to greet the public just outside the facility. Nearby, on Hwy. 4, is a small, reasonably priced public campground, Under 8 Flags Campground, with 40 sites, about half of which have full and partial hookups. Dry camping is available. Call 403-421-0200 for this and the Milk River RV Park.

Farther up the road, in the heart of Milk River, multiple grain elevators alongside the railroad tracks sure look like a row of milk cartons. Expect to see little else but farm country on both sides of the road all the way to Lethbridge—irrigated fields and grain elevators, ranging from the classic wooden buildings to new, shiny metal structures.

Just past Milk River, you can take a tour of ancient petroglyphs by turning east for 26 miles (42 km) on Hwy. 501 and following the signs to Writing-on-Stone Provincial Park, which was declared a national historic site in 2005. This archaeological preserve features huge sandstone outcrops with petroglyphs and pictographs inscribed by ancient Shoshone and Blackfoot Indians. A camping area includes sites with or without electricity, coin-operated showers, and sani-dump. There is swimming, and interpretive programs. For more information, call 403-647-2364, or check for reservations online at www.albertaparks.ca.

Devil's Coulee Dinosaur Heritage Museum is located in Warner, about 12 miles (19 km) north of Milk River, or about a 30-minute drive from the US border. In the early 1990s, scientists discovered the world's largest dinosaur nesting site in this incredible land formation. Guided site tours twice daily, at 10 AM and 1 PM, allow visitors to view the excavation site, which includes intact embryos and eggs of hadrosaur (duckbill) dinosaurs. Call ahead to join a tour. Work continues here as paleontologists search for more clues to this area's prehistory dating from 230 to 65 million years ago. Admission is charged. For more information, call 403-642-2118 or see www.devilscoulee.com.

LETHBRIDGE

From the Montana border: 63 miles (101.5 km)
To Fort Macleod, AB: 33.5 miles (54 km)

A lovely settlement along the Oldman River, Lethbridge offers the attractions of a big city in a little package. All services and facilities are available in this city of nearly 87,000 people, from top-rated golfing to a natural history center, art galleries, a theater, beautifully landscaped gardens, and a university and archives. Shopping malls, vast retail outlets, and little shops provide plenty of shopping opportunities. Dine in style or eat on the run, choosing from among dozens of cafés, restaurants, and fast-food establishments.

The Chinook Country Tourist Association operates a visitor center year-round near the junction of Scenic Dr. (Hwy. 4) and Mayor Magrath Dr. (Hwy. 5). Call 800-661-1222 or see www.chinookcountry.com for information. A second center, open March through October, is located on Scenic Dr. off Hwy. 3, near Indian Battle Park.

EVERY ROCK IN PLACE

Nikka Yuko Japanese Garden in Henderson Lake Park was established in 1967, celebrating Canada's centennial. With a name that translates to "Japan-Canada friendship," this unique treasure has fully matured and can be found on the corner of 9th Ave. South and Mayor Magrath Dr. Don't enter the garden expecting a rush of floral sights and scents. A true Japanese garden offers quietude and the opportunity for meditation, not overstimulation of the senses. In these four acres, you will appreciate the beauty in simplicity, in a garden designed by respected landscape architect Tadashi Kubo, assisted by Masami Sugimoto.

At the center, an authentically built Japanese teahouse—shoes off at the door, please—is surrounded by carefully groomed grounds with pruned trees and paths that have been meticulously landscaped. Nothing is out of place, not even the rocks in the pond or the pebbles along its shore, specially chosen for their size and shape, then laid in an overlapping design. Everything about this controlled landscape reflects the Japanese desire to express an understanding of humanity's place in the environment.

In the distance, you'll occasionally hear the low, muffled toll of a huge bell. You will find it at eye level near the end of a path, and you may move the clapper if you like. The weight of the bell hanging inside a unique gazebolike structure actually keeps the walls and beams together. Like the Japanese house, this perfectly engineered and fitted structure contains no manufactured nails. All of it was handcrafted in Kyoto.

Kimono-clad women of Japanese heritage guide the way and explain cultural practices as well as relate how this lovely place came to be. Admission is charged. For more information, call 403-328-3511 or see www.nikkayuko.com.

Other attractions within Henderson Lake Park include a picnic area, bowling green, golf course, swimming pool, campground, and rose gardens.

A jogger ascends the steps near Lethbridge's High Level Bridge, the longest and highest steel viaduct railroad bridge in the world.

Among the premier attractions in Lethbridge is its beautiful High Level Bridge, the longest and highest steel viaduct railroad bridge in the world. It spans the Oldman River valley and soars above the site of a historic trading post. At Indian Battle Park, the last of the intertribal battles of North America took place, between the Cree and Blackfoot Indians. Besides picnic areas and playgrounds, the park features walking trails.

Also beneath the High Level Bridge is Fort Whoop-Up National Historic Site and Interpretive Centre, a great place to learn about the city's beginnings. With its log construction, old-time displays, and friendly gift shop, historic Fort Whoop-Up today seems like a tame tourism stop. Although this is a replica of the original, don't forget that log walls such as these have seen passion, fury, and acts of utter lawlessness.

Workmen move a piece of glass inside Fort Whoop-Up. A walk through the restored fort lends a sense of everyday life in the old days, from the shelves in the company store to the tools in the blacksmith's forge.

Built in 1869 by two American fur traders, the fort originally was established as Fort Hamilton and became known as a critical post for whiskey runners. At that time, trade in buffalo robes flourished between Montana and Alberta. Payment with guns or illegal alcohol was commonplace, and powerful men took advantage of those who were addicted to the drink—trappers and pioneers, as well as members of local tribes. Because of the ensuing bedlam, people began calling the post Fort Whoop-Up.

With the arrival of the North West Mounted Police in 1874, the lawlessness was contained, but the name stuck. A sign in northern Montana—the southern end of the whiskey trail—offered this explanation for the unusual name: "Origin of the name Whoop-Up is possibly from a conversation by a trader on the whiskey-for-furs trade route. Upon his return to Fort Benton, Johny LaMotte was asked 'How's business?' His reply, 'Aw, they're just whoopin' 'er up!'" Call about the dinner theater and historical reenactments at the present-day fort: 403-329-0444. See more at www.fortwhoopup.com.

ONCE A COWBOY...

"I've been cowboying for years," said Phil Still, the teamster and carpenter at Fort Whoop-Up. These days, Phil helps keep the place in shape and true to its period with his carpentry skills, and he also takes visitors on horse-drawn wagon rides. Off duty, Phil and his wife load the wagon and harness the horses when they go camping. The advantages are obvious: when they go on vacation, they can leave right from home and don't have to trailer their horses.

Phil demonstrated a little roping exercise for us, explaining that as a cowboy, he often practiced roping as he rode with the herd, roping a rock here, a branch there—just keeping limber.

"So if you had a sick animal, you could pull out the rope and get it out from the others. It felt natural because you'd been practicing."

After watching Phil and his rope, I tried my hand on Fort Whoop-Up's sawhorse with horns. I think I just need more practice.

Phil Still shows how it's done.

For outdoor enthusiasts, the Helen Schuler Coulee Centre is an urban nature retreat that includes interpretive programs and touchable displays, as well as self-guided trails through the coulees and cottonwood forests on a 200-acre reserve. Watch for great horned owls, deer, and porcupines that make their homes in the reserve. The city offers numerous other hiking and biking opportunities, too, especially around Henderson Lake Park.

Events that draw big crowds are hosted at the Lethbridge Exhibition Park at 3401 Parkside Dr. South, east of Henderson Lake. More than a million visitors will roam the 67-acre grounds during events such as the Dodge EXtreme Pro Rodeo and, in December, the Big Christmas Trade Show. The big daddy of them all, Whoop-Up Days, is held in August, with a parade, chuckwagon races, midway rides, and a professional rodeo. The event line at the park is 403-317-3222, or browse www.exhibitionpark.ca.

The Galt Museum & Archives is located in what was once the Galt Hospital, overlooking the Oldman River valley at the west end of 5th St. off Scenic Dr. Sir Alexander Galt was founder of North Western Coal and Navigation Company. Displays and interactive programs teach about the history of Lethbridge, the settling of southern Alberta, and the area's first people. Some claim the museum is haunted. Call 403-320-GALT for recorded information or browse www.galtmuseum.com.

Golfers will be thrilled to play at the championship course of Paradise Canyon Golf Resort, once rated among Alberta's top seven golf courses by Canada's *Golf Course Ranking Magazine* and one of the best in North America by *Golf Digest*. The course is located at 107 Canyon Blvd.

Members of the Blackfoot Confederacy call the Medicine Stone "That Which Has Become Red-Holy." The legend tells of a man who saw a figure descend the coulee and sit, but when the man reached the spot, he found only this rock. In a dream he was told that he and his descendents were to come here and offer peace offerings. It remains a holy place, tended to by First Nations people who leave meaningful offerings within the circle of small stones surrounding the rock: coins, a cigarette, a large pebble, some foil.

West. Call 403-381-4653 or see www.paradisegolfresort.com. Another option is a round at the Henderson Lake Golf Club at 2727 S. Parkside Dr. South, in the heart of the city. Call 403-329-6767 or see www.hendersonlakegolfclub.com.

The annual Alberta International Airshow is one of the region's favorites, scheduled for early August at the Lethbridge Airport, south on Hwy. 5 from Lethbridge. The show features military and civilian aircraft in flying demonstrations, while ground displays invite visitors for a closer look. Admission is charged. For details, call 403-380-1222. Browse www.albertaairshow.com. The 2010 air show made the news in the United States as well as Canada when a military pilot, engaged in a difficult maneuver, ejected

A dusky sky is reflected in a southern Alberta lake.

from his jet four seconds before it crashed and burned. No spectators were harmed, and the pilot suffered only minor injuries.

For more information about Lethbridge, call the Chinook Country Tourist Association at 800-661-1222, or browse www.chinookcountry.com.

LODGING

Canada's Best Value Inn Lethbridge
1030 Mayor Magrath Dr.
403-328-6636
56 air-conditioned units, Internet, cable TV with free movies. Family rates. Discount at adjacent restaurant.

Chinook Motel
1245 Mayor Magrath Dr.
800-791-8488 or 403-329-0555
20 air-conditioned rooms, telephone, cable TV, Internet. Vehicle plug-ins.

Comfort Inn
3226 Fairway Plaza Rd. South
866-554-4110 or 403-320-8874
58 units, cable TV, Internet, fridge/microwave, pool, hot tub, exercise room. Free continental breakfast, coffee. Family rates.

Days Inn Lethbridge
100 3rd Ave. South
800-DAYSINN or 403-327-6000
www.daysinn.ca
91 units including nonsmoking rooms. Cable TV, movies, exercise room, whirlpool. Free continental breakfast, coffee. Winter plug-ins, coin laundry. Senior discount.

Econo Lodge & Suites
1124 Mayor Magrath Dr.
403-328-5591
www.choicehotels.ca
44 air-conditioned units with fridge, cable TV. Vehicle plug-ins. Adjacent to restaurant/lounge.

Heidelberg Inn Lethbridge
1303 Mayor Magrath Dr. South
800-791-8488 or 403-329-0555
66 air-conditioned rooms with cable TV, Internet, fitness room, sauna, pub, liquor store, restaurant.

Holiday Inn Express Hotel & Suites
120 Stafford Dr. South
877-508-1762 or 403-394-9292
102 air-conditioned units with fridge, Internet, cable TV. Exercise room. Family rates, vehicle plug-ins.

Howard Johnson Express Inn
1026 Mayor Magrath Dr.
800-597-1114 or 403-327-4576
www.hojo.com
37 air-conditioned units with fridge, hair dryer, iron and board, Internet, cable TV. Bridal suites available. Pool, vehicle plug-ins, free continental breakfast.

Lethbridge Lodge Hotel and Conference Centre
320 Scenic Dr.
800-661-1232 or 403-328-1123
www.lethbridgelodge.com
Full-service hotel with 190 rooms around tropical courtyard, indoor pool, hot tub, fitness facility. Two restaurants, lounge, downtown location. Free shuttle service.

Lethbridge Village Inn
207 4th Ave. South
800-416-0305 or 403-327-2104
32 units with fridge, hair dryer, Internet, cable TV. Park Café, lounge, and night club. Vehicle plug-ins. Family rates.

Parkside Inn Lethbridge
1009 Mayor Magrath Dr. South
800-240-1471 or 403-328-2366
65 air-conditioned rooms, cable TV, room service, laundry service, whirlpool, exercise room, sundeck. Lounge with live entertainment. Adjacent to Henderson Lake Golf Club and Nikka Yuko Japanese Garden.

Peppertree Inn Lethbridge
1142 Mayor Magrath Dr.
800-708-8638 or 403-328-4436
56 air-conditioned rooms with fridge, fax jack, VCR, cable TV, and movies. Nonsmoking available.

Premier Inn & Suites Lethbridge
2225 Mayor Magrath Dr. South
403-380-6677
50 rooms, business center, fitness room, shuttle, laundry facilities, free continental breakfast.

Ramada Hotel & Suites Lethbridge
2375 Mayor Magrath Dr. South
403-380-5050
Well-appointed rooms, full business and fitness facilities. Close to attractions. Two waterslides, kiddie pool, wave pool.

Sandman Hotel Lethbridge
421 Mayor Magrath Dr.
800-266-4660 or 403-328-1111
www.sandmanhotels.com
139 air-conditioned rooms with nonsmoking available. Cable TV and movies. Executive floors, exercise room. Restaurant, room service, lounge, hair salon, vehicle plug-ins.

CAMPGROUNDS

Bridgeview RV Resort
1501 2nd Ave. West (.3 miles west of Oldman River)
403-381-2357
www.holidaytrailsresorts.com/bridgeview
150 full hookups, 63 partial, 30- to 50-amp service, 70 pull-throughs, Internet access. Laundry, country store, heated pool, restaurant. Reservations recommended in summer months.

Henderson Lake Campground
3419 Parkside Dr. South (next to Henderson Lake Park)
403-328-5452
www.hendersoncampground.com
92 sites with full or partial hookups, 23 tent sites. Showers, laundry, restrooms. Grocery store, canoeing. Shopping and dining nearby. Next to golf course.

RESTAURANTS

Also note that most major hotels in the Lodging list include restaurants and lounges.

Abyssinian Restaurant
313 5th St. South
403-327-3315
Ethiopian dining, beautiful decor.

Cheesecake Café
904 2nd Ave. South
403-394-2253
www.cheesecakecafe.ca
Full menu, family dining, fireplaces, outdoor seating, lounge. Sunday brunch.

Earl's Restaurant
203 13th St. South
403-320-7677
Family dining, indoor and outdoor seating.

East Side Mario's
3720 Mayor Magrath Dr. South
403-331-0123
Italian American food in a fun eatery.

El Comal Mexican
1020 Mayor Magrath Dr. South
403-380-6836
Mexican favorites and specialties.

Georgio's Contemporary Dining
1502 3rd Ave. South
403-328-0676
Modern and traditional cuisine.

Keg Steakhouse & Bar
1717 Mayor Magrath Dr.
403-327-2727
Steaks and more on upscale menu; lounge.

Luigi's Pizza & Steak House
1119 Mayor Magrath Dr. South
403-329-8322
Casual atmosphere with meat and pasta dishes; close to hotels.

MIRO Bistro
313 5th St. South
403-394-1961

O-Sho Japanese Restaurant
311 4th St. South
403-327-8382
www.oshojapanese.com
Extensive menu for diners at tables, booths, tatami
rooms, or sushi bar.

Penny Coffee House
331 5th St. South
403-320-5282
Coffee and other beverages, sandwiches,
baked goods.

Prebbie's Place
1604 2nd Ave. South
403-328-3979
Burgers and such.

Ric's Grill
103 Mayor Magrath Dr. South
403-317-7427
Award-winning cuisine and stunning views from the
top of the old Lethbridge Water Tower; lounge.

The Slice Bar & Grill
314 8th St. South
403-320-0117
www.theslice.ca
Pizza and more.

Smitty's Pancake House
1020 Mayor Magrath Dr. South
403-320-7950
Family dining with special breakfast combinations.

Streatside Eatery
317 8th St. South
403-328-8085
Salads, burgers, steaks, Greek food, and pasta in
relaxed, downtown setting.

Top Pizza & Spaghetti House
11th St. and 4th Ave. South
403-327-1952
Pizza and pasta in a casual setting.

TABER: WHERE CORN IS KING

One of the pleasures of road travel is stopping at a roadside stand and picking up fresh fruits or vegetables for the evening meal. Or you may choose to just eat a sweet, juicy peach right there over the grass and let the juice drip off your chin and fingers. I quickly became obsessed with finding the best sweet corn.

Driving through this part of western Alberta, or west in British Columbia, you'll see many fruit and vegetable stands with crudely made signs declaring TABER CORN! *What in the world is Taber corn,* we wondered, *and what makes it better than any other?* We got our answers when we stopped where a woman was selling several corn varieties from the back of her truck—and was giving out corn recipes and information with each purchase. She knew a lot about flavor differences among varieties, and she solved for us the mystery of Taber corn.

It seems that the Taber area, east of Lethbridge on Hwy. 3, has become known far and wide for its sweet corn: delicate and white, bulky yellow, or multicolored beauties. With an average of more than 2,300 hours of sunshine a year and up to 120 frost-free days, the Taber area grows much more than just corn. It is known as the Market Garden of Canada, with crops that include beets, potatoes, grains, and many types of vegetables.

"The area has near-perfect growing conditions," says farmer Carl Valgardson, "with sandy loam soil, long warm summers, and irrigated fields." We picked up half a dozen ears and immediately learned why Taber is the corn capital. The kernels fairly exploded with sweetness. If you appreciate a good ear of corn or other fresh vegetables and fruits, make road-stand shopping part of your drive.

If you're traveling through the area in late August, make a point of joining the end-of-season harvest celebration at the Taber Cornfest, with four days of carnival rides, motocross, fireworks, a cruise-in, a beer garden, and contests for corn tasting, corn eating, and making corn stuffing and cornbread. For more information, call 403-223-2265 or check out www.aroundtaber.com.

Road Notes

You won't see a lot of rest stops as you drive west from Lethbridge on Hwy. 3, then north from Fort Macleod on Hwy. 2, so plan your stops around these bigger towns instead.

The prairies of southern Alberta are windy. The prevailing wind ruffles through the crops on either side of the road, and it takes only a little imagination to see the surface of the grain fields as sea waves or a living thing that ripples with movement. Lift your eyes and enjoy the prairies and badlands beneath this big sky.

About 18 miles (29 km) west of Lethbridge, you'll enter the Oldman River valley. Note where, over time, the river has created coulees: treeless valleys beneath high ridges. To the west, the Canadian Rockies are visible.

Costumed interpreters greet visitors to Fort Macleod's historic fort and its museum and gift shop. In summer months, local riders in Mountie red perform with their horses in The Musical Ride.

FORT MACLEOD

From Lethbridge, AB: 33.5 miles (54 km)

To Calgary, AB: 103 miles (165.5 km)

This friendly city of about 3,000 people is centrally located on the crossroads of hwys. 2 and 3. One of Alberta's oldest communities, Fort Macleod (muh-CLOUD) was founded in 1874 by the North West Mounted Police when the patrol established a post on the Oldman River. Today, the downtown historic district includes more than 30 historic and architecturally significant buildings dating from 1880 to 1920. Guided or self-guided walking tours are fun, and shopping is plentiful. Stay on Hwy. 3 west and it will become a one-way street through the downtown core.

We always enjoy a visit to the Fort Museum of the North West Mounted Police and First Nations, located at 219 25th St. This is a replica of the original fort that depicts pioneer and Native life in the late 1800s and is a highly recommended stop for history buffs. July and August bring a local version of the nationally celebrated Musical Ride, in which horses and riders perform choreographed movements to music. In the fort's performance, local youth dressed in NWMP's classic red uniforms perform with their mounts. Check for details at www.nwmpmuseum.com.

WEST TO A NATIONAL TREASURE

Consider a side trip to Waterton Lakes National Park, which lies about 75 miles (120 km) south and west of Lethbridge on Hwy. 5, or the same distance traveling due west from Milk River on hwys. 501 and 5. This area is rich with biological diversity and is extraordinarily beautiful, marked by vast lakes, waterfalls cascading from dramatic mountain peaks, and streams full of fish. Upper Waterton Lake is the deepest lake in the Canadian Rockies.

The park's southern boundary lies adjacent to Glacier National Park, in Montana. Like Waterton Lakes, Glacier National Park is a natural beauty worthy of exploration. Of course the two national parks are part of a single landscape onto which political boundaries have been drawn—and that was only yesterday in geologic time. Indeed, billion-year-old rocks have been identified in this glacier-carved region.

In 1932, Waterton Lakes National Park and Glacier National Park were together designated as the first International Peace Park, commemorating the friendship between the countries and their commitment to shared resource management. Since 1995, the combined national parks have been on a list of modern-day wonders of the world as a UNESCO World Heritage Site. Both parks offer backcountry hiking, camping, horseback riding, rafting, biking, and other recreation. For more information on Waterton Lakes National Park, call 403-859-2224 or visit www.pc.gc.ca/eng/pn-np/ab/waterton. For more on Glacier National Park: 406-888-7800 or www.nps.gov/glac.

Other historic buildings include the Fort Macleod Empress Theatre on Main St. (which doubles as 24th St.). The original theater opened in 1912 and is still in operation, featuring touring shows and lighthearted plays staged throughout the summer. The Empress is Canada's oldest continually operating theater west of Winnipeg. Ask about Ed, the resident ghost.

Even the local golf course is rooted in history. This is western Canada's oldest course, established in 1890. For more on this and other area attractions, check www.fort macleod.com.

The provincial government operates a recreation area on the Oldman River, north of town on Hwy. 2 near the bridge (see Campgrounds), and a wildlife reserve adjacent to the Oldman River offers hiking, biking, birding, and fishing. The reserve habitat supports deer, many species of birds, and beaver. Spend a few hours berry picking for local varieties such as saskatoon, chokecherry, and buffalo.

A side trip to the municipality of Crowsnest Pass—56 miles (91 km) west of Fort Macleod on Hwy. 3—has much to offer. A nearby interpretive center provides a slide show, self-guided walks, and programs that recall the Frank Slide, the 1903 disaster that wiped out half the town of Frank as it dumped 90 million tons of rock. Nearby Leitch Collieries features the ruins of a powerhouse, a mine manager's residence, coke ovens, and other signs of earlier life in this coal-mining valley. An admission fee is charged. For more information: 403-562-7388 or www.frankslide.com.

Elsewhere in Crowsnest Pass, you may go underground for a tour of the Bellevue Mine. Throughout the guided tour, each visitor wears a hard hat equipped with a miner's lamp. You will descend through about 330 feet (100 m) of the main rock tunnel and into 660 feet (200 m) of the coal seam. Admission is charged. Call 403-564-4700 or see www.bellevuemine.ca.

LODGING

Century II Motel
462 Main (24th) St. East
403-553-3331
14 air-conditioned units, cable TV, coffee upon request. Barbecue rental. Close to museum.

DJ Motel
416 Main (24th) St.
403-553-4011
www.djmotel.com
15 air-conditioned units, some nonsmoking. Cable TV and movies, Internet, free local calls, in-room coffee, barbecue area.

Fort Motel
451 and 433 Main (24th) St.
403-553-3115
14 air-conditioned units, cable and satellite TV, kitchenettes, Internet. Free coffee, free local calls. Nonsmoking facility.

Heritage House Motel
140 Col. Macleod Trail (west end)
403-553-4205
12 units, some with air-conditioning. Cable TV, coffee, family plan. No phone in rooms. Senior rates. Pets upon approval.

Queen's Hotel
207 25th St.
403-553-4343
Guest rooms and lounge. Cold beer store.

Red Coat Inn
359 Main (24th) St.
403-553-4434
www.redcoatinn.com
28 air-conditioned guest rooms, fridge, microwave. Indoor pool, sauna, spa. Cable TV, free movies, barbecue area, senior and family rates. Pets upon approval.

Sunset Motel
104 Hwy. 3 West
888-554-2784 or 403-553-4448
www.sunset-motel.ca
22 air-conditioned units. Refrigerator, free coffee. Internet, cable TV and movies, winter plug-ins. Gift shop, free continental breakfast. Adjacent to self-service laundry. Close to golf, recreation complex, attractions.

CAMPGROUNDS

Buffalo Plains RV Park & Campground
7.5 miles (12 km) west of Fort Macleod via Rte. 785
403-553-2592
www.buffaloplains.com
23 sites with views of foothills and mountains, partial hookups. Tenting area, firewood, community fire pit. Showers, laundry, restrooms, sani-station. Playground, Wi-Fi. Open May–early September. Near Head-Smashed-In Buffalo Jump.

Daisy May Campground & RV Resort
249 Lyndon Rd. (intersection of Hwy. 2 and Hwy. 3)
888-553-2455 or 403-553-2455
www.daisymaycampground.com
110 sites with full and partial hookups, cabin rentals, free Wi-Fi. Laundry, camp kitchen. Heated pool, game room, minigolf. Across from golf course. Store, beach volleyball, horseshoes. Open May–October.

John Zoeteman Park
1 mile (3 km) north on Hwy. 811
403-625-3351
Dry camping or tenting. Camp kitchen, firepits. Open May–October.

Oldman River Provincial Recreation Area
.3 miles (.5 km) northwest of Fort Macleod on Hwy. 2
403-627-3765
40 sites on Pincher Creek. No services. Sheltered picnic areas, dump station, fishing, canoe access. Open May–mid-October.

River's Edge RV Park & Campground
Near junction of Hwy. 2 and Hwy. 3 on the Oldman River
403-553-0334
Partial hookups or dry camping. Open mid-April–mid-October.

RESTAURANTS

Aunty Lynda's Dining Room
170 24th St., #2
One-half block from Fort Museum
403-553-2655
Casual dining featuring steaks, seafood, pasta, soups, salad.

Johnny's Restaurant
225 24th St.
403-553-3939
Family dining.

Head-Smashed-In Cafeteria
11 miles (18 km) northwest of Fort Macleod at Buffalo Jump
403-553-2029
Cafeteria-style dining at interpretive center.

HEAD-SMASHED-IN BUFFALO JUMP

For centuries, the buffalo hunters of the Plains Indians counted on this region's topography to help them kill their prey. Incited to stampede, a portion of the herd would follow the natural contours of the land along a route that gradually narrowed until the animals encountered an escarpment in this place, 37 feet high and 1,000 feet (305 m) long. The buffalo would fall headlong to their deaths, and the waiting party at the bottom of the cliff would immediately set to work on the meat and hides. Only the bones were left behind to disintegrate with time.

The Plains Indians hunted buffalo this way for more than 6,000 years. At the first arrival of Europeans, there were an estimated 16 million bison on the North American plains. By 1879, they were virtually extinct due to hunting by non-Natives.

Head-Smashed-In, a UNESCO World Heritage Site, is one of the largest and best-preserved buffalo jumps on the continent. Most jumps were disturbed prior to World War II, because they held centuries of bones, which are high in phosphorous, a necessary ingredient for munitions, explosives, and gunpowder. Through these hurried and haphazard excavations, most archaeological sites of the Plains Indians were destroyed.

To reach Head-Smashed-In, turn off from Hwy. 2 about 4.5 miles (97 km) north of Fort Macleod. Then take Hwy. 785 west for 10 miles (16 km) to the RV parking area.

A five-level interpretive center built into the cliffside is open year-round. Displays include a diorama with full-size mounted buffalo, films explaining the traditional hunt, a restaurant, and a gift store. Visitors can handle objects such as a stone club, an arrow, a buffalo robe, tools made from bone, a hide scraper, and a flint knife. Native interpreters are on duty to add to the store of information. A wheelchair-accessible trail leads to the buffalo jump along the edge of the escarpment.

In the museum, objects and documents tell tragic stories. Artifacts include a payment book from 1890 listing names of reservation residents and what they were paid annually. Men, women, boys, and girls were paid differently, amounts ranging from $1 to $7. Also on display is a historic register of passes giving permission to leave the reservation, which required the signature of a Department of Indian Affairs agent. Each name is filled with meaning: One Owl, Rises with the Sun, No Account Woman.

The name Head-Smashed-In comes from the story of a young man, many years ago, who hid beneath the escarpment during a buffalo hunt and died from a skull fracture.

Westerly winds are nearly constant at Head-Smashed-In, blowing 314 days of the year, sometimes with almost hurricane force. Wear a scarf or a secure hat and clothes that you can button up or zip shut. Bring your sunglasses, too.

Every Wednesday in July and August, First Nations people gather on the plaza for dancing and drumming. The public is invited to the celebrations, at 11 AM and 1:30 PM.

For more information, call 403-553-2731, or visit the center's website at www.head-smashed-in.com.

To mark the years, First Nations people recorded events on a buffalo skin, called a Winter Count Robe, with figures to remember milestones. This example stretches from 1764, the year of the big smallpox scare, to 1879.

Luigi's Pizza & Steak House
537 24th St.
403-553-4555
Pasta and steak, lounge.

Macleod's Restaurant & Lounge
271 23rd St.
403-553-8841
Full menu for family dining.

New Hong Kong Restaurant
510 25th St.
403-553-3838
Family dining with Chinese- and Western-style meals.

Silver Grill
246 24th St.
403-553-3888
Chinese- and Western-style dining in family atmosphere.

Westerner Family Restaurant
404 24th St.
403-553-4066
Restaurant, ice cream. Lounge.

In Claresholm, Jan Daley described Top Hand Western Shop's "back door policy." Located next door to the community's Agriplex, the shop invites cowboys to drop over during an event, pick out a rope, and try it out. Later they can buy it or try another one. Here, too, a local man sells recycled rope, that's been shaped into bowls, birdhouses, and clocks.

Road Notes

This semiarid region seems like a Hollywood Western back lot. There is little shade from the sun, the soil is dry and rocky, and hot wind snaps your clothing when you step outside. It's easy to imagine that this place was once thick with buffalo, and you can picture nomadic Indian tribes setting up seasonal hunting camps as they traveled and hunted.

Just ahead is a UNESCO World Heritage Site called Head-Smashed-In Buffalo Jump, where the hunting practices of the Plains Indians, as well as their cultural history, are presented in a beautiful interpretive center. (See sidebar.)

As you continue driving north, the road divides Claresholm, a town of 3,700 people at the edge of beautiful foothills. The townspeople call their place "Where the wheatlands meet the range." The Claresholm Museum and visitor information are found in an elegant old sandstone railroad station at 5126 Railway Ave. You can also visit the town's original 1903 schoolhouse and a nearby log cabin dating from 1902. Other local offerings include bowling, billiards, motels, auto repair, a car dealer, and a grocery store. Camping with a dump station and playground is available in the town's Centennial Park. A new full-service, 18-hole golf course called The Bridges at Claresholm rounds out the recreational offerings, along with the town's swimming pool and curling and skating rinks. It's a lovely little town. For more details, call 403-625-3381 or see www.townofclaresholm.com.

About 25 miles (40 km) beyond Claresholm, you'll enter the village of Nanton, a little town with lots to see. Downtown Nanton's historic shops hold uncountable antique treasures, crafts, and collectibles, plus the town's old blacksmith shop, the

The Bomber Command Museum of Canada can be found in Nanton, AB, with an impressive and growing collection of aircraft and related displays that began with a single Lancaster warplane.

Willow Creek Forge. Also downtown: a tearoom, restaurants, and auto repair and gas services. World War II aircraft buffs will enjoy a stop at the Bomber Command Museum of Canada (formerly the Nanton Lancaster Society Museum) on Hwy. 2 South at 17th St. The star of the tour is the Lancaster Bomber, one of few left in the world. Open daily, 9 AM to 5 PM, from mid-April to mid-October; weekends in the off-season. See www.bomber commandmuseum.ca. Other local attractions include the Ultimate Trains/Big Sky Garden Railway, a display of 22 model trains constantly running in a miniature world of 7,000 square feet. Plus there's a ride-on train, Nanton's "Steamin' Demon," for kids and grown-up kids. Open during the summer from 11 AM to 5 PM weekdays and 10 AM to 5 PM Saturday. You'll find them at 2121 18th St., or browse www.ultimatetrains.com.

Nanton is also doing its part to educate the public about grain elevators—their history, use, and place in the culture of rural communities all over North America. In summers Thursday to Monday, you can arrange for an informational tour through the Canadian Grain Elevator Discovery Centre at 403-646-1146 or 403-646-5893.

Driving north of Nanton, keep your eye out for buffalo. One year we spotted a small herd grazing in the roadside grass. Numbering about a dozen, they didn't seem to mind the traffic or the idea of having their picture taken by a woman hanging out of an RV window. Remember, that's the best advice—stay in your vehicle, and if you want close-ups, get a longer lens. But don't risk your safety or harass the wildlife by approaching on foot.

Alberta's open skies are spectacular in this region, with shades of blue from delicate to rich, velvety hues—and the natural artistry in the clouds, in their streaks, layers, balls, and fingers in tones from gray to bleach white. It's a pleasure to just gaze at the heavens.

About 163 miles (262 km) north of the Canadian border, you'll see the turn onto Hwy. 23 west for High River, where more than 11,000 people make their home. Architects, geologists, and historians alike will enjoy touring High River's sandstone buildings. You can also take a guided tour of local murals. Each summer, the city hosts four straight days of championship chuckwagon racing during the third week of June. Another favorite local event, the Little Britches Rodeo & Parade, highlights Victoria Day (the first Monday preceding May 25, also termed the "Long Weekend"). Campers will find 56 sites, 40 with electric, at George Lane Park, along with washrooms and showers. For reservations, call 403-652-2529. The visitor information center can be found at 1201 5th St. SE, on the lower level of the Munroe Barn in Sheppard Family Park. For tourism information, call the Business & Tourism Development office at 403-652-8622.

High River is the last stop before Calgary, 37 miles (59.5 km) to the north. However, if your family likes to track down natural wonders, there's one more place to see: the Okotoks Erratic, locally called "Big Rock," the largest known glacial erratic in the world. This gigantic feature sits alone on this flat landscape, an oddity that was transplanted here by advancing glaciers and left on the prairie when the glaciers retreated 10,000 years ago. Actually, it's part of a train of erratics that trail from Jasper National Park to northern Montana. Look for the exit to Okotoks via hwys. 7 and 547.

CALGARY

From Fort Macleod, AB: 103 miles (165.5 km)

To Red Deer, AB: 88 miles (141.5 km)

To Edmonton, AB: 190 miles (305.5 km)

The little prairie town that boomed, Calgary sits at the confluence of the Bow and Elbow rivers, with the purple Rocky Mountains to the west. It's a marvelous place to work and play, and judging from the city's calendar of events, it seems that there's plenty of both here.

With a population of 1.1 million, making it the fourth-largest metro area in Canada, this town is experiencing a growth spurt, but it hasn't forgotten its roots in the Wild West. It is that unusual contrast of wilderness and metropolis, cowboys and businessmen, a rodeo among the skyscrapers, that makes Calgary such a unique destination. Throughout western Canada, this city has gained a winning reputation for its restaurants, shopping, museums, festivals, art, music, and flowers. And in the world of professional rodeo throughout North America, it is famed for its main event, the Calgary Stampede.

In the summer of 1875, when an expedition of North West Mounted Police arrived to establish a fort here, the place very nearly was named Fort Brisebois. Inspector Ephraim Brisebois, an unpopular leader of the troop, intended to name the new fort for himself. Instead, Col. James Macleod, a Scotsman, suggested the name Fort Calgary in remembrance of his ancestral castle on the island of Skye. His choice prevailed.

The presence of white settlers was troubling and unwelcome to the local Niitsitapi, which means "real people" in the Blackfoot language. More than a century of resistance had already passed in bloody and destructive warfare. In 1877, the tribes

Downtown Calgary is an invigorating mix of modern skyscrapers and heritage buildings. Horse sculptures at the Calgary Police Officers and Firefighters Tribute Plaza recall the city's western roots.

TAKE A WALK THROUGH HISTORY

Canada's largest living-history village, Heritage Park, is sprinkled over 66 acres with an entrance at 1900 Heritage Dr. SW. Explore an 1860s fur-trading post, an 1880s prerailway pioneer settlement, a street of businesses, and residences set in about 1910. You are free to mill in and out of the buildings, relax in the grassy areas, or travel on a steam railway, a riverboat, or an antique carnival ride.

Antique machinery is well oiled and working at the old wooden oil rig. Elsewhere, the village blacksmith is hard at work, but willing to share his knowledge with visitors. A schoolmarm invites you into the old one-room school. Other costumed interpreters reenact a suffragette march, a wedding, a shoot-out. Children play on the antique carnival rides while parents read about how these attractions were the hit of their day.

Take a ride on the riverboat SS *Moxie* as it cruises the adjacent reservoir. Peek into every room in the circa-1904 Burnside Ranch House, and wander through the Hudson's Bay Company fort and an aboriginal encampment across the way. Buy goodies at the bakery, see how a printing press worked, step inside the historic church, savor an ice cream cone in the heat of the day.

It's a lot of walking, but you can pick up a ride on the train or a horse-drawn buggy. Plan your time well and make a day of it. On weekends, there's a musical melodrama on stage and old-timey lawn games outdoors.

The entire park is a simple pleasure. Follow suggested walking trails if you want to soak it all in. Parking may be some distance from the park entrance, but you can hop on an antique trolley to shorten the trip. It's open from late May to early September. For more information, contact 403-268-8500 or browse www.heritagepark.ca.

Calgary Heritage Park Historical Village is one of the city's most popular attractions, a living history museum that's a joy to explore.

of the Blackfoot Confederacy signed an important peace agreement, called Treaty 7, which designated boundaries for Native land reserves. Representing the North West Mounted Police for the queen of Great Britain and Ireland was James Macleod. Timing was important to the government, which planned to build a railway across aboriginal land by 1881.

Alberta's Blackfoot Confederacy tribes—Kainai (Blood), Piikani (Peigan), Siksika (Blackfoot), and Tsuu T'ina (Sarcee)—continue to practice traditions handed down from generation to generation. Learn more about the First Nations people at the Tsuu

T'ina Culture Museum inside the Sarcee Seven Chiefs Sportsplex, 3700 Anderson Rd. SW. The museum features artifacts from Edmonton's Provincial Museum, among others, and from area residents whose ancestors traded with aboriginal people. Open weekdays, 9 AM to 4 PM. Book your tour by calling 403-238-2677. Explore www.treaty7.org to gain insight on this Calgary-area Nation, its history, customs, and spiritual life.

A must-see, must-do during your trip to Calgary: take an elevator ride up to the top of the Calgary Tower, a 525-foot (160-meter) torch-shaped tower that has overlooked this sprawling city since it opened as "The Husky Tower," in June 1968. The red-topped landmark stands in the downtown core at 101 9th Ave. SW, and it's easy to spot from the ground. Elevators hold 18 passengers, and it takes only a minute to reach the top, where you can peer straight down through a glass floor as well as take in the distant horizon. There's a gift shop on the observation deck; dinner is served in the revolving restaurant. Call 403-266-7171 or visit www.calgarytower.com.

The Calgary Exhibition and Stampede, held in mid-July each year, has earned the name "Greatest Outdoor Show on Earth," filling the town with rodeo fans, cowboys, and cowgirls who come from all over North America for some of the hottest competition on the continent. Events include saddle bronc riding, bull riding, chuckwagon races, bareback riding, wild cow–milking events, and wild pony races. Rodeo clowns, parades, agriculture exhibitions, square dancing, a midway, and lots of food fill out the 10-day celebration. For more information, call the ticket office at 800-661-1767 (toll-free in North America) or 403-269-9822. See more at www.calgarystampede.com.

Calgary was the host city for the 1988 Winter Olympic Games, and the ski jump, bobsled run, and slopes have since been converted to Canada Olympic Park, a place for families to ski, sled, bike, ride the zip line, scrabble up the climbing wall, and experience even more extreme fun. You may even meet one of tomorrow's Olympic champions among the many skiers who train here year-round. In summer, daring mountain bikers ride the ski lift with their bikes hooked on the side of their chairs. They virtually fly back down on two wheels. And the variety of terrains and obstacles in the expansive bike park attracts all levels of experience. The Mountain Bike School is open for all ages, seven days a week. Bike rentals are available. You can enjoy the slopes, the 295-foot ski jump, and the bobsled run from November through March. The Olympic Hall of Fame and Museum in the park honors the stars of Olympic history. Bobsled and ski jump simulators make the experience real, and exhibits teach about developments in snow sports through the decades. Admission into Canada Olympic Park is free, but there are fees for activities within the park. Call 403-247-5452 or see more at www.winsportcanada.ca.

Wondering where to take the kiddies to work off some energy? Let 'em run wild at Calaway Park, the largest outdoor amusement park in western Canada, with 34 rides, minigolf, and live musical productions for the whole family. It's located 6 miles (10 km) west of Calgary on Trans-Canada Hwy. (Hwy. 1). Call 403-240-3822 or browse www .calawaypark.com.

Fort Calgary Historic Park, at 750 9th Ave. SE, is a reconstruction of the original 1875 fort and 1888 barracks on a 40-acre site at the confluence of the Bow and Elbow rivers, Calgary's birthplace. Interpreters share the stories of the early settlers and of this site. For information, call 403-290-1875 or see www.fortcalgary.com.

Even if you were just an average student in science, you'll reawaken a sense of discovery during a visit to the TELUS World of Science–Calgary. Hands-on, discovery-oriented exhibits make science fun again. Enter a world of adventure in the Discovery

Dome theater, a surround-your-senses journey. A new facility is under construction and set to open on St. George's Dr. in Fall 2011. Until then, the center can be found at 701 11th St. SW. Call 403-268-8300 for more information or see www.calgaryscience.ca.

The world-class Calgary Zoo is home to more than 1,000 animals, including some rare and endangered species, and a tropical aviary. Walk among spectacular, life-size replicas of dinosaurs in a vast park that's a re-creation of their surroundings. It's all found at 1300 Zoo Rd. NE on St. George's Island in the middle of the Bow River. Open year-round. Call the zoo at 403-232-9300 or 1-800-588-9993; visit www.calgaryzoo.com.

Bird lovers can explore the Inglewood Bird Sanctuary and Nature Centre, at 2425 9th Ave. SE, an attraction that features more than 270 species of birds and some mammals. Natural history programs for families introduce children to these natural wonders. Admission is free, and they're open year-round. They ask that visitors not bring bird food or pets, and plan to walk on the trails—no bikes, Rollerblades, or skateboards. However, most trails are accessible for wheelchairs and strollers. Call 403-269-6688.

Take time out to visit Olympic Park, constructed as the site for medal presentations in the 1988 Olympics. It's a downtown centerpiece, winter or summer, bordered with flowers, sculpture, restaurants, shopping, and folks just relaxing in their outdoor living room. In 2010, the City of Calgary Parks celebrated its centennial, and in the celebratory spirit unveiled six interactive gardens within the park, featuring the work of Canadian landscape architects. See more at www.calgary.ca/parks.

Golfers, just 25 minutes from downtown Calgary you'll find The Links of GlenEagles at the 100 GlenEagles Dr., in Cochrane. This 18-hole course designed by Les Furber is a challenge for any level—a gorgeous championship-length par-72 course. Call 403-932-1100 or go to www.gleneaglesgolf.com. In Calgary itself, stop by the McKenzie Meadows Golf Club, a championship 18-hole public course in Fish Creek Provincial Park, offering power- and pull-carts, pro shop, restaurant, lounge, and patio. It was designed by Gary Browning. Call 403-257-2255 to book a tee time or go online at www.mckenziemeadows.com.

If you're up for outdoor adventure, there are plenty of options: motor sports, world-class fly-fishing, photo safaris, hunting, horseback riding, rafting, hiking, and mountain biking. For more details on anything the city has to offer, call Tourism Calgary at 800-661-1678 or 403-263-8510. Visit their website at www.tourismcalgary.com.

In celebration of Calgary's first 100 years, six landscape artists were invited to create works for downtown's Olympic Park. This playful approach, titled "I'm Not a Gopher," was designed by Kristina Meehan-Prins and Jonathan Sagi. (They're Richardson's ground squirrels, if you're wondering, unnaturally pinked.)

LODGING

For information on local bed-and-breakfasts, contact the B&B Association of Calgary at www .bbcalgary.com.

Best Western Calgary Centre Inn
3630 Macleod Trail South
877-287-3900 or 403-287-3900
www.bwcalgarycentre.com
Air-conditioned units in full-service hotel. Cable TV, hair dryer, business center, indoor heated pool, kiddie pool, deluxe continental breakfast, Internet.

Best Western Port O' Call Calgary Airport Hotel
1935 McKnight Blvd. NE
800-661-1161 or 403-291-4600
www.bestwesternportocall.com
201 rooms, nonsmoking floors, movies, laundry service. Indoor pool, whirlpool, fitness center, AAA rated. Restaurant and two lounges. 15 minutes from downtown. Free shuttle service.

Best Western Suites Downtown
1330 8th St. SW
800-981-2555 or 403-228-6900
www.bestwesternsuitescalgary.com
123 suites with kitchens, cable TV, Internet, laundry, fitness center, sauna. 3-Diamond rating, AAA. Close to downtown attractions and Stampede grounds.

Blackfoot Inn Calgary
5940 Blackfoot Trail SE
403-252-2253
Modern luxury hotel minutes from Stampede grounds, close to downtown. Restaurants, lounges, Wi-Fi, fitness facilities, whirlpool, sauna, seasonal pool. Pet friendly.

Carriage House Inn Calgary
9030 Macleod Trail South
403-253-1101
165 well-appointed rooms, Wi-Fi, writing desks. Fitness center, outdoor swimming pool. Choice of five restaurants, lounges.

Coast Plaza Hotel & Conference Centre
1316 33rd St. NE (Off Hwy. 1 at 36th St.)
800-661-1464 or 403-248-8888
www.calgaryplaza.com
248 rooms, cable TV, movies, voice mail, Internet, coffee. Indoor pool, sauna, whirlpool. Restaurant, lounge, gift shop. Free shuttle.

Comfort Inn & Suites–Calgary South
4611 Macleod Trail SW
403-287-7070
Air-conditioned rooms, suites. Fitness facility, swimming pool, whirlpool. Coffee, free continental breakfast.

Deerfoot Inn & Casino Calgary
11500 35th St. SE
403-236-7529
188 elegant rooms, themed suites, business class with flat-screen TVs, Internet. Exercise facility, pool. Lounge, dining, entertainment.

Delta Bow Valley Calgary
209 4th Ave. SE
403-205-5459
www.deltabowvalley.com
398 rooms in landmark facility, nonsmoking floors. Cable TV, Internet, minibar, exercise facilities, gift shop.

Delta Calgary South
135 Southland Dr. SE
403-278-5050
Guest rooms and suites with cable TV, data port, laundry service, fitness facility, two indoor pools, whirlpool. Business center, restaurant, lounge.

Econo Lodge Inn & Suites–University
2231 Banff Trail NW
800-55-ECONO or 403-289-1921
www.econolodgecalgary.com
62 rooms, cable TV, free movies, hair dryer, iron and board, Internet. Swimming pool, whirlpool, hot tub.

Econo Lodge–Motel Village
2440 16th Ave. NW
800-55-ECONO or 403-289-2561
56 rooms and kitchenettes, hair dryer, Internet, laundry. Fitness center, pool, free movies. Restaurant, free continental breakfast.

Executive Royal Inn North Calgary
2828 23rd St. NE
403-291-2003
Air-conditioned, Internet, coffee, dining, lounge. Nonsmoking facility. Free airport shuttle.

Fairmont Palliser
133 9th Ave. SW
800-441-1414 or 403-262-1234
www.fairmont.com
405 rooms in historic downtown landmark, full-service hotel, cable TV, health club, hot tub, covered parking. Room service, saltwater pool.

5 Calgary Downtown Suites
618 5th Ave. SW
403-451-5551
Nicely appointment, air-conditioned rooms in downtown location. Fitness center, pool, Internet, room service, continental breakfast. Restaurant, lounge.

Four Points Sheraton Calgary West
8220 Bow Ridge Crescent NW
877-288-4441 or 403-288-4441
www.fourpointscalgarywest.com
118 units, suites with fireplaces and Jacuzzis available, cable TV, fridge, hair dryer, Internet, microwave. Gift shop, covered parking, room service. Indoor pool and waterslide.

Glenmore Inn & Convention Centre
2720 Glenmore Trail
403-279-8611
www.glenmoreinn.com
169 well-appointed guest rooms, business suites, laundry, exercise facility. Three-and-a-half-star facility. Dining, lounge, room service. Downtown location.

Greenwood Inn & Suites
3515 26th St. NE
888-233-6730 or 403-250-8855
www.greenwoodcalgary.com
213 units, full-service hotel. Cable TV, nonsmoking floors, laundry, room service. Indoor pool, whirlpool, steam room, gift shop. Restaurant, lounge. 3-Diamond rating, AAA. Close to airport.

Hampton Inn & Suites–Calgary
2231 Banff Trail NW
888-432-6777 or 403-289-9800
www.hamptoncalgary.com
96 units, cable TV, free movies, fridge, microwave, hair dryer, free Wi-Fi. Exercise facility, hot tub, gift shop. Waterslide, deluxe continental breakfast, free shuttle service.

Holiday Inn Calgary Macleod South Hotel
4206 Macleod Trail South
403-287-2700
Recently renovated guest rooms, free local calls, Internet. Indoor pool, 24-hour fitness room. Nonsmoking property. Restaurant, lounge. Minutes from downtown and attractions.

Holiday Inn Express Hotel & Suites
1020 8th Ave. SW
877-508-1762 or 403-508-1762
56 rooms in downtown location, some nonsmoking units. Refrigerator, cable TV, Internet, heated parking.

Hotel Arts Calgary
119 12th Ave. SW
403-266-4611
Air-conditioned rooms, Internet, coffee, laundry, exercise facility. Restaurant, lounge, room service.

Howard Johnson Express Inn
5307 Macleod Trail SW
403-258-1064
Corporate suites, deluxe guest rooms, private chalets on Macleod Trail. Wi-Fi, continental breakfast.

Inn on Crowchild
5353 Crowchild Trail NW
800-735-7502 or 403-288-5353
www.innoncrowchild.com
58 units, cable TV, hair dryer, iron and board, Internet. Exercise room, hot tub, room service. ATM, sports bar, vehicle plug-ins.

International Hotel of Calgary
220 4th Ave. SW
403-265-9600
Air-conditioned rooms and suites, kitchenettes. Hot tub, swimming pool, dining.

Lakeview Signature Inn Calgary Airport
2622 39th NE
403-735-3336
Studio, one-, and two-bedroom suites with full kitchens, some with fireplaces. Internet, indoor swimming pool, free hot breakfast, shuttle service.

The Pointe Inn
1808 19th St. NE
800-661-8164 or 403-291-4681
www.pointeinn.com
151 units, cable TV, fridge, Internet, laundry. Room service, vehicle plug-ins. Some pet rooms available.

Quality Inn University
2359 Banff Trail NW, off Hwy. 1
800-661-4667 or 403-289-1973
105 rooms. Indoor heated pool, whirlpool, sauna, steam room. Lounge, poolside restaurant. Wi-Fi and 24-hour business center. Free continental breakfast. Nonsmoking facility.

Ramada Limited Calgary
2363 Banff Trail NW
800-272-6232 or 403-289-5571
www.ramada.com
70 units, close to university, cable TV, Wi-Fi, free movies, hair dryer, iron and board, laundry. Hot tub. Free continental breakfast. Nonsmoking facility.

Red Carpet Inn & Suites
4365 16th Ave. NW
403-286-5111
Newly renovated guest rooms, microwave, fridge, free Wi-Fi. Some suites with full kitchens. Close to shopping, Canada Olympic Park, mall.

Regency Suites Hotel Calgary
610 4th Ave. SW
403-231-1000
Spacious efficiency, one-, and two-bedroom suites in downtown, cable TV, Internet, in-room coffee, private phone with voice mail. Fitness facility, business center, babysitting services available.

Sandman Hotel Downtown

888 7th Ave. SW
800-726-3626 or 403-237-8626
www.sandmanhotels.com
301 rooms, cable TV, movies, Internet, voice mail. Indoor pool, whirlpool, sauna, fitness center. Restaurant, lounge, room service.

Service Plus Inns & Suites Calgary

3503 114th Ave. SE
403-256-5352
136 rooms in newer facility, iPod alarm clock, flat-screen TV, free Wi-Fi, hot breakfast buffet. Indoor water park, hot tub. Pet friendly.

Sheraton Cavalier Hotel

2620 32nd Ave. NE
1-800-325-3535 or 403-291-0107
www.starwoodhotels.com/sheraton
306 units in full-service hotel. Cable TV, hair dryer, hot tub, Internet, concierge, room service, sports bar. Indoor water park. Shuttle service.

Sheraton Suites Calgary Eau Claire

255 Barclay Parade SW
403-266-7200
325 all-suite rooms, Internet, exercise facility, pool, whirlpool. Restaurant and lounge on-site. Close to shopping and attractions.

Super 8 Motel Village Calgary

1904 Crowchild Trail NW
403-289-9211
Air-conditioned rooms, suites, kitchenettes, free coffee. Swimming pool.

Travelodge Hotel Calgary Macleod Trail

9206 Macleod Trail South
403-253-7070
254 guest rooms in full-service hotel. Cable TV, Wi-Fi, in-room coffee, free hot breakfast, indoor pool. Fully licensed comedy club.

The Westin Calgary

320 4th Ave. SW
800-937-8461 or 403-266-1611
525 deluxe air-conditioned rooms in full-service hotel. Cable TV, Internet, business center, gift shop. Pool, whirlpool, exercise facility. Senior discount. Downtown location.

Wingate by Wyndham Calgary Hotel

400 Midpark Wy. SE
403-514-0099
Well-appointed, air-conditioned rooms, suites. Exercise facility, pool, whirlpool. Coffee, laundry, Internet, nonsmoking rooms available. Business center.

CAMPGROUNDS

Calaway RV Park and Campground

6 miles (10 km) west of Calgary on Hwy. 1
403-249-7372
www.calawaypark.com
84 sites in country setting, full and partial hookups. Showers, laundry, dump station. Grocery store. Walking distance to amusement park. Shuttle service to Stampede grounds.

Calgary West Campground (KOA)

On western city limits, Hwy. 1 south side near Olympic Park
800-562-0842 or 403-288-0411
www.calgarycampground.com
More than 300 sites, with and without hookups. Showers, laundry, flush toilets, dump station. Picnic grounds, outdoor pool, minigolf, store. Wheelchair access. Downtown shuttle.

Camp 'n' Water Park

Near Chestermere Lake
888-899-2267 or 403-273-5122
180 full-service sites; 50 unserviced; 10 tent sites. Firepits, picnic tables, Internet. Lake nearby. Waterslide. Adults-only section. Shuttle during Calgary Stampede.

Mountainview Camping

2 miles (3 km) east of Calgary on Hwy. 1
403-293-6640
www.calgarycamping.com
160 sites with and without full hookups. 15- and 30-amp service. Propane, showers, restroom, campfire pits, shelter. Minimart. Playground, petting zoo, fishpond, minigolf. Tours available by coach or van. Open year-round. Reservations recommended.

Symon's Valley RV Park

26001 Symons Valley Rd.
403-274-4574
140 campsites, open year-round. General store, showers, 15 minutes from downtown.

South of Calgary:
Nature's Hideaway Campground

DeWinton, on Highwood River
403-938-8185
http://trommex.net/natures
Tent and RV campsites. Fishing, swimming, playground, free showers, sani-station. 15 minutes from Calgary.

Okotoks Lions Sheep River Campground

Okotoks, off Hwy. 2A at 99 Woodhaven Dr.
403-938-4282
www.okotokslionscampground.com
55 sites with full service; 6 with power only. Some pull-throughs. Washrooms, firepits, coin-op showers, laundry, dump station. Wading in Sheep River. Playground and bike trails. Handicap accessible. Open May 1–October 1.

RESTAURANTS

Bear's Den
254028 Bearspaw Rd. NW
403-241-7611
Upscale dining, service in sophisticated setting.
Live entertainment, parking, licensed.

The Belvedere
107 8th Ave. SW
403-265-9595
Reviewers' choice for continental fine dining and
service. One of *Wine Spectator*'s top 500 wine lists
worldwide.

Blink Restaurant and Supper Club
111 8th St. SW
403-263-5330
Fine dining, service, wine list.

Brava Bistro
723 17th Ave. SW
403-228-1854
www.bravabistro.com
Modern Mediterranean. Honored in *Calgary Magazine*.

Brewsters Brewing Company & Restaurant
834 11th Ave. SW
403-265-2739
www.brewsters.ca
Pizza, burgers, entrées, premium beers brewed
on-site. Three other locations in Calgary.

Broken Plate Kitchen & Bar
302 10th St. NW
403-283-6300
Contemporary Greek cuisine; two other locations.

Buchanan's
738 3rd Ave. SW
403-261-4646
www.buchanans.ca
Fine dining. Steaks, chops, seafood. Wine and 200
choices of single-malt whiskies.

Buon Giorno Ristorante Italiano
823 17th Ave. SW
403-244-5522
Northern Italian cuisine. Fireplace, private
dining area.

Buzzards Cowboy Cuisine
140 10th Ave. SW
403-264-6959
www.cowboycuisine.com
Cowboy restaurant featuring steaks, burgers,
pub fare.

Calgary Tower Panorama Dining Room
101 9th Ave.
403-266-7171
Above downtown Calgary, a revolving restaurant
with a 360-degree view of city and mountains;
breakfast, lunch, and dinner.

Catch Oyster Bar & Seafood Restaurant
100 8th Ave. SE (Stephen Ave. Walk)
403-206-0000
www.catchrestaurant.ca
Oyster bar, dining room, Calgary skyline view.

Ceili's Irish Pub & Restaurant
803 8th Ave. SW
503-265-1200
www.ceilis.com
Irish pub sprawling over four floors with theme
decor. Rooftop and street patios. Lunch and dinner.

Centini Restaurant & Lounge
160 8th Ave.
403-269-1600
Italian/continental European cuisine, extensive
wine selection.

Conga Room
109 8th Ave. SW
403-262-7248
Traditional Latin cuisine served in historic 1888
building on Stephen Ave. Walk.

Dakota Bar & Grill
310 8th Ave. SW
403-262-4967
Cuisine inspired by American Southwest. Pub
atmosphere, patio, pool table.

Eat! Eat! in Inglewood
1325 9th Ave. SE
403-532-1933
Family dining in bright atmosphere.

Ed's Restaurant
202 17th Ave. SE
403-262-3500
www.edsrestaurant.com
Traditional steakhouse menu featuring Alberta
beef, pasta, seafood. Six dining rooms in 1911
house.

Divino Wine & Cheese Bistro
113 8th Ave. SW
403-410-5555
Seasonal menu, pizza, pasta, entrées, lounge/
entertainment.

Fionn MacCool's Irish Pub
255 Barclay Parade SW
403-517-6699
Traditional Irish and Canadian cuisine. Steak, seafood, sandwiches. Live Celtic entertainment.

Fiore Cantina
638 17th Ave. SW
403-244-6603
Seafood, Italian, pizza.

1410 World Bier Haus
1410 17th Ave. SW
403-229-1410
www.1410bierhaus.com
Beers from around the world, lively menu, live music.

Glory of India
515 4th Ave. SW
403-263-8804
www.gloryofindia.com
Fine dining in downtown location. Authentic East Indian and Pakistani cuisine.

Il Sogno
24 4th St. NE
403-232-8901
www.ilsogno.org
Upscale dining, fine wines, Italian cuisine. Features Alberta beef, house-made pasta. Reservations recommended.

Japanese Village Restaurant
317 10th Ave. SW (second floor)
403-262-2738
Teppanyaki-grill dining, tableside cooking. Steak, chicken, seafood.

La Casa d'Italia Ristorante
2820 Centre St. NE
403-277-7556
Homemade pasta, sauces, bread.

The Living Room
514 17th Ave. SW
403-228-9830
Oysters, seafood, Alberta beef, cheese and chocolate fondues.

The Metropolitan Grill
880 16th Ave. SW
403-802-2393
Steaks and other daily features, upscale casual. Sunday brunch, dancing and DJ weekend eves.

Mother Tucker's Food Experience
345 10th Ave. SW
403-262-5541
Famed salad bar. Prime rib, steaks, ribs, children's menu. Expansive Sunday brunch.

Murrieta's Bar & Grill
200–808 1st St. SW (in historic Alberta Hotel Building)
403-269-7707
www.murrietas.ca
Pacific crab cakes and other seafood, pastas, steaks. Comprehensive wine list.

Oriental Phoenix North
2493 27th NE
403-253-8383
Vietnamese cuisine. One of three locations. Reservations recommended.

The Ranche
15979 Bow Bottom Trail SE
403-225-3939
www.theranche.com
Located in Fish Creek Provincial Park. Rocky Mountain cuisine served in historic mansion built in 1896. Seafood, game specialties.

River Café
Prince's Island Park
403-261-7670
www.river-cafe.com
Canadian fare, wood-fired cuisine. Organic, locally grown ingredients. Park setting. Casual fine dining.

Rouge
1240 8th Ave. SE
403-531-2767
www.rougecalgary.com
French cuisine in former home of A. E. Cross. Seafood, game, beef, lamb. Private rooms, garden patio.

Selkirk Grill at Heritage Park
1900 Heritage Dr. SW
403-268-8607
Continental, Canadian cuisine.

Sushi Hiro
727 5th Ave. SW
403-233-0605
Sushi, sashimi, teriyaki dishes, and more.

Teatro
200 8th Ave. SE
403-290-1012
Italian-inspired regional cuisine. Wood-burning oven, extensive wine selection.

Trib Steakhouse
100–118 8th Ave. SW
403-269-3160
Elegant surroundings; continental dining in historic Tribune Block of Stephen Ave.

DINO DELIGHTS

If you have an extra day in your travel schedule, by all means take a side trip to the Alberta Badlands and the city of Drumheller, 83 miles (134 km) east of Crossfield and the Queen Elizabeth II Hwy. (Hwy. 2), via Hwy. 72. Experience a dramatic shift in scenery as the land around you changes from farms and field to canyonlands, rocks walls, and hoodoos. You can't miss the dinosaur sculptures on nearly every corner of the town, and a true giant presides over the grounds of the visitor center. He's many stories high, and after climbing many stairs inside, visitors can peek out through his dino teeth. Tourism information can be found at www.traveldrumheller.com or call 403-823-8100.

The town is named for American businessman Sam Drumheller, who in 1911 launched the area's first coal-mining operation. Now his name is synonymous not with coal, but with dinosaurs. Just outside town, follow the Dinosaur Trail on a 33-mile (53-km) loop from the north side of the river off Hwy. 9 into the Valley of the Dinosaurs.

Along the way, in Midland Provincial Park, you'll find the Royal Tyrrell Museum of paleontology. In 1884, Joseph Burr Tyrrell found a fossil of a dinosaur nearly as large as the famed tyrannosaur; in 1905, the year Alberta became a province, it was named *Albertosaurus*. Tyrrell's discovery launched even more digging as other paleontologists arrived to launch their own excavations. The museum features more than two dozen complete dinosaur skeletons, along with finds of other prehistoric creatures. Little is left to the imagination in the walk-through diorama-style exhibits and Cretaceous Garden. It's as if you were entering the days of the dinosaurs. Admission is charged. Call 403-823-7707 or browse www.tyrrellmuseum.com.

A mammoth roams the earth again at the Royal Tyrrell Museum, outside Drumheller.

Road Notes

The Queen Elizabeth II Hwy. (QEII Hwy., or Hwy. 2) between Calgary and Edmonton follows the route of a century-old trail. In the mid-1880s, entrepreneur John Dickson established several stopping houses along this rude trail. When he abandoned the southernmost stopping house, a neighboring homesteader, Johnston Stevenson, claimed the site and building and reopened it. The roadhouse that served travelers during the decades that followed bore a merging of their names: Dickson-Stevenson Stopping House.

Although that building no longer stands, southbound motorists can still pull over near its original site for rest and refreshment at the modern Dickson-Stevenson Stopping House, located about 24 miles (38 km) north of Calgary on the QEII Hwy. The rest stop offers snacks, fast food, visitor information, and historical plaques about the Old Calgary Trail. The first automobile journey over the decaying trail between Calgary and Edmonton took place in 1906.

A distinct line exists between city and farmland as you travel north out of Calgary. Clearly, controlled growth is under way, as subdivision homes are tightly clustered in the middle distance while cows graze alongside the road. The speed limit is 110 kmh on this six-lane highway. It's easy driving on a flat landscape. You can see a rain shower coming for miles before the first drop hits the windshield.

As you continue north, dairy cattle become more and more a part of the landscape and the road is no longer a superhighway. The land begins to roll in low hills, and more sections are wooded. Here and there, you'll see evidence of the oil industry, with solitary pumpjacks at work in fields and pastures.

I still remember the time we entered Red Deer and spied a hawk perched on the sign that gave the name of the town. We laughed because he looked like a grossly mislabeled stuffed bird in a museum exhibit. He just glared into space as we drove by, obviously not getting the joke.

RED DEER

From Calgary, AB: 88 miles (141.5 km)
To Edmonton, AB: 102.5 miles (165 km)

Calgary is two hours to the south; Edmonton, two hours to the north. Right here in the middle is beautiful Red Deer, government seat for a county of the same name. A city of nearly 88,000, it offers full services for travelers, from automotive repair to major shopping areas, entertainment, lodging, campgrounds, and an abundance of restaurants. And it's a golfer enthusiast's dream—within 20 miles (32 km), there are no fewer than 10 courses with beautiful settings and challenging greens. See www.golflink.com for details.

In 2003, Red Deer was honored by the minister of Canadian heritage when it was named a Cultural Capital of Canada. With the award comes a grant that the city tagged for expanding its already abundant arts and culture programs and celebrations.

Red Deer also takes pride in its area parklands, which range from swimming beaches and wooded trails to an equestrian facility, those many golf courses, and (surprisingly) a ski area amid these low, rolling hills. The Red Deer River cuts a canyon through the fertile farms and parklands and flows through the center of town.

The visitor center exit for northbound travelers on Hwy. 2 is north of 32nd St. It's open year-round, and inside you'll find restrooms, a gift shop, and a café. The adjacent Heritage Square, with a playground and picnic area, is a gateway to the Waskasoo Park system, which lies at the heart of Red Deer. From here, you can walk, skate, or cycle the vast corridor of river valley nature trails. Within the park you'll find picnic areas, playgrounds, and fishing ponds. To find out more on the Red Deer & District Museum and Heritage Square historic site, visit www.tourismreddeer.net or call 800-215-8946 or 403-346-0180. You can browse their visitor guide online, flipping pages as if it were on your lap.

The Kerry Wood Nature Centre hosts nature walks and canoe tours, as well as presentations for children. An exhibit gallery, theater, and bookstore are on site at 6300 45th Ave. Admission is free. Call 403-346-2010 or see www.waskasoopark.ca.

Take an hour or more to wander through the original James Bower homestead on a lovely 10-acre site bordering Piper Creek. The homestead is at the Sunnybrook Farm Museum and Agriculture Interpretive Centre, 4701 30th St., and offers self-guided or guided tours on the ways that rural life changed from 1880 to 1950. Studying these pioneers and their workload makes you wonder why you ever complain about your own life. Admission by donation. Call 403-340-3511 or see www.sunnybrookfarmmuseum.ca.

Another county jewel is Sylvan Lake, 10 miles (16 km) west of Red Deer on Hwy. 11, which has been a holiday destination since 1901. Each summer, the lake is dotted with fishermen and water-skiers, boaters and windsurfers. Even parasailors can be seen flying overhead. Its sandy beaches are perfect for family fun, and playing on the Wild Rapids waterslides will consume a whole day before you know it. Nearby are several private campgrounds and Sylvan Lake Provincial Park.

Red Deer has much to be proud about with its Collicutt Centre, billed as a "state-of-the-art leisure and wellness centre." The Collicutt houses the ENMAX Water Park, with a wave pool, water park, waterslide, lazy river, and water playground. You won't want to leave. The facility also includes an ice arena, climbing walls, and much more. Located south of 32nd St. on 30th Ave., it's a terrific place for families. Other indoor and outdoor pools can be found throughout town. And be sure to investigate Red Deer's historical treasures as well.

LODGING

Aladdin Motor Inn
7444 Gaetz Ave.
403-343-2711
www.aladdinmotorinn.ca
80 air-conditioned units, some family suites and kitchenettes. Refrigerator, laundry, cable TV. Dining and sports bar. Family rates.

Best Western Red Deer Inn & Suites
6839 66th St.
403-346-3555
www.bestwesternreddeer.com
Comfortable rooms with free Internet, fridge, microwave, cable TV, free local calls. Indoor pool, whirlpool, exercise facility, deluxe continental breakfast. Near shopping and parks.

Black Night Inn
2929 Gaetz Ave.
403-343-6666
www.blackknightinn.ca
98 deluxe rooms, suites, cable TV, Internet, fridge, ATM. Whirlpool, indoor/outdoor pool, spa. Restaurant, lounge.

Capri Centre Hotel
3310 50th Ave.
403-346-2091
www.capricentre.com
219 air-conditioned luxury rooms in full-service hotel. Cable TV, movies, Internet, hair dryer, iron and board. Exercise room, hair salon, gift shop, business center. Winter plug-ins.

Comfort Inn & Suites Red Deer
6846 66th St.
403-348-0025
www.comfortinnreddeer.com
Spacious accommodations, free Internet, deluxe continental breakfast. Indoor pool, waterslide, fitness room. Near restaurants. Ask about pets.

Coronation Inn
4707 50th St.
403-347-5551
www.coronationinn.com
62 air-conditioned rooms, hair dryer, iron and boards, cable TV, Internet, ATM. Family restaurant, bar, and grill. Downtown location.

oil is more difficult and more expensive to extract, but if the price per barrel is high enough, it's worth that expense. That accounts for the boom-city feel all over Alberta in recent years.

The dollars from oil also have been poured into the culture and comfort of the citizenry. The city has two dozen art and history museums and more than a dozen theater companies (more per capita than any other city in Canada). Rain or shine, downtown pedestrians can freely move about in elevated, enclosed walkways or through underground and street-level pedways.

There are dozens of golf courses in the Edmonton area, hundreds of shops, scads of hotels, and more than 2,000 dining establishments. If you want to spend money and feel like you're getting something for it, this is the place to visit. And by the way, Alberta has no provincial sales tax.

Edmonton is a city that loves to play—every month, it seems, the city hosts a festival, rodeo, carnival, anniversary, or other celebration, earning it yet another title: Canada's Festival City, with more than 30 festivals per year. See www.festivalcity.ca for the calendar. These celebrations of music, food, theater, history, horsemanship, and home land in every season, among them: Silver Skate Festival (mid-February); Edmonton Poetry Festival (late May); Canada Day celebrations (July 1); A Taste of Edmonton (late July); Klondike Days (late July); Edmonton Dragon Boat Festival (late August); Latin Festival (late August); Canadian Country Music Week (mid-September) and Accordion Extravaganza (late September); Edmonton International LitFest (early October); Canadian Finals Rodeo (mid-November); and Festival of Trees (early December).

The Royal Alberta Museum is one of Canada's most popular museums, at 12845 102nd Ave., just west of downtown, with exhibits on a broad range of subjects, from the province's aboriginal people to dinosaurs, geology, insects, ice age mammals, and more. There's a café and gift shop here, too. Admission is charged. Call 780-453-9100 or visit www.royalalbertamuseum.ca.

At Muttart Conservatory, take in the weird and wonderful sight of four massive glass pyramids in western Canada. Each one houses plant life particular to a climate, such as tropical, arid, and temperate. The fourth pyramid is reserved for seasonal displays, which regularly rotate. You'll find it at 9626 96A St. Call 780-442-5311 or visit www.muttartconservatory.ca.

Fort Edmonton Park, at Fox and Whitemud drives, is a 158-acre living-history park, the country's largest, with 60 period buildings to explore. Walk through time at the 1846 Hudson's Bay Trading Post, or down streets from 1885, 1905, and 1920. Watch a blacksmith or an old-fashioned rope maker at work. Catch a ride on a stagecoach or the steam train. This is a great place to teach kids about history while they're having fun. You'll find plenty of gift shops and restaurants. The park is owned by the City of Edmonton. For more information, call 780-442-5311 or visit the website www.fort edmontonpark.ca.

A futuristic building at 11211 142nd St. houses the TELUS World of Science, Edmonton's space and science museum with exciting, interactive galleries and permanent and traveling exhibits. Science is anything but a boring subject here. Inside, kids and adults alike will enjoy observation and hands-on play—from learning more about wildfires and the weather to other wonders of space. Features include a planetarium—the largest in North America—laser shows, mock Challenger missions, and fantastic you-are-there films in the IMAX theater. Call 780-451-3344 or visit www.edmontonscience.com.

BIG SHOPPING AT BIGGEST MALL IN NORTH AMERICA

The West Edmonton Mall is billed as The Greatest Indoor Show on Earth and Alberta's Number One Attraction. Sprawling over a 110-acre site, this remarkable indoor megamall counts 800 stores and services, an ice arena, thrill rides, kiddie rides, a water park, and aquariums. Located at 87th Ave. and 107th St., it's not hard to find. Roadside signs will lead the way, especially as you travel north on Hwy. 2—it rounds the city limits and practically lands you in the parking lot. And once you're inside, you'll pick up a map to figure your way from there. Wear your walking shoes, and be sure to bring your swimsuit, ice skates, and maybe your bowling ball. (Never mind, they have skates and bowling balls.)

Kids in Edmonton have no excuse for saying, "There's nothing to do!" More likely it's "There's too much to do!"

Choose from nine attractions, any one of which could stand alone as big deal outside the mall. There's the Galaxyland Amusement Park, with two dozen rides and attractions, including the spinning roller coaster called the Orbiter; World Waterpark, with slides, a wave pool, and kiddie water play; the Deep Sea Adventure, with submarine rides; Sea Life Caverns; Professor Wem's Adventure Golf, a miniature course; and the Ice Palace, an ice rink that's occasionally used by the Edmonton Oilers hockey team. There's an entire pirate ship in the middle of one wing.

Hungry? Dine at any of 110 restaurants. This is, after all, a mall. You'll find a wide selection, from cheap eats in various food courts to an elegant evening at a live dinner theater, and dozens in between. Entertainment options for kids to adults are likewise broad, including Space Race, Lazer Extreme, and the Wild West Shooting Theatre.

Not to mention the shopping.

For more information, call 780-444-5300 or visit www.wem.ca. And remember, this is the only province with no provincial sales tax, so spend to your heart's delight!

A pirate ship afloat in a shopping center—the famous Edmonton Mall. North America's biggest mall holds several theme parks under one roof, not to mention hundreds of stores.

Church St. (officially 96th St.) was once listed in *Ripley's Believe It or Not* for the 16 churches you'll find in one small section. Another local oddity, although it's not listed in *Ripley's*, is Edmonton's prized four-story-high cowboy boot, installed in 1989 at a boot factory that later closed, 10007 167th St. NW. Made of fiberglass, it weighs 40 tons. The new business there is taking good care of it. This city also claims the distinction of having the longest stretch of urban park in Canada: the North Saskatchewan River valley park system.

The Alberta Legislature Building, at 10800 97th Ave., is an architectural beauty built in 1912 on the site of Fort Edmonton. An interpretive center follows the building's history and provincial politics. Guided tours are available several times a day. Call for scheduled times at 780-427-7362 or visit the website at www.assembly.ab.ca.

Take a cruise on the *Edmonton Queen* riverboat, which offers daily cruises through the river valley. Dinner cruises with Dixieland entertainment are available, too. Call 780-424-BOAT or see www.edmontonqueen.com.

For more information on local events and attractions, call Edmonton Tourism at 800-463-4667 or visit www.edmonton.com.

LODGING

The Aladdin Motel
15425 111th Ave.
780-484-0071
www.thealaddinmotel.com
37 air-conditioned units, free movies, microwave, fridge, free local calls. Small dogs accepted.

Alberta Place Suite Hotel
10049 103rd St.
780-423-1565
www.albertaplace.com
85 units, all with fully equipped kitchens, cable TV, Internet, free local calls, laundry. Exercise room, indoor pool. Nonsmoking facility. Pets welcome. Discounts to West Edmonton Mall attractions.

Argyll Plaza Hotel
9933 63rd Ave.
800-737-3783 or 780-438-5876
48 rooms, kitchenettes, suites, cable TV, movies. Whirlpool, sauna, lounge, restaurant. Free continental breakfast.

Best Western Cedar Park
5116 Gateway Blvd.
800-661-9461
Comfortable accommodations with cable TV, Internet, swimming pool, pet-friendly rooms. Licensed restaurant, lounge, 24-hour gift shop. Close to shopping and attractions.

Best Western City Centre
11310 109th St.
800-666-5026 or 780-479-2042
www.bestwestern.com
109 air-conditioned rooms, indoor pool, whirlpool, laundry, data ports. ATM, restaurant, lounge. Close to shopping. Children under 18 stay free.

Best Western Westwood Inn
18035 Stony Plain Rd.
800-557-4767 or 780-483-7770
169 air-conditioned rooms, cable TV, movies, laundry service. Indoor pool, sauna, whirlpool, steam room, squash court. Restaurant, lounge. Handicap-accessible rooms.

Campus Tower Suite Hotel
11145 87th Ave.
780-439-6060
Located near university, fine dining, entertainment, park system. On-site restaurant and lounge.

Canterra Suites Executive Hotel
11010 Jasper Ave.
877-421-1212 or 780-421-1212
www.canterrasuites.com
44 apartments, 1–3 bedrooms, cable TV, free movies. Fridge, microwave, washer/dryer, free Internet, hair dryer, iron and board. Close to food and shopping.

Century Casino and Hotel Edmonton
13103 Fort Rd.
780-643-4000
26-room hotel in facility with casino, two fine dining rooms, and a deli. Waterfalls and stone fireplaces in casino.

Chateau Louis Hotel
11727 Kingsway
800-661-9843 or 780-452-7770
140 rooms, suites, family rooms in European-style boutique hotel. Cable TV, Internet, hair dryer, iron, wheelchair-accessible shower. Business center, 24-hour room service, restaurant, piano bar, gaming room. Outdoor courtyard and gazebo.

Coast Edmonton House
10205 100th Ave.
800-716-6119 or 780-420-4000
www.coasthotels.com
1- and 2-bedroom luxury suites with amenities.
Fitness center, Internet, indoor pool, sauna, steam
rooms. Restaurant, lounge, covered parking.
Downtown location.

Coast Edmonton Plaza Hotel
10155 105th St.
780-423-4811
www.coasthotels.com
299 deluxe rooms, suites, cable TV, laundry service. Exercise room, indoor pool. Lounge, family
restaurant. Downtown, close to business and government.

Coliseum Inn
11845 Wayne Gretzky Dr. South
877-471-1231 or 780-471-1231
www.coliseuminn.ca
98 recently renovated units with cable TV, Internet,
laundry. ATM, exercise room, sports bar, room
service.

Comfort Inn & Suites Downtown Edmonton
10425 100th Ave.
800-384-6835 or 780-423-5611
www.comfortinnedmonton.com
108 guest rooms, cable TV, free Internet, movies,
indoor pool, iron, restaurant.

Continental Inn & Suites
16625 Stony Plain Rd.
888-484-9660 or 780-484-7751
www.continentalinn.ca
100 units with amenities, cable TV, free movies,
data ports, laundry. Dining, lounge, coffee shop,
room service. Vehicle plug-ins.

Courtyard by Marriott
1 Jasper Ave. NW
780-423-9999
www.marriott.com
Well-appointed, air-conditioned rooms with coffee,
minibar, room service, free continental breakfast,
Internet. Fitness facility, restaurant, lounge on site.

Crowne Plaza–Chateau Lacombe
10111 Bellamy Hill NW
800-661-8801
www.chateaulacombe.com
307 rooms, downtown luxury hotel overlooking river
valley. All amenities included. Revolving restaurant.

Days Inn Downtown Edmonton
10041 106th St.
800-267-2191 or 780-423-1925
www.daysinn.com
71 units, cable TV, hair dryer, Internet, ATM.
Covered parking, room service. Airport shuttle.

Days Inn & Suites West Edmonton
10010 179A St.
780-444-4440
84 guest rooms and 24 suites, some with kitchenettes. Three-minute drive to West Edmonton Mall.
Business center, free Internet, laundry. Restaurant
and fitness center.

Delta Edmonton Centre Suite Hotel
10222 102nd St.
800-890-3222 or 780-429-3900
www.deltaedmontoncentre.com
169 deluxe suites and rooms. Internet, business
center, babysitting. Whirlpool, sauna, restaurant,
lounge. In City Centre Shopping Complex.

Eastglen Inn Edmonton
6918 118th Ave.
888-411-2610 or 780-471-2610
www.eastgleninn.com
47 units with cable TV, fridge, data ports. Vehicle
plug-ins. Some pets accepted. Close to attractions.

Executive Royal Inn West Edmonton
10010 178th St.
800-661-4879 or 780-484-6000
www.executivehotels.net
236 units, cable TV, games, Internet. ATM, business center, executive wing. Room service. Gift
shop.

Fairmont Hotel Macdonald
10065 100th St.
800-441-1414 or 780-424-5181
www.fairmont.com
198 luxury units in downtown 4-Diamond hotel.
Cable TV, minibars, hair dryer, Internet. Exercise
room, hot tub, business center, ATM. Saltwater
pool.

Fantasyland Hotel at West Edmonton Mall
17700 87th Ave.
800-RESERVE or 780-444-3000
www.fantasylandhotel.com
355 units with 11 theme rooms (African, Polynesian,
Roman, etc.), cable TV, games, Internet, fridge, hair
dryer. Health club/spa, hair salon, vehicle plug-ins.
Adjacent to World Waterpark.

Four Points by Sheraton Edmonton South
7230 Argyll Rd. NW
780-465-7931
www.starwoodhotels.com/fourpoints
Grand waterfall and pond greets guests entering
139-room deluxe hotel. Business center, free Wi-Fi,
pool, whirlpool, fitness center. Restaurant and pub.

Glenora Inn
12327 102nd Ave. NW
780-488-6766
Historic 1912 hotel with 21 rooms and suites, each
decorated with antiques. In Art Gallery District of
west Edmonton.

Grand Hotel

10266 103rd St. NW
888-422-6365 or 780-422-6365
71 units, cable TV, Internet. Liquor store, vehicle plug-ins. Free breakfast.

Greenwood Inn

4485 Gateway Blvd. (Hwy. 2)
780-431-1100
www.greenwoodinn.ca
224 rooms in south-side hotel. Cable TV, movies, laundry service. Indoor pool, whirlpool, steam room, exercise room. Gift shop, restaurant.

Hilton Garden Inn West Edmonton

17610 Stony Plain Rd.
780-443-2233
www.hiltongardeninn.com
160 units, cable TV, free movies, Internet, fridge, hair dryer, iron and board. Exercise room, hot tub, sports bar, room service.

Holiday Inn Hotel & Suites West Edmonton

11330 170th St.
780-444-3110
www.hiedmonton.com
Comfortable, air-conditioned rooms with coffee, laundry, Internet. Pool, fitness room, whirlpool.

Hotel Selkirk

1920s St., Fort Edmonton Park (park located at Whitemud and Fox drives)
877-496-7227 or 780-496-7227
www.hotelselkirk.com
Deluxe hotel furnished in 1920s style echoes an earlier building that stood from 1903 to 1962. Now with air-conditioning and fully restored to its grand days. Restaurant and lounge on-site.

Howard Johnson Hotel

15540 Stony Plain Rd.
780-446-4656
www.hojoedmonton.com
60 air-conditioned rooms, nonsmoking floor, Internet, cable TV, free movies. Family restaurant, lounge, room service. Free parking.

Inn on 7th

10001 107th St. NW
780-421-7363
172 units, cable TV, wireless Internet, data ports. Free local calls. Room service.

Jockey Motel

3604 118th Ave.
780-479-5981
52 units, cable TV, free movies, free local calls. Family rates.

Lodge Motor Inn

18125 Stony Plain Rd.
780-489-3321
54 units, cable TV, free movies, Internet, free local calls. Family rates. Close to West Edmonton Mall.

Mayfield Hotel & Suites

16615 109th Ave.
800-661-0984 in North America or 780-484-0821
www.mayfieldinnedmonton.com
327 units, cable TV, games, Internet. ATM, health club/spa, lounge with live music/entertainment, saltwater swimming pool, room service. Shuttle to West Edmonton Mall.

Quality Inn West Harvest

17803 Stony Plain Rd.
780-484-8000
160 guest rooms with air-conditioning, free Internet in some rooms, coffee, wheelchair access. Restaurant and lounge on-site.

Ramada Hotel & Conference Centre

11834 Kingsway Ave.
780-454-5454
www.ramadaedmonton.com
316 units, cable TV, games, hair dryer, iron, laundry, Internet. Hair salon, gift shop, sports bar, room service.

Ramada Inn & Waterpark

5359 Calgary Trail
800-661-9030 or 780-434-3431
www.ramada.com
123 rooms, nonsmoking floor, cable TV, Internet, movies, laundry service. Two giant waterslides, pool, exercise room, hot tub. Restaurant, lounge.

Rest E-Z Inn

21640 Stony Plain Rd. NW
780-447-4455
40 units, most with air-conditioning. Cable TV, free movies, Internet. Next door to waterslide and restaurant.

Rosslyn Inn & Suites

13620 97th St.
877-785-7005 or 780-476-6241
92 units, some wheelchair accessible, cable TV, free movies, Internet, hair dryer, iron, laundry. ATM, exercise room, wheelchair-accessible shower. Restaurant, close to shopping.

Sands Hotel and Conference Center

12340 Fort Rd.
888-444-3402 or 780-474-5476
www.sandshoteledm.com
54 units with cable TV, free local calls, hair dryer, Internet. ATM, family restaurant, room service.

The Sutton Place Hotel Edmonton
10235 101st St.
866-378-8866 or 780-428-7111
www.suttonplace.com
313 deluxe units, cable TV. ATM, hair salon, health club, spa, pool, hot tub. Restaurant and lounge on-site. Handicap accessible.

Travelodge Edmonton South
10320 45th Ave. South
800-578-7878 or 780-436-9770
219 rooms with cable TV, Internet, movies, hair dryer, room service. Indoor pool, whirlpool. Restaurant. Close to shopping, dining, nightclubs.

Travelodge West
18320 Stony Plain Blvd.
780-474-6031
85 rooms, cable TV, adjoining units. Barbershop, restaurant, lounge. Cold-weather hookups.

Union Bank Inn
10053 Jasper Ave.
888-423-3601 or 780-423-3600
www.unionbankinn.com
34 units in full-service hotel. Cable TV, free movies, PC friendly, fireplaces and goose-down bedding in all rooms. Exercise room, free full breakfast.

West Edmonton Mall Inn
17504 90th Ave.
780-444-9378
In the great West Edmonton Mall; features 88 well-appointed rooms with voice mail, cable, Internet, coffee, hair dryer.

Westin Edmonton
10135 100th St.
800-228-3000 or 780-426-3636
www.westin.com/edmonton
413 deluxe units, cable TV, free movies, fridge, hair dryer, iron and board, PC friendly. Exercise room, pool, hot tub. Business center, babysitting. Downtown location.

CAMPGROUNDS

Edmonton:
Glowing Embers Travel Centre & RV Park
2 miles (3.2 km) west of Edmonton on Hwy. 16A and Hwy. 60
780-962-8100
268 full-service sites. Internet, RV wash, laundry, washrooms, store. Close to West Edmonton Mall. Reservations accepted.

Rainbow Valley Campground
Whitemud Park off 122nd St., south of Whitemud Frwy.
888-434-3991 or 780-434-5531
88 sites, with and without power; tent camping. Showers, washrooms, laundry, dump station. Store, playground, nature trails.

Royal Scot Motel & Trailer Park
20904 Stony Plain Rd.
780-477-3088
33 fully serviced sites; 33 sites with power only. Close to West Edmonton Mall and downtown.

Shakers Acres
21530 103rd Ave. (off Hwy. 16A)
877-447-3565 or 780-447-3564
www.shakersacresrvpark.com
165 sites with full or partial hookups, showers, laundry, groceries, public phone.

Whitemud Creek Golf & RV Park Resort
3428 156th St. SW
780-988-6800
125 sites. Access to course makes this a golfer's delight. Boat launch, store, pit toilets, and water pump.

Leduc:
Lions Campground
20 miles (32 km) south of Edmonton (South on 50th St. then east on Rollyview Rd.)
780-986-1882
69 sites with full hookups, tent area. Washroom, phone, dump station. Heated picnic shelter. Open in summers. Reservations accepted.

Devon:
Lions Campground
520 Haven Ave., 20 miles (32 km) southwest of Edmonton
780-987-4777
www.devonlionspark.com
200 sites with and without full hookups; tent camping. Restrooms, firepits. Playgrounds, baseball diamond, gold panning, horseshoe pits. Adjacent to Devon Golf & Country Club.

Sherwood Park:
Half Moon Lake Resort
16 miles (25.5 km) east of Edmonton via 23rd Ave.
780-922-3045
www.halfmoonlakeresort.ca
196 sites, with and without power. Hayrides, ponies, horseback rides, petting zoo, wading pool, lake, playground, trout pond, minigolf, boat rentals. Reservations accepted.

Sherwood Forest Campground & RV Park
23242 Hwy. 14
780-467-3329
40 sites, with and without power. Café. Adjacent to golf course and bird sanctuary.

Spring Lake:
Spring Lake Resort & RV Park
499 Lakeside Dr., 30 minutes west of Edmonton off Hwy. 16A
780-963-3993
160 sites with full and partial hookups or dry camping. No tenting sites available. Dump station, swimming, trout fishing, concession, picnic area. Boat and log cabin rentals.

RESTAURANTS

ABC Country Restaurant
4485 Gateway Blvd.
780-786-5411
Homemade is the watchword on full menu, including baked goods. Family dining, kids' menu.

Barb & Ernie's Restaurant
9906 72nd Ave.
780-433-3242
German buffet restaurant famed for its extensive selection of breakfast foods. There's always a line, so come early.

Brits Fish & Chips
6940 77th St.
780-485-1797
Classic British-style fish and chips.

Characters
10257 105th St.
780-421-4100
www.characters.ca
Elegant fusion dining, seasonal menu items.

The Copper Pot Restaurant
9707 110th St., #101
780-452-7800
www.copperpot.ca
Specializing in Canadian fare.

The Creperie
10220 103rd St. NW
780-643-2321
French country, crêpes. Award-winning restaurant in downtown location.

Delux Burger Bar
9682 142nd St. NW
780-420-0101
The burger goes chic, along with premium wine, beer, and spirits. Other inventive menu items. Eat indoors or on the heated patio.

Doan's Restaurant
Downtown: 10130 107th St.
780-424-3034
South side: 7909 104th St.
780-434-4448
Vietnamese and Thai cuisine.

Famous Steak and Pizzeria
13128 82nd St.
780-475-2473
Casual steakhouse, pizza, lounge.

4th & Vine Wine Bar
11358 104th Ave.
780-497-7858
Food and wine in a friendly atmosphere.

Hardware Grill
9698 Jasper Ave.
780-423-0969
Upscale restaurant features award-winning cuisine and impressive wine list. Reservations recommended.

Haweli Restaurant & Lounge
10220 103rd St.
780-421-8100
Authentic East Indian cuisine.

Highlevel Diner
10912 88th Ave.
780-433-0993
Health food, vegetarian dishes, brunch. Located at the foot of the High Level Bridge.

Japanese Village
10126 100th St.
780-422-6083
Sushi, steak, seafood.

The King and I Thai Cuisine
8208 107th St.
780-433-2222
Thai cuisine with vegetarian, meat, seafood, and poultry selections.

La Spiga Ristorante Italiano
10133 125th St.
780-482-3100
Fine Italian dining in 1913 mansion. Award-winning menu.

Montana's Cookhouse Saloon
10330 GA MacDonald Ave.
780-434-2886
Casual restaurant with cabin decor, extensive menu.

New Asian Village
10143 Saskatchewan Dr.
780-433-3084
www.newasianvillage.com
East Indian dining. Top honors among Canada's ethnic restaurants.

Pepper 'n' Chili
10406 Mayfield Rd.
780-487-6688
Szechuan and Cantonese selections in large, modern restaurant.

Ruth's Chris Steak House
9990 Jasper Ave. #100
780-643-2372
Top-of-the-line steaks, seafood, award-winning
wine list. Reservations recommended.

Tom Goodchild's Moose Factory
4810 Calgary Trail South
780-437-5616
Alberta beef plays a central role in the menu, along
with seafood, alligator, even sushi.

Smokey Joe's Hickory Smoke House
15135 Stony Plain Rd.
780-413-3379
Hickory-smoked beef, chicken, and pork, and side
dishes.

Road Notes

To leave Edmonton, take Hwy. 16A west toward Spruce Grove and Stony Plain and connect with Hwy. 43 north. You'll stay on Hwy. 43 all the way across northern Alberta as it wends north and west.

A series of small towns along Hwy. 43 forms a dot-to-dot line between Edmonton and Whitecourt. Services and facilities such as gas stations, self-service laundries, restaurants, motels, and campgrounds are available all along this stretch.

(A few miles past Stony Plain is the junction for the westbound Yellowhead Hwy. 16A. For more information, see the section on the Yellowhead-Cassiar Highways in Chapter 7, Western Canada's Northbound Byways.)

WHITECOURT

From Edmonton, AB: 104 miles (167 km)

To Valleyview, AB: 104 miles (167 km)

To Grande Prairie, AB: 173 miles (278.5 km)

The confluence of the Athabasca and McLeod rivers, two major transportation routes, seemed a natural place for a settlement to spring up in rich, forested land. A family-operated sawmill was established here by James William Millar in 1922 and has since grown into a major employer, along with two other timber-related companies. Forestry, oil and gas, sand and gravel, and tourism keep Whitecourt's 9,000-plus people happy and hard at work. Nearly half of all adults are involved in some form of volunteerism.

At the east end of town, at 3002 33rd Ave. (off Hwy. 43), informational help for tourists is housed in a beautiful newer building with a very long name: Whitecourt and District Forest Interpretive Centre, Heritage Park and Tourist Information Centre. For information by phone, call 800-313-7383 or 780-778-3433. For walk-ins, they're open seven days a week in the summer, and the center's staffers can help with directions and ideas as well as plenty of printed material. Multimedia museum displays inform about the city's beginnings and its natural history, particularly in forestry, and outside an interpretive trail through the forest rounds out your education.

If you're looking for outdoor fun, go swimming at Rotary Park, at the end of 51st Ave. The River Slide is open all summer long, and the pond is stocked for kids to enjoy some fishing. Pick up a guide to Alberta's fishing regulations wherever licenses are sold. Find details at 780-778-2273.

Other choices for local recreation include horseback riding, boating, fishing, or

Museum, just east of Beaverlodge, where antique farm equipment has been restored to working order. Also, Pouce Coupe is proud of its museum in the old railroad station, which houses artifacts tracing this community's beginnings as a trading post in 1908.

These roadside communities also offer fuel, meals, and lodging. Multiple camping opportunities lie along this stretch of the road, from small municipal campgrounds to provincial parks. Watch for the signs.

As you near Dawson Creek and enter British Columbia, be sure to set your clocks back one hour to reflect Pacific time. If you follow the Alaska Hwy. through British Columbia and the Yukon Territory, you won't have to change the time again until you cross the Alaska-Yukon border.

DAWSON CREEK, BRITISH COLUMBIA

From Grande Prairie, AB: 86 miles (138.5 km)

From the Montana border: 753 miles (1,212 km)

To the Alaska border: 1,190 miles (1,915 km)

To Fairbanks, AK: 1,488 miles (2,395 km)

Symbolically, Dawson Creek is the end of this road and the beginning of another. You have arrived at Mile 0 of the famed Alaska Hwy., and a new leg of your adventure is about to begin. For a complete description of Dawson Creek and its services, facilities, and attractions, see Chapter 6, The Alaska Highway.

Posing with the Milepost 0 cairn and sign, Kerstin Drees and Jurgen Muller of Moers, Germany, made another tick on their Pan-American drive from the tip of South America to as far north as roads would take them.

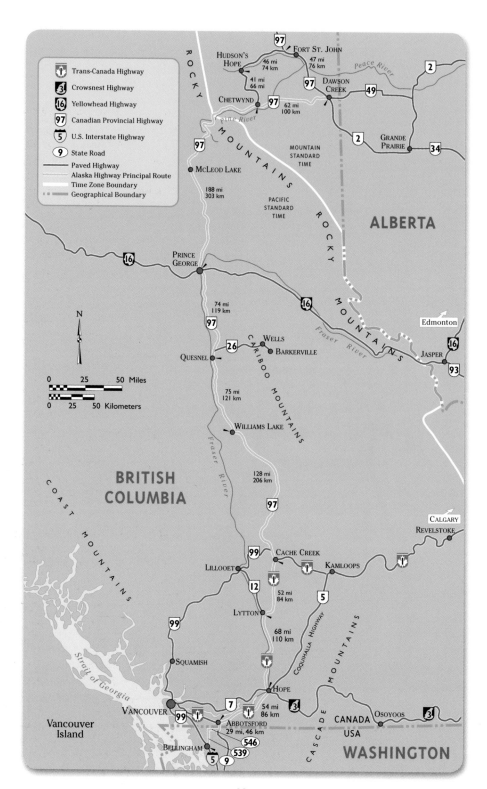

CHAPTER 5

THE WESTERN ROUTE:
THROUGH BRITISH COLUMBIA TO DAWSON CREEK, BC, AND MILE 0

See for yourself why British Columbia was chosen to host the 2010 Olympics and Para-lympic Winter Games. If natural beauty were measured on a scale of one to ten, British Columbia would easily break out the top, like an overheated thermometer. Canada's westernmost province is flat-out gorgeous from south to north, west to east.

Motoring along the northbound highways that lead to Dawson Creek, you can't miss the fascinating juxtaposition of the cultivated and uncivilized: orderly farms and untamed rivers, formal street grids beneath a tumble of mountains, and logging trucks rumbling by tearooms.

Evidence of British, French, and American influence is also visible in this province. But do not overlook the region's rich and ancient cultures. In museum exhibits and in daily practice, the First Nations people demonstrate the continuation of centuries-old tradi-tions. Learn about life in this country before contact with Europeans, along with customs and traditions in dance, art, and storytelling that continue today. Planning can begin at the Aboriginal Tourism Association of BC. Browse their site at www.aboriginalbc.com.

This traditional homeland of Canada's first people remains rich in resources such as big game, fish, birds, and small furbearers. As you drive, take care to watch for wildlife-viewing opportunities. We saw caribou, bears, stone sheep, bison, eagles, hawks, and other birds, plus numerous species of fish during our trip. In the case of big game on the road, keep your eyes open for safety's sake, as well as for photographic opportunities.

British Columbia is widely known for its magnificent coastline and islands, the Fraser and other wild rivers, fruitful farmlands, mountain lakes, glaciers and ice fields, and the longest stretch of the Canadian Rockies. Victoria and Vancouver, its major cities in the southwestern part of the province, rival many in Europe for cultural attraction and architectural wonder. Fertile farms in the south feed British Columbia and con-tribute to the province's export economy. Inland, the historic Cariboo Country holds stories of a gold rush that lingered well past that of the Klondike.

Crossing the border from Sumas, WA, into Canada. For a shorter wait, try to time your crossing so you're not with the weekend vacationers.

BRITISH COLUMBIA AT A GLANCE

Size: 365,948 square miles, or 947,800 square km

Population in 2006: 4,310,452

Capital: Victoria

Tourism and lodging: 800-435-5622 or www.hellobc.com

Provincial and national park camping: 800-689-9025 or www.discovercamping.ca

Sport fishing: www.env.gov.bc.ca/fw/fish

Hunting: www.env.gov.bc.ca/fw/wildlife

Canada border information: 204-983-3500 (outside Canada) or www.cbsa-asfc.gc.ca

Road reports: 800-550-4997 (anywhere in North America) or www.drivebc.ca

As you travel toward Cache Creek, the landscape turns drier and rockier, and the scent of sagebrush and juniper lingers in the air, bringing with it a sense of the Old West. Indeed, Canada's Old West holds as much wonderful and bizarre history as that of the United States, with ranchers, cowboys, miners, outlaws, and the women who loved them. You can visit Historic Hat Creek Ranch or Barkerville to learn more about the Cariboo Wagon Rd. and the stagecoach line that once connected the western towns.

Like elsewhere in western Canada, the northernmost reaches are the rough-and-ready regions, where timber, oil, and natural gas take economic precedence over farming. This is not surprising, considering that the number of frost-free days shrinks with every northbound step in latitude, and the soil tends toward spotty sections of permafrost. As you drive, you'll also see incredible evidence of mankind's ability to harness energy through building dams and extracting oil and gas.

WASHINGTON–BRITISH COLUMBIA BORDER

To Chilliwack, BC: 17.5 miles (28 km)
To Dawson Creek, BC: 692 miles (1,113.5 km)

To begin your northward journey through British Columbia, make your way to north–south I-5 in western Washington. Take I-5 north from Seattle to Bellingham, the southernmost port city on the Alaska Marine Highway System. (See Chapter 9, Alaska Marine Highway System, for more information on ferry routes.)

Just north of Bellingham, I-5 connects with northbound WA 539 (Guide Meridian Rd.). From the I-5 turnoff to the international border, it's about 25 miles (40 km). Recent road improvements and new roundabouts on Guide Meridian Rd. have made driving these two dozen miles so much more smooth and efficient. Along here, you might want to top off the tank or stop for groceries as a last-chance measure to spend those US dollars.

Northbound travelers, continue on Guide Meridian to the junction with WA 546 (Lynden-Sumas Hwy.) and turn right—this eastbound route is later designated as Badger Rd. Eight miles of driving brings you to the junction with WA 9, but there's no need to turn. Continue straight, and within a few minutes you'll reach Sumas, the border town on the US side. On the Canada side, it's Huntington, BC. The border crossing is open 24 hours a day. (See the section on Border Crossings in Chapter 2, What You Need to Know, A to Z.)

Road Notes

Heading north from the border, stay on Hwy. 11 for 3 miles (5 km) to Abbotsford, a fast-growing community of 124,000 folks who live snug between the Fraser River on the north and the US border on the south. Abbotsford is widely known for its temperate climate, which feeds the region's abundant crops of raspberries, blueberries, and strawberries. You can pick your own at area farms and in early July enjoy a taste of desserts and berry entrées at the Berry Beat Festival in historic downtown Abbotsford. Later in the month, cowboys, farmers, and fairgoers congregate at the Abbotsford Exhibition Park for the Agrifair and Mighty Fraser Rodeo, what local folks call "The Best Little Country Fair."

In mid-August, the Abbotsford International Airshow features flying stunts by Canadian and international pilots, plus ground displays of fixed-wing, military, war-bird, homebuilt, and civilian planes. It's been drawing fans since 1962. For information, call 604-852-8511 or see www.abbotsfordairshow.com.

Unleash your daring side—give skydiving a try in the safest possible way. The Abbotsford Skydive Centre can arrange for a tandem jump, so you're attached to an experienced diver, making that first jump virtually danger free, if not fright free. And they'll take pictures of you while you're airborne. Call 888-738-5867 or 604-327-5867, or browse www.vancouver-skydiving.bc.ca.

Grab a taste of cultural history at The Xá:ytem Longhouse Interpretive Centre in Mission, an important archaeological site that revealed evidence of its occupation thousands of years ago. The Stó:lō Nation erected a longhouse at the site and offers First Nations culture and history tours. From Abbotsford, turn north on the Trans-Canada Hwy. (Hwy. 1) and cross the Fraser River to reach Mission via Hwy. 11. Learn more at www.xaytem.ca.

Mechanically oriented members of the family will enjoy a tour of the Barrowtown Pump Station, 10 miles (16 km) east of Abbotsford off Hwy. 1, where since 1923, pumps have drained what once was Sumas Lake, opening up 30,000 acres of land for farming. There's a picnic area here, too. Call for information at 604-823-4678.

Abbotford's mild climate also allows golfers to stay in the game 12 months of the year. You'll find dozens of courses within a 50-mile radius. Consult www.golflink.com for details.

To learn more about area attractions, events, lodging, and dining, stop by the Abbotsford Visitor Center at 34561 Delair Rd. (take Exit 92, Sumas Wy.), or call 888-332-2229. Visit their website at www.tourismabbotsford.ca. To purchase tickets to sporting events, symphonies, or theater events, Tourism Abbotsford operates a box office on-site and is open from 9 AM to 5 PM. You can order tickets by phone at 604-859-1701.

From Abbotsford, follow Hwy. 1 east for 15 miles (24 km) to Chilliwack.

CHILLIWACK

From the Washington border: 17.5 miles (28 km)
To Hope, BC: 35.5 miles (57 km)

The Fraser River valley is a suitable setting for a painting, with snowcapped peaks as a backdrop to widespread farms and a pretty city. This is a place for folks who appreciate life in a rural setting with the convenience of a nearby metropolis. Vancouver is just an hour's travel to the west.

PHOTOGRAPHERS' PARADISE

Minter Gardens bills itself as a "world-class show garden," and now that I've seen it in person, I second the vote. Paths wend through, under, and around 32 acres of perfectly groomed hillsides that look as if an artist has applied color to the foliage in sweeps of paint, not plantings. Eleven themed gardens feature creative topiary, water gardens, and serene rest stops. Allow at least two hours to walk the paths among the gardens, aviary, and bonsai displays.

With 7,000-foot Mt. Cheam as a backdrop, skilled gardeners show off their talents in artfully pruned shrubbery, an archway of trained boughs, and topiary sculptures. My favorites included the "Floral Lady," a shrub woman whose southern belle hoopskirt was a blaze of flowers; another was a peacock whose body was a piece of topiary art, with his tail feathers swept across a downward slope in a rush of color.

One of the most photographed gardens is a tidy hillside with the words *Minter Gardens* snipped with sharp-edged precision in letters so large, you have to stand half a football field away just to get your picture. You'll come away with dozens of photos, each one an inspiration for your own gardening efforts. On the grounds, you'll also find a gift shop, snacks, and coffee, plus an on-site plant shop. (Keep in mind that you'll have to declare these agricultural products when you cross the US-Canada border, and officials may or may not allow certain plants, so you might shop here with your eyes only.) The Envision Conservatory Café is open daily, and the Trillium Restaurant serves a buffet lunch as well as a Sunday buffet brunch. Call 604-794-7044 for reservations. Minter Gardens is open April to mid-October and is located is off Hwy. 1 at Exit 135. Call 604-794-7191 or browse www.mintergardens.com.

Mt. Cheam, a prominent peak in the Canadian Cascades, is the wild backdrop for a tidy formal garden in Chilliwack's Minter Gardens.

Home to about 80,000 people, Chilliwack, "The Great Outside," prides itself on its recreational opportunities as well as its agriculture-based economy. Water is the tie that binds—the Fraser River, Chilliwack River, and Cultus, Chilliwack, and Harrison lakes are playgrounds for locals and visitors.

Generous water sources, along with southern BC's climate and good soil, have made agriculture king here. In local fields, you'll find flowers, grain, corn and other vegetables, herbs, pumpkins, and, like in the northwest United States, apples.

If golf is your game, you'll find more than 10 courses within a half hour of downtown Chilliwack. Among them is the full range of challenge, up to world-championship level, and in southern BC's mild temperatures you can easily golf into late autumn.

At the Chilliwack Museum and Archives, objects and artifacts help tell the story of this community's beginnings and the diverse people who have lived in this valley. Rated one of the top 10 museums in British Columbia by *Westworld Magazine*, the Chilliwack Museum is located downtown at 45820 Spadina Ave., in a 1912 structure that was the former city hall. From Hwy. 1, take the Yale Rd. exit north and follow Yale until you reach the museum at Spadina Ave. Open Monday through Friday, 9 AM to 4:30 PM. Call 604-795-5210.

Over Labor Day weekend, Chilliwack hosts the annual Bluegrass Festival at Chilliwack Heritage Park, Hwy. 1 at Lickman Rd. (Exit 116). It's a popular weekend, full of music, crafts, and free nightly corn roasts. There's even bluegrass church on Sunday morning. Check www.chilliwackartscouncil.com for dates and the list of performers.

For family fun, look just 10 miles (16 km) east of Chilliwack, where Bridal Falls offers Dinotown, a dinosaur theme park, golfing, waterslides, and bumper boats. There's something for every family member, from tots to adrenaline-seeking teens to adults who could use a little less adrenaline. Campsites for tents or RVs are nearby. Call Dinotown at 800-491-ROAR or visit www.dinotown.com. To reach the Bridal Falls Water Park and other neighboring attractions, take Exit 135 on Hwy. 1 east. Call 888-883-8852 or 604-794-7455 for rates and hours. The falls themselves are gorgeous—at 400 feet (122 meters), they are the sixth-highest in Canada.

Families also love to visit the Cultus Lake area, where either the provincial park or resort accommodations offer more fun. On the water: canoeing, kayaking, and fishing. On land: hiking, horseback riding, biking, and walking trails. Or in the resort park, which is open rain or shine, take on water features with names like Adventure River, Valley of Fear, or Radical Rapids. To reach the family-owned Cultus Lake Waterpark from eastbound Hwy. 1, take Exit 104 through Yarrow to Cultus Lake, about a 10-minute drive. Browse www.cultus.com or call 604-858-7214.

Anglers make the Chilliwack area a destination for lots of reasons—nearly all of them scaly. The Fraser River and multiple area lakes each represent a fishing adventure. It's just a question of whether you want to fish independently or arrange for a guide. Either way, provincial, regional, and seasonal regulations will apply, as well as those for a specific body of water. For more on local fishing, see www.fishchilliwack.com.

For more on local heritage, events, and activities, visit the Tourism Chilliwack Visitor Centre, 44150 Luckakuck Wy., or call 800-567-9535 or 604-858-8121. Visit www.tourismchilliwack.com.

LODGING

Best Western Rainbow Country Inn
43971 Industrial Wy.
800-665-1030 or 604-795-3828
www.rainbowcountryinn.com
74 air-conditioned rooms. Laundry, coffee, sauna, whirlpool. Indoor pool, family restaurant, coffee shop, lounge. Golf packages available.

Chilliwack Motor Inn
8120 Young Rd.
604-792-8501
24 units and kitchenettes with cable TV, outdoor pool, playground, laundry facilities. Smoking rooms available. Wheelchair access. Pets allowed.

Coast Chilliwack Hotel
45920 1st Ave.
604-795-4788
www.coastchilliwackhotel.com
110 newly remodeled rooms in a full-service hotel located downtown, overlooking park. Air-conditioned, fitness facility, Jacuzzi, indoor pool, free Wi-Fi, free laundry service. Restaurant, lounge. Close to shopping and entertainment.

Comfort Inn
45405 Luckakuck Wy.
800-228-5150 or 604-858-0636
www.choicehotels.ca/cn235
83 air-conditioned rooms, nonsmoking property. Cable TV, Internet, hair dryer, iron and board. Continental breakfast, business center. Restaurants, shopping, gardens, golf nearby.

Days Inn–Chilliwack
8583 Young Rd. South
800-329-7466 or 604-792-1955
www.daysinn.ca
29 newly remodeled, air-conditioned units. Cable TV, fridge, microwave, Internet. Business center, Continental breakfast, newspaper. Free local calls; near attractions.

Parkwood Lodge
8600 Young St.
877-793-1234 or 604-795-9155
www.besthotel.ca
30 deluxe air-conditioned rooms, some kitchenettes, cable TV, Internet, coffee. Nonsmoking property. Heated outdoor swimming pool, playground. Close to restaurants, shopping, attractions.

Rainbow Motor Inn
45620 Yale Rd.
800-834-5547 or 604-792-6412
www.rainbowmotorinn.com
40 newly renovated, air-conditioned rooms, efficiencies, free local calls, movies, laundry. Adjacent to restaurants, garden.

Royal Hotel
45886 Wellington Ave.
888-434-3388 or 604-792-1210
www.royalhotelchilliwack.com
29 units in circa 1908 inn, private bath, cable, air-conditioning, vintage furniture. Honeymoon suite with Jacuzzi. Internet. Full breakfast included. Restaurant.

Travelodge Hotel Chilliwack
45466 Yale Rd.
800-566-2511 or 604-792-4240
www.travelodgechilliwack.com
82 air-conditioned units, some kitchenettes. Cable TV, coffee. Indoor pool, Jacuzzi, laundry, arcade, restaurant.

Vedder River Inn
5788 Vedder Rd.
800-591-0181 or 604-824-7999
www.vedderriverinn.com
52 rooms and kitchenettes with microwave, fridge, Internet, coffeemakers, and TV. Some two-bedroom suites with full kitchens. Wheelchair accessible. Close to river and walking trail, shopping. Pet-friendly.

CAMPGROUNDS

For a detailed directory of provincial, city-operated, and private RV parks, browse the City of Chilliwack website at www.gov.chilliwack.bc.ca and type "camping" in the search box.

Bridal Falls Camperland RV Resort
53730 Bridal Falls Rd.; Hwy. 1, Exit 135
604-794-7361
www.holidaytrailsresorts.com
180 sites for high-quality resort camping with amenities: pool, hot tubs, clubhouse, restaurant. Near dining, attractions, golf, entertainment.

Cottonwood Meadows RV Country Club
44280 Luckakuck Wy.
604-824-7275
120 level sites with full hookups, pull-throughs, cable hookup, Internet, security gate. Free showers, clubhouse, steam room. Close to services.

Cultus Lake Provincial Park
Columbia Valley Hwy.; Hwy. 1 to Cultus Lake Rd.
604-795-6169; reservations: 800-689-9025
296 sites with mountain views, flush and pit toilets, firepits, hiking, swimming, sani-station. Open April to October. Reservations accepted at this provincial park.

Orchard Trailer Park
46289 Yale Rd. East; Hwy. 1, Exit 119A
604-795-7634
20 sites three blocks east of downtown, off highway, treed sites, full hookups, pull-throughs, showers, cable, laundry.

Sunnyside Campground
3405 Columbia Valley Hwy.; Hwy. 1, Exit 119.
604-858-5253
www.cultuslake.bc.ca
348 seasonal campsites, 108 full hookups, 133 tenting sites. Showers, bathrooms, firewood. Boat launch, fishing, canoeing, hiking, go-carts, waterslide, beaches. Restaurants. Operated by City of Chilliwack. Reservations available 12 months in advance.

Vedder River Campground
5215 Giesbrecht Rd.; west from Hope, Exit 119A
604-823-6012
www.cultuslake.bc.ca
270 sites, full hookups, pull-throughs, showers,
sani-station, laundry. Group sites, playground,
horseshoe pits. Operated by City of Chilliwack.

RESTAURANTS

Bozzini's
45739 Hocking Ave., # 4
604-792-0744
Casual family dining; open daily from 11 AM. Live
music in the lounge.

Bravo Restaurant & Lounge
46224 Yale Rd.
604-792-7221
Casual fine dining with Pacific Northwest fare.
Reservations accepted.

Dakota's Restaurant
45850 Yale Rd., #200
604-795-2215
Angus beef, prime rib, ribs, seafood. Bar, two
patios, private dining room.

Earls
45585 Luckakuck Wy.
604-858-3360
www.earls.ca
Pizza, pasta, burgers, creative soups and salads.
Wine, beer, spirits.

Garden Court Atrium Dining Room
43971 Industrial Wy., in Best Western Rainbow
Country Inn
800-665-1030 or 604-795-3828
Continental menu featuring aged steaks, seafood.
Live entertainment on weekends. Sunday brunch
buffet.

Greek Islands Restaurant
45781 Hocking Ave.
604-702-1881
www.greekislandsrestaurant.com
Greek cuisine, steaks, seafood. Open Tuesday–
Saturday, 11 AM–10 PM.

La Mansione
46290 Yale Rd. East
604-792-8910
Dinner service. Steak and seafood; historic setting
in nearly century-old mansion decorated with collectibles and fine art.

Mill Street Café
9381 Mill St.
604-795-4640
Casual fine dining. Organic and whole foods, Old
World wines. Original art.

The Pantry
45610 Yale Rd. West
604-792-2110
Family dining, breakfast all day. Sunday brunch
buffet. Seniors' and children's menus.

Preston's
45920 1st Ave.
604-701-3070
Fine dining featuring innovative dishes and cocktails.

The Reef Restaurant
46675 Yale Rd. East
604-392-4444
Caribbean-style lunch and dinner, seven days a
week. Weekend brunch. Live entertainment.

Rustica's Ristorante Italiano
9339 Main St., downtown
604-792-7081
Casual fine dining with the flavors of Italy.

Shandhar Hut
8835 Young Rd.
604-793-0188
Indian cuisine.

White Spot Restaurant
45373 Luckakuck Wy.
604-858-0602
Well-known BC restaurant serves breakfast, lunch,
dinner. Burgers, pasta, steak, chicken.

Yonnies Family Restaurant
45905 Yale Rd., #60, inside Southgate Shopping
Center
604-792-2512
Breakfast, lunch, and dinner, seven days a week.
Seniors' and children's menus.

Road Notes

Wouldn't a nice soak in a mineral hot springs do the trick right now? If you're willing to follow that urge, just past Chilliwack take Exit 135 to Hwy. 9 and east to Hwy. 7.

Harrison Hot Springs is a lovely resort village in the mountains and only about a half hour away from Chilliwack. The city bills itself as the "Sand Sculpture Capital of the World." Little more than 1,500 people live here on the shores of Harrison Lake, but water enthusiasts come from miles around for boating, windsurfing, swimming, or camping. At 37 miles (60 km) long, this is the largest body of freshwater in southwestern British Columbia. And anglers have discovered that this lake and the connecting Harrison and Fraser rivers offer fantastic fishing opportunities: salmon, sturgeon, trout, and steelhead. For online licenses and regulation information, go to www.gofishbc.com. The visitor information center at 499 Hot Springs Rd. can help direct you to guided fishing outfits in the area.

The hot springs themselves are a rare treat, with water coming out of the ground so hot that it must be cooled to between 85°F and 104°F (30°C to 40°C). The public pool is open year-round. For more information on the resort and spa, call 866-638-5075 or see www.harrisonresort.com.

Right out in front of the resort, you can book a day cruise with Shoreline Tours & Charters (604-819-3418), or you'll find a full range of water-sport rentals, from power boats to bumper boats and Sea-Doo rentals. Check with Harrison Watersports at 604-796-3513 or www.harrisonwatersports.com; or Killer's Cove Boat Rentals at 604-819-5398 or www.killerscoveboatrentals.com.

Information on hotels, shopping, and dining is available through the visitor center at 604-796-5581 or visit www.tourismharrison.com.

If you go, retrace your route back to Hwy. 1 for the best, fastest access to Hope.

HOPE

From Chilliwack, BC: 35.5 miles (57 km)

To Lytton, BC: 68 miles (109.5 km)

This charming community at the confluence of the Fraser and Coquihalla rivers is home to nearly 7,000 people. Hope seems surrounded by mountains as well as by rivers, and its beautiful natural setting has made it a vacation destination as well as the site for two major motion picture productions. The area and its temperate climate attract a unique variety of coastal and interior birds, so birders often arrive hoping to add to their life lists. Adventure sports lovers find plenty to do here, too.

The confluence of the two rivers has been a population center and transportation hub for thousands of years, and as a First Nations village, it was known as Ts'qó:ls. The term, meaning "bare" or "bald," referred to trees that have been shaped by prevailing winds, making them nearly bare on one side.

With the arrival of Europeans and the discovery of gold, newcomers renamed the settlement. For all the possibilities of how they settled on "Hope," there is no agreement. One of our favorites was attributed to old-time gold miners who wintered here between lousy mining seasons: "They lived in Hope and finally died in despair."

In 1981, Hollywood transformed Hope into a movie set for its filming of *First Blood* at sites all over town. A hundred locals were cast as extras, and for a while, actors

Hope's downtown park, with its distinctive chainsaw carvings, is a delightful place to relax and play. It's right across the street from shops and restaurants.

Sylvester Stallone and Brian Dennehy were small-town regulars. Just outside the visitor center, a full-size wooden cutout of Stallone (minus the face), wearing warfare gear and muscles, allows visitors to photograph each other in good humor. Once more, in 1988, Hope was starstruck during the filming of *Shoot to Kill*, starring Sidney Poitier and Kirstie Alley.

This little city vies with Chetwynd, BC, as Chainsaw Sculpture Capital of British Columbia, and pieces from a chainsaw sculpture competition each September can be found in Rotary Park along the river and in installations outside businesses all over town. But it all began in Hope's grassy, treed downtown park. In 1991, when a few of the giant old trees in Memorial Park began to die, local artist Pete Ryan made a proposal. He asked the city to leave 12-foot stumps rather than raze the trees. From them he carved detailed works of art depicting miners, burros, rams, and, best of all, bears. His work and that of other talented artists such as Randy Swope have become town treasures.

Mixing history and hiking, one must-see lies east of town: Coquihalla Canyon Provincial Recreation Area, where you can walk through five tunnels that were cut through solid granite for the long-abandoned Kettle Valley Railway, built from 1911 to 1918. Because the chief engineer was a Shakespeare fan, he used Shakespearean names on railroad bridges, waysides, and these, the Othello Quinette Tunnels. The railroad ties are long gone, and walkers and bikers enjoy the easy trail these days, creeping through high-ceilinged, dark tunnels that open up to impressive trestles over the rushing Coquihalla River.

For the more adventurous, try out a jet boat tour of the beautiful Fraser Canyon on a 4.5-hour run from Hope to Hell's Gate. Contact STS Guiding Service at 604-671-3474 or check out www.hellsgatejetboattours.com. No surprise—you *will* get wet.

Hiking trails for all levels of fitness can be found throughout the area, and the Hope Visitor Information Centre has detailed maps of local trails, plus maps of nearby Manning and Skagit Valley provincial parks. Other maps include walking tours to the various chainsaw sculptures and to locations where *First Blood* was filmed.

There's rafting, fishing, golfing, a leisure center, all kinds of fun. The helpful people at the visitor center will tell you about local activities and attractions and answer questions about highway conditions and weather, as well as direct you to lodging and restaurants. The center is at 919 Water Ave., along Hwy. 1. Call 604-869-2021, or browse www.hope.ca.

LODGING

Alpine Motel
505 Old Hope Princeton Wy.
877-869-9931 or 604-869-9931
14 air-conditioned, ground-level rooms, kitchenettes. Coffee, fridge. At-door parking.

Best Continental Motel
860 Fraser Ave.
604-869-9726
13 air-conditioned units, cable TV, free movies, fridge, coffee, Internet. Near shopping, bus depot. Senior discount.

City Centre Motel
455 Wallace St.
604-869-5411
16 air-conditioned rooms, cable TV, fridge, coffee/tea, movies. Senior discount. Close to park, grocery. Small pets okay.

Colonial 900 Motel
900 Old Hope Princeton Wy.
604-869-5223
www.colonial900motel.com
16 air-conditioned, nonsmoking rooms with mountain views. Cable TV, fridge, coffee, landscaped grounds. Adjacent to restaurant.

Coquihalla Motel
724 Old Hope Princeton Wy.
604-869-3572
18 recently renovated units in quiet setting, air-conditioned 1-, 2-, or 3-bedroom suites, some with kitchens. Cable TV, movies, coffee.

Heritage Motel
570 Old Hope Princeton Wy.
604-869-7166

Holiday Motel & RV Resort
63950 Old Yale Rd.
604-869-5352
www.holiday-motel.com
20 cabins and kitchenettes with 1 or 2 bedrooms in quiet neighborhood. Outdoor heated pool, playground. Near restaurant, pub.

Inn Towne Motel
510 Trans-Canada Hwy.
800-663-2612 or 604-869-7276
26 air-conditioned rooms, deluxe suites, kitchenettes, nonsmoking available. Laundry, indoor pool, whirlpool, sauna, garden patio. Close to attractions.

Lake of the Woods Resort
22805 Trans-Canada Hwy.
604-869-9211
www.lakewoods-resortmotel.com
Motel rooms, cabins, cottages in private woods, with mountain and lake views. Canoe rentals. Five minutes from downtown Hope.

Lucky Strike Motel
504 Old Hope Princeton Wy.
604-869-5715
www.luckystrikemotel.com
14 air-conditioned units, cable TV, movies, mountain views, landscaped grounds. Near restaurant, shopping. Senior discount.

The Maple Leaf Motor Inn
377 Old Hope Princeton Wy.
888-530-1995 or 604-869-7107
38 quiet, air-conditioned rooms, kitchenettes, cable TV, movies. Indoor pool, whirlpool, sauna. Dining, coffee shop.

Park Motel
823 4th Ave.
888-531-9933 or 604-869-5891
19 air-conditioned units with fridge, cable TV, Internet, coffee. Nice landscaping in downtown location.

Quality Inn

350 Old Hope Princeton Wy.
800-424-6423 or 604-869-9951
25 air-conditioned rooms, cable TV, free continental breakfast. Indoor hot tub, pool, sauna. 3-Diamond rating, AAA. Walk to downtown.

Red Roof Inn

477 Fraser
604-869-2446
27 air-conditioned units, some nonsmoking. Cable TV, indoor spa, whirlpool. Mountain views, restaurant, indoor swim spa, whirlpool.

Royal Lodge Motel

580 Old Hope Princeton Wy.
604-869-5358
http://royallodgemotel.ca
20 air-conditioned units, some connecting. Movie and sports channels, coffee, wireless, continental breakfast, ATM.

Skagit Motor Inn

655 3rd Ave.
888-869-5228 or 604-869-5220
www.skagit-motor-inn.com
30 air-conditioned ground-level rooms in wooded setting. Cable TV, Internet, free movies, Continental breakfast, pool, whirlpool, spa. Mountain views, close to downtown. Near restaurants. Senior discount.

Slumber Lodge

250 Fort St.
800-757-7766 or 604-869-5666
www.slumberlodgehopebc.com
34 air-conditioned rooms, suites. Downtown location. Indoor swimming pool, sauna, restaurant.

Swiss Chalets Motel

456 Trans-Canada Hwy.
800-663-4673 or 604-869-9020
www.swisschaletsmotel.com
26 air-conditioned rooms, family chalets, kitchenettes. Fireplace, cable TV, coffee. Near Fraser River.

Windsor Motel

778 3rd Ave.
888-588-9944 or 604-869-9944
www.bcwindsormotel.com
24 air-conditioned rooms in downtown setting. Family units, kitchenettes, nonsmoking available. Cable TV, coffee, senior discount.

CAMPGROUNDS

Coquihalla Campsite Hope

800 Kawkawa Lake Rd.
888-869-7118 or 604-869-7119
Full or partial hookups, riverfront sites, 24-hour security. Laundry, dump station, store. Recreation area, playground. Video games, covered picnic area. Senior discount. Pets allowed.

Holiday Motel & RV Resort

63950 Old Yale Rd.
604-869-5352
www.holiday-motel.com
14 sites with full hookups, 4 with partial hookups. Cable, heated outdoor pool. Near restaurant, pub. Surcharge for pets.

Hope Valley Campground

62280 Flood Hope Rd.; Hwy. 1, Exit 168
604-869-9857
130 sites with full or partial hookups, pull-throughs, tent sites. Showers, laundry, restrooms. Store, ice, gift shop. Game room, swimming pool, playground.

Kawkawa Lake Resort

55427 Kawkawa Lake Rd.
604-869-9930
www.kawkawalake.net
Full hookups, fire rings, picnic area, swimming, store. No dogs, no boats.

Othello Tunnels Campground & RV Park

67851 Othello Rd.; Hwy. 5, Exit 183
604-869-9448
www.othellotunnels.com
40 sites with full and partial hookups, tent sites, firepits. Laundry, free showers, barbecue area, rainbow trout fishing pond. Store, playground. Near Othello Quinette Tunnels.

Telte Yet Campsite

600 Water Ave.
604-869-9481
29 full hookup sites, tent camping. Showers, laundry, dump station. Group rates. Acres of trees along Fraser River. Walking distance to Hope.

Whistlestop RV Park

59440 St. Elmo Rd.; Hwy. 1, Exit 160
877-869-5132 or 604-869-5132
39 sites, full and partial hookups, tent sites, firepits. Wheelchair access. Free showers; laundry, dump station. Store, playground, grass and shade.

Wild Rose Campground & RV Park

62030 Flood Hope Rd.; Hwy. 1, Exit 165 or 168
604-869-9842
www.wildrosecamp.com
68 sites with full and partial hookups. 15 and 30 amp. Cable TV, Internet, showers, laundry, dump station. Discount for Good Sam, KOA, CAA/AAA, seniors.

RESTAURANTS

Blue Moose Coffee House
322 Wallace St.
604-869-0729
Sandwiches, soups, espresso, desserts, high-speed wireless.

Darrell's Place Family Restaurant
241 Wallace St.
604-869-3708
Hearty breakfasts, old-fashioned burgers, fries, homemade pies.

Driftwynd Bistro & Dining Room
273B Wallace St.
640-860-4950
Fine international dining. Alberta beef, wild Pacific salmon and scallops.

Home Restaurant
665 Old Hope Princeton Wy.
604-869-5558
Home-cooked burgers, ribs, baked goods, family dining.

Hope Drive-in & Restaurant
590 Old Hope Princeton Wy.
604-869-5380
Family owned since 1962, seating for 100.

Kan Yon
800 3rd Ave.
604-869-2212
Chinese and Canadian fare.

Kibo Japanese Restaurant
267 King St.
604-869-7317
Teriyaki, ribs, tempura, and Canadian fare.

Kimchi Japanese & Korean Restaurant
821A 6th Ave.
604-869-0070
Asian cuisine.

Little Tokyo Japanese Restaurant
259 Wallace St.
604-869-5628
Sushi, sashimi, teriyaki, tempura, Canadian cuisine.

New Golden Star Restaurant
377 Old Hope Princeton Wy.
604-869-9588
Chinese and Western cuisine with no MSG. Lunch and dinner buffets.

Papandreas Greek Taverna
904 Old Hope Princeton Wy.
604-869-7218
Family-owned restaurant serving Greek cuisine.

Rolly's Restaurant
888 Fraser Ave.
604-869-7448
Breakfast all day, casual dining. Great for families.

Skinny's Grille
63810 Flood Hope Rd.
604-869-5713
Music and menu items such as lasagna, prawns, ribs.

Yale is one of BC's oldest mining communities, and its historic church, St. John the Divine Anglican Church, is still standing on its original foundation.

Road Notes

Fifteen miles (24 km) north of Hope, you'll come upon Yale, a historic village site along the gold rush trail. In its advantageous position at the southern entrance of Fraser Canyon, Yale was the site for paddle wheelers to unload cargo that would continue its journey to the goldfields on the Cariboo Wagon Road, built between 1861 and 1863. The Cariboo gold rush was still going strong by 1863, when the Church of St. John the Divine was constructed. It is now the second oldest church on the BC mainland, still sitting on its original foundation, and designated a BC Heritage Site. As you take a tour of the town, peek inside the church and get an eyeful of its magnificently carved pump organ. Visit the pioneer cemetery with its unique grave markers. Nearby, camping is available at the Yale Campground or Emory Creek Provincial Park, both on your approach to Yale.

The circa 1962 Alexandra Bridge over the Fraser River is the world's second-largest fixed archspan.

In these parts or farther along in the canyon, you can arrange a rafting trip on the mighty Fraser, the Thompson, or other area rivers, spending anywhere from hours to days on a river. Not all trips are the heart-in-your-throat variety. Rafting companies offer trips in powered or paddled rafts and in water as wild or mild as you like it. Contact these operators:

- Fraser River Raft Expeditions in Yale at 800-363-RAFT or 604-863-2355, or see www.fraserraft.com
- Hyak River Rafting, 800-663-7328 or www.hyak.com
- Kumsheen River Rafting in Lytton at 800-663-6667 or http://kumsheen.com
- REO Rafting, 800-736-7238 or 604-461-7238, or see www.reorafting.com

Fraser Canyon is postcard beautiful from one end to the other. Just past the first of seven tunnels in the canyon, note the historical marker at a pullout to the east. This explains more about the Cariboo Wagon Road and the difficulty of transportation during that mid-1800s gold rush. Railroad tracks on each side of the canyon mark the routes of the Canadian Pacific and National Pacific railways.

Hell's Gate trams carry sightseers over a fast-and-furious narrowing in the Fraser River.

Some 40 minutes east of Hope on Hwy. 1, you will encounter the natural wonder called Hell's Gate, where the Fraser River virtually explodes in a churning rush of wild white water through a 108-foot-wide narrowing in the canyon. In 1808, Simon Fraser, the first white man to descend the canyon, wrote, "We had to travel where no human being should venture for surely we have seen the gates of hell." Look over the edge, watch 211 million gallons of water thunder past in one minute, and you'll know why the name stuck. Hell's Gate Airtram offers a thrilling look at the river from above. For a fee, you can ride the tram across the canyon while descending 502 feet. On the opposite side, explore the family-oriented boardwalk village that's built into the cliff. You'll learn more about migrating salmon and their habitat, and you'll find a snack bar and restaurant, gift shop, and gold panning. And for the intrepid, a suspension bridge lets you walk back over the river and enjoy an unadulterated view of the swirling current beneath your feet. We were amazed to learn that nearly 2 million salmon swim up the Fraser River each summer. Open from mid-April to mid-October. For more information, call 604-867-9277 or visit www.hellsgateairtram.com.

Two campgrounds operate within the 10 miles (16 km) north of Hell's Gate. Canyon Alpine RV Park & Campground offers 31 sites, with full hookups and pull-throughs, Wi-Fi, firepits, washrooms, and showers. The facility is close to a restaurant, store, phone, and self-service laundry. For information, call 604-867-9734. Anderson Creek Campground at Boston Bar is located alongside the Fraser and Anderson rivers in a 30-acre setting with lots of trees. They offer full and partial hookups, showers, and a sani-dump. No pull-throughs. Call 604-867-9089.

LYTTON

From Hope, BC: 68 miles (109.5 km)
To Cache Creek, BC: 52 miles (84 km)

Situated at the confluence of the Thompson River and the powerful Fraser River (Canada's third largest), Lytton is the place to park and play—a river rafter's dream. Looking down at the rivers' confluence from above, you can see a distinct edge where the clear blue Thompson blends into the cloudy gray of the Fraser. A third, the Nahatlatch River, is smaller and steeper, offering dramatic class 4 and class 5 rafting.

As the white-water rafting capital of British Columbia, Lytton offers plentiful outfitter choices. You can go with a group, hire a guide for your own group, or rent what you need to go on your own. You can't miss rafting company signs all along this stretch of road. Among them is Kumsheen Raft Adventures, which also offers other adventures, such as rock climbing, kayaking, and bike touring, along with comfortable or rustic overnight accommodations. Call 250-455-2296 or visit their website, www.kumsheen.com.

This meeting place of the rivers has been a gathering place for centuries, as evidenced in ancient pictographs and rock paintings. First Nations people chose the spot for its abundance of wildlife, water, and trees for food and building material. During the annual Lytton Days in late May, you can learn more about First Nations culture through art, dance, and storytelling. Native arts and crafts, including soapstone carvings, baskets, and beaded leather, can be purchased in Lytton. Call 250-455-2523 for more information.

The Lytton Museum & Archives is located at 425 Fraser St. Phone 250-455-2254 for details. A walking tour of the community is a good way to learn more about the people and their special place. Ask at the visitor information center, or go online and take a virtual walking tour at www.lytton.ca. We enjoyed spotting the silhouette murals on buildings all over town. They depict people in gold-rush-era costume.

After prospector Billy Barker discovered gold on Williams Creek in 1862, more than 100,000 people

China Bar Bluff, near Spuzzum on the Fraser Canyon. One of the most dangerous stretches of the trans-Canada railway ran through the canyon, and most of those miles were built by Chinese laborers from Kwangchow, China, and the played-out California gold rush. They hand-drilled blasting holes in the sheer cliffs above the river, removed the debris after the blast, and laid track, all for fewer wages and in more perilous conditions than the white workmen. One estimate claims that for every foot of track, a Chinese man died. Image A-03867 courtesy of Royal BC Museum, BC Archives

ROCK-HARD JELLYROLL

Sedimentary geologists and other earth scientists will appreciate an unusual attraction in the heart of downtown Lytton. Across from Lytton's visitor information center, at 400 Fraser Ave., is the tiny Caboose Park, where a retired Canadian National Railway caboose is parked alongside a picnic table and grassy area. But it's the thing on the exterior wall of an adjacent building that makes scientists and curiosity seekers walk closer and squint. The "thing" is called the Lytton Jellyroll, a cast of a geological formation that was discovered south of the village. The unusual structure is a rolled layer of silt encased in coarse sands and gravel. Scientists believe it was created from 11,000 to 25,000 years ago during an event in the last glaciation period. That makes it very young by geological standards. But it is the size of the formation that makes it special. Normally a find such as this would be measured in inches, not feet. Erected by the Lytton and District Chamber of Commerce, this detailed replication of the real thing could fool an amateur.

All around Lytton, silhouettes speak of the same place, but of another time in the town's history. The street names are posted in English and in the First Nations language. And downtown, there's an awesome view of the Fraser and Thompson rivers meeting. This is BC's rafting capital.

joined the ensuing rush and swarmed into British Columbia to mine for gold, traveling the famed Cariboo Wagon Road to reach the goldfields. As one of the early stops, Lytton thrived as a place for the stampeders to outfit themselves.

In 1881, intrepid railway builders arrived to cut a rail bed into the sides of this canyon. The Canadian Pacific Railway and the Canadian National Railway continue to move freight and passengers on this route that parallels the river and the road through Fraser Canyon.

This area is still rich with wildlife. Along the back roads and hiking trails, you may see elk, bighorn sheep, deer, eagles, and ospreys. Hidden from sight are the more human-shy animals: coyotes, bears, cougars, bobcats, and lynx.

For more information on the area, stop by the Lytton Visitor Information Centre, open year-round at 400 Fraser St. Call 250-455-2523 or visit www.lytton.ca.

Road Notes

In the 52 scenic miles (84 km) between Lytton and Cache Creek, you'll find two provincial parks and several private campgrounds.

Just 5 miles (8 km) beyond Lytton is Skihist Provincial Park, with 58 campsites, a picnic area, restrooms, and an RV dump station. Another 12 miles (19 km) later, less-developed Goldpan Provincial Park lies to the west, with 14 sites along the Thompson River. You can go fishing or put your canoe in the water here.

Along the way, pay attention to the historic buildings and opportunities to stop for coffee, pie, or a meal and learn more about the area's gold rush history. Less than 10 miles (16 km) south of Cache Creek, the oldest roadhouse in British Columbia is

The manor of Ashcroft Manor Historic Site no longer stands, due to a fire, but the old roadhouse of the Cariboo Wagon Road is still here, along with accommodations, food, and a small museum.

still in business—since 1862. During summer months, the restored Ashcroft Manor & Teahouse offers rooms, meals, campground (with pull-through sites for RVers), jade gifts, and an invitation to walk the grounds and visit the historic outbuildings. For more information, call 250-453-9983. The nearby village of Ashcroft invites visitors to tour their historic downtown, Heritage Place Park, and to stop by the farmers' market every Saturday morning from June to October.

Seven miles (11 km) south of Cache Creek is the Nl'akapxm Eagle Motorplex, a quarter-mile drag strip sanctioned by the National Hot Rod Association. Racers come from around the world to race and show their cars. Check www.eaglemotorplex.com for details.

During Cache Creek's Graffiti Days, the second weekend in June, restored vehicles are paraded and parked for the Show & Shine celebration. Festivities include a dance, a barbecue, and racing at the motorplex.

CACHE CREEK

From Lytton, BC: 52 miles (84 km)
From Hope, BC: 120 miles (193 km)
To Williams Lake, BC: 126 miles (203 km)

Set in a semiarid region of low, rolling hills, Cache Creek is home to a scant 1,140 people who live at the confluence of the Bonaparte River and Cache Creek. Here, too, is the junction of Hwy. 1 with Hwy. 97.

The scent of sagebrush wafts through the air on hot summer days, and at the town's main intersection, a wooden gold miner stands, arms extended, welcoming you to this frontier town that was built on the backs of gold miners.

These days there's less gold mining than there is cattle ranching and farming.

Cache Creek services include lodging, restaurants, grocery stores, a post office, and a golf course. Most visitors are passing through on their vacations. But 150 years ago, this town was overrun with miners and business owners who wanted to trade gold for goods and services.

GREEN AND GOLD

Just outside Cariboo Jade Shoppe, where the Trans-Canada Hwy. (Hwy. 1) joins Hwy. 97 North, you'll find a massive jade boulder, an obviously valuable piece of inventory that just sits out on the porch, day and night. Managers Ben Roy and Bill Elliott don't worry too much about shoplifting. It would take a Caterpillar D9 to move the 2,850-pound slice away from 1093 Todd Rd.

Inside, these two brothers-in-law manage the business traffic that the boulder generates, like a billboard that says Come Inside. The green cast of jade pieces—polished jewelry, raw jade, sculptures large and small—is reflected on nearly every glass shelf. They also offer other quality Canadian gifts and Native crafts in a wide price range.

In the back of the shop, behind a glass partition, Ben cuts British Columbia jade on a special rock saw to accommodate its extreme hardness. Bill's specialty is working in gold. Together they create jewelry and other specialty pieces.

British Columbia jade is nearly as prized as gold and known throughout the world. Four times harder than marble, this jade is difficult to cut and finish into sculpture and jewelry. For more information on BC jade, call 250-457-9566.

The scale of this giant slice of nephrite jade is realized next to Bill Elliott, co-owner of the Cariboo Jade Shoppe in Cache Creek. The business has been there for 40 years, and Bill and his partner have had it for 25 of them. According to Bill, they're seeing return customers who came as kids and are now parents bringing their own kids.

A small, jade *inukshuk* for sale at the Cariboo Jade Shoppe in Cache Creek. During the 2010 Olympics, the world learned more about the traditional man-shaped form. *Inukshuk* means "resembling Inuit." Through time, these rock-slab formations have guided travelers in the wild places.

Stan Roberts and Charles Tremblay are two Cache Creek men who were enjoying the sun and pulling fish out of Six-Mile Lake, just outside of town. It's a stocked lake—rainbows and eastern brook trout ("Yanks call 'em 'speckled,'" Stan explained). Using worms and a float, Stan had caught a couple of one-pounders.

As a major point on the Cariboo Wagon Road, Cache Creek grew quickly. After the rush, some mining continued, along with farming, logging, and cattle ranching. Tourism helps keep Cache Creek cooking, too. There's a public park, pool, golf course, and other recreational opportunities.

To stock up on fresh fruits and veggies, stop by Horsting's Farm Market, just north of Cache Creek, where the scent of freshly baked bread and pies fills their country store. Local jams, syrups, honey, and gifts are for sale, along with all kinds of fresh produce. The 80-acre farm and country market is family owned. The kids will love visiting the rabbits and chickens and getting a peek inside a working farm. Call 250-457-6546 for more information.

A few miles farther on your journey is an 1860 landmark of the Cariboo Wagon Road: the Historic Hat Creek Ranch, at the intersection of hwys. 97 and 99. This 320-acre ranch was once an important roadhouse stop for horse-drawn wagons along the BC Express Stage line (also known as the BX) that led to the gold-rush town of Barkerville and beyond. More than 20 buildings dating from 1863 to 1915 may be found on the grounds. Explore the Victorian-style rooms of the main house, visit the BX Barn, watch the blacksmith at work, and view a First Nations pit house. You can also take a trail ride or climb into a stagecoach for a horse-drawn ride on the famous Cariboo Wagon Road. Educational programs are available, as well as overnight accommodations: tent camp, park your RV, rent a cabin, or stay overnight in a Native pit house. Phone 800-782-0922 or browse their website, www.hatcreekranch.com.

LODGING

Best Value Inn Desert Motel
1069 Trans-Canada Hwy. South
800-663-0212 or 250-457-6226
45 air-conditioned units, kitchenettes. Cable TV, coffee. Grass courtyard with outdoor pool. Wheelchair accessible. Winter plug-ins. In town center, close to shops and restaurants.

Bonaparte Motel
1395 Cariboo Hwy. 97 North
250-457-9693
24 air-conditioned rooms and kitchenettes with refrigerator, cable TV, fax service. Outdoor pool, indoor whirlpool. Close to restaurants and golf.

The Good Knight Inn
827 S. Trans-Canada Hwy.
800-736-5588 or 250-457-9500
20 deluxe rooms with cable TV and movies, data phones, e-mail. Whirlpools, continental breakfast, picnic area.

The Oasis Hotel
1064 S. Trans-Canada Hwy.
250-457-6232
Full hotel facilities, banquet room, lounge, restaurant.

Sage Hills Motel
1379 Cariboo Hwy. 97 North
888-794-9494 or 250-457-6451
18 air-conditioned units, cable TV, coffee. Pool with slide and shower, grassy courtyard. Senior discount.

Sandman Inn Cache Creek
Intersection of hwys. 1 and 97
800-726-3626 or 250-457-6284
www.sandmanhotels.com
35 air-conditioned units, cable TV, coffee.
Restaurant. Senior discount.

Sundowner Motel
1085 Trans-Canada Hwy.
250-457-6216
18 air-conditioned units, cable TV, movies, kitchens, fridge, microwave. Near restaurants, golf.

Tumbleweed Motel
1221 Quartz Rd.
800-667-1501 or 250-457-6522
25 deluxe air-conditioned rooms in parklike setting, cable TV, free movies, picnic area. Near restaurants, golf.

CAMPGROUNDS

Brookside Campsite
1621 E. Trans-Canada Hwy.
.6 mile (1 km) east of Cache Creek on Hwy. 1
250-457-6633
Pull-through sites, tent sites, free showers, free Wi-Fi, heated pool. Washroom, sani-dump. Playground, arcade, store. ATV trails nearby. Adjacent to 9-hole golf course.

Evergreen Fishing Resort
1820 Loon Lake Rd.
250-459-2372
www.evergreenfishingresort.ca
Furnished lakeside log cabins, tenting campsites, full and partial hookups, store, laundry. Boat rentals, moorage.

Historic Hat Creek Ranch
Junction of hwys. 99 and 97
800-782-0922 or 250-457-9722
www.hatcreekranch.com
8 campsites with electrical hookups only. Flush toilets, hot showers. Near historical roadhouse, Native interpretation site, restaurant, gift shop. Also available are 2 sleeping units. Open May–September.

RESTAURANTS

Chum's Restaurant
1108 E. Trans-Canada Hwy.
250-457-6735
Family dining.

Horsting's Farm
1.25 miles (2 km) north of town on Hwy. 97
250-457-6546
www.horstingfarms.com
Farm market, bakery, with sandwiches, ice cream, long list of fresh-baked pies.

Hungry Herbie's Drive-In
Hwy. 97 North
250-457-6644
Burgers, fries, and more.

North End Petro-Can Restaurant
Cariboo Hwy. 97
250-457-6261

Oasis Restaurant
1064 S. Trans-Canada Hwy., in the Oasis Hotel
http://oasiscachecreek.com
250-457-6232
Canadian fare, entertainment.

Sandman Inn Family Restaurant
Junction of hwys. 1 and 97
250-457-6284
Pasta, steaks, Greek dishes, coffee shop, dining room, cocktail lounge.

Wander Inn Restaurant
Junction of hwys. 1 and 97
250-457-6511
Sterling Silver AAA steaks, Cantonese food, coffee shop, dining room, cocktail lounge.

Road Notes

Immediately north from Cache Creek, a handful of small towns bear names that indicate their places along the historic route known as the Cariboo Wagon Road, beginning with Clinton, "Gateway to the Cariboo," which was once known as 47 Mile. Farther along are the communities of 100 Mile House and 150 Mile House and others, former locations of stopping houses known by their distance from Lillooet, which was Mile 0 on the early road, dating from mid-1880s.

100 Mile House today is a lumber town that also claims the title of Handcrafted Log Home Capital of North America *and* International Nordic Ski Capital. It hosts

the Cariboo Marathon each February, attracting skiers from around the world. Outside the town's information center, you can see the world's longest cross-country skis, 39-foot-long Karhu racers, and around back is a protected marsh that's a haven for birds and travelers alike. Learn more about this district, its history, natural history, as well as local dining and lodging at the South Cariboo Visitor Info Centre, at the corner of Hwy. 97 and Airport Rd. in 100 Mile House (just watch for the gigantic skis!). Call 877-511-5353 or 250-395-5353 or see www.southcaribootourism.com.

WILLIAMS LAKE

From Cache Creek, BC: 126 miles (203 km)

To Quesnel, BC: 75 miles (120 km)

To Prince George, BC: 146 miles (235 km)

For the northbound traveler on Hwy. 97, the gateway to Williams Lake is marked by the inviting Tourism Discovery Centre, a two-story, 15,000-square-foot beauty that opened in 2006. This beautifully designed and built log facility is a can't-miss-it stop as you enter town from the south. Entertaining displays and exhibits include an "exploding" view of a camper's overpacked car, a lodge living room with informational videos, and area wildlife displays. Open year-round, the center is staffed by friendly, knowledgeable folks who'll help you line up a stay at a guest ranch or arrange for some horseback riding.

During construction of the Cariboo Wagon Road in 1863, a Williams Lake landowner would not lend money to road builders, so the new road bypassed the town, routed instead through 150 Mile House. There's that story, and then there's the one about how one road builder in particular stood to gain financially by rerouting the trail. Either way, the decision nearly killed the young town's economy, kicking it off the major transportation route for the thousands of people moving in and out of the goldfields.

Williams Lake was nearly abandoned, except for two business partners, William Pinchbeck and William Lyne, who built a lumber mill, a gristmill, and a farm. But their real income earner was the sale of home-brewed whiskey. You might assume that this town took its name from the two Williams, but it is attributed to Chief William of the local Shuswaps.

Excellence in craftsmanship is evident in every inch of the Tourism Discovery Centre at Williams Lake. For northbound travelers, it'll be on your right just as you enter town. Inside, the center-post tree was harvested from Bella Coola and estimated at 745 years old.

"ARE WE THERE YET?"

Parents traveling with children, please try to recall your own family trips as a kid. Seriously, did you gaze out the window and gush over the glorious landscape when your parents cried, "What a beautiful sunset!"?

That's why we figured Abra and Fernando Pintor would have some insider ideas. We found them and their three girls, Shiloh, 8, Nophia, 7, and Keakoa, 6, in the parking lot of the 100 Mile House Visitor Centre. They'd already come a long way from California, and were many miles from their destination of Glennallen, Alaska, but the Pintors seemed to have it figured out. Behind the visitor center was a cultivated marsh, where even those of us who know nothing about birds are drawn in by the songs and bustle of common and more rare birds. Interpretive signage informs the viewer very well. That's a good thing for the grown-ups, but what about wiggly kids?

In this case, it *was* all about the bike. The Pintor family was taking a break for peanut butter and jelly sandwiches and some bike riding around the parking lot, Fernando following after his girls on foot. (Dads can get pretty cramped after hours behind the wheel, too.) Fernando grew up in Santa Rosa, California; Abra was born in Hawaii, as were two of their daughters. And that's where they'd been living—on the Big Island—for the last eighteen months. They were headed for Glennallen and a summerlong construction job. There, the travel trailer would continue to serve as home in an RV park, where Abra had arranged to work in exchange for rent. After the job was over, the family would head south again, but where, they didn't know. That adventure was still ahead.

This family trip had been in the works for years. The couple bought the travel trailer and deliberately sought work far away from home, with plans to drive there. Abra had always homeschooled, so that continued on the road and in their to-be-determined future. As for now, the Pintors' tips for traveling with kids: bring along crafts, a DVD player for movies, and especially bikes.

"We break and they ride out all that energy," says Fernando.

Another piece of advice from the experts: get up at 2:30 in the morning and drive while the kids are sleeping. Otherwise, says Fernando, "we could never get a 10-hour travel day out of them. We want to get through Canada pretty quick, so today we're going to try and power out some miles."

Bottom line, Fernando advises "plenty of patience and knowing your own frustration level. Try to be temperate."

Fernando Pintor and his daughters played off some pent-up energy in the parking lot of the 100 Mile House Visitor Centre. Behind them, the world's longest cross-country skis.

The world-famous Williams Lake Stampede attracts top competitors from across North America. Competing in the July 2010 event, Beau Waters of Darwell, AB, made the eight-second whistle on John Duffy's saddle bronc horse, Aristocrat. Photo by Liz Twan

By the 1940s, 20 years after the railway arrived, this was a ranching town that had grown into the largest cattle-shipping center in British Columbia. Today about 11,000 people call Williams Lake home, and more than 25,000 live in the wider area, called "The Hub of the Cariboo." Ranching and timber remain important aspects of the economy.

Williams Lake is the Old West in action, and at no time of the year is there more action than during the Williams Lake Stampede. Counting the spectators, the town's population doubles for the Stampede, held during the early July long holiday weekend (Canada Day is July 1). This family event includes chuckwagon races, barn dances, mountain horse races, and the crowning jewel: the world-famous rodeo featuring top cowboys from throughout Canada and the United States. A parade and midway are part of the fun, too. Camping is available right next to the Stampede grounds. For more information, call 800-71 RODEO or 250-398-8388; www.williamslakestampede.com.

The Museum of the Cariboo Chilcotin is a full-fledged ranching and rodeo museum that is entrusted with the story of the Williams Lake Stampede, which dates back to 1919, and the history of this region, the Cariboo Chilcotin, the First Nations people, and those who followed. It's also home to the BC Cowboy Hall of Fame and is located on the corner of 4th and Borland St. Call 250-392-7404 or visit www.cowboy-museum.com.

The First Nations people of the Interior Cariboo have dwelt in this region for at least 5,000 years. The Xat'súll Heritage Village, located some 23 miles (37 km) north of Williams Lake on Hwy. 97, is an excellent place to learn about Shuswap language, art, celebrations, history, and more. You're invited to make it a day trip, or arrange a longer stay, overnighting in a pit house, teepee, or under the stars. Hear the stories and view the village site, artifacts, petroglyphs, and a sweat lodge. Stop by the Williams Lake office at 3405 Mountain House Rd. for more information or call 250-989-2323. You can

Wood bison, or mountain bison, are a subspecies of North American bison. We saw this giant right outside our window.

browse www.xatsull.com, or call the village site at 250-297-6502.

Williams Lake—the actual lake itself—lies along a major flyway for migrating waterfowl. Scout Island Nature Centre, at the west end of the lake off S. Mackenzie Ave., offers bird-watching opportunities along a corridor of trails, open from 8 AM to dusk. The Nature House there is chock-full of displays and more information about this habitat and the creatures that inhabit it. Between the Fraser River and the lake, you can see sandstone hoodoos— mushroom-shaped formations still standing after the forces of erosion removed the rock all around them.

Golfers have two courses to choose from, and there's minigolf for the minigolfers and their parents.

For more information on Williams Lake and the surrounding district, call 877-967-5253 or browse www.williamslake.ca.

LODGING

Coast Fraser Inn
285 Donald Rd.
800-716-6199 or 250-398-7055
www.coasthotels.com/hotels/canada/bc
79 luxury air-conditioned units, cable TV, movies, room service, free Wi-Fi. Overlooks Williams Lake. Gift shop, whirlpool, sauna, free hot buffet breakfast. Restaurant, lounge, patio. Walk to city center.

Drummond Lodge & Motel
1405 Hwy. 97 South
800-667-4555 or 250-392-5334
www.drummondlodge.com
18 regular and deluxe air-conditioned units and 6 large suites with views of Williams Lake. Movie and sports channels, Internet, coffee, continental breakfast, laundry facilities.

Lakeside Motel
1505 Hwy. 97 South
800-663-4938 or 250-392-4181
32 units overlooking Williams Lake and Scout Island Nature Centre. Coffee/tea, local calls, barbecue grills for family picnics. Minigolf. Small pets welcome.

Overlander Hotel
1118 Lakeview Crescent
800-663-6898 or 250-392-3321
www.overlanderhotel.com
57 air-conditioned units in full-service hotel. Free Internet, free Wi-Fi. Fitness facilities, tour packages. Restaurant, pub, gym pass. Downtown location, near shopping. Senior discount.

Sandman Inn Williams Lake
664 Oliver St.
800-726-3626 or 250-392-6557
www.sandmanhotels.com
105 air-conditioned units, executive suites, kitchenettes. Cable TV, laundry, room service, Internet, indoor pool, sauna, pub. Near shopping, adjacent to 24-hour restaurant.

Super 8 Motel (Williams Lake)
1712 Broadway Ave. South
800-800-8000 or 250-398-8884
www.super8williamslake.com
53 air-conditioned units, nonsmoking available. Cable TV, whirlpool, complimentary breakfast, free Internet.

Valleyview Motel & Jamboree
1523 Hwy. 97 South
250-392-4655
www.valleyviewmoteljamboreemotel.bcmotels.com
18 sleeping and housekeeping units with mountain and lake views. Cable TV, coffee, near restaurant. Senior discount. Pets welcome.

Williams Inn Hotel
55 6th Ave. South
250-392-7747
www.williamsinnhotel.ca
43 newly renovated, air-conditioned rooms, kitchenettes. Free high-speed Internet, cable TV, fridges, microwaves. Free hot breakfast. Close to attractions. Senior discount.

CAMPGROUNDS

Big Bar Lake Provincial Park
26.5 miles (42 km) northwest of Clinton off Hwy. 97
800-689-9025
www.env.gov.bc.ca/bcparks
46 sites in two campgrounds: Lakeside
Campground and Upper Campground. Full
and partial hookups, pull-throughs, tent sites.
Swimming, fishing, boat launch, hiking.

McLeese Lake Resort
6721 Cariboo Hwy. 97 North
250-297-6525
www.mcleeselake.com
Located north of Williams Lake. Cabins, tent sites,
RV pull-throughs and back-ins. Full and partial
hookups. Camp store, restrooms, bathhouse,
swimming, fishing, boat rental.

Springhouse Trails Ranch
3061 Dog Creek Rd.
250-392-4780
www.williams-lake.travel.bc.ca/listings/spring-
house-trails-ranch/21301
12 RV full-hookup sites, showers, washrooms.
Horseback riding and lessons.

Williams Lake Stampede Campground
850 S. Mackenzie St.
250-398-6718
www.williamslakestampede.com
74 sites with full or partial hookups, phone, cable
hookup. Tent sites, free firewood. Showers, restrooms. Four blocks to downtown.

RESTAURANTS

Alley Katz Bistro
27 7th Ave. South
250-398-8700

Carmen's Restaurant
1118 Lakeview Crescent, inside the
Overlander Hotel
800-663-6898 or 250-392-3321
Local specialties, hilltop view from downtown
restaurant, adjacent to hotel. Sunday brunch.

Great Cariboo Steak Company
285 Donald Rd., inside the Coast Fraser Inn
800-452-6789 or 250-398-7055
Breakfast, all-you-can-eat lunch buffets, steak,
chicken, seafood, pasta. Outdoor seating available, lounge.

Gringo's Restaurant
112 N. 2nd Ave.
250-392-6012

The Hearth Restaurant
99 3rd Ave. South
250-398-6831
Sandwiches, soups, salads.

Hong She NG Restaurant
770 Oliver St.
250-398-6888

Joey's Grill
177 Yorston St.
250-398-8727
Pasta, steak, chicken.

Laughing Loon Neighbourhood Pub
1730 S. Broadway
250-398-5666
Beef, chicken, pork dishes.

Leone's Pizza & Steak House
36 3rd Ave. North
250-398-8299
Family-style dining.

Panama Red's
160 N. 2nd Ave.
250-392-1113

Porky's Deli
83 S. 2nd Ave.
250-392-5629

Sam's Restaurant
179 N. 3rd Ave.
250-392-7181

Santa Fe Café
24F S. 2nd Ave.
250-392-7166

Sir Bob's Fish and Chips
3015B N. Mackenzie
250-398-6633

Stockmen's Café
4665 N. Mackenzie
250-398-5366

Trattoria Pasta Shop
23A S. 1st Ave.
250-398-7170

Road Notes

Seventy-five miles (120 km) north of Williams Lake is Quesnel (kwi-NELL), which, like many area towns, boomed during the Cariboo gold rush of the early 1860s. Today this town of more than 11,000 people is supported by lumber, pulp and plywood manufacturing, cattle ranching, mining, and, of course, tourism. All travelers' services may be found here, from shopping, lodging, and dining to assistance in planning your trip. Learn more about Quesnel's history, which really began long before the gold rush, at the Quesnel Museum in the Visitor Centre, at the south entrance to the city center on Hwy. 97. You can go on a self-guided walking tour of historic Quesnel, or take in the city's illustrated history of more than a century in photos and see Mandy, the famed "haunted doll" in their collection. Since the antique doll came to live at the museum, strange

Quesnel's unique welcome sign plainly states this town was founded on the pursuit of gold.

things stopped happening at the donor's home and began instead at the museum. The staff will tell you about her and let you judge for yourself. There's much to see in the 11,000-square-foot facility. The visitor center and museum lobby offers free public Wi-Fi. They're open daily from 9 AM to 6 PM from late May to early September. See www.quesnelmuseum.ca.

If you're feeling hot and dusty, you'll find a swimming pool at the Quesnel & District Arts and Recreation Center, 500 N. Star Rd. A weight room, saunas, and a whirlpool are here, too, as well as an art gallery. Off the deck, enjoy the Japanese garden.

On the third weekend of July, Quesnel celebrates Billy Barker's discovery of gold with Barker Days, four days of river races, dances, games, concerts, and contests for pie eaters and watermelon-seed spitters. Snowmobile races—without the snow—are a kick. A midway multiplies the family fun. An amateur rodeo draws big crowds to Alex Fraser Park. Learn more at http://billybarker days.netbistro.com or call 250-992-1234.

West of Quesnel, the Blackwater River flows almost 200 miles (322 km) from the Coast Mountains to the Fraser River. Its pristine waters attract fly-fishers, canoeists, and kayakers. The Alexander Mackenzie Heritage Trail parallels the river; in 1793, Mackenzie followed this First Nations trading trail to the Pacific Ocean.

End of the driving day and time to build a campfire along the Fraser River. The smoke is a natural deterrent for mosquitoes, too.

THE RUSH TO BARKERVILLE

For a worthwhile side trip, take the Hwy. 26 turnoff just beyond Quesnel and follow it north and east for 55 miles (88 km) to Barkerville, where the gold-rush past comes alive again.

Founded in 1862, Barkerville first sprang to life when Billy Barker discovered gold in Williams Creek. Now more than 120 heritage buildings and displays on the original town site celebrate the past. Also on-site are two cemeteries, thousands of artifacts, a resource library, and archives, all operated by a nonprofit called Barkerville Heritage Trust.

As you stroll through town, costumed interpreters can be found in the buildings and on the boardwalks, staying in character as they answer questions and join conversations with visitors.

Museum displays about mining and Barkerville and its namesake are in the main building through which you access Barkerville—which is kind of like a Hollywood back lot, except that this town was and is for real. And at each house or business, you learn about its former owner. Street performances add to the feeling that this was once a busy town of miners, Chinese immigrants, churchmen, and partygoers. The cemeteries hold the remains of former residents. A stagecoach driver invites passengers to ride to the other end of the town. Guided tours begin at regular intervals, and musical comedy is on the bill for evenings in the Theatre Royal. There's a new show each year.

At restaurants, snack shops, gift stores, and an old-time photo studio, the shopkeepers and waitstaff are dressed in gold-rush-era clothing, all lending to the sense of stepping back in time. There's even a judge on the bench in the courthouse, pontificating about justice in his wild and woolly town.

We were pelted by a hailstorm while visiting Barkerville, and people rushed into the saloon, candy store, general store, or museum building. Others huddled beneath building overhangs until the storm passed. This was in August—an indicator of this place's elevation of about 4,200 feet (1,280 m) above sea level. Museum docents explained that snow comes early in these mountains. The mining was hard work; the living was just as hard.

This is a great place for families and solo travelers alike. For more information, call 888-994-3332 or 250-994-3332. Online, learn more at www.barkerville.ca.

As for overnight accommodations, two bed-and-breakfast businesses operate in the town: Kelly

Barkerville is no movie back lot—the buildings in this town are the real deal, restored to their earlier glory to teach us about the lives of the pioneers. With costumed interpreters roaming the streets, it feels like we've entered their world.

House and King House, both in restored homes (866-994-0004), and there's the 1880s-era St. George Hotel on Main St. (250-994-0008), where an overnight stay includes a gourmet breakfast. Tent or RV campers will find plenty of sites and services in the three campgrounds at the entrance to the gold-rush town. Horses and pets are welcome. For more information, call 866-994-3297 or 250-994-3297, or visit online at www.barkervillecampgrounds.ca.

The White Cap Motor Inn & RV Park is 5 miles before Barkerville, just a few minutes from Wells. Full-service motel, service RV sites, and tent sites are available with everything else you'd want for a comfortable night. Call 800-377-2028 or 250-994-3489, or visit www.whitecapinn.com.

Heading north toward Prince George, you will be within range of some excellent lake fishing for rainbow and brook trout, char, burbot, and more. There are about 1,600 lakes within a 100-mile radius of Prince George. Contact Tourism Prince George at 800-668-7646 or 250-562-3700 for a free fishing guide and info on licensing.

Ten Mile Lake Provincial Park, 7 miles (11 km) north of Quesnel, offers two campgrounds with a total of 108 campsites accessible by vehicle, including 22 pull-throughs. There's water, showers, restrooms, and an RV dump station. You'll find a playground, a swimming beach on the lake, and a boat launch, as well as nature trails for walking and wildlife viewing. Thirty sites can be reserved through the Discover Camping reservation service at https://secure.camis.com/Discovercamping; all others are first come, first served. Watch for several private campgrounds just south of Prince George, too.

PRINCE GEORGE

From Quesnel, BC: 73 miles (118 km)

To Chetwynd, BC: 168 miles (270 km)

To Dawson Creek, BC: 252 miles (406 km)

Here in what is known as the Lakes and Rivers District, Prince George is viewed as the capital of northern British Columbia. It is home to about 83,000 people who understand and enjoy the natural treasure that's around them and the city they helped to create. Inside the city limits alone, you can count 120 parks!

Just minutes from downtown in any direction, you'll find some form of outdoor recreation: walking, fishing, swimming, horseback riding, boating, backpacking. The local lakes and streams are rich with trout, salmon, burbot, Dolly Varden, char—for a fly-fisher, this is world-class water. And there's no shortage of campgrounds, provincial and private. Hunkering in the distance is Mt. Robson, highest peak in the Canadian Rockies, inviting those who prefer a lot of challenge in their outdoor adventure.

In winter, visitors and residents head out for downhill skiing, cross-country skiing, hockey, ice skating, even dogsledding. Snow typically begins in November and stays on the ground into late March.

Fur trader Simon Fraser, an intruder in the lands of the Lheidli T'enneh people, built a fur-trading post here in 1807. Fraser named it Fort George, to honor King George III, but the city that later bloomed at the trading post was named for another George: the fourth son of King George V.

A big piece of the local economy lies in wood, with employment in forestry, plywood manufacturing, sawmills, pulp mills,

Prince George's mascot, an oversized log man, towers outside the visitor center.

A taste of a big city in the heart of the wilderness, Prince George's inviting amenities include great shopping and dining, as well as theater, art galleries, music festivals, a science museum, aquatic center, farmers' market, and plenty of walking trails through its green spaces.

and log home construction. Other employers include two chemical plants, an oil refinery, and an aluminum boat manufacturer. From its unique place as a transportation crossroads, Prince George also serves outlying mining and prospecting operations.

This is a frontier city at its roots, yet it cleans up real nice, with its own brand of polish. Just as you finish a half-day trail ride, Prince George's nightlife offerings will revitalize you with concerts, art galleries, theater openings, or an evening of jazz. The city claims several resident theater groups, a symphony orchestra, and many dance troupes. The Two Rivers Art Gallery, featuring work by local, regional, and national artists, can be found in the downtown Civic Complex. There are art classes, special events, hands-on experimental art fun for kids, and a gift shop. See www.tworiversartgallery.com.

Also downtown, the Centennial Fountain at 7th Ave. and Dominion St. depicts the early history of Prince George in mosaic tile, from life among the First Nations people to the arrival of explorers, settlers, the railway, and forward into 20th-century life.

Along the banks of the Fraser River, at the end of 20th Ave., Fort George Park is the place where locals bring their visiting friends and relatives, so you should see it, too! Come down to the river to picnic, enjoy the free water park, or follow the Heritage Trail, which links this park with several others. Inside the park, you'll find The Exploration Place Museum and Science Centre, which accelerates learning by linking it with entertainment. Explore prehistory and human history as the family scrambles around dinosaurs or through an exhibit on the last days of the *Titanic*. Open seven days a week, year-round. For more details, call 250-562-1612 or see www.theexplorationplace.com.

Nearby, stop by the Prince George Railway and Forestry Museum, an 8-acre park that's an outdoor repository for antique or merely retired railcars, engines, and more.

There are more than 70 pieces of rolling stock. Ride the Cottonwood Miniature Railway. The full-size train depot was faithfully moved piece by piece from a spot along the British Columbia Railway between Quesnel and Prince George. Steam locomotives, cranes, sleeping cars, cabooses, snowplows, and even logging and agricultural machinery are part of the walkabout display. Located at 850 River Rd., the museum is open from mid-May to September, five days a week; limited hours in winter. Call 250-563-7351 or visit www.pgrfm.bc.ca.

If you're in Prince George on Canada Day, July 1, you'll be in for a real treat. Join nearly 12,000 folks in historic Fort George Park, where everybody gathers for the Canada Festival, celebrating the country's birthday and the city's multicultural makeup with music, dance, and food in the colors and flavors of countries throughout the world.

Golfers are welcome to choose from a nice variety of courses, and you won't have to drive far. You'll find links within the city limits and others that are just a few miles away. Check out the Aberdeen Glen Golf Course (250-563-8901), Alder Hills Golf Course (250-963-7500), Aspen Grove Golf Course (250-963-9650), Links of Maggie May (250-963-7588), Pine Valley Golf Centre (250-562-4811), and the Prince George Golf and Curling Club (250-563-0357).

The city and its people are busy year-round. Almost like a city unto itself, the Treasure Cove Casino & Hotel can be found at the junction of Yellowhead Hwy. 16 and Hwy. 97. It boasts Las Vegas–style entertainment, spas, shopping, water park, restaurants, and, of course, a gaming area.

One of Prince George's most-photographed spots is located near the casino at the intersection of hwys. 16 and 97, where a visitor information center is open during the summer months only. There you'll find the three-story log man, whose friendly wave welcomes you to town. A second visitor center, open year-round from 8 AM to 8 PM, can be found at 1300 1st Ave., #101, in the VIA Rail Station.

For more information on the city's attractions and events, contact Tourism Prince George at 800-668-7646 or 250-562-3700 or www.tourismpg.com. (For more on Yellowhead Hwy. 16, see Chapter 7, Western Canada's Northbound Byways. If you're heading to Dawson Creek, however, you will continue your journey north on Hwy. 97.)

LODGING

For information on Prince George bed-and-breakfast accommodations, call 877-562-2626 or browse www.princegeorgebnb.com.

Best Western City Centre
910 Victoria St.
250-563-1267
www.bestwesternbc.com
53 air-conditioned units in downtown location. Free local calls, cable TV, indoor pool, sauna, fitness room, laundry. Restaurant. Next to Civic Centre. Senior discount.

Bon Voyage Motor Inn
4222 Hwy. 16 West
888-611-3872 or 250-964-2333
www.bonvoyageinn.ca
96 air-conditioned units, kitchenettes, suites. Cable TV, coffee, Internet. Gift shop, spacious restaurant, RV parking, winter plug-ins. Adjacent to gas, diesel station, car wash.

Camelot Court Motel
1600 Central St.
800-668-3361 or 250-563-0661
www.camelot.prince-george.com
69 well-appointed suites with refrigerator, cable TV, Internet. Swimming pool, Jacuzzi, winter plug-ins. Close to shopping, restaurants, recreation, public transportation.

Canadas Best Value Inn (formerly Anco Motel)

1630 E. Central St.
250-563-3671
www.ancomotel.ca
62 extra-large rooms, 5 one-bedroom, kitchenettes. Free local calls, free wireless. Restaurant.
Fee for pets.

Carmel Motor Inn

1502 Hwy. 97 South
800-665-4484 or 250-564-6339
www.carmelinn.ca
90 air-conditioned rooms and 50 kitchenettes.
Cable TV, movies, Internet, RV parking. Gift shop,
adjacent to restaurant, diesel station, car wash.

Coast Inn of the North

770 Brunswick St.
800-663-3290 or 250-563-0121
www.coastinnofthenorth.com
153 air-conditioned deluxe units. Three restaurants,
pool, sauna, gym, hair salon, free Wi-Fi, lounge.
Senior discount.

Days Inn Prince George

600 Quebec St.
800-292-8333 or 250-562-7072
www.daysinnpg.com
Well-appointed units with queen beds, microwave,
fridge, cable TV, and Wi-Fi. Close to Civic Centre,
art gallery, leisure pool, and shopping.

Downtown Motel

650 Dominion St.
800-663-5729 or 250-563-9241
www.downtownmotel.ca
43 air-conditioned rooms, cable TV, movies.
Outdoor patio. Winter plug-ins. Close to Civic
Centre, downtown shopping, entertainment, and
pool. Senior discount. Limo service to airport or
railway.

Economy Inn

1915 3rd Ave.
888-566-6333 or 250-563-7106
www.economyinn.ca
30 air-conditioned rooms, kitchenettes, wireless
Internet, cable TV, coffee. Whirlpool, exercise
room. Winter plug-ins. Near restaurants, shopping,
entertainment.

Esther's Inn

1151 Commercial
800-663-6844 or 250-562-4131
www.esthersinn.com
122 air-conditioned rooms in quality hotel.
Whirlpools, sauna, exercise club, indoor pool with
waterslides. Dining room, lounge. Close to attractions, shopping.

Four Points by Sheraton

1790 Hwy. 97 South
888-564-7105 or 250-564-7100
www.fourpointsprincegeorge.com
74 well-appointed, air-conditioned guest rooms,
cable TV, refrigerator, microwave, free Internet,
turndown service, coffee and tea, Jacuzzi, bathrobes, and more. Dining lounge, saltwater pool.

Grama's Inn

901 W. Central St.
877-563-7174 or 250-563-7174
www.gramasinn.com
60 air-conditioned rooms, kitchenettes, hospitality
room. Guest laundry, wireless Internet, homestyle
restaurant. Guests may use facilities of sister hotel,
Esther's Inn: pool, whirlpool, exercise club. Pet
friendly.

97 Motor Inn

2713 Spruce St.
250-562-6010
17 air-conditioned rooms, suites, and kitchenettes
in downtown location. Cable, movies. Close to
restaurants, shopping.

PG Hi-Way Motel

1737 20th Ave.
888-557-4557 or 250-564-6869
45 budget and deluxe rooms, kitchenettes. Winter
plug-ins. Near restaurants, laundry, shopping.

Ramada Hotel Downtown

444 George St.
800-830-8833 or 250-563-0055
www.ramadaprincegeorge.com
193 air-conditioned units and executive suites
in downtown location. Cable TV, movies, indoor
pool, sauna, whirlpool, fitness center. Dining, pub,
casino, gift shop. Airport shuttle.

Sandman Inn & Suites

1650 Central St.
800-SANDMAN or 250-563-8131
www.sandmanhotels.com
144 units, from 1- and 2-bedroom suites to kitchenettes. Coffee, indoor pool, sauna, 24-hour restaurant, room service. Senior discount.

Spruceland Inn

Hwy. 97 and 15th Ave.
800-553-3295 or 250-563-0102
www.sprucelandinn.com
Air-conditioned rooms with cable TV, free Wi-Fi,
coffee. Indoor pool, sauna, and Jacuzzi. Winter
plug-ins, pet friendly. Close to restaurants and
shopping.

Travelodge Goldcap
1458 7th Ave.
800-663-8239 or 250-563-0666
www.travelodgeprincegeorge.com
77 air-conditioned units in downtown location.
Cable TV and movie channel. Laundry, beauty
salon, sauna. Family restaurant, lounge. Close to
Civic Centre.

Treasure Cove Hotel & Casino
2005 Hwy. 97 South
877-614-9111 or 250-614-9111
www.treasurecovehotel.net
82 well-appointed rooms, suites, complimentary
continental breakfast. Exercise facility, day spa,
waterslide and pool, fitness center and Jacuzzi.
Restaurants, casino, entertainment.

CAMPGROUNDS

Bednesti Lake Resort
Mile 33 Hwy. 16 West
250-441-3500
7 rooms and 3 cabins, along with 40 campsites
with full or partial hookups, some pull-throughs,
satellite TV, flush toilets, showers, laundry, picnic
area, playground. Dining, café, lounge. Swimming,
boating, boat launch, convenience store, fishing
licenses. Fuel, propane.

Bee Lazee RV Park and Campground
15910 Hwy. 97, 9 miles (15 km) south of Prince
George
866-963-7263 or 250-963-7263
49 sites with full hookups, pull-throughs, tent
camping. Free showers; laundry, washrooms, car
and RV wash. Playground, heated pool.

Blue Spruce RV Park and Campground
3 miles (5 km) west on Hwy. 16 from intersection
with Hwy. 97
877-964-7272 or 250-964-7272
128 sites with full hookups, pull-throughs, cable
TV, tent camping, cabins. Showers, laundry, store.
Heated pool, minigolf, playground, sani-station.
Near golf, gas, shopping.

Hartway RV Park
7729 Kelly Rd. South, 6 miles (10 km) north of
Prince George on Hwy. 97
866-962-8848 or 250-962-8848
40 landscaped sites with full and partial hookups,
pull-throughs, cable TV, free Wi-Fi. Free showers,
self-service laundry, gift shop, near restaurants
and shopping.

The Log House Guest Ranch and RV Park
11075 Hedlund Rd.
250-963-3477
Lakeside resort 12 minutes from downtown.

MamaYeh RV Park
5235 White Rd.
866-961-6828 or 250-963-8828
www.mamayeh.com
Newly opened in 2010, offering 32 sites including
pull-throughs and back-ins with water and sewer.
Forest setting. Wi-Fi. Pets on leash welcome.

Sintich RV Park
7817 Hwy. 97 South, 3 miles (5 km) south of Prince
George on Hwy. 97
250-963-9862
www.sintichpark.bc.ca
50 spacious landscaped lots for adult campers,
pull-throughs, power, cable TV. Wi-Fi. Free showers; laundry. Near golf, store, and gas station.

Southpark RV Park
9180 Hwy. 97 South
877-963-7275 or 250-963-7577
www.southparkrv.com
Extra-long pull-throughs, free hot showers, Internet,
satellite TV, golf nearby.

RESTAURANTS

Cariboo Steak & Seafood
1165 5th Ave.
250-564-1220
Steaks, seafood, salad bar.

Cimo Mediterranean Grill
601 Victoria St.
250-564-7975
Pasta, grill, seafood, wine.

De Dutch Pannekoek House
101-910 Victoria St.
250-563-2946
www.dedutch.com
Continental dining, breakfast, burgers and more.

Earl's Place
1440 Central St. East
250-562-1527
Family dining, appetizers, desserts. Licensed.

Japanese Wasabi Sushi Wonton House
395 Quebec St.
250-562-8111
Japanese cuisine.

The Keg
582 George St.
250-563-1768
Steak, prime rib, other favorites.

The Loghouse Restaurant
11075 Hedlund Rd.
250-963-9515

Mai Thai
484 Douglas St.
250-563-7779
Thai cuisine. Seafood, appetizers, curries.

Moxie's Classic Grill
1804 Central St. East.
250-564-4700
Burgers, pasta, daily entrées. Mixed drinks.

Nancy O's
1261 3rd Ave.
250-562-8066
Canadian cuisine in the heart of downtown.

Ric's Grill
547 George St.
250-614-9096
Steak, chicken, seafood.

Sgt. O'Flaherty's Pub
770 Brunswick St.
250-563-0078
Pizza and other pub grub, beer, and wine. Entertainment.

Spicy Green
1215 5th Ave.
250-564-3509
Flavors of India, Sri Lanka, Singapore.

Temptations Restaurant
409 George St.
250-563-7109
Nouveau French cuisine.

Winston's
770 Brunswick St., inside the Coast Inn
250-563-0121
Quality dining in well-appointed restaurant.

Road Notes

Ready for a side trip to see something extraordinary? How does hiking through an ancient rain forest strike you? From Prince George, take Hwy. 16 (Yellowhead Hwy.) east for an hour to a quiet little turnoff near Slim Creek that leads to what some call one of BC's best-kept secrets. This rare inland rain forest is a place where location, climate, and other factors have protected stands of ancient western red cedars from destruction. Many of the giant trees are more than a thousand years old and 10 feet in diameter, dwarfing the travelers who walk among them on newly constructed trails. An interpretive sign stands at the trailhead, pointing the way from the gravel parking lot (a former quarry that can be a bit challenging for longer rigs). Discovered by a University of Northern British Columbia graduate student, the ancient rain forest is still under study. Learn more about the science of this unique place. Visit the university's website at http://web.unbc.ca/~wetbelt/af-trail.htm.

For those who'll pass on the side trip, keep your grill pointing north as you leave Prince George, continuing on Hwy. 97 (John Hart Hwy.) to Chetwynd, 168 miles (270 km) away. About 25 miles (40 km) outside of Prince George is the turnoff to see the oldest home in this area, Huble Homestead Historic Site. Through summer and early fall, you can take a guided tour and learn about early life in this remote place. It's a great place for families, with picnic areas, a gift shop, food concession, and farm animals. On weekends, enjoy a pancake breakfast and blacksmith demonstrations. Call 250-564-7033 or visit www.hublehomestead.ca.

At the Salmon River, about 25 minutes north of Prince George, Rockin's River Resort (250-971-2223, www.rockinsriverresort.com) offers treed campsites with pull-throughs, conveniences, a camp store, and easy access for fishing on this tributary of the Fraser.

The Rocky Mountain Trench, 95 miles (153 km) north of Prince George, marks the western boundary of the Rocky Mountains. This land of lakes, rivers, and fertile valleys beneath snowcapped peaks will have you shooting pictures in every direction. There are plenty of pullouts for a short rest, most with garbage cans, some with picnic tables or toilets.

A trio of carved bears welcomes motorists to Chetwynd, where you'll find chainsaw carvings on many corners. An annual competition here draws some of the top artists in the field.

CHETWYND

From Prince George, BC: 168 miles (270 km)
To Dawson Creek, BC: 63 miles (102 km)

Chetwynd is proud of the dozens of chainsaw sculptures you'll see around town, beginning with the welcome sign that features a family of curious bears carved by Terry McKinnon. Nearby is the Chetwynd Visitor Information Centre (www.gochetwynd .com) at 5217 North Access Rd., just off Hwy. 97, where you can pick up a driving map that shows where more than 60 sculptures are on display at the Chainsaw Sculpture Park as well as businesses around town. For lovers of chainsaw sculpture, you can't do better than watching the artists at work. Come and observe during the annual Chetwynd International Chainsaw Carving Championship Invitational, held annually in the second week of June at the recreation center, off Hwy. 97 at 48th St.

Chetwynd lies in coal and timber country in Little Prairie Valley. In fact, early fur traders originally called it Little Prairie. The name Chetwynd honors Ralph Chetwynd, a government minister who helped bring the Pacific Great Eastern Railway to town. In 1966, his grandson, Richard Chetwynd, visited the community and donated an impressive wood sculpture, known locally as "The Little Giant." At 9 feet tall and 1,200 pounds, the statue of a bearded woodsman has become the town's mascot, representing its roots and as well as its future. Recently, the original statue was replaced by a replica by Ken Sheen, a local artist.

Many of Chetwynd's 2,600 people are employed at the sawmill, the coal mine, or the two dams up Hudson's Hope Loop. If you want to learn more about mining and forestry, industrial tours are available. Check at the visitor center for reservations.

DINOSAURS AND DAMS

On the map, the Hudson's Hope Loop road—Hwy. 29 running north from Chetwynd—looks like a great way to shave off time and miles from your Alaska Hwy. trip. Don't be fooled by the two-dimensional aspects of the map. The 87-mile route will lead you through some beautiful country, but it is a narrow, winding affair that's best left to the sports-car set. And besides, if you take this cutoff, you'll miss Dawson Creek completely, along with the fun of seeing your way around the Mile 0 City.

But do make a side trip along Hudson's Hope Loop to enjoy the countryside and visit two massive dams across the Peace River: the Peace River Dam and the W.A.C. Bennett Dam. See the dams, and then come back to Chetwynd so you can launch your Alaska Hwy. adventure at Dawson Creek.

Along Hudson's Hope Loop, the landscape changes from pasture to aspen forest to wheat fields in a broad river valley. The narrow road is patchy at times, and elevation changes can be rather steep, so you may just decide to pass on this side trip if you're driving a big rig.

Dinosaur footprints are part of an outside display at the W.A.C. Bennett Dam, and more interactive displays can be found inside the visitor center. The dam itself is 600 feet (183 m) tall and 1.25 miles (2 km) long, creating Williston Lake, a 230-mile-long (370-km) reservoir that's the 10th largest in the world. In the modern visitor center theater, a film shows historical footage of the river before the dam's construction, explains why it was built here, and how it all came together. Hands-on science experiments demonstrate how much energy is needed to light a bulb. Take a tour of the underground powerhouse. Parking is plentiful, and there are excellent views and photo opportunities. For information on tours of the Bennett Dam, call 888-333-6667.

Farther along the loop road is Peace Canyon Dam. While this is the more modest of the two dams, the visitor center here includes museum dioramas that depict early life for settlers in this area. Just inside the front door are full-size replicas of dinosaurs that once roamed the region. An upper deck allows a generous view of the dam and the valley. For information on the Peace River Dam, call 250-783-9943.

Take a walk along any of the extensive trails in the Chetwynd Greenspace Trail System. They range from a five-minute walk to an hour or more on trails varying from rustic to improved. A popular route is the Baldy Hiking Trail, which leads to the summit of Mt. Baldy. A viewpoint halfway offers excellent views of the country and is a good spot to rest for the push to the summit, or a turnaround point. The Community Forest has interpretive walking and trails, a tree registry, and a demonstration forest, along with picnic areas in forested settings. You can pick up a detailed trail map at the visitor center.

Take the kids for a few hours of water fun at the Chetwynd Leisure Pool, one of the best in the area, located at 46th St. and the North Access Rd. off Hwy. 97. Other local recreation includes golfing, mountain biking, and terrific fishing. You can obtain your mandatory fishing license and all the tackle you need at Lonestar Sporting Goods, 5028 50th Ave. Call 250-788-1850.

For more information on what to see and do in Chetwynd, call the Chetwynd Visitor Centre at 250-788-1943 or visit www.gochetwynd.com.

LODGING

Brookside Inn
5112 50th St.
250-788-9123
Rooms and on-site restaurant.

Chetwynd Court Motel
5104 North Access Rd.
250-788-2271
17 rooms, kitchenettes, cable TV, laundry facilities, wheelchair access, pet friendly. Restaurant.

Country Squire Motor Inn Chetwynd
5317 South Access Rd.
250-788-2276
51 deluxe units, Internet, air-conditioning, kitchenettes. Fitness center and sauna. Pet friendly. Close to restaurant.

High Country Inn
5000 North Access Rd.
250-788-9980
32 air-conditioned rooms, pets allowed, coach parking. On-site restaurant and liquor store.

Lakeview Inns & Suites
4820 North Access Rd.
877-355-3500 or 250-788-3000
Full-kitchen units, wheelchair-accessible rooms, free movies. Business center, Internet, fitness center and pool, free continental breakfast, laundry.

Pine Cone Motor Inn
5224 53rd Ave.
800-663-8082 or 250-788-3311
52 air-conditioned units, including kitchenettes. Wheelchair accessible. Cable TV. Pets allowed. Coffee shop, dining room.

Pomeroy Inns & Suites
5200 North Access Rd.
800-424-4800 or 250-788-4800
Well-appointed units. Pool, waterslide, continental breakfast. Close to shopping and restaurants. Pet friendly.

Stagecoach Inn
5413 South Access Rd.
250-788-9666
55 air-conditioned rooms, kitchenettes, nonsmoking available, wheelchair access. Cable TV, sauna, whirlpool, laundry. Winter plug-ins. Pets on approval. Restaurant.

The Swiss Inn
4812 North Access Rd.
250-788-2566
Quality, comfortable accommodations for weekly or monthly rental. Pet friendly. Kitchenettes, cable TV. CAA Diamond rated. On-site restaurant.

Westwind Motel
4401 53rd St.
877-988-3344 or 250-788-3344
Rooms and kitchenettes. Continental breakfast, business center.

Windrem Motel Chetwynd
5201 South Access Rd.
250-788-9808
Rooms and tenting sites with showers in downtown Chetwynd.

CAMPGROUNDS

Caron Creek RV Park
On Hwy. 97, 10 miles (16 km) west of Chetwynd
250-788-2522
40 sites with full and partial hookups, pull-throughs on gravel and grass. Free showers; washrooms. Pay phone. Senior discount. Open May–October.

Westwind RV Park
4401 53rd Ave., 1 mile (1.6 km) north past junction of hwys. 97 and 29
250-788-2190
50 pull-through sites with full hookups. Showers, laundry, restrooms, dump station. Grassy sites, tent sites, picnic tables, firepit area, playground, fishing. Open May–October.

RESTAURANTS

Dee's Diner
4741 51st St.
250-788-3778
Homestyle cooking.

Dixie Lee Chicken Fish n' Chips
5200 52nd St.
250-788-9511
Casual family fare.

Dragon Palace
5317 South Access Rd.
250-788-3700
Chinese cuisine. Eat in or take out.

High Country Inn
5000 North Access Rd.
Adjacent to Chetwynd Court Motel
250-788-9980
Dining, cocktails.

June's Country Kitchen
4632 North Access Rd.
250-788-2612
Home-cooked meals.

New Blue Sky Restaurant
5217 South Access Rd.
250-788-2777
Full menu, family dining.

Stagecoach Restaurant
5413 South Access Rd.
250-788-3388
Dining with views of Sukunka Valley.

The Swiss Inn Restaurant
4812 North Access Rd.
250-788-2566
Steaks, pizza, European cuisine.

The distinctive red buildings of Northern Alberta Railway (NAR) Park house art and photography exhibits. Nearby is the Alaska Hwy. sign that draws so many travelers with their cameras.

DAWSON CREEK, BRITISH COLUMBIA

From Chetwynd, BC: 63 miles (102 km)
From the Washington border: 692 miles (1,113.5 km)
To the Alaska border: 1,190 miles (1,915 km)
To Fairbanks, AK: 1,488 miles (2,395 km)

Symbolically, Dawson Creek is the end of this road and the beginning of another. You have arrived at Mile 0 of the famed Alaska Hwy., and a new leg of your adventure is about to begin.

For a complete description of Dawson Creek and its services, facilities, and attractions, see Chapter 6, The Alaska Highway.

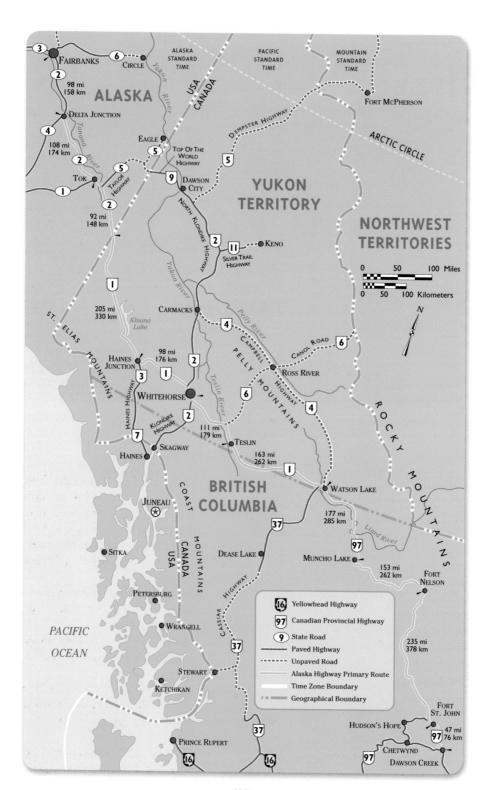

ALASKA

FAIRBANKS
CIRCLE
ALASKA STANDARD TIME
PACIFIC STANDARD TIME
MOUNTAIN STANDARD TIME
USA
CANADA
FORT MCPHERSON

98 mi
158 km

DELTA JUNCTION

Tanana River

Yukon River

108 mi
174 km

EAGLE
TOP OF THE WORLD HIGHWAY

DEMPSTER HIGHWAY

ARCTIC CIRCLE

TOK
Taylor Highway

DAWSON CITY

YUKON TERRITORY

NORTHWEST TERRITORIES

92 mi
148 km

North Klondike Highway

KENO
SILVER TRAIL HIGHWAY

0   50   100 Miles

0   50   100 Kilometers

N

205 mi
330 km

Kluana Lake

CARMACKS

Yukon River

Pelly River

CANOL ROAD

ST. ELIAS MOUNTAINS

98 mi
176 km

HAINES JUNCTION

Campbell Highway

PELLY MOUNTAINS

ROSS RIVER

ROCKY MOUNTAINS

WHITEHORSE

Teslin River

Haines Highway

Klondike Highway

111 mi
179 km

TESLIN

163 mi
262 km

HAINES
SKAGWAY

BRITISH COLUMBIA

WATSON LAKE

Liard River

JUNEAU

COAST MOUNTAINS

CANADA
USA

177 mi
285 km

SITKA

DEASE LAKE

MUNCHO LAKE

153 mi
262 km

FORT NELSON

PETERSBURG

Cassiar Highway

WRANGELL

PACIFIC OCEAN

235 mi
378 km

STEWART

KETCHIKAN

Yellowhead Highway
Canadian Provincial Highway
State Road
Paved Highway
Unpaved Road
Alaska Highway Primary Route
Time Zone Boundary
Geographical Boundary

FORT ST. JOHN

PRINCE RUPERT

HUDSON'S HOPE

47 mi
76 km

CHETWYND

DAWSON CREEK

CHAPTER 6

THE ALASKA HIGHWAY

Welcome to Dawson Creek, BC. Right about now, you're probably thinking, *I thought we'd never get here!* It's true that the starting line of the Alaska Hwy., or Mile 0, is more than 800 miles from the Canada border, whether you came up through British Columbia or Alberta. So if you're saying "Finally!" join the crowd. But if you're like most people, here you'll shed any lingering road weariness and find revival in a sense of excitement and anticipation.

Now, don't expect the wilderness adventure part to begin immediately, for the road really doesn't change for many more miles. It's still paved and easy to navigate and is basically a continuation of what you've been seeing for a long distance already—farmlands—for some travelers, not too different from the place they started.

Yet as you visit the historic sites of Dawson Creek and make final preparations, you'll realize that you'll be following the footsteps of those intrepid workers who laid the groundwork for this highway seven decades ago—and enduring a frigid winter, no less—pushing a route through forests and over mountains, skirting jewel-colored lakes, battling the quagmire of newly exposed permafrost, to complete one of the world's greatest road-building projects. Carry those images with you as you travel, and be sure to stop at the historic signposts and pullouts to learn more about this incredible road north.

DAWSON CREEK, BRITISH COLUMBIA

Mile 0 of the Alaska Hwy.

To Fort St. John, BC: 45 miles (73 km)

To the Alaska border: 1,186 miles (1,908 km)

To Fairbanks, AK: 1,488 miles (2,395 km)

Tucked into the far northeast corner of British Columbia, little Dawson Creek gained international attention in March 1942 when thousands of US troops "invaded" to begin construction of the Alaska Hwy. from the south end of the route. For a brief time, Dawson Creek's sparse population of 650 was overrun with 10,000 GIs, straining local accommodations and food services, filling its sidewalks, and clogging the only movie theater in town. The boom was short-lived, however, as most of the men and equipment trailed northwest in the months to come.

Dawson Creek, BC, and Dawson City, YT, farther north, were both named for George Mercer Dawson, a geologist who surveyed these parts of Canada in 1879. His work paved the way for settlement and development in both Dawsons.

Dawson Creek was a village of 800 people when the Northern Alberta Railway made it a terminus in 1931. Incorporated as a city in 1958, Dawson Creek remains a small town, with fewer than 13,000 residents.

At the city limits, near Dawson Creek Airport, stands a welcome sign declaring Mile Zero City, Where the Adventure Begins! And at the traffic circle in Dawson Creek that connects Hwy. 2 to Hwy. 97, you'll spot the oft-photographed sign proclaiming: You Are Now Entering the World Famous Alaska Highway.

Just inside the roundabout connecting hwys. 2 and 97, a metal sculpture by Carl Mattson points the way to Alaska and honors the surveyors of the historic Alcan. This

Jay and Delphine Gage of Anchorage, AK, were headed Outside for a family visit, driving their family car and staying in hotels along the way. In 1942, while others of Jay's generation were building the Alaska Hwy., he was serving in Patton's army.

is such a busy, dangerous traffic area, visitors are well advised to stay on the safe side of the street and forego posing by the sculpture. It's not worth the risk.

Behind you towers another Dawson Creek classic, dressed in red: a historic wooden grain elevator that was relocated to this place in the Northern Alberta Railway Park (NAR Park). Today it houses a gift shop and art gallery and features a spiral ramp, making access to the exhibits easy for everybody. The building of the Alaska Hwy. is portrayed in historic photos.

On any given summer day, the NAR Park lot is filled with RVs from all over the US and Canada—a true cross section of the North American camping world. These are people who are always ready for conversation and to compare travel notes, and new friendships have been forged here. According to Tourism Dawson Creek, some 320,000 visitors travel up the highway each year.

From the NAR Park parking area, it's an easy stroll to the Dawson Creek Visitor Information Centre at 900 Alaska Ave. Just follow the brick footpath past the railcar to the renovated 1931 railway station, which is now a combination visitor center/museum. Tens of thousands visit the center each year to get answers, pick up free brochures, freshen up in the public restrooms, and buy books and souvenirs to mark this memorable trip. Access to the South Peace Historical Society museum is a nominal fee. See more on the history of the Peace River Region at www.calverley.ca. With a free copy of the self-guided historic walking tour pamphlet, you'll stroll by the buildings that were standing when the American soldiers began arriving in March of 1942. A mural project enhances the beauty and history of the downtown core.

The Mile 0 milepost is a couple of blocks from NAR Park's must-see sites. It is situated in the middle of an intersection, so take care when you grab your picture.

Just one block due south of the Station Museum is another not-to-be-missed landmark, the Mile 0 milepost. Erected in 1946, it's in an unfortunate place—dead center in the busy intersection of 10th St. and 102nd Ave., making posed photos a dangerous proposition. We saw others like us, passing off their cameras to friendly strangers and dodging traffic, trying to keep an eye on the crossing signals as well as vehicles that might ruin the photo shoot. Still, it's a must-have shot. So if the weather's lousy, get it on a postcard. In form, it matches mileposts at Delta Junction, AK, the official end of the Alaska Hwy., and Fairbanks, AK, the unofficial end.

Atop the monument, sign makers have painted the number of miles from Dawson Creek to Fort St. John (48), Fort Nelson (300), Whitehorse (918), and Fairbanks (1,523). The numbers no longer match the actual driving distances, because the road has been straightened (and shortened) since it was first constructed. At that time, Canada used miles to measure distance. The country has since switched to the metric system, and kilometerposts have replaced mileposts along the highway.

The Alaska Highway House is a new attraction in town, just steps from the Mile 0 milepost on 10th St. Step inside to see and hear the stories of the people who built the highway, and view some amazing film footage, maps, interpretive displays, and other visitor information. Call 250-782-4714 or see www.alaskahighwayhouse.com.

This town of nearly 13,000 people supports a wide-ranging community of farming families. Agriculture and tourism are the leading economic drivers. If you're visiting during early August, be sure to make it to the Dawson Creek Fall Fair, Exhibition & Pro Rodeo, which includes farming exhibits, horse shows, handicrafts, a food fair, and rodeo events. And for the fright of your life, watch the professional chuckwagon drivers' race.

Mile Zero Park (oddly enough, located at Mile 1 of the Alaska Hwy.) includes the Walter Wright Pioneer Village and some beautiful botanical treats, shops, and a restaurant. A picnic area, swimming lake, and adjacent RV park and campground round out the attraction.

Golfers can test their skills on two local courses. In town is the 18-hole, par-70 Dawson Creek Golf & Country Club (with at least three driveable par-4s). Cart and equipment rentals are available, and tee time reservations are recommended. Located at 2121 Alaska Hwy.; call 250-782-7882. Just 10 miles along the Alaska Hwy. in Farmington is a 9-hole, well-treed course. Farmington Fairways also offers an on-site campground with pull-throughs and tent sites so you can stick around if the clubs are hot. Cart and club rentals, driving range, pro shop, and clubhouse round out your holiday. For tee times, call 250-843-7774.

Dawson Creek has many restaurants, hotels, campgrounds, bakeries, car and RV washes—anything you need for resting up or stocking up before beginning your journey up the Alaska Hwy. For more information on the area's attractions and services, call 866-645-3022 or 250-782-9595, or visit www.tourismdawsoncreek.com.

LODGING

Please browse www.bbcanada.com to locate a bed-and-breakfast.

The Alaska Hotel
10209 10th St.
250-782-7998
www.alaskahotel.com
12 modest units, shared bathrooms, Old World decor. Common kitchen and TV room. Restaurant, pub, entertainment. Just 55 paces south of the historic Mile 0 milepost.

Aurora Park Inn & Suite
12004 8th St.
877-782-8006 or 250-782-8006
www.auroraparkinn.com
45 deluxe rooms, suites. Free breakfast. Near airport and highway.

Best Western Dawson Creek
500 Hwy. 2
800-528-1234 or 250-782-6226
www.bestwesternbc.com
100 deluxe air-conditioned rooms, kitchenettes, cable TV, Internet. Laundry service, exercise facility, whirlpool/sauna. Pet friendly. Free breakfast.

Cedar Lodge Motel
801 110th Ave.
250-782-8531
41 units, with kitchenettes, refrigerator, cable TV, laundry. Pet friendly. Across from mall.

Central Motel & RV Park
1301 Alaska Ave.
250-782-8525
15 air-conditioned units, cable TV, Internet, convenient location.

Dawson Creek Super 8 Motel

1440 Alaska Ave.
888-482-8884 or 250-782-8899
66 business suites and kitchenettes. Free Internet, microwave, refrigerators, iron, cable TV. Fitness center. Pet friendly. Free breakfast.

George Dawson Inn

11705 8th St.
800-663-2745 or 250-782-9151
www.georgedawsoninn.bc.ca
80 well-appointed air-conditioned rooms, executive suites, flat-screen televisions, cable, free Wi-Fi. Coffee shop, lounge, dining room, fitness center. Small pets. Senior rates. Walking tours of historic Mile 0 sites.

Inn on the Creek

10600 8th St.
888-782-8136 or 250-782-8136
www.innonthecreek.bc.ca
48 air-conditioned deluxe rooms and kitchenettes. Fridge, microwave, family restaurant. Adjacent to mall, close to attractions.

The Lodge Motor Inn & Café

1317 Alaska Ave.
800-935-3336 or 250-782-4837
www.lodgemotorinn.com
40 modern air-conditioned rooms, cable TV, free local calls. Dining. Centrally located, near mall.

North Country Inn (Airport Inn)

800 120th Ave.
800-555-2809 or 250-782-9404
www.airportinn.ca
40 air-conditioned rooms, suites, cable TV, Internet, laundry. Pet friendly.

Northwinds Lodge

623 103rd Ave.
www.northwindslodge.com
800-665-1759 or 250-782-9181
20 newly renovated air-conditioned units; kitchenettes. Cable TV, fridge, free Internet, winter plug-ins.

Peace Villa Motel

1641 Alaska Ave.
877-782-8175 or 250-782-8175
48 air-conditioned rooms, movies, laundry, office services, sauna. Senior discount. Near golf course and restaurants.

Pomeroy Inns & Suites

540 Hwy. 2
866-782-3577 or 250-782-3500
www.pomeroyinnandsuites.com
Suites with luxury mattresses and linens, fully equipped kitchens, separate living areas, free Internet. Free breakfast, indoor pool, waterslide, business center, fitness center, hot tub. Pet friendly.

Ramada Limited Dawson Creek

1748 Alaska Ave.
800-663-2749 or 250-782-8595
www.ramada.com
41 units on one level, fridge, coffee, iron and board, cable TV, Wi-Fi. Free deluxe continental breakfast. Close to restaurants, downtown, and tourist information.

Travellers Inn

800 112th Ave.
250-782-5333
36 air-conditioned rooms, kitchenettes, cable TV, Internet. Pet friendly. Free breakfast.

Voyageur Motor Inn

801 111th Ave.
877-782-8006 or 250-782-1020
19 air-conditioned rooms, cable TV. Pet friendly. Restaurant.

CAMPGROUNDS

Alahart RV Park

Junction of Hwy. 97 and Alaska Hwy.
250-782-4702
Full hookups, pull-throughs, tent camping. Free showers, self-service laundry, cable TV, dump station, free ice. Windshield repair. Close to downtown, next to restaurant.

Central Motel & RV Park

1301 Alaska Ave.
250-782-8525
Motel also offers 10 back-in RV sites with full hookups. Close to parks, picnic area, swimming pool, visitor center, and museum.

Mile 0 RV & Campground

Mile 1.5, next to Rotary Lake and Walter Wright Pioneer Village
250-782-2590
Partial hookups, pull-throughs, Wi-Fi, shady sites. Free showers; laundry, dump station, Mile 1 Café. Near golf course.

Northern Lights RV Park
On Hwy. 97 South, just west of junction with Hwy. 97 North
888-414-9433 or 250-782-9433
55 sites, spacious pull-throughs, full and partial hookups. Free satellite TV and wireless Internet, modem hookup, free showers, self-service laundry, washrooms. RV wash; full service for Alaska Hwy. preparation. Gift shop, trout-fishing pond. Large groups welcome.

Tubby's RV Park
1913 Hart Hwy. (Hwy. 97 South)
250-782-2584
97 full-hookup sites, pull-throughs, tenting. Free showers, self-service laundry, restrooms, dump station. Car and RV wash, auto services. Internet. Near swimming pool and Pioneer Village.

RESTAURANTS

Dew Drop Inn Pub
10209 10th St., in the Alaska Hotel
250-782-7040
www.alaskahotel.com
Lunch and live music, near Mile 0 milepost.

Caruso's
1025 Alaska Ave.
250-782-4938
Steak, seafood, pasta, beer and wine. Reservations accepted.

China Kitchen
10600 8th Ave.
250-782-1596
Chinese favorites, full menu or take-out.

Dawson Co-op Cafeteria
11300 8th St.
250-782-4858
Full menu and take-out.

Dawson Creek Diner & Deli
10221 10th St.
250-782-1182
Burgers, sandwiches, pizza.

Dawson Creek Golf & Country Club
Mile 2 Alaska Hwy.
250-782-5156
Breakfast, lunch, dinner, views. Reservations accepted.

Fireside Steakhouse & Lounge
1029 102nd Ave.
250-782-4881
Full menu for lunch and dinner. Full bar. Reservations accepted.

Le's Restaurant
801 111th St.
250-782-1020
Western gourmet dining.

Lily's Dining Room
11705 8th St., in the George Dawson Inn
250-782-9151
Breakfast, lunch, dinner.

Lodge Café
1317 Alaska Ave.
250-782-4837
Full menu, breakfast specials. Beer and wine.

Men Fan
800 120th Ave.
250-782-9798
Chinese fare.

Mr. Mike's West Coast Grill
1501 Alaska Ave.
250-782-1577
Seafood, steak; full menu or take-out. Patio seating. Reservations accepted.

New Dragon Palace Restaurant
11400 8th St.
250-782-8222
Asian cuisine.

Noodle Hut
1405 102nd Ave.
250-782-9484
Asian menu; eat in or take out.

Orion Restaurant
910 102nd Ave.
250-782-1020
Asian menu.

Panago Pizza
10508 8th St.
250-310-0001
Pizza, wings, salads. Eat in or take out.

Replace Restaurant
1100 102nd Ave.
250-782-2240

Rockwell's Pub Club
1729 Alaska Ave.
250-782-2994

Road Notes

The price of gas in Dawson Creek is typically higher than in the smaller towns to the south. And generally, the farther north you go in Canada, the more you pay. In the summer of 2010, we found Fort Nelson the most expensive stop, where, after converting Canadian dollars to US and liters to gallons, we were paying more than $5 US per gallon.

As you drive north toward Fort St. John, notice the pumpjacks in the fields. These mechanisms draw the oil out of the ground and into a pipeline or a storage tank. Most of the oil and gas is sold to markets in Canada and the United States.

Get sweeter than honey just south of Fort St. John at The Honey Place, which boasts the world's largest glass beehive. You can learn about bee behavior and what makes quality honey. Get your honey here, or pollen or other souvenirs. It's on the west side of the road, about 5 miles (8 km) before Fort St. John. Call 250-785-4808.

FORT ST. JOHN

From Dawson Creek, BC: 45 miles (73 km)

To Fort Nelson, BC: 240 miles (387 km)

Fort St. John calls itself The Energetic City and the Oil & Gas Capital of British Columbia, with a nod to the industries that power the city's economy: natural gas and oil extraction, hydroelectric power, forestry, agriculture, and tourism. In addition, in 2009 the city was designated BC's Music Capital. This community of more than 19,000 people is the oldest non-Native settlement on the British Columbia mainland, its beginnings rooted in the 1794 trading post named Rocky Mountain Fort. Another 60,000 people live throughout the North Peace region, where the Peace River snakes through a broad, green valley. These rural residents and First Nations communities look to Fort St. John as a regional hub for business and services. The city offers shopping, dining, and cultural attractions such as live theater, dance, and music at the North Peace Culture Centre, 10015 100th Ave. Call 250-785-1992. And it's a pet-friendly town—your traveling pets are welcome in nearly every hotel, motel, or lodge in Fort St. John.

As the main town of the North Peace region, Fort St. John lies within a diverse landscape, from rolling farmlands and valleys to canyons carved by rivers. Near the entrance to the city, the staff at the visitor information center, open year-round at 9523 100th St., will help you plan an outdoor adventure. You can jump on the Internet, buy a fishing or hunting license, and get up-to-date information on weather, roads, and events. Call 877-785-6037 or 250-785-3033, or visit www.fortstjohn.ca. The center offers a list of local guides and outfitters and their specialties. Think about a day of hiking on Fish Creek Community Forest trails, swimming, horseback riding, or fishing for walleye or northern pike in Charlie Lake. And golfers may choose from several excellent courses within easy driving distance from town.

Check with the folks at Backcountry, one of BC's largest hunting, fishing, and outdoor supply stores, for mandatory fishing licensing as well as outdoor clothing and gear— plus advice on where to find the fish. They can book a guide for you, too. Backcountry is located at 10120 Alaska Rd. Call 250-785-1461 or see www.backcountryfsj.com. In Charlie Lake, stop by the General Store at Mile 52 Alaska Hwy., or call 250-787-0655.

The North Peace Leisure Pool complex, at 9505 100th St., is a modern addition to the recreational possibilities in Fort St. John. Every Saturday, RVers are invited to park

Charlie Lake was the site of a grave tragedy during highway construction. This memorial honors twelve American soldiers who died in an accident at this place.

here and mosey around this busy part of town. Stroll through the farmers' market, take a walking tour, shop, or enjoy a picnic in Centennial Park. Nearby is the free Rotary Spray Park, perfect for kids on hot, sunny days. And inside the Leisure Complex, you'll find a six-lane lap pool, wave pool, rapids channel, waterslide, hot tub, and a kiddie pool. Relax in the steam room or sauna and the road miles will melt away. Call 250-785-8178.

Exhibits at the Fort St. John-North Peace Museum reflect on the region's First Nations roots, its settlement by fur traders, and its development into the regional power that it is today. Back in 1942, Fort St. John was the unofficial starting line for the builders of the Alaska Hwy. A gravel road already existed between Dawson Creek and this outlying community, and that road was incorporated into the route. Six thousand troops descended on what was then a town of 200 people. You'll find the museum at the foot of the landmark oil derrick at 9323 100th St. Open Monday through Saturday. Call 250-787-0430.

Golf enthusiasts can play a 9-hole course with bent-grass greens at Fort St. John Links, 12707 86th St. You'll find cart rentals, club repairs, lessons from a CGPA pro on staff, and a licensed clubhouse. For information, call 250-285-9995. North of town at Charlie Lake is Lakepoint Golf & Country Club at Mile 54 Alaska Hwy., offering an 18-hole championship course, pro shop, rentals, and restaurant. Call for tee times at 250-785-5566; visit www.lakepoint.ca.

Charlie Lake, almost 4 miles (6 km) northwest of Fort St. John, is a friendly community of about 1,000 people, with another 1,250 in the outlying areas. This was also the site of a large work camp during the Alaska Hwy. construction. Its history holds a sad story about a day in May 1942 when the waters of Charlie Lake took the lives of 12 men who were crossing the lake on a pontoon barge with some heavy equipment. At

Mile 52, a memorial to those men, including each of their names, serial numbers, and hometowns, stands along the shore near the Rotary RV Park.

At Charlie Lake, you can turn west to access Hwy. 29, Hudson's Hope Loop, from the north end. This road leads to some beautiful driving country, but the road does get narrow and patchy in places. Steep grades and switchbacks are not advisable for over-size RVs. Two dams along this loop road are major area attractions, as is Hudson's Hope Museum. For more information, see the section on the town of Chetwynd in Chapter 5, The Western Route.

LODGING

Please browse www.bbcanada.com to locate a bed-and-breakfast.

Blue Belle Motel
9795 Alaska Rd., Mile 47 of the Alaska Hwy.
866-833-2121 or 250-785-2613
40 air-conditioned units, kitchenettes, fridge, microwave, cable TV, Internet. Free coffee, laundry, barbecue grills.

Caravan Motel
9711 Alaska Rd.
250-787-1191
28 air-conditioned suites; some kitchenettes. Cable TV, Internet, coffee, laundry, wheelchair access.

Cedar Lodge Motor Inn
9824 99th Ave.
800-661-2210 or 250-785-8107
47 air-conditioned units, some kitchenettes. Fridge, microwave, cable TV, Internet. Pet friendly. Winter plug-ins.

Coachman Inn
8540 Alaska Rd.
888-388-9408 or 250-787-0651
70 deluxe rooms, nonsmoking and pet rooms available. Cable TV, Internet, sauna, whirlpool, fitness room.

Econo Lodge
10419 Alaska Rd.
800-4CHOICE or 250-787-8475
www.choicehotels.ca
42 air-conditioned units, coffee, fridge. Cable TV, Internet, laundry services, health club, swimming pool. Free hot breakfast. Winter plug-ins. Restaurant, coffee shop, pub.

Fort St. John Motor Inn
10707 102nd St.
888-988-8846 or 250-787-0411
www.fortstjohnmotorinn.com
83 air-conditioned rooms, cable TV, free local calls, fridge, Internet, laundry, winter plug-ins. Quiet surroundings.

Four Seasons Motor Inn
9810 100th St.
800-523-6677 or 250-785-6647
60 air-conditioned rooms, kitchenettes, cable TV, Internet, winter plug-ins. Close to shopping, restaurants. Senior discount.

Lakeview Inns & Suites
10103 98th Ave.
877-355-3500 or 250-787-0779
www.lakeviewhotels.com
73 deluxe rooms, suites, kitchenettes, fridge, microwave, iron and board. Cable TV, Internet, guest laundry. Fitness facility, winter plug-ins. Free airport shuttle. Free light breakfast.

Northwoods Inn
10627 Alaska Rd.
250-787-1616
120 comfortable air-conditioned rooms, cable TV, Internet. Dining, coffee shop, lounge, pub, entertainment.

Pomeroy Hotel & Conference Center
11308 Alaska Rd.
866-618-3233 or 250-262-3233
www.pomeroyhotel.com
125 rooms, 48 suites, fridge, microwave, free Internet, 32-inch plasma TV. Fitness room, indoor pool, whirlpool, waterslide. Restaurant. Airport shuttle. Pet friendly.

Pomeroy Inns & Suites
9304 Alaska Rd.
888-264-3030 or 250-262-3030
www.pomeroyinnandsuites.com
92 rooms with fireplaces, full kitchens, Internet, deluxe breakfast, fitness facility.

Quality Inn Northern Grand Hotel
9830 100th Ave.
800-663-8312 or 250-787-0521
www.qualityinnnortherngrand.com
125 units in full-service hotel, free breakfast, suites, cable TV, Internet. Fitness facility, swimming pool, sauna, whirlpool. Restaurant, lounge, pub. Downtown location.

Roost Motel
9207 Alaska Rd.
250-785-2906
13 units, including nonsmoking rooms. Internet, laundry service. Pet friendly.

Stonebridge Hotel
9223 100th St.
888-419-4657 or 250-785-8364
www.stonebridgehotel.ca
127 recently renovated luxury rooms, kitchenettes, suites, Wi-Fi, 42-inch LCD TVs. Complimentary breakfast, pillowtop mattresses, coffee. Central location near attractions, shopping, entertainment.

Super 8 Motel
9500 Alaska Wy.
866-828-8885 or 250-785-7588
www.super8.com
93 units with comfortable beds, Internet, continental breakfast, indoor pool and waterslide, restaurant and pub.

CAMPGROUNDS

Corner RV Park
8428 Alaska Rd.
250-785-4218
41 sites, including pull-throughs and tent sites, with full or partial hookups. Coin-op showers and laundry. Pets welcome. Open year-round.

Charlie Lake:
Charlie Lake RV & Leisure
Mile 52 Alaska Hwy.
250-787-1569
Full or partial hookup campsites among shade trees, minutes north of Fort St. John. Some pull-throughs, coin-op showers, laundry, phone, playground, firepits. Boat rentals on Charlie Lake.

Rotary RV Park
6 miles (9.5 km) north of Fort St. John
Across from Charlie Lake General Store
250-785-1700
40 sites with full or partial hookup, pull-throughs. 30-amp service, showers, laundry, picnic tables, dump station. Boat dock on Charlie Lake. Next to nature reserve. Open May–September.

The province manages two easy-access parks north of Fort St. John. For more information, contact the Parks District Office in Fort St. John at 250-787-3407. The parks are:
Beatton Lake Provincial Park
2 miles (3 km) north, then 5 miles (8 km) east of Fort St. John
800-689-9025
37 RV and tent sites, with Charlie Lake access. Swimming, playground, fishing, boat launch.

Charlie Lake Provincial Park
7 miles (11 km) north of Fort St. John
800-689-9025
58 treed sites with picnic tables, outhouses, dump station. Playground, short hiking trail to Charlie Lake.

RESTAURANTS

Also stop by major local hotels, which feature full lunch and dinner menus in their dining rooms.

Centre Dining
10228 100th St.
250-785-2812
Cantonese dishes with eat in, take-out, delivery.

Copper Creek Grill
10608 100th Ave.
250-787-7147
Breakfast and lunch specialties.

Egan's Irish Pub
9404 Alaska Rd.
250-263-9992
Appetizers, soups, salads, burgers, sandwiches.

Forty-niner Steakhouse
8111 100th Ave.
250-787-9292
Steak and more on the western-style menu.

Mings Kitchen
9005 100th Ave.
250-787-1177
Lunch, dinner buffet, eat in or take out.

Mr. Mike's Steakhouse
9324 Alaska Rd.
250-262-4151
Beef is king; choose your cut and extras.

Northern Star Restaurant
8540 Alaska Rd.
250-787-1454
Western-style cuisine. On-site lounge.

Northwoods Inn Pizza & Steakhouse
10627 Alaska Rd.
250-787-1616

Ship to Shore Seafood
9520 93rd Ave., #4
250-785-3839
Seafood in a family dining atmosphere.

Silver Creek Cookhouse
10104 Alaska Rd.
250-785-4888
Lunch restaurant with sandwiches and meals.

Uptown Grill
9924 101st Ave.
250-787-9085
Lunch and evening dining.

Whole Wheat and Honey Café
10003 100th St.
250-787-9866
Healthy specialties.

Yoko Beef
9600 93rd Ave., in the Totem Mall
250-787-8778
Chinese take-out and delivery. No MSG.

Charlie Lake:
Charlie Lake General Store
Mile 50.6 Alaska Hwy.
250-787-0655
Take-out chicken and ribs.

Jackfish Dundees
Mile 52 Alaska Hwy.
250-785-3233
Seafood, sirloin burgers, prime rib.

Road Notes

Certain mileposts you may see at roadside represent the distance from Dawson Creek on the original Alaska Hwy.—they show the Historical Miles. Many were erected in 1992, the road's 50th-anniversary year, as a way to provide markers with historical information about the significance of various places. These mileposts do not take into account the road improvements and shortening that have taken place over the years. Many towns and businesses refused to give up their former addresses when the road was shortened, so they now refer to themselves as being at Historic Milepost such-and-such, further muddying the question of just exactly where you are. And as British Columbia and the Yukon work on the road, milepost markers are often missing. So if you are following the numbers closely and your math is coming out funny, it's not you.

The next major city, Fort Nelson, is 240 miles (387 km) down the road. That's the longest segment of the Alaska Hwy. without a town of 1,000 residents or more. Nonetheless,

The Sikanni Lodge is watched over by this very relaxed guard dog.

on this wilderness drive you'll find the occasional roadhouse, gas station, restaurant, or campground tucked in quaint little places along the way, so don't worry about heading into the unknown. You won't starve, and you will find a safe place to camp or lay your head. Services are available at these locations with their Historic Milepost addresses: Shepherd's Inn (Mile 72), Wonowon (Mile 101), Pink Mountain (Mile 143–147), Sasquatch Crossing (Mile 147), Sikanni Chief (Mile 162), Buckinghorse (Mile 175), and Prophet River (Mile 233). Plus, there's so much beauty to behold: this country is crisscrossed with rivers, and the Rocky Mountains to the west will keep you company.

A few miles before the Sikanni Chief River, at Mile 145.5 (Km 234), is the first of the historical stops on the Northwest Staging Route, the series of airstrips that were used during World War II to deliver supplies and Lend-Lease program airplanes to Fairbanks. From there, Russian pilots ferried the planes over the Bering Sea. The Sikanni Chief flight strip, at the southernmost end of the Northwest Staging Route, lies on the east side of the road. Another of those WWII airstrips, now abandoned, can be seen near Mile 217 (Km 349), where a side road crosses the old airstrip. As you drive, you'll also notice segments of the original road that have been abandoned to the weeds through the years as the route has been straightened (and shortened).

Use extra caution as you approach Sikanni Chief, as there's a 9 percent grade with a 50 km/hr speed corner as you descend this dangerous hill—really tough if you're pulling a big rig. In winter, northbound truckers pause at the top to put on chains for their descent on this section of road. Down below, at the campground along the Sikanni River, you can see the remains of the original wooden bridge crossing this stream—also indicating the original route of the highway. During road construction, as temporary bridges were replaced with permanent spans in 1943, this was the first bridge to be replaced. The historic structure was burned by an arsonist in 1992.

The Muskwa Bridge at Mile 281 (Km 452), just a couple of miles before Fort Nelson, is the lowest point on the Alaska Hwy., at an elevation of only 1,000 feet (305 m).

While driving the road for the fourth edition of this book, we traveled in late May and saw several black bears on various occasions before we reached Fort Nelson. The bears were feeding at the forest edge, well away from the roadside, but clearly visible. They were intently munching on the new grasses of spring, and while they kept a wary eye on slow-moving vehicles with cameras pointed their way, they didn't instantly scramble away. Again, we stayed in the camper and took pictures from a distance.

FORT NELSON

From Fort St. John, BC: 240 miles (387 km)

To Muncho Lake, BC: 154 miles (248 km)

To Watson Lake, YT: 330 miles (531 km)

Fort Nelson boasts that it has the longest main street in the world: the Alaska Hwy. And the city's address is Historical Mile 300 (Km 483)—a reference to the town's distance from Dawson Creek on the original Alaska Hwy. (Road realignment now puts Fort Nelson just 283 miles, or 455 km, from Dawson Creek.)

Established in 1805 as a fur trading post, this community in the northeast corner of British Columbia was named for Admiral Horatio Nelson, famed for the Battle of Trafalgar. About 4,700 people live in this town near the convergence of four rivers:

the Muskwa, Prophet, Sikanni, and Fort Nelson. Another 1,300 live outside the city. It's not like your typical small town, Anywhere, USA, however, especially when you figure that 320,000 people drop in for a visit between April and September. Fort Nelson has the services—hotels, restaurants, campgrounds, recreational options—to keep residents and visitors hopping.

The extraction of natural resources fuels the local economy, with diverse industries represented on the city's snowflake-shaped emblem: gas and oil, mining, lumber, wildlife, agriculture, tourism, and trapping.

Like other small towns of the north, the emphasis is on opportunity and friendliness. Each Monday through Thursday from June through August, travelers are invited to stop by the Visitor Centre at 5430 50th Ave. North, on the corner of the Alaska Hwy. and Simpson Trail, for a free "Welcome Visitor" evening of entertainment loaded with local information. For details, call 250-774-6400. Check out their website at www.tourismnorthernrockies.ca.

Cash machines and US currency exchanges are available at banks located along the frontage road of the highway. This is a good place to restock the RV with groceries, gas, and propane.

A don't-miss attraction is the Fort Nelson Heritage Museum, on the west end of town, along the highway. You can't miss it—a bronze statue of a ram stands out front. Inside, the museum features a mounted white moose in

Fort Nelson's Marlin Brown is a World War II veteran whose love for "mechanic-ing" has never waned, demonstrated by his amazing collection of working antique cars, trucks, and motorcycles. Marl's appreciation for local history and highway history is also evidenced in the Fort Nelson Heritage Museum, a nonprofit that he founded and helps to shepherd.

its display of local wildlife, and film footage taken during the building of the Alaska Hwy. can be seen in the museum's Muskwa Theatre. On the grounds are several historic buildings that have been recovered and moved here, as well as a vintage car collection. Nearly every year we drop in and find Marl Brown, the man responsible for this enormous collection, visiting with tourists and answering questions about his cherried-out antique autos and motorcycles. He's an old man with a long memory—you'll come away smarter. Browse through the trapper's log cabin, gift shop, and an old-time general store. And leave a big fat donation. This is a nonprofit. Call 250-774-3536.

Golfers can play a 9-hole, par-35 course with grass greens at Poplar Hills Golf and Country Club, just outside town. Take advantage of the midnight sun and play from 8 AM to dusk in summer. Call 250-774-3862.

Winter visitors will marvel at the northern lights in these parts. Aurora borealis displays above Fort Nelson draw scientists who observe and record the events. The northern lights can occur year-round, but are easiest to see during the winter months.

LODGING

Please browse www.bbcanada.com to locate a bed-and-breakfast.

The Bluebell Inn
4203 50th Ave. South, Mile 300 Alaska Hwy.
800-663-5267 or 250-774-6961
www.bluebellinn.ca
57 air-conditioned rooms, kitchenettes. ATM, cable TV, self-service laundry, store, winter plug-ins. Restaurant, fuel station. Senior rates.

Fort Nelson Hotel
5110 50th Ave. North
800-663-5225 or 250-774-6971
www.fortnelsonhotel.com
134 air-conditioned rooms, kitchenettes. Cable TV, gift shop, indoor pool, saunas. Dining room, cocktail lounge, entertainment and dancing.

Fort Nelson Super 8
4503 50th Ave. South
888-888-5591 or 250-233-5025
142 units, microwave, fridge; Internet, pool, hot tub, waterslide, gym. Fee for pets.

Kacee's Northern Suites
Main St.
866-769-6606 or 250-233-4800
22 air-conditioned rooms, suites, kitchenettes. Cable TV, coffee, Internet. Pets welcome.

Pioneer Motel
5207 50th Ave. South
250-774-5800
12 units; kitchenettes and cabins available. Cable TV, movie channel, laundry facilities. Senior rates. Pets welcome.

Ramada Limited Fort Nelson
5035 51st Ave., Mile 300 Alaska Hwy.
866-774-2844 or 250-774-2844
41 units, some kitchenettes, in central downtown location. Cable TV, coffee, iron and board, Internet. Free continental breakfast, hot tubs. Winter plug-ins.

Thriftlodge Fort Nelson
4711 50th Ave. South
250-774-3911
www.travelodge.com
More than 70 air-conditioned rooms, plus laundry service, office services, winter plug-ins. Sauna, whirlpool. Small pets welcome. Restaurant, dining room, lounge with TV and fireplace. Free airport shuttle.

Woodlands Inn
3995 50th Ave. South
866-966-3466 or 250-774-6669
www.woodlandsinn.bc.ca
131 spacious air-conditioned rooms, suites, kitchenettes. Cable TV, Internet, coin-op laundry, steam bath, hot tub, fitness room. Restaurant, sports lounge. Free shuttle.

CAMPGROUNDS

The Bluebell Inn
4203 50th Ave. South, Mile 300 Alaska Hwy.
800-663-5267 or 250-774-6961
42 full-service sites, laundry, fuel, store, ice, ATM. Sleeping rooms also available. Restaurant, Internet café.

Fort Nelson Truck Stop & RV Park
5 miles (8 km) south of downtown Fort Nelson on Alaska Hwy.
250-774-7270
44 RV sites with full hookups, some pull-throughs, 14 tent sites. Showers, laundry, store, fuel, restaurant. Cable TV, Internet.

Pioneer Motel
5207 50th Ave. South
250-774-5800
RV spaces with full hookups, cable TV, showers, laundry facilities.

Triple "G" Hideaway
West end of town on Alaska Hwy., next to Heritage Museum
250-774-2340
More than 160 sites with full and partial hookups, pull-throughs, grassy tent sites, free firewood, free wireless. Showers, laundry, cable TV, dump station. Gift shop, free car wash, RV supplies and wash. Walking distance to local attractions. Auto services, tours.

RESTAURANTS

Also stop by major local hotels, which feature full lunch and dinner menus in their dining rooms.

Backroads Sports Bar & Grill
4607 55th St.
250-774-2000
Full menu and bar.

Coachhouse Restaurant
4711 50th Ave. North
250-774-3929
Full-menu dining room, fully stocked bar.

Dan's Neighborhood Pub
4204 50th Ave. North
250-774-3929
Full menu, daily lunch specials. Seating indoors or on the patio

Dixie Lee Chicken
5011 50th Ave. South
250-774-6226
Hamburgers, chicken, fish and chips, ice cream.

Fort Pizza
5148 Liard St.
250-774-2405
Pizza, fast food, ice cream; eat in, take-out, or delivery.

Fort Restaurant
5100 50th Ave. North
250-774-7840
Full menu of dining choices and adult beverages.

Pantry Restaurant
3896 50th Ave. South
250-774-7060
Dining room seating; beer and wine.

P&T Restaurant
4103 50th Ave. South
250-774-6244
Family dining, full menu.

Pizzarama Pizzaria
12 Landmark Plaza
250-774-7100
Eat-in or take-out pizza.

Don't leave town without visiting the Fort Nelson Heritage Museum, where the collection sprawls from the main log building out to a spacious garage that houses gorgeous restored antique autos. Other historic buildings on the property have been moved here, too.

ONE WOMAN, EIGHT TONS OF TRAILER, AND A CRUDE HIGHWAY

Iris Woolcock documented her travels to Alaska and back to the East Coast in 1947–48, when the Alaska Hwy. had just opened to the public. Traveling alone, she towed a 16,000-pound trailer that was outfitted with a darkroom for processing the photos she took along the way. Iris Woolcock, Iris Woolcock Collection; Anchorage Museum, B89.4.210

Steamboat Mountain lay ahead. I had been warned many times about it. It sure was a long stiff climb up a series of steep hills. I succeeded in pulling myself up one after another and was just relaxing and thinking I had conquered it when I rounded one of those million curves to find the last and most precipitous grade of all looming up in front of me. I had barely stopped when a big bright orange meat truck came along and pulled me over the top.

It rained that afternoon and I decided that if there were any more steep hills ahead I'd have less chance of making them if they were the least bit slippery. I was following along the Racing River and at Mile 378 I pulled off to the side to park.

Seeing three little white tents off down by the water's edge, I strolled down to investigate. A small crew of government surveyors were stationed there. They had been working up and down the highway all summer surveying all the many plots which had been leased along the roadside for gas stations, cabin courts, and lunch rooms. It will not be long before one will find a hamburger or a gas pump around every curve.

—Iris Woolcock, excerpted with permission from *The Road North:
One Woman's Adventure Driving the Alaska Highway, 1947–1948*

Iris Woolcock paused during her 1948 southbound trip on the Alaska Hwy. to shoot this image of her rig above the Trout River, near the Liard, in northern BC. She noted, "Where the trailer went over and *down*." Iris Woolcock, Iris Woolcock Collection; Anchorage Museum, B89.4.233

Road Notes

Over the years, we've seen fewer mileposts and kilometerposts along the road, mainly because they aren't always replaced after road maintenance. Again, be aware that the mileposts won't necessarily jibe with mileage showing on your odometer. Mileage and kilometer figures used in this text are based on the actual current number of road miles from Dawson Creek.

Fifty-three miles (85 km) past Fort Nelson, at the summit of 3,500-foot (1,067-km) Steamboat Mountain, you'll gain spectacular views of the Muskwa River valley and the Rocky Mountains. Looking at the shape of Steamboat Mountain from a distance, you'll see how it got its name.

Another 5 miles (8 km) along, look high up in the craggy rocks of Indian Head Mountain and you'll see the small but distinctive shape of a classic Indian profile. Stop for a photo at the turnout in another mile. In another couple of miles, at the Teetering Rock viewpoint, there's another turnout with a litter barrel and trailheads.

Tetsa River Regional Park lies just beyond the viewpoint, with 25 gravel sites for dry camping, plus a tenting area, along with pit toilets, fire rings, and free firewood. Anglers will find grayling or Dolly Varden in the river.

Again, while at times it may feel like you're alone in this unspoiled wilderness, you'll find rest stops along this long stretch. A few of the longtime businesses are no longer open, but Tetsa River Services (250-774-1005), nearly 75 miles (121 km) west of Fort Nelson, has been in the family for three generations, renting rooms, cabins, and RV campsites, and cooking for travelers since the highway was young. The price of gas is higher here than before or after Tetsa, but as the sign says, No Sniveling. I liked that—either buy it or don't buy it, but don't complain to the help. I have to recommend their cinnamon rolls, too. Served warm and gooey, they're divinely good. Baker Ben Andrews advertises Tetsa as the "Cinnamon Bun Center of the Galactic Cluster." He may be right.

About 340 miles (547 km) from Dawson Creek, the road affords this view, another reason to have your field glasses handy. Way off in the distance, that rocky point is the classic Indian profile, jutting out from Indian Head Mountain.

Tetsa River Services advertises its cinnamon buns as the best on the highway, the country, the continent, the world. Heck, they're the best in the galactic cluster, according to baker Ben Andrews, a third-generation family member who helps run the roadhouse, RV park, gas island, and guiding service.

One more note on wildlife, which seemed especially abundant on this late spring trip of ours. This time of year in the Northland, you may still find snow and ice at the river's edge, as well as in the higher reaches, so we were not surprised to see one or two dead moose at various spots along the road. By the looks of them, they probably died during the snowy months and had only been revealed at breakup, but collisions with big game are possible and you do need to keep an eye out for crossings.

I've already mentioned that we'd seen several black bears before Fort Nelson. In the miles to come, we would see another two brown bears, five black bears, a dozen

stone sheep, a red-tailed hawk, and several gigantic bull bison—all this without opening the door to the camper. The signs that advise watching out for wildlife are serious and especially useful when animals such as stone sheep come right down to the shoulder of the road to sample the natural mineral licks, which is common in the coming miles.

The highest point on the Alaska Hwy. (4,250 feet) occurs at Summit, 90 miles (145 km) from Fort Nelson. Snowy patches linger into June at this elevation, and the view seems endless. You can look back at the rise and fall of the highway miles you've just covered. Summit Lake Provincial Campground, along the water, has 28 gravel sites, with water and picnic tables as well as a boat launch. Again, it's dry camping and can be chilly, so be prepared.

Heading toward Muncho Lake, you'll cross or parallel several rivers—the MacDonald River, the Racing River—but the most beautiful has to be the Toad River,

In this area, stone sheep can be seen up close, enjoying natural mineral licks along the roadside.

From Summit Pass, the highest point on the route, you can see distant snowcapped peaks well into summer, along with a ribbon of the highway that lies before you.

A squall moves over the Racing River in northern British Columbia.

which accompanies the highway for many miles. It's hard to keep your eyes on the road rather than watch its fast-moving water and its peculiar, beautiful blue green. Grayling and "Dollies" may be found in these waters, too.

The Toad River Lodge at Historical Mile 422 had always been a favorite stopping place for pie and coffee for my aunt and uncle, who drove the road every summer for twenty years. On their recommendation, we enjoyed a lakeside campsite on a couple of our trips. They wrap the base of their campground trees with plastic to keep the beavers from munching on them. One year we enjoyed watching a moose browsing at the water's edge. Rooms and cabins are available, too. In the restaurant, owners keep a running tally on a whiteboard behind the cash register, tracking the ever-expanding baseball cap collection. Rows and rows of caps cover the ceiling in this room and the next.

The lodge at Toad River displays its collection of hats, brim to brim, on the ceilings of the café and gift shop.

Another attractive business is just a few more miles down the road: Stone Mountain Safaris, a 500-acre ranch with a massive cedar lodge as its centerpiece. They offer adventure tours, housing, and meals. Call 250-232-5469 for reservations, or see www.stonemountainsafaris.com.

Lift your eyes to the incredible geologic formation known as Folded Mountain, and imagine the force it took to bend those rock layers as if they were fabric. You'll find a parking area and signage about this unique mountain at Mile 410, just before Muncho Lake Provincial Park.

Jewel green Muncho Lake makes for standout photos. Workers had to blast portions of this route out of the mountainside.

MUNCHO LAKE

From Fort Nelson, BC: 154 miles (248 km)
To Watson Lake, YT: 176 miles (283 km)

With the crown of the Rocky Mountains towering above, and the jewel-colored waters of Muncho Lake at roadside, the highway here lies at an elevation of 2,680 feet (817 m). The province has developed campgrounds right along the lake. What a wake-up view. Copper oxide leaching into the lake is what creates these dramatic deep greens and blues. Anglers pull in Dolly Varden, rainbows, whitefish, lake trout, and the occasional grayling.

Muncho means "big lake" in Tagish, the aboriginal language. At 7.5 miles (12 km) long, it is one of the largest natural lakes in the Canadian Rockies. To the west lies the Terminal Range. *Terminal* refers to the geographic position of the range—the northernmost section of the Rocky Mountains. The total length of the Rockies is almost 1,850 miles (2,977 km), from here to Santa Fe, New Mexico.

At Double G Service, at the south end of Muncho Lake, you can get a room or a campsite and enjoy homestyle cooking. Call 250-776-3411 for information. Fishing, rafting, and flightseeing trips are available at various businesses in this stretch of the road, too. See below for details.

LODGING/CAMPGROUNDS/MEALS

Muncho Lake is 435 miles (700 km) from Dawson Creek, but its Historical Milepost number is 456. For the locations of the following four highway stops, we provide the actual distances from Dawson Creek. However, some of them prefer to use their Historical Milepost distances in advertising. Just be aware that all of these places lie along a 7-mile stretch of road on the eastern shore of the lake.

Double G Service
Historical Milepost 456
250-776-3411
Motel rooms, store, campsites, café. Narrated tours on the lake aboard the MV *Sandpiper* expected to begin again in 2011.

Muncho Lake Provincial Park
Strawberry Flats Campground
Mile 438 Alaska Hwy.
250-427-5452
15 sites with picnic tables on lakeshore amid spectacular natural beauty. Pit toilets. Swimming, boat launch. Pets on leash. Walk the old highway roadbed, a mile-long trail.

Northern Rockies Lodge Ltd.
Mile 442 Alaska Hwy.
Historical Milepost 462
800-663-5269 or 250-776-3481
www.northernrockieslodge.com
45 units in modern log lodge, some wilderness cabins. 35 lakeshore RV sites with full or partial hookups. Laundry, restaurant, bakery, service station. Guided fly-in fishing, photo safari, floatplane service, flightseeing. Open year-round.

Muncho Lake Provincial Park
MacDonald Campground
Mile 443 Alaska Hwy.
250-427-5452
15 campsites on the lake. Pit toilets, water pump. Swimming, boat launch. Pets on leash.

Territorial Canada geese were vocal and engaged in aerial warfare at Liard hot springs.

Whether camping at Liard hot springs, or just parking in the day-use area, you'll check in at the gate.

A WELL-DESERVED SOAK

Try to work your travel schedule so that you have time to visit Liard River Hot Springs Provincial Park, about a half hour's drive past Muncho Lake at Mile 478 (Km 765). If you're planning to spend the night, check in early, as 33 of the 53 campsites are on a first-come, first-served basis, and they fill up quickly. Reserve one of the 20 sites on www.discovercamping.com. Interpretive programs about area

wildlife and the Liard (pronounced LEE-ard) hot springs attract large numbers of day-use people as well.

The big draw here: the wondrous hot springs, which lie at the end of a board-walk that crosses a superheated marsh. On either side of the walk, you can see the slow bubbling action of the mud beneath a clear layer of warm water. This is no cement-lined pool or pond. It's gravel under your toes. At the swimming hole, there are simple his-and-hers bathhouses with wooden benches and hooks for your clothes. Outside, more benches and a wooden deck overlook naturally heated pools in the river. Take care on the slippery steps leading into the water. Depending on how hot you like it, you move around to different levels of the pools until you are sufficiently cooked. The experience was heavenly after a day on the road.

This is bear country, and one day when we visited, another pool farther up the walkway was closed due to bear activity. A park ranger with a noisy popgun was

Liard hot springs is delightfully rustic and accessible.

headed in that direction to encourage the bears to move out. Bears that are regularly fed by humans lose their natural fear and, in fact, become demanding to the point of being dangerous. Many have to be shot simply because they've been "trained" to come to people for food. Signs at the campground read A fed bear is a dead bear.

After our wonderful soak, we did cross paths with a black bear—a little fellow that ran across the road at full tilt and headed into the woods on the other side. I remember thinking how awkward he looked, like a guy in a bear suit.

Nearly 170,000 people come through this campground each year, and the day-use fee of $10 Canadian per vehicle is well worth the price. However, no matter how popular it becomes, as one park ranger told us, the government will not develop it further. The plan is to keep the boardwalk and campground in good shape, but the rustic facilities will not be enlarged or upgraded. There is no electricity, no running water—except for that old friend, the Liard River.

Road Notes

The Trout River follows the road beyond Muncho Lake, with swift, clear water that foams over the rapids. For several miles, this part of the highway seems to echo the old days: it's paved, but it's curvy. Left, right, left, right.

Watch for the 1,143-foot (348-m) suspension bridge over the Liard River, built in 1943, the last of its kind on the highway. All others have been replaced in the last seven decades.

The must-stop on this section of the road is Liard River Hot Springs Provincial Park at Mile 478 (Historical Mile 496), where motorists can soak in naturally heated mineral waters, wash off a layer of dust, and ease that neck tension. It's an easy stroll from the parking lot along a boardwalk to the springs. Watch for signs of bear—park rangers are vigilant and will notify campers immediately. (See sidebar.) The privately owned Liard Hotsprings Lodge is right across the highway from the park, if you're looking for a room and a hearty meal. Call 250-776-7349. They're open all year.

The US Army built more than 200 bridges during construction, often using pontoon bridges as temporary crossings while a more permanent structure was placed. US Army Corps of Engineers photo

The Coal River Lodge, Mile 514 (Km 823), clings to its old address from 1949 and the early days of tourism on the highway: Historical Mile 533. The lodge offers gas, lodging, camping, a laundry, and a pay phone. And in the café, order a full breakfast or a buffalo steak or burger, and desserts. You'll find them at www.coalriverlodge.com, or call 250-776-7306.

Later on down the road, a couple of pullouts provide good views of rapids along the Liard River and of surrounding vistas. In the miles that follow, note several sections of the old Alcan where the former roadbed is buckled, broken, and overgrown with weeds.

For a panoramic view of the Liard River, stop at Mile 551 (Km 880), where there's a gravel wayside with signage, a bench, and garbage containers. Take a short walk to the overlook for unsurpassed vistas both up- and downriver. It's called Allen's Lookout. It's told that bandits used this site for a lookout and dropped down to attack oncoming riverboats.

Within a few miles you'll enter the Yukon with little fanfare, as it's the first of six crossings.

At Mile 566 (Km 910), or Historical Mile 588, is Contact Creek, marked with a modest plaque that remembers September 24, 1942, a key day in construction of the Alaska Hwy. On that day, road builders from two regiments, the 35th Engineer Combat Regiment, working north from Fort Nelson, and the 340th Engineer Combat Regiment,

Allen's Lookout affords a long view up and down the Liard River. It is said that from here outlaws used it to spot riverboats to rob.

working south from Whitehorse, met here. The southern segment of the highway, from Dawson Creek to Whitehorse, was complete. Two trucks, each marked with signs reading Fairbanks Freight had arrived a day earlier and were waiting in the camp to drive the completed road. Chester Russell was a young soldier who'd been trained to knock over trees with a Caterpillar D-8. He later wrote about that day in his memoir, *Tales of a Catskinner*, a best seller in gift shops along the highway today.

"There was no official ceremony and no champagne to mark the occasion," Russell wrote. "Charles Flambo was there with his camera along with a few other men, so the officers got up on the Cats to get their pictures taken. I don't think anyone took pictures of the catskinners on that memorable day; I know for sure that they didn't take mine." After building their portion of the Alaska Hwy., the 35th went on to help build the road to Fort Simpson, known as the Winter Trail, and the Canol Pipeline Road. It wasn't over for them yet. The regiment was next shipped out to the European theater, where they served in combat in the Battle of the Bulge and crossed the Rhine River. On September 15, 1945, Russell and the others who survived set foot on American soil again, three years after Contact Creek.

In September 1942, this place was 590 miles (950 km) from Dawson Creek; road improvements now put it 568 miles (914 km) from Dawson Creek. Evidence of the 1982 Eg Fire, which burned more than 400,000 acres, is still visible in the distant regrowth. It was the second-largest fire in the history of British Columbia. The fresher-looking burned areas were from a smaller event in 2009.

Just over the Yukon border, Contact Creek Lodge, at Historical Mile 590, sells fuel, coffee, souvenirs, fishing licenses for both British Columbia and the Yukon, and groceries; call 867-536-2262. There's Internet access, and a wrecker is available for 24-hour road help, too.

At the north end of the Hyland River Bridge, you'll find parking for accessing the river. Locals say there's good fishing here for rainbow trout, Dolly Varden, and arctic grayling.

In the mid-2000s, motorists had to contend with extensive roadwork in the far-north reaches of British Columbia as a large realignment project was under way. Fortunately, the project is completed and this section is in great shape. If you see large piles of brush alongside the road, that's where land has been cleared for more work.

And, to make things even more challenging for the motorist who pays close attention to kilometerposts, the British Columbia and Yukon governments are not on the same schedule for replacing their roadside signage. Many posts were not replaced after construction, so you'll rely more on point-to-point readings, or keeping close watch on your own odometer as you travel.

YUKON TERRITORY

Just before Contact Creek, the Alaska Hwy. begins a zigzagging westerly route, crossing the British Columbia-Yukon border six times before it finally plunges fully into that immense northern territory—home to some 65,000 to 70,000 moose (twice as many moose as there are people); 159,000 caribou; 22,000 mountain sheep; 6,000 to 7,000 grizzlies; 10,000 black bears; 4,500 wolves; and 223 species of birds.

The Yukon was made famous by writers such as Jack London and Robert Service, each of whom had firsthand knowledge of this land's stark, gripping beauty in winter, and how its people, flora, and wildlife flourish under the midnight sun in summers. Tourism, mining, forestry, trapping, and fishing remain leading industries. The Yukon River, with its headwaters in British Columbia, flows through Canada for 714 miles (1,149 km), the second-longest river in the country.

As you approach Watson Lake, the trees are shorter, with pine and shrubby deciduous trees. Their uniform height suggests regrowth from a great fire some 40 years ago.

YUKON TERRITORY AT A GLANCE

Size: 186,660 square miles, or 483,450 square km

Population in 2007: 32,212

Capital: Whitehorse

Tourism and lodging, government campgrounds: Tourism Yukon, 800-661-0494; www.travelyukon
.com

Fishing and hunting: Environment Yukon, 867-667-5721; www.environmentyukon.gov.yk.ca. Hunters should consult Client Services at 867-667-5652.

Canada border information: 204-983-3500 (outside Canada); www.cbsa-asfc.gc.ca

Road report: 511 (in Yukon); www.511yukon.ca

WATSON LAKE, YUKON TERRITORY

From Fort Nelson, BC: 330 miles (531 km)
From Muncho Lake, BC: 176 miles (283 km)
To Teslin, YT: 163.5 miles (263 km)
To Whitehorse, YT: 275 miles (442.5 km)

You've arrived at Canada's Gateway to the Yukon, located at Historical Mile 635. Driving through Watson Lake, you'll see the Stars and Stripes and the Maple Leaf paired on light posts down the main drag, reflecting the spirit of cooperation between Canada and the United States, not only in building the Alaska Hwy., but also in using it for the last half century. Watson Lake, population about 1,600, is also the junction city for the

MAKING YOUR MARK

The Watson Lake Signpost Forest began with a single sign placed by Carl K. Lindley, an Illinois soldier, during construction of the Alaska Hwy. By 1978, when I first came by this place, the addition of signs through the years had expanded to cover a row of tall poles at a gravel pullout along the gravel road. (And we were covered in gravel dust!) Each pole was studded with signs from all corners of the world, placed there by passersby as the signpost forest had gained notoriety.

Today's forest is astonishing in its size, poles studding the ground in all directions, in rows that make up walkways that course over, up, and down small hills. By June 2010, there were more than 67,983 signs, and gaining. There is so much to see that it's hard to take in all of the colors, words, and messages that were meaningful to somebody, somewhere, at some time in this road's history.

If you're planning to drive the highway, be sure to bring along a sign—hopefully not an ill-gotten one from your hometown's city limits—but something durable to show where you're from or who you are. The folks inside the Alaska Highway Interpretive Centre will direct you on where to add your sign, and you can view photos of that soldier, Carl K. Lindley, who returned to Watson Lake for the Alaska Hwy.'s 50th anniversary in 1992. Seeing what he'd started, he was nearly speechless.

On a recent trip on the highway, I asked a staff member if anybody knew the site of Lindley's original post. She told me it would have been out in the middle of the nearby intersection. But she also told me their maintenance man believes he found the buried post bottoms of the first row, "not 10 feet from our door." Modern archaeology?

The signpost forest, as garish as it is, has become a living testament to the road travelers, a guest book for people who want to tell the world: I WAS HERE.

At Watson Lake, what began with a single sign erected by a homesick soldier has overgrown into a forest of signage from all over the world.

Alaska Hwy. and Campbell Hwy. 4, an unpaved northbound highway.

When the Alcan was under construction, Watson Lake was not much more than an air terminal on the Northwest Staging Route, a fueling and maintenance stop for American pilots of warplanes on their way to Fairbanks. (Russian pilots ferried the planes onward from Alaska to the front lines.) In the late 1940s, a small town began to grow as Watson Lake was linked to the outside by road and air.

Stop by the Alaska Highway Interpretive Centre, at the heart of the Watson Lake Signpost Forest (see sidebar), for information about the birth of the signpost forest and to see a small exhibit that details the building of the Alcan in pictures and artifacts. A film on the road's construction is worthwhile. You'll also enjoy a free cup of coffee, clean restrooms, and lots of printed material on towns and attractions still ahead. The center's hosts are friendly and knowledgeable. Call 867-536-7469.

Across the highway, check out the Northern Lights Centre, decorated outside with banners that simulate the aurora borealis. Inside, learn about the science behind the phenomenon and the stories that it has inspired through time. Electric Sky theater, with panoramic video and surround sound, presents shows six times daily until early September. Call 403-536-7827 or visit www.northernlightscentre.ca.

The town's recreation department maintains 18 multiuse trails in and around Watson Lake. They are color-coded with green for the beginner level, blue for intermediate, and black for advanced. Call 867-536-2246 with your questions.

A good place for a picnic and a stroll can be found at Wye Lake Park, 64 acres (26 ha) in the heart of town on 8th St. off the Alaska Hwy. The handicap-accessible trail around First Wye Lake is 1.6 miles (2.5 km) long and includes interpretive signs on local birdlife and wildflowers. RVers may use the dump station and water refill station at Wye Lake Park.

Another favorite local place to play is Lucky Lake, just east of town on the highway. Picnic, swim, play ball, or hike the trails. If you're there on a weekend afternoon, take a run down the enormous waterslide: a 60-foot drop and 500 feet long!

You can also arrange to go fishing, take a helicopter ride, or play nine holes of golf at Greenway's Greens, a 9-hole, par-35 course up the highway at Liard Village. This was the Yukon's first golf course to support grass greens. Full rentals are available, and a tee time is not required. Call 867-536-2477. Watson Lake's local shops sell art and jewelry pieces in gold, jade, and ivory. Truck and RV service and repairs are available in Watson Lake.

For tourism information, call 867-536-8000 or visit www.watsonlake.ca.

LODGING

Please browse www.yukonbandb.org to locate a bed-and-breakfast.

Air Force Lodge
Adela Trail at south end of town
867-536-2890
www.airforcelodge.com
Comfortable, quiet rooms, Wi-Fi, in restored historic building.

Belvedere Motor Hotel
On the Alaska Hwy.
867-536-7712
31 rooms, suites, satellite TV, whirlpools, Internet, coffee. Cocktail lounge, coffee shop, dining room.

Big Horn Hotel
On Frank Trail, 1 block south of Alaska Hwy. in Watson Lake
867-536-2020
www.yukonweb.com/tourism/bighorn
29 rooms, wheelchair-accessible suite, kitchenettes, Jacuzzi rooms. Satellite TV, Wi-Fi, coffee. Pet friendly.

Cedar Lodge Motel
Junction of Adela Trail and Stubenberg Blvd.
867-536-7406
www.cedarlodge.yk.net
12 rooms, suites, kitchenettes, coffee.

Gateway Motor Inn
Junction of Frank Trail and 8th St. South
867-536-7744
50 rooms, kitchenettes, coffee. Restaurant.

CAMPGROUNDS

Baby Nugget RV Park
Nugget City
Historical Mile 650, west of Watson Lake
888-536-2307 or 867-536-2307
www.nuggetcity.com
130 pull-throughs, 15-, 30-, and 50-amp service.
Room for big rigs. Satellite TV, Wi-Fi, laundry, RV
wash. Cabins, restaurant, bakery, gift shop. Gold
panning, hiking, fishing. 24-hour fuel, licensed
mechanic, horse corral.

Campground Services
Mile 632 Alaska Hwy.
867-536-7448
140 full and partial hookups. Laundry, food mart,
RV wash, RV repairs, fuel.

Downtown RV Park
Lakeview Ave. and 8th St. North, at center of town
867-536-2646
84 full hookups, including 26 pull-throughs, free
Wi-Fi, showers, laundry, RV wash. Walking distance
to shopping, restaurants, visitor information.

Junction 37 RV Park
Mile 649 (Km 1002) Alaska Hwy.
867-536-2794
Full hookups, 30-amp service, some pull-throughs,
showers, laundry. Restaurant, gift shop, fishing
licenses, store, saloon, gas, diesel, propane. Free
RV dumping.

Watson Lake Recreation Park (provincial campground)
2.5 miles (4 km) west of town center via Alaska Hwy.
55 gravel RV sites, including 12 pull-throughs. Tent
sites, hiking, kitchen shelter, pit toilets. Playground,
trails, swimming, fishing, boat launch.

RESTAURANTS

Bee Jay's Café
Adela Trail near 3rd Ave.
867-536-2335
Full menu, lunch and dinner specials. Pastries,
bread, ice cream.

Belvedere Motor Hotel
On the Alaska Hwy.
867-536-7712
Hotel restaurant with full-service dining room and
coffee shop.

Gateway Motor Inn
Junction of Frank Trail and 8th St. South
867-536-7744
Pizza Palace take-out available; full-service restaurant and lounge.

Junction 37 Services
Mile 649 (Km 1002) Alaska Hwy.
867-536-2794
Dining and bar at campground, fuel station.

Nugget Restaurant
Nugget City
Historic Mile 650 Alaska Hwy.
867-536-2307
Breakfast, lunch, dinner, baked goods. Fine dining
and bar, restaurant with deck.

A hungry cinnamon bear digs into a juicy thicket
of dandelions. In the universal language (above),
never feed a bear. You could be training it to open
your camper like it was a can of SpaghettiOs.

Road Notes

West of Watson Lake on the Alaska Hwy. is the junction with Canada Hwy. 37, which leads southbound to Dease Lake and the Cassiar Hwy. This is the way to the coastal communities of Stuart, BC, and Hyder, AK. Call ahead for road conditions to save yourself some time and frustration. In midsummer 2010, the north end of the Cassiar was closed due to forest fires; other southerly sections were in the process of seal-coating, so delays were expected. Check www .drivebc.ca or call 800-550-4997. (See the section on the Yellowhead-Cassiar Highways in Chapter 7, Western Canada's Northbound Byways.)

The Nisutlin Bay Bridge at Teslin is the longest water span on the highway.

As you journey north, you'll see another form of the signpost forest idea on the slopes along the highway. For the past 20 years, "natural" graffiti artists have been writing messages using lines of small rocks.

Several day-use or recreation sites and viewpoints can be found in the beautiful miles between Watson Lake and Teslin, as well as a historic lodge that has served Alaska Hwy. motorists since 1949: the Rancheria Lodge.

Big Creek Yukon government campground at Mile 561 (Km 1042) is small—15 sites with 7 pull-throughs—and rustic, with pit toilets and a water pump, but it's on the water and lovely. The Rancheria Lodge at Mile 687 (Km 1100) holds on to its historical address of Mile 710. The year-round business includes an RV park with all the amenities, including Internet, pull-throughs, showers, and fuel, plus a restaurant and lounge. Call 867-851-6456. Just a few miles farther, Rancheria Falls Recreation Site at Mile 695 (Km 1118.5) is a park-and-rest area with a boardwalk trail that leads to a waterfall. As with other local streams, the Rancheria holds Dolly Varden and grayling.

As you approach the Continental Divide, the mountain peaks become sharper and more crowded. At the crossing, a pullout includes signs with points of interest, maps, and outhouses. Readers learn that water in the streams west of here eventually finds its way to the Yukon River and empties into the Pacific Ocean. To the east, water drains into the Mackenzie River watershed, flowing north for thousands of miles to the Arctic Ocean.

The Continental Divide Lodge and Riverside RV Park may be found within miles of the geographic divide at Mile 721 (Km 1118). You can refuel your vehicle or your stomach. (The homemade baked goods are calling, too.) Stay in the motel or camp overnight. Call 867-851-6451.

On the way to Teslin, the highway moves in gentle, winding curves through forest. A few miles before town, one of the newer lodges on the highway, Dawson Peaks Resort & RV Park, can be found at Mile 769.5 (Km 1232).

Prepare to cross the longest bridge on the Alaska Hwy., the Nisutlin Bay Bridge, which spans the Nisutlin River where it enters Teslin Lake. This is a gorgeous body of water—narrow and long: 86 miles (138 km).

TESLIN

From Watson Lake, YT: 163.5 miles (263 km)
To Whitehorse, YT: 111.5 miles (179 km)

Teslin is an Inland Tlingit (pronounced KLINK-it) Indian village of fewer than 500 people, many of whom are related to members of the Alaskan coastal Tlingit tribes. Although it is a small town, it offers much in the way of visitor services. You'll find a couple of major motels with in-house restaurants and lounges, groceries and general merchandise, RV parks, gift shops, and a trading post. Teslin's two cultural museums are good reasons to linger in this little town, and both have ample parking for RVs.

At the Teslin Tlingit Heritage Centre, you will come away with insights about the culture, traditions, and lifestyles of this unique people. Outstanding totem pole carvings are on display outside. Open June through September, the museum can be reached at 867-390-2526, or visit www.yukonmuseums.ca/cultural/teslin/teslin.html.

And the George Johnston Museum & Heritage Park is named for an exceptionally resourceful Tlingit man who lived from 1884 to 1972. In 1928, Johnston ordered a Chevrolet, which was to arrive in Teslin aboard a paddleboat. While he waited, he built four miles of road on which to drive his new car. Those four miles were joined to the Alaska Hwy. in 1942. See Johnston's Chevy and learn more about this amazing man, Teslin, and the area's natural and cultural history, and view some machinery used to build the highway. The museum is operated by the Teslin Historical Museum Society. Call 867-390-2550 or see www.gjmuseum.yk.net.

LODGING/CAMPGROUNDS/MEALS

Dawson Peaks Resort & RV Park
Mile 769.5 (Km 1232) Alaska Hwy.
866-402-2244 or 867-390-2244
www.dawsonpeaks.ca
Rooms, lakefront cabins with private baths and decks. Campsites with pull-throughs, water, dump station, firepits, showers. Tenting area. Free firewood. Restaurant, gift shop, fishing charters, boat rentals.

Nisutlin Trading Post
Mile 776.5 (Km 1244) Alaska Hwy.
867-390-2521
Motel rooms, groceries, bakery, fuel, propane, fishing licenses, pay phone.

Teslin Lake Provincial Campground
Mile 783 Alaska Hwy.
27 RV and tent sites, 6 pull-throughs, hand-pump water, shelter, boat launch, fishing.

Yukon Motel and RV Park
Mile 804 Alaska Hwy.
867-390-2575
www.yukonmotel.com
Rooms with satellite TV. 40 pull-through RV sites, some at the water's edge, with full hookups, Wi-Fi, laundry, RV wash, fuel. Restaurant, lounge, gift shop, liquor store. Fishing charters. Wildlife gallery of mounted animals.

Road Notes

At Mile 808.5 (Km 1295.5), you'll cross the Teslin River Bridge, 1,770 feet (539.5 m) long and high enough to accommodate the steamers that once navigated the river between Whitehorse and Teslin. At the north end of the bridge, Johnson's Crossing Campground Services claims that its cinnamon buns are world famous. They also offer motel rooms, camping, deli items, laundry, fuel, and fishing licenses. Foot-long grayling run in the river here from spring to late fall. Call 867-390-2607.

Ravens are much larger than crows, and the farther north you go, the more you'll see of these loud and playful rascals.

HAPPY TRAILS

Caitlin Lougheed and Josh Baron, both of Fort Nelson, BC, were the sole tent campers along the bay in Teslin, YT, where they'd collected wood and banked an impressive campfire. The couple had left Fort Nelson that morning to see how far they'd get. For a few days, Caitlin and Josh were leaving behind their everyday lives. She would soon leave to study nursing in Halifax; he'd return to his law enforcement work with the Royal Canadian Mounted Police. But for this weekend, Whitehorse and Kluane—and more camping and hiking—lay ahead.

Asked to recommend some favorite hiking trails, Caitlin and Jason had two to share. BC's Wokkpash Valley–McDonald Creek Trail in Stone Mountain Provincial Park would be rated difficult, Caitlin said, as the 44-mile (71-km) loop takes about four to seven days, but is well worth it. According to the park's website, the recommended start is at Old Churchill Mine Rd. at Mile 401 (Km 645.25) of the Alaska Hwy., and it ends back on the highway, but at Mile 392.5 (Km 632). Caitlin's recommendation for an easy 5-km day hike was Baba Canyon, accessed on the north side of the Alaska Hwy. at Mile 378 (Km 609).

For other ideas on where to go biking, hiking, or horseback riding in the region, you can check out www.tourismnorthernrockies.ca.

Caitlin and Josh enjoyed a quiet evening with a roaring campfire and a view of the bay at Teslin.

One year, we chose to camp at Squanga Lake, a Yukon government campground at Mile 821 (Km 1316). We'd heard there was good fishing for northern pike, grayling, burbot, rainbow trout, and whitefish (which are called *squanga* in the local Native language). The setting sun cast a brilliant pink across the sky and the lake's surface, silhouetting the spruce trees in black. That late-August night was dark, superbly quiet, and cool—a great combination for sleepy travelers. The next morning we saw (and heard) loons out on the lake in the rain.

Farther up the highway comes an opportunity for an exciting side trip to the historic Alaska community of Skagway. To drive there, leave the Alaska Hwy. at Jake's Corner (Mile 837; Km 1341.5) and go west on Yukon Hwy. 8 for 34 miles (55 km) to Carcross and Klondike Hwy. 2. Skagway is then a scenic 66 miles (106 km) to the south. For

ROLLIN', ROLLIN', ROLLIN'

Bruce McDowell of Amana Colonies, IA, delivers to five big-box stores in the Anchorage area, driving the highway with a second man so the truck is always moving, one man at the wheel while the other's in the bunk.

In the early summer, the going is easy. But in the thick of tourist season, truckers can be frustrated by slow campers, and vice versa. Bruce said good-naturedly, "That's the way it is." This driving job

beats any other trucking work he's had so far.

"I always wanted to connect to Alaska, and when this opportunity came up, I took it," he said.

As for the southbound trip, the trailer won't be going back empty. After delivering goods to those five Anchorage-area stores, the two drivers headed down Alaska's Kenai Peninsula, where they picked up a load of black cod from a Seward processing plant. They were pointed south when we met them. Now that's not deadheading. That's fishheading.

Southbound on the Alaska Hwy., Bruce McDowell pauses to fill up in the Yukon.

The Canyon Creek bridge has a long history. The original was built about 1920 by a pair of traders and brothers named Jacquot. It was rebuilt by the US Army during road construction in 1942, and twice more by the territorial government, in 1987 and 2005.

details on the highway and on the history, attractions, lodging, and restaurants of Skagway, see the section on Klondike Highway 2 in Chapter 8, Alaska's State Highways.

If you choose to stay on the Alaska Hwy., Marsh Lake Yukon government campground lies ahead at Mile 860 (Km 1379). It offers 41 sites, including some pullthroughs, on a gravel loop road near the lake. Like other government campgrounds, it's well-maintained, and campers can build a nice fire for making s'mores. Not a whole lot of other amenities, but the $12 per night price tag can't be beat.

Now, if you're looking for amenities, turn around and retrace your path for 6 miles to Mile 854.5 (Km 1370) and the turnoff for Inn on the Lake, a red-roofed log beauty that was voted among "129 Hotels We Love" by *National Geographic Traveler* in 2009. Suites overlook Marsh Lake and include Internet access, fitness facility, hot tub, and sauna, as well as free use of kayaks, bikes, canoes, and golf clubs. And, wait for it… Martha Stewart slept here. Call 867-660-5253 or visit www.innonthelake.ca.

WHITEHORSE

From Watson Lake, YT: 275 miles (442.5 km)

From Teslin, YT: 111.5 miles (179 km)

To Haines Junction, YT: 100 miles (160 km)

To Alaska-Yukon border: 298 miles (463.5 km)

The beautiful capital of the Yukon Territory is situated on the banks of the Yukon River, along the route of the stampeders who were headed for the goldfields more than a century ago. One of the city's landmarks is a lovely giant: the 210-foot SS *Klondike*, a restored paddleboat that is dry-docked on the west bank of the Yukon. Named a National Historic Site, the *Klondike* is a tangible reminder of this region's history—a retired workhorse left from a fleet of more than 250 riverboats that reigned in transportation until construction of the highway. Restored to its 1937–1940 appearance, the *Klondike* remains a figure of elegance and grace. Come aboard for a tour of the decks, cargo holds, and passenger accommodations; RV parking, a gift shop, and a visitor center are located nearby.

One of only two federal heritage sites in the Yukon, the SS *Klondike* has been restored to its glory and is open for tourists. Most of the old paddleboats of the gold-rush days were pulled ashore and left to rot over time.

More than 26,000 people live in Whitehorse year-round, and it also serves as the economic base for outlying communities. This is an economy that was built on mining and transportation services, and those industries remain important, along with tourism and government. Major airlines connect Whitehorse to the rest of the world, and the Alaska Hwy. brings thousands of visitors to its doorstep, mostly during the summer.

As is the case in other Far North cities, living in Whitehorse sometimes means sharing the streets with wildlife. As we drove through a Whitehorse neighborhood, we spotted a small family of coyotes trotting across mowed lawns. One of the local constables said he'd seen them often, that they were part of the urban landscape. Almost every morning, he said, they were out and about at the same early hour. You could almost set your clock by them.

The expansive Whitehorse Visitor Information Centre, at 2nd Ave. and Lambert St., offers films, advice, and printed materials on attractions throughout the area, as well as maps and displays. There's easy access for RV parking, and it's a good place to plan your day. For the active set, you'll find directions to golfing, fishing, nature hikes, trail rides, swimming, biking, canoeing, kayaking, and more. French and German speakers are on-site. Ask about the convenient downtown trolley to get around town. Call 867-667-6401 or browse www.visitwhitehorse.com.

Downtown Whitehorse retains much of its old-time charm, with log structures and false-front buildings sharing city blocks with more modern stores and offices. Learn about local characters and the city's history, and view architectural marvels such as the Old Log Church at 3rd Ave. and Elliott St., built in 1900 and now a museum housing artifacts from early northern missionary and whaling history. Ask about the bishop who ate his boots, and take a walking tour of the Pioneer Cemetery. Learn about the First Nations people. For information, call 867-668-2555.

A hydroelectric dam built in 1959 created Schwatka Lake, which is now a floatplane base. Beneath this stretch of deep water, there still exists the boulder-strewn river bottom once known as Whitehorse Rapids. The town was named after those rapids—the plumes of foamy water were as white as the mane of a white horse.

For gold seekers on the trail to the Klondike, the roaring water and hundred-foot sheer rock walls of Miles Canyon were a formidable challenge, often smashing the homemade boats against the rocks. Those who were successful were next met with the Devil's Punchbowl, a swirling mess of confused current, which then led to the most perilous stretch of the Yukon River: Whitehorse Rapids. After such a frightening river run, shaken and no doubt relieved, the miners often pulled ashore to dry out their goods and rest.

Entrepreneurs arrived with the miners, eager to find ways to make money without digging in the ground. In 1897, two men devised a way around the natural obstacles by building tramways on either side of the rapids and canyon. During a short-lived boom, a tent city called Canyon City sprang up, with businesses such as a saloon and roadhouse to further mine the pockets of the thousands who passed through. North West Mounted Police arrived to maintain order as more than 20,000 stampeders used this gateway to the Klondike.

The historic site of Canyon City is accessible by walking trail, and interpretive signs mark the way. To get there, take Miles Canyon Rd. from Mile 910 (Km 146.5) of the Alaska Hwy. At the lookout, enjoy a spectacular view, then drive down to the suspended footbridge and walk over the bridge to the site where Canyon City once stood.

With completion of the White Pass & Yukon Route Railway on July 29, 1900, miners could travel in comfort to a point beyond the rapids. However, by then, all claims had been staked and the rush was in decline. The little railway was called into service during the construction of the Alaska Hwy. in 1942. The US Army leased the railway and it became a main transportation corridor for supplies arriving by ship in Skagway en route to Whitehorse, the halfway mark between Dawson Creek and Fairbanks. Although the WP&YR no longer offers rail service between Skagway and Whitehorse, it connects with Fraser, BC, and Carcross, YT, where bus service to Skagway is available between May and September. The historic depot stands on 1st Ave. near the river in downtown Whitehorse. The WP&YR remains one of the only operating narrow-gauge railroads in North America, an International Historic Civil Engineering Landmark, and riding in the restored railcars is a rare treat. For tickets and reservations for daily departures in combination train and motorcoach service to Skagway, call 867-633-5710 or see www.wpyr.com.

The MacBride Museum of Yukon History, at 1st Ave. and Wood St., provides mining displays, natural history, First Nations culture, artifacts from the gold rush, and geology of the area. Lectures for Yukon history hounds vary each week, but are always exciting. And kids' camps infuse adventure into learning. Exhibits teach about different kinds of gold deposits, where they are found, and how they are taken from the ground. You can pan for gold here, too. And during the summer months, visit with a real Mountie and his horse in the Historical Horse and Rider Program. In the summer of 2010, Superintendent Hank Moorlag of the North West Mounted Police and his steed Titan could be found at the museum for a few hours on Monday and Thursday. For more on the museum's offerings, call 867-667-2709 or see www.macbridemuseum.com.

Yukon Beringia Interpretive Centre, at Mile 915 (Km 1473) on the Alaska Hwy., highlights a time when this land belonged to mastodons, saber-toothed cats, and lions. Call 867-667-8855 or see www.beringia.com. The Yukon Transportation Museum, next to the Beringia Centre, features displays on the various modes of transportation used

The entertaining vaudeville-style *Frantic Follies*, performed nightly in Whitehorse, showcases dance, song, and the macabre humor of the Robert Service poem "The Cremation of Sam McGee."

on the Trail of '98, then and now, from snowshoes to dogsleds and paddleboats and trains. Murals painted by Yukon artists serve as backdrops. Call 867-668-4792 or see www.goytm.ca.

The Yukon First Nations Tourism Association invites visitors to learn more about the 14 ancient cultures of this region. Art, dancing, storytelling, and drumming often are part of important annual events such as the Moosehide Gathering, held every other year in Dawson City, and the International Storytelling Festival, held in Whitehorse each June. Visitors are always welcome.

Many museums and interpretive centers share the stories and artifacts of the First Nations people. To gather more information on cultural tourism opportunities, visit the YFNTA's website at www.yfnta.org.

The Frantic Follies has entertained audiences since 1970, so we expected a corny, tired stage show. Instead, we discovered a first-class vaudeville show by talented performers. On the bill: ragtime piano, cancan girls, red-hot-mama singing, banjo extravaganzas, magic, family-oriented comedy—and some wild Robert Service poetry. You've never heard "The Cremation of Sam McGee" quite like this. The revue shows nightly from late May through early September at 8:30 PM. Reservations are not necessary, as most seating is first come, first served in the Westmark Whitehorse, 2nd Ave. and Wood St. Groups larger than 10 can make advance reservations through 867-668-2042 or see www.franticfollies.com.

The Whitehorse Fishway is one of Whitehorse's most popular visitor sites, attracting 25,000 to 30,000 people each summer. Here is the world's longest fish ladder, along with three underwater viewing windows, underwater cameras and viewing monitors, an interpretive center, and lots of salmon action. Watch the migration of the Yukon River chinook salmon and other species, including trout and arctic grayling. An aboriginal interpretive program also shares the story of how First Nations people interacted with this river and its resources through centuries past. The site is open from June through August, and admission is free. Take 2nd Ave. from downtown, cross the bridge over the Yukon River to Lewes Blvd., then follow the signs to Nisutlin Dr. and the fish ladder. Call 867-633-5965.

Take a ride on the Yukon aboard the MV *Schwatka*, which twice a day offers a two-hour narrated cruise that begins at Schwatka Lake. The dock is five minutes from the city center via Miles Canyon Rd. on the north side of town. Just follow the signs. The lake serves as a floatplane base, so you'll see lots of traffic in the air and on the water.

The route takes you through Devil's Punchbowl and into Miles Canyon. You can wave to the foot traffic above you on the Robert Lowe Suspension Bridge. Points of interest include an old fox farm and the historic site of Canyon City. An evening dinner cruise is available as well. The trip is popular, so advance tickets are recommended. Call 867-668-4716 or make a reservation online at www.yukonrivercruises.com.

Whitehorse is either the start or finish line every February during the annual running of the Yukon Quest International Sled Dog Race, one of two major long-distance races in the Far North that attract competitors from all over the world. At the other end of the race's grueling 1,000 miles is Fairbanks, AK. The Whitehorse headquarters can be found in the White Pass depot building at Main St. and 1st Ave. To learn more about the race, see www.yukonquest.com, and to shop for memorabilia visit the store at 205 Main St. or go online to www.yukonqueststore.com. Call 867-668-4711.

Local shopping is an adventure unto itself. Customized gold nugget jewelry is a regional specialty, and several shops will sell you raw nuggets or fashion a piece just for you. Check along Main St. as you prospect for your own gold.

The North End Gallery (across from the White Pass depot) offers artwork, sculpture, jewelry, and ceramics made by Yukon artisans. Or stop by Northern Wonders Gift Shop, inside the Westmark Hotel at 1st Ave. and Wood St. (867-393-9700), for scrimshaw, Inuit sculpture, and other original art. Your art purchases may be shipped anywhere in the world. Mac's Fireweed Books, at 203 Main St. (www.macsbooks.ca), specializes in books, calendars, art cards, music, and videos from the Far North. And nearby Murdock's Gem Shop, at 207 Main St. (www.murdochs.ca), not only fashions gold nugget and mammoth ivory jewelry, they also have unique displays of gold-rush artifacts and photos.

Services and parts for autos and RVs are available in Whitehorse. Twenty-four-hour cash machines may be found at banks all along Main St. For information on city attractions and services, write the City of Whitehorse, 2121 2nd Ave., Whitehorse, YT, Canada Y1A 1C2, or call 867-668-TOUR. Their website can be found at www.city.whitehorse.yk.ca or see www.travelyukon.com.

The famous Yukon River flows through Whitehorse.

LODGING

*Please browse www.yukonbandb.org to locate a
bed-and-breakfast.*

Airline Inn Hotel
16 Burns Rd. (across from the airport)
867-668-4400
30 rooms, some kitchenettes, cable TV, laundry,
lounge, restaurant. Adjacent to convenience store
and gas station.

Airport Chalet
91634 Alaska Hwy.
867-668-2166
29 units, offering gas, diesel, RV dump, and self-
service laundry for guests. Restaurant and lounge.

Best Western Gold Rush Inn
411 Main St.
800-661-0539 or 867-668-4500
www.goldrushinn.com
106 deluxe rooms, suites, spas, barbershop,
beauty salon, laundry and dry-cleaning services.
Restaurant and lounge.

Bonanza Inn
4109 4th Ave.
867-668-4545
52 rooms, some kitchenettes, TV, wheelchair
accessible. Dining facility.

Canada's Best Value Inn/River View Hotel
102 Wood St.
888-315-2378 or 867-667-7801
www.riverviewhotel.ca
Comfortable guest rooms with views of river and
mountains. Free Wi-Fi, fridge, microwave, laundry
facilities, shuttle service. Heated indoor parking.
Guest office and computer room, restaurant on-
site, shuttle service.

Capital Hotel
103 Main St.
867-667-2565
17 rooms in historic downtown setting, restaurant,
entertainment.

Casa Loma Motel
1802 Centennial, Mile 921 (Km 1482) Alaska Hwy.
867-633-2266
28 rooms, some kitchenettes, wheelchair access.
Dining.

Chilkoot Trail Inn
4190 4th Ave.
867-668-4190
32 rooms, some kitchenettes.

The Edgewater Hotel
101 Main St.
877-484-3334 or 867-667-2572
www.edgewaterhotelwhitehorse.com
30 deluxe rooms and suites, restaurant overlooking
Yukon River. Cable TV, DSL, and Wi-Fi, coffee, hair
dryers. Downtown location.

High Country Inn
4051 4th Ave.
800-554-4471 or 867-667-4471
www.highcountryinn.yk.ca
Jacuzzi or executive suites and kitchenettes with
view. Cable TV, coffee, hair dryer, iron and board,
laundry. Dining. Downtown location.

Mountain Ridge Motel & RV Park
Mile 912 Alaska Hwy.
888-667-4202 or 867-667-4202
www.mtnridge.ca
Guest rooms, kitchenettes, cabins. TV, laundry
facilities, wireless. Pet friendly. Close to downtown.

98 Hotel
110 Wood St.
867-667-2641
Popular historic building dating from the 1940s has
been converted into a hotel and bar.

Pioneer Inn
2141 2nd Ave.
867-668-2828
Hotel in downtown location; restaurant on-site.

SKKY Hotel
Across from Whitehorse Airport
866-799-4933
www.skkyhotel.com
Luxury air-conditioned guest rooms and suites with
fireplace, rain showers, free Wi-Fi, TV, Jacuzzi.
Free shuttle.

Stop In Family Hotel
314 Ray St.
867-668-5558
44 air-conditioned rooms in full-service hotel.
Laundry, hair salon, sauna, hot tub. Close to shopping and Yukon River.

Stratford Motel
401 Jarvis St.
867-667-4243
50 affordable units, some kitchenettes, suites,
laundry. Wheelchair accessible.

Town & Mountain Hotel
401 Main St.
800-661-0522 or 867-668-7644
www.townmountain.com
Boutique hotel with 30 executive-style suites and
family suites, fridge, microwave, iron and board.
Cable TV, parking, restaurant.

202 Motor Inn
206 Jarvis St.
867-668-4567
32 rooms, coffee, Internet. Dining room, lounge with entertainment. Discount for miners.

Westmark Klondike Inn
2288 2nd Ave.
800-544-0970 or 867-668-4747
www.westmarkhotels.com
99 deluxe rooms, suites, coffee, guest sauna, laundry facilities. Gift shop, restaurant, lounge. Free parking. Gray Line Tour desk.

Westmark Whitehorse Hotel & Conference Centre
201 Wood St.
800-544-0970 or 867-393-9700
www.westmarkhotels.com
180 deluxe rooms, suites. Gift shop, restaurant, lounge, box office of *The Frantic Follies*.

Yukon Inn
4220 4th Ave.
800-661-0454 or 867-667-2527
www.yukoninn.com
98 luxury guest rooms, suites, kitchenettes, with Internet, fridge. Laundry, dry cleaning, hair salon, office services, winter plug-ins. Gift shop, exercise facilities. Café, two lounges, big-screen TVs. Walking distance to local attractions. Handicap access.

CAMPGROUNDS

Whitehorse:
Hi Country RV Park
91374 Alaska Hwy.
877-458-3806 or 867-667-7445
www.hicountryrvyukon.com
130 roomy, treed sites with power. Showers, self-service laundry, cable TV, free Wi-Fi, store, gift shop. Close to downtown. French and German spoken.

Mountain Ridge Motel & RV Park
Mile 912 Alaska Hwy.
867-667-4202
www.mtnridge.ca
Full and partial hookups, pull-throughs, store, Internet, shower, sani-dump. French spoken.

Robert Service Campground
120 Robert Service Wy.
867-668-3721
www.robertservicecampground.com
68 treed sites along the Yukon River with showers, water, store, barbecue, playground. Close to downtown. French and German spoken.

North of Whitehorse:
Tahkini Hot Springs
Mile 6 (Km 10) Hotsprings Rd.
867-456-8000
www.takhinihotsprings.com
88 treed sites, with 15- and 30-amp service, full and partial hookups. Sani-dump, showers, water, store, café. Horseback riding, swimming, hiking, sauna. Climbing wall and zip line. Cabin rentals available.

Outside of Whitehorse:
Caribou RV Park
Mile 904 Alaska Hwy., 14 miles (22.5 km) south of downtown Whitehorse
867-668-2961
www.caribou-rv-park.com
47 treed pull-through sites with power, private showers, satellite TV, free wireless, car wash, sani-station, laundry, firepits, tent camping available. Canoe rentals. Wolf's Den Restaurant on-site.

MacKenzie's RV Park
18 Azure Rd., junction of Alaska Hwy. and Azure
867-633-2337
79 spacious sites with full or partial hookups, 22 tent sites. Cable hookup, showers, laundry, store. Playground, horseshoe pit, free gold panning. Wheelchair access. Vehicle wash. On city bus route.

Pioneer RV Park & Campground
Mile 878.5 (Km 1414) Alaska Hwy. (Historic Mile 911)
866-626-7383 or 867-668-5944
www.pioneer-rv-park.com
150 sites, including full and partial hookups, some pull-throughs. Showers, laundry, restrooms, store, gift shop. Gold display, book exchange, pet wash. Coin-op Internet kiosk. Car and RV wash, licensed mechanic on duty, windshield chip repairs. Tickets and reservations for local attractions.

Wolf Creek Government Campground and Recreation Site
Mile 877 (Km 1408) Alaska Hwy.
40 RV sites, including 11 pull-throughs and tent sites. Pit toilets, hand-pump water, shelters, playground, trails.

RESTAURANTS

Alice's Restaurant
1802 Centennial
867-633-2961

Arizona Charlie's
2288 2nd Ave., inside the Westmark Klondike Inn
867-668-4747
Fine dining, Yukon-style.

Blackstone Café
302 Wood St.
867-667-6587

The Cellar Steakhouse & Wine Bar
101 Main St., in Edgewater Hotel
877-484-3334 or 867-667-2572
Fine dining, specializing in salmon, crab, halibut,
arctic char, prime rib.

Cheechako's Sourdough Steakhouse
204B Main St.
867-393-2555
www.cheechakos.com
Steaks, seafood, salads, and more.

China Garden
301 Jarvis St.
867-668-2899
Chinese and Western menus; lunch buffet, dinner,
take-out.

The Chocolate Claim
305 Strickland St.
867-667-2202
Soups, salads, sandwiches, coffee bar.

City's Steak and Pizza House
4092 Quartz Rd.
867-667-4963
Steaks, pizza, pasta, and more.

Cranberry Bistro
302 Wood St.
867-456-4898
European.

G & P Steak House & Pizza
238 Alsek Rd.
867-668-4708
Greek and Italian specialties, seafood, pasta.

Giorgio's Cuccina
206 Jarvis St.
867-668-4050
www.grogioscuccina.com
Italian cuisine.

Green Garden Restaurant
1612 Centennial St.
867-633-6089
Chinese dining.

Iron Horse Grill
151 Industrial Rd., #3
867-668-7871
Casual dining.

Klondike Rib & Salmon BBQ
2116 2nd Ave., across from Westmark Whitehorse
867-667-7554
Fresh local fish, Yukon-style BBQ ribs, caribou and
musk ox Stroganoff.

La Gourmandise
4121 4th Ave.
867-456-4127
Fine dining, French and other world cuisines.
Sunday brunch and dinner.

Legends Smokehouse & Grill
4220 4th Ave., inside Yukon Inn
800-661-0454 or 867-667-2527
Dining in convenient downtown location.

North Dragon Restaurant
2058 2nd Ave.
867-456-2182
Chinese, eat in or take out.

Pandas European Dining
212 Main St.
867-667-2632
European fine dining without the dress code.
Northern seafood specialties, steaks, schnitzels,
pasta.

Pasta Palace
201 Main St.
867-667-6888
Full selection of pastas and sauces, tapas.

Robbyn's Highway Grill
867-334-5259

Sam 'n' Andy's Tex Mex Bar & Grill
506 Main St.
867-668-6994
Mexican and Canadian food; outdoor patio.

Steele Street Restaurant and Lounge
201 Wood St., in the Westmark Whitehorse
867-393-9700
Daily lunch and dinner specials. Arctic char, cedar
plank salmon, locally brewed ales and beers.

Tung Lock Chinese Restaurant
404 Wood St.
867-668-3298
Casual dining, specializing in seafood, daily lunch
and weekend dinner buffets.

Wolf's Den Restaurant
Mile 904 Alaska Hwy., at Caribou RV Park, 14 miles
(22.5 km) south of downtown Whitehorse
867-393-3968

Yukon Mining Company
4051 4th Ave., in the High Country Inn
867-667-4471
Salmon, halibut, wild game. Barbecue on the deck,
local beer specialties.

The little resort of Takhini Hot Springs, several miles outside of town, offers delicious soaks in their naturally heated cement pools, camping, a café, trail rides, a climbing wall, and a zip line.

Road Notes

Just north of Whitehorse, the Alaska Hwy. connects with the North Klondike Hwy. (Hwy. 2), which heads north to Dawson City. (See the section on the North Klondike Highway in Chapter 7, Western Canada's Northbound Byways.)

Takhini Hot Springs, with its naturally heated outdoor swimming pool, is a star any time of year, but it's especially attractive when the temperature drops below freezing. To get there, drive several miles north of Whitehorse, turn right onto the North Klondike Hwy. (Hwy. 2), and follow it for about 4 miles to the turnoff to the hot springs; follow the 6-mile spur road to the west. Out of the ground, the source water is 117°F, so it is mixed with cool water to maintain a temperature around 100°F for the swimming pool. While it is rich in minerals such as calcium, magnesium, and iron, no sulfur is present to foul the air or your swimsuit. A café, campground, climbing wall, zip line, and horseback riding are also on the grounds. Call 867-456-8000 or see www.takhinihotsprings.yk.ca.

It's 100 miles (160 km) between Whitehorse and Haines Junction. In 1958, more than 1.5 million acres of forest burned in this region, and even now you can still see evidence of that fire in the landscape around you.

At Mile 933 (Km 1502), a sign reads: You are leaving the 911 service area. Feels a bit ominous, doesn't it? But rest assured, it's still populated, and help is available when you need it. More homes along the roadside are decorated with caribou and moose

Sharing the road through the Yukon with truckers.

antlers. You'll see more log cabins, more outbuildings, and places where homeowners have something of a collection on their property. While some might call this junk, people of the North call it storage, defending it with: "You never know when I might need this." The blue tarp—more essential here, it seems, than at many points south—may cover a broken appliance, a woodpile, or inoperable equipment that truly is of value to its owner.

About halfway to Haines Junction, the road used to pass through the First Nations village of Champagne. The highway was rerouted in 2002, and that surely brought traffic relief for this tiny community. A turnoff leads to the town now. Travelers are asked to be respectful of the villagers' private property and of their cemetery, which is not open to visitors. If you'd like to learn more about the Champagne and Aishihik Indian Band, see www.cafn.ca.

Yukon Hwy. 1, leaving Haines Junction on the main route of the Alaska Hwy. A four-wheeler kicks up a dust plume on the side trail that's also used by snowmobiles in the winter months.

Pay close attention to the intersection at Haines Junction, at Mile 985 (Km 1585). To continue on the Alaska Hwy., you must make a right turn, the first in many miles. Hundreds of wayward travelers have ignored the turn and ended up instead on Hwy. 3, heading south toward Haines, AK, instead of Fairbanks, AK. In the last decade, Canadian customs officials at the border before Haines reported more than 1,000 irate wrong-turners, even though signs at the intersection have gotten bigger. (See the section on the Haines Highway in Chapter 8, Alaska's State Highways.)

This community of fewer than 1,000 people lies 205 miles (323.5 km) away from the border crossing on the Alaska Hwy. If you choose to pause here, you'll find several choices for lodging and places to eat. See more at www.hainesjunctionyukon.com or call 867-634-7100. Learn more about Kluane National Park at the visitor information center just east of the highway junction. They're open daily between May and September. Call 867-634-2345.

Headed toward Whitehorse, the mountain views are photo worthy for many miles. Keep your camera

This black bear looked up from his lunch momentarily, then continued to munch on greens along the road.

A derelict boat rests on the shore of Kluane Lake.

handy, as the Alaska Hwy. crosses Bear Creek Summit, elevation 3,294 feet (1,004 m), and Boutillier Summit, elevation 3,294 feet (1,004 m), en route to the picturesque Kluane Lake. The Alaska Hwy. skirts this vast and beautiful body of water for more than 60 miles (96.5 km), making this drive worthy of a few extra lines in your travel journal. Extensive road repairs that were under way in 2007 have wrapped up, and the road is a Sunday drive, but it will change soon.

On the way to the communities of Destruction Bay and Burwash Landing (where all services are available), take a few minutes to pull over at Mile 1061 (Km 1707.5), the historical wayside for Soldiers Summit. A trail from the parking lot leads to the site of the Alaska Hwy.'s official opening ceremonies, on November 20, 1942. Try to imagine how, at this location, officers in full-dress uniforms (with inadequate footwear) endured deep cold and snow while officials made grand speeches and cut the ribbon. Another ceremony here in 1992 celebrated the highway's 50th anniversary. Unlike the Alcan's early years, today it's easy to find motels, lodges, campgrounds, and restaurants from Haines Junction to Beaver Creek, which lies ahead. Gas and other services are available, too. While many miles through the Yukon may appear wild and unsettled, help

A cow moose feeds on vegetation in a Yukon pond.

A devastating fire ripped through Burwash Landing in the late 1990s. At the natural history museum, outdoor exhibits teach about the scope of the burn.

is never far away. Small communities along these miles can meet most of your service and shopping needs.

A few words about the road itself in this last stretch in the Yukon: in summary, batten down the hatches and hang on. The road traverses some of the poorest subsurface for road builders that you can imagine. When ice-riddled soil is compressed by the weight of a road surface, it melts, and the blacktop sinks in places. Plus, seasonal freezing and thawing action creates a roller-coaster effect on the road surface. The best engineers in the country have been at the washboard problem since they put in the road, and have been experimenting with heat exchange fins, subsurface coverings, paint—they're working on it. For now, just know that you should drive slower, because conditions may change in a matter of minutes. In my notebook, I wrote, "Not a stretch for drinking coffee, putting in your contacts, or writing a postcard, or, if you're the driver, looking at scenery—and it's particularly beautiful on the approach to Beaver Creek." My scrawl is barely legible, by the way.

Burwash Landing was once a seasonal fish camp that lay on a major trading trail used by the Southern Tutchone people to trade with others in the region. During the Kluane gold rush of 1904, a pair of traders (and brothers), Eugene and Louis Jacquot, established a trading post here, giving it the name Burwash, for Lachin Burwash, the mining recorder back at Silver City, across Kluane Lake. They were still in business in 1942, trading and guiding hunters, when the Alaska Hwy. was under construction.

A forest fire in 1999 blackened the landscape near Burwash Landing and beyond it for several miles. Stop by the Kluane Museum of Natural History, at Historic Mile 1093, and you'll see how close the fire came to burning down this structure and many others in the town. The fire line came within 30 feet of the museum's back door, sparing world-class wildlife exhibits and displays on the Southern Tutchone people. For unexplained reasons, the winds changed direction and the town was spared. Get your picture by the World's Largest Gold Pan next to the museum. Call 867-841-5561.

The northernmost town on the Alaska Hwy. in Yukon Territory is Beaver Creek, and it's also Canada's most westerly community. Its year-round population of 115 is swamped by visitors in summer season. Across from the visitor center is the Westmark Inn, a classic dark brown log lodge, where you can also catch the "Rendezvous Dinner Show" on summer evenings. Located at Mile 1202 (Km 1934.5), the Westmark has 174 well-appointed guest rooms, a restaurant, lounge, and an RV park. Call 867-862-7501 or www.westmarkhotels.com.

In 1942, here, as at Contact Creek, construction crews working from opposite directions met and completed a stretch of the Alaska Hwy. US Customs is just 20 miles (34 km) north from here. Last chance to mail a letter or postcard with a Yukon postmark!

We noticed during early summer that just about every southbound vehicle in these parts is an escaping Alaskan—heading Outside for vacation or, for many military families, relocating south.

Few motorists can sail past the border without stopping for a picture as Perry and I did in 2010.

At the Alaska-Yukon border, the international boundary marker, and the swath of cleared brush in the distance, designates the otherwise invisible line. The US-Canada International Boundary Commission ordered surveys of the 141st meridian from Mount St. Elias to the Arctic Ocean, working from 1907 to 1913.

ALASKA-YUKON BORDER

From Whitehorse, YT: 298 miles (463.5 km)

From Haines Junction, YT: 205 miles (323.5 km)

To Tok, AK: 128 miles (206 km)

To Fairbanks, AK: 300.5 miles (483.5 km)

Crossing into Alaska is an achievement, and you're due for another round of photos. There's a wonderful place to pull over and record this moment, right at the demarcation line that separates the United States and Canada. Alaska and the Yukon Territory have each erected impressive welcome signs, massive wooden affairs that are beautifully painted. Between them is a parking area with a gazebolike structure over the international border marker. Stand here and look north, then south, and you'll see the border as a brushed-out band in the scrubby trees, signifying the 141st meridian. At this wayside, most people like to pose with a foot in each country or sit on the nearby bench that's divided by a carved line with the word *Yukon* on one side, *Alaska* on the other.

We found Barbara and Benny Hawkins of Alabama at the Alaska border, headed south, with hard-earned knowledge about seriously taking it easy on those poor sections of road. A hitch problem had caused the front end of their rig to bounce so badly that it was pretty torn up when they finally reached Tok, AK. "The mechanic told me that he'd already replaced fifteen hitches so far," Barbara said, "and it's still early in the season." Benny did repair work to the trailer body using bolts, screws, and good old-fashioned duct tape. "I'm going to invest in the company!" he joked. "I've got another roll *this* big." As for Barbara, she had questions for us about the cost of a one-way rental, adding sweetly, "It's been an experience."

Just ahead is the US Customs and Border Protection station, which is open 24 hours a day. Turn your watch back an hour to reflect the Alaska time zone.

Gas, RV camping, and tire services are available at the border and just beyond it. Extensive road maintenance was ongoing in the summer of 2010.

Road Notes

For the first 65 miles (104.5 km) into Alaska, the highway follows the border of 730,000-acre Tetlin National Wildlife Refuge in the Upper Tanana (pronounced TAN-nuh-nah) River basin, a sparsely treed region of marshes and lakes that attracts thousands of nesting waterfowl and migrating sandhill cranes. The refuge lies on a major migratory pathway between Alaska and Canada as well as the Lower 48, and as far south as South America. Watch for other birds, too, including ptarmigan, trumpeter swans, loons, and some species of raptors. Mammals include black and brown bears, moose, caribou, and smaller furbearers such as lynx, red foxes, and coyotes. The Forest Service maintains two campgrounds, Lakeview and Deadman Lake, along the Alaska Hwy., both before Northway Junction. In the distance are the

A gorgeous log building is the headquarters for the Tetlin National Wildlife Refuge. Outside, an example of a traditional cache, a storage outbuilding on stilts that pioneers typically used to keep food supplies safe from animals.

Mentasta Mountains, to the west, the Nutzotins. For information on accessing the refuge, call 907-883-5312 or see www.fws.gov/refuges.

One hundred and fifteen miles (185 km) from the border, at Tetlin Junction (not to be confused with Teslin, YT), you'll find the northbound turnoff to Alaska Hwy. 5 (the Taylor Hwy.), a road that's closed in winter and occasionally suffers washouts in the summer months. Be sure to check road conditions before setting out. Call 511 in Alaska or visit http://511.alaska.gov. This route is paved for 66 miles (106 km), to the Alaska village of Chicken, then turns to gravel (the village of Eagle lies at the end of a spur off the Taylor). The customs station is not open at night. Hours are 8 AM to 8 PM Alaska time; 9 AM to 9 PM Yukon time. Certain paved sections are severely disturbed by frost heaves and the effects of

Tok was dubbed Alaska's Main Street for its location, where the Alaska Hwy. meets the Glenn (known as the Tok Cutoff). A few miles away, motorists can reach the communities of Chicken or Eagle on the Taylor Hwy.

permafrost in the soil. This rustic road connects with the Yukon's Top of the World Hwy., the northern route to Dawson City and another instance in which *highway* is used loosely. (See the section on the Taylor Highway in Chapter 8, Alaska's State Highways. Also see the section on the Top of the World Highway in Chapter 7, Western Canada's Northbound Byways.)

Twelve miles (19 km) beyond Tetlin Junction is Tok, which was a construction camp during the building of the Alaska Hwy.

TOK

From Alaska-Yukon border: 128 miles (206 km)

To Delta Junction, AK: 108 miles (174 km)

To Fairbanks, AK: 206 miles (331.5 km)

Surrounded by stands of spruce trees, Tok (pronounced TOKE) is a junction city. Motorists can continue northwest on the Alaska Hwy. toward Fairbanks or veer southwest onto the Glenn Hwy. (known by Alaskans as the Tok Cutoff). This panoramic shortcut for southbound drivers leads to Glennallen or Valdez on the Richardson Hwy., or to Anchorage at the end of the Glenn Hwy. In November 2002, the Tok Cutoff was temporarily closed when east-central Alaska was rocked by a magnitude 7.9 earthquake that damaged roads, homes, and businesses. Portions of the Richardson and Parks hwys. also were shut down until repairs could be made.

A gigantic Eskimo boot, called a mukluk, marks the entryway to Mukluk Land, a family-fun attraction outside Tok.

With a population of about 1,400, Tok is geared toward travelers' services and stays and is especially busy in the summer months. Alaska's Mainstreet Visitors Center is housed in a massive log structure at the junction of the two highways. Cultivated flower beds around the center and elsewhere in town flourish in the long, sunny days of Alaska's Interior. At the center, you can learn about Tok's strategic role during the building of the Alaska Hwy. and about area wildlife, events, and attractions. Today it is known as Alaska's dog mushing capital.

Take the kiddies to Mukluk Land at Mile 1317 of the Alaska Hwy., just 2 miles (3 km) west of the highway junction. You'll find a lovely Alaska garden (mixing cabbages and flowers), videos on the Trans-Alaska Pipeline and the northern lights, golf, and a chance to do some gold panning (Mukluk Land guarantees the gold). Call 907-883-2571.

Tok is a great place to rest and restock. You'll find many choices here for comfortable accommodations, meals, gifts, groceries, and filling up the gas tank. Some campgrounds even offer a free breakfast for their guests.

LODGING

Burnt Paw Gift Shop and Cabins Outback
Mile 1314 Alaska Hwy.
907-883-4121
www.burntpawcabins.com
Modern log cabins with sod on the roof and private baths. Breakfast included. Display of mushing equipment, along with husky pups.

Golden Bear Motel & RV Park
Mile 123.5 Glenn Hwy. (Tok Cutoff)
866-883-2561 or 907-883-2561
www.alaskagoldenbear.com
60 rooms, private baths. Cable TV, gift shop, coffee bar, Alaska displays, restaurant. Senior discount.

Snowshoe Motel

Mile 1314 Alaska Hwy.
907-883-4181
http://alaskasnowshoemotel.homestead.com
24 units, satellite TV, phones. Continental breakfast, picnic area, gift shop. Pets welcome.

Tok Motel

800-883-3007 or 907-883-2852
www.tokmotels.com
Clean, affordable rooms with cable TV. Minimart and liquor store.

Westmark Tok

Junction of Alaska and Glenn hwys.
800-544-0970 or 907-883-5174
www.westmarkhotels.com
92 deluxe rooms, nonsmoking available. Guest laundry. Shop for unique Alaskan gifts. Restaurant and lounge. Adjacent to visitor center.

Young's Motel

Mile 1313 Alaska Hwy.
907-883-4441
43 rooms, private baths, nonsmoking available. Satellite TV, Wi-Fi. Check-in inside Fast Eddy's Restaurant, next door.

CAMPGROUNDS

Alaskan Stoves Campground

Mile 1313 Alaska Hwy.
907-883-5055
www.alaskanstovescampground.com
RV parking and tenting area next to 40-Mile Air. Showers, dump station, group firepit.

Gateway Salmon Bake & RV Park

Mile 1313 Alaska Hwy.
907-883-5555
Space for big rigs to tenting campers. Water, electric, showers, restrooms. Lunch and dinner.

Golden Bear Motel & RV Park

Mile 123.5 Glenn Hwy. (Tok Cutoff)
866-883-2651 or 907-883-2561
www.alaskagoldenbear.com
Full and partial hookups, pull-throughs, tent sites. Showers, laundry, restaurant, gift shop, phone.

Sourdough Campground

Mile 123 Glenn Hwy. (Tok Cutoff)
907-883-5543
www.sourdoughcampground.com
Full hookups, shaded area, dump station, Wi-Fi, laundry, showers, RV wash, vacuum. Sourdough pancakes and reindeer sausage breakfast. Live music nightly in the campground theater. Gift shop, outdoor museum. Sites available for winter campers.

Tok RV Village

Mile 1313.5 Alaska Hwy.
800-478-5878 in Alaska or 907-883-5877
www.tokrv.net
161 sites, full and partial hookups, pull-throughs. Showers, laundry, dump station, vehicle wash. Cable TV, Wi-Fi. Fishing licenses. Evening entertainment, gift shop.

Tundra Lodge & RV Park

Mile 1315 Alaska Hwy.
907-883-7875
78 forested sites with full or partial hookups, pull-throughs, tent sites, fire rings, dump station, laundry, RV wash. Internet, Wi-Fi. Cocktail lounge.

RESTAURANTS

Fast Eddy's Restaurant

Mile 1313 Alaska Hwy.
Next to Young's Motel
907-883-4411
Steaks, seafood, pasta, burgers, pie.

Golden Bear Restaurant

Mile 123.5 Glenn Hwy. (Tok Cutoff), adjacent to motel and RV park.
866-883-2651 or 907-883-2561
www.alaskagoldenbear.com
Luncheon and dinner specials. Senior discount.

Tok Gateway Salmon Bake

Mile 1313 Alaska Hwy.
907-883-5555
King salmon, halibut, reindeer sausage, buffalo burgers. Shuttle pickup available.

Young's Café

Junction of Alaska and Glenn hwys.
907-883-2233
Breakfast all day. Lunch specials, dinner, beer and wine, baked goods.

Westmark Inn Tok

Junction of Alaska and Glenn hwys.
907-883-5174
www.westmarkhotels.com
Fine dining and lounge, boasting Alaska's largest margaritas.

Road Notes

From Tok to Delta Junction is 108 miles (174 km) of almost unpopulated wilderness. The road follows or crosses several streams, the biggest of which is the Tanana River. Many of these streams were formed by runoff from glaciers in the Alaska Range. That's why the water tends to be a cloudy gray; in it are particles of suspended rock, called rock flour, carried by glaciers. The forest here is largely spruce. Watch for moose and caribou.

DELTA JUNCTION

From Dawson Creek, BC: 1,422 miles (2,288.5 km)

From Alaska-Yukon border: 236 miles (380 km)

From Tok, AK: 108 miles (174 km)

To North Pole, AK: 84 miles (135 km)

To Fairbanks, AK: 98 miles (158 km)

At Delta Junction, the Alaska Hwy. joins the Richardson Hwy.—marking the official end of the Alcan. Stop by the end-of-the-road milepost outside the visitor center at the junction of the two highways. (This may be the official end, but for most travelers, Fairbanks is still the destination that marks completion of their journey up the Alaska Hwy.) A nearby log structure is the old Sullivan Roadhouse, which houses historical exhibits from the late 19th century, when the Richardson Hwy. was a crude route known as the Valdez–Fairbanks Trail and roadhouses were spaced about every 15 to 20 miles. Built in 1905, the Sullivan is the oldest of the roadhouses that are still standing. Guided tours are free, inside and out in the beautiful flower and vegetable gardens. For information, call 907-895-4415 or 907-895-5068.

The Sullivan Roadhouse in Delta Junction, once an important link in a chain of businesses along the old Valdez–Fairbanks Trail, has had a second life as a museum devoted to those early days of transportation.

Addresses for Delta Junction are Mile 1422 Alaska Hwy. or Mile 266 Richardson Hwy. This crossroads town is an agricultural community of 5,760, where hardy strains of barley flourish in the short growing season and long hours of sunshine. More than 130,000 acres of land are in cultivation. Other crops include oats, wheat, grass seed, canola, and potatoes. Local farmers raise dairy cows, Tibetan yaks, elk, and reindeer. And Delta Junction is the site of a maintainence station for the Trans-Alaska Pipeline.

In Alaska, this little town is well known for its buffalo herd. Twenty-three plains bison, or buffalo, were transplanted to the area from Montana in 1928, and they flourished. A 90,000-acre bison range was established in 1978, with enough habitat to support between 400 and 500 animals. An annual hunt by permit keeps the population in line and helps feed families. New calves arrive in spring. In early summer, you're most likely to see the free-ranging herd browsing on the west side of the Delta River, but they move back over to the bison range in August. The Alaska Department of Fish and Game plants barley, oats, and hay on the range to keep the animals there and out of private fields. (Fences, as you can imagine, do not work when a headstrong herd wants to cross to the other side, especially if a meal is waiting.)

Locals advise that a good spot to view the bison in the summer months is at Mile 242.5 Richardson Hwy., about 20 miles south of Delta. You may need your binoculars.

Yes, they seem that big in the Far North.

DIVE-BOMBERS OF OLD

Some of the boys might have preferred the extreme cold of mid-winter to the mosquitoes. I was fortunate in missing the mosquitoes, but ran into many a tale about the "dive-bombers," as they were usually called. There were the two soldiers who pumped a couple of hundred gallons of gasoline into one before they realized it wasn't a Douglas transport. And there were the two small mosquitoes who were feasting on a couple of boys inside a tent when one mosquito said to the other, "Let's take 'em outside to finish 'em."

"Naw," said the first, "if we do, the big fellers'll get 'em."

—Iris Woolcock, *The Road North: One Woman's Adventure Driving the Alaska Highway, 1947–1948*

At Mile 274.5, a historic site along the Tanana River, Rika's Roadhouse has been restored and put to good use as a favorite community gathering spot and visitor attraction. Built in 1913 at a ferry crossing on the old Valdez–Fairbanks Trail (now the Richardson Hwy.), the log roadhouse is on the National Register of Historic Places. The grounds include museum displays, a barn, a gift shop, a restaurant, and a bakery. It's all part of Big Delta State Historical Park, managed by Alaska State Parks. The gift shop concessionaire specializes in luxury fur coats, hats, and accessories, as well as gold pieces and wood carvings. A roomy parking area is perfect for turning around those big RVs, and a few campsites are available, as well as a dump station. Call 907-895-4201 or visit http://dnr.alaska.gov/parks/units/deltajct/bigdelta.htm.

Just a quarter mile past the turnoff for Rika's Roadhouse, the Tanana River crossing is a fantastic photo op for a picture of the Trans-Alaska Pipeline. Here, a suspension bridge supports the pipeline as it parallels the highway's Big Delta Bridge over the Tanana River. There's a pullout here for a quick photo.

Summertime events in town include Friendly Frontier Days in late May, and Old-Fashioned 4th of July Celebration, and the Deltana Fair in late July and early August.

Sample smoked reindeer, buffalo, elk, and yak sausage at Delta Meat & Sausage Co. at Mile 1413 Alaska Hwy. They welcome RVers and have a picnicking site. See www.deltameat.com or call 907-895-4006. Taste a buffalo burger, chili, or barbeque at the Buffalo Center Drive-In, located by the big ice cream cone, south of the visitor center. Or try fishing in one of the more than 40 stocked lakes in the area. Local rivers hold trout and grayling, too. Outfitters are available to guide you on land and by air on your outdoor adventure.

Check in at the Delta Junction Visitor Information Center at the junction of the Alaska and Richardson hwys. for more on what to see and do. While you're there, don't forget to ask for your end-of-the-road certificate. You can call the center at 877-895-5068 or 907-895-5068, or visit www.deltachamber.org.

LODGING

Alaska 7 Motel
Mile 270 Richardson Hwy.
907-895-4848
www.alaska7motel.com
Rooms, kitchenettes available. Satellite TV, Wi-Fi, fridge, microwave, full bath. Daily and weekly rates.

Alaskan Steak House & Motel
Mile 265 Richardson Hwy.
907-895-5175

The Bunkhouse
1555 Richardson Hwy.
907-895-5422
Modest single and double rooms with fridge, microwave, shared bathroom. Laundry, satellite TV, free Wi-Fi. Game room, kitchen.

Clearwater Lodge
7028 Remington Rd.
907-895-5152
Comfortable rooms on the Clearwater River. Restaurant, campground.

Kelly's Alaska Country Inn
1616 Richardson Hwy.
907-895-4667
www.kellysalaskacountryinn.com
Rooms with private bath, fridge, microwave, TV, Wi-Fi, kitchenettes.

Tanana Loop Country Inn
2775 Tanana Loop Extension
907-895-4890
www.tlcalaska.com
16 rooms in four country homes.

Trophy Lodge
1420 Alaska Hwy.
907-895-4685
100 rooms, single and double beds, satellite TV, Wi-Fi, game room, buffet breakfast.

CAMPGROUNDS

Clearwater Lodge
7028 Remington Rd.
907-895-5152
RV and tent camping, cabins, restaurant open for dinner 7 days a week.

Smith's Green Acres RV Park & Campground
Mile 268 Richardson Hwy.
800-895-4369 or 907-895-4110
Full and partial hookups, pull-throughs, tent sites. Showers, self-service laundry, restrooms, phone, vehicle wash. Can arrange here for a pipeline pump station tour.

Alaska State Parks system maintains five nearby campgrounds on the Richardson Hwy. They are:
Delta State Recreation Site. 1 mile past visitor center, at Mile 267, with 25 campsites, water, picnic tables, and toilets.

Clearwater State Campground. 2 miles past visitor center, turn right on Jack Warren Rd. for 10.5 miles. Offers 17 campsites, some along the river, on 46 acres. Picnic tables, toilets, water, fishing, and a boat launch.

Donnelly Creek Wayside. Mile 238 Richardson Hwy. 12 campsites, with picnic sites, pit toilets, picnic shelter, and trails.

Fielding Lake State Recreation Site: Mile 200.5 Richardson Hwy. 17 campsites on 605 acres with picnic sites, water, toilets (including handicap accessible).

Quartz Lake Recreation Area: Mile 278 Richardson Hwy. This 600-acre park includes two campgrounds (Lost Lake and Quartz Lake) and a handicap-accessible fishing dock, picnic shelter, water. 12 miles past visitor center, turn right on Quartz Lake Rd. for 3 miles.

RESTAURANTS

Alaskan Steak House & Motel
Mile 265 Richardson Hwy.
907-895-5175
Breakfast, lunch, dinner. Specializing in all-you-can-eat barbecue rib dinner.

Birch Brothers Pizza Place
1591 Quartz Ave.
907-895-9999
Pizza, salads, shakes, arcade.

Buffalo Center Drive-In
South of the visitor center
907-895-4383
Burgers, fries, and shakes. Buffalo burgers, chili, barbecue.

Clearwater Lodge
7028 Remington Rd.
907-895-5152
Open for dinner 7 days a week; live music on weekends.

Packhouse Restaurant
Rika's Roadhouse & Landing
Big Delta State Historical Park
907-895-4938
Soups, sandwiches, salads, and baked goods.

Poor Boy Restaurant
Across from the library, downtown
907-895-1308
Open weekdays for breakfast and southern-style cooking.

Taquitos
Next to the post office, downtown
907-895-4048
Authentic Mexican food and ice cream. Closed Sunday.

Trophy Lodge
1420 Alaska Hwy.
907-895-4685
Fine dining, cocktails.

Road Notes

The Richardson Hwy. between Delta Junction and Fairbanks is a four-lane route, but certain sections remain challenging because it was built over permafrost. With Interior Alaska's extreme seasonal cycles of hot and cold damaging the road, you've got a roller-coaster ride in places. About 10 miles northwest of Delta Junction, you'll cross the Tanana River where the Big Delta Bridge parallels the suspension bridge supporting the Trans-Alaska Pipeline at this crossing. The bridge was built to withstand an earthquake measuring up to a magnitude of 7.5 and temperatures as low as −60°F.

About 7 miles (11 km) before you reach the town of North Pole, you'll see Eielson Air Force Base, home to nearly 3,000 people in a major military installation named for Carl Ben Eielson, an early day Fairbanks pilot. Eielson AFB is the northernmost fighter wing in the United States, "Red Flag-Alaska," and has more airspace for training than any other military facility in the country. Guided tours of the base are free every Friday

Near Tetlin, AK, the Robertson River stays locked in winter's grip even in late May.

at 10 AM. with displays of military aircraft, antique and new. Advance clearance is necessary, so for a Friday tour, reserve a spot by noon on Wednesday. Call 907-377-2116 or see www.eielson.af.mil.

A few miles later, note the eastbound turnoff for Chena Lake Recreation Area at Mile 346 Richardson Hwy. This popular park includes 80 campsites in two campgrounds, without utility hookups, but there is a dump station. Picnickers and swimmers enjoy the sandy beach at Chena Lake; canoeists can navigate the lake or the Chena River, which flows through at one end. Boat rentals are available, and there's fishing, biking, hiking, and nature walks for outdoor fun. The Fairbanks North Star Borough charges a nominal use fee for first-come, first-served campers, with a 10-night maximum at the Lake Park Campground or the River Park Campground. This isn't the Yukon, so you'll have to pay for the firewood: $3 a bundle. The lake is stocked, and you can rent a boat to go after grayling, pike, whitefish, and burbot.

NORTH POLE

From Delta Junction, AK: 84 miles (135 km)
To Fairbanks, AK: 12 miles (19 km)

It's Christmas all year long in North Pole. That's because Santa doesn't disappear after Christmas Eve. On December 26, you can track him to North Pole and tell him what you want for next Christmas.

North Pole's roots reach back to Bon Davis, who homesteaded here in 1944. Later, he and several other homesteading families sold their property for town lots, calling it North Pole, hoping to attract a toy manufacturer. Nobody took the bait, however. Nellie and Con Miller were among those early settlers, and Con often flew into neighboring villages to trade for furs. He enjoyed wearing a Santa suit and bringing treats for the village kids. Miller came to be called Santa. Later, when he was at work building a trading post, a little boy came by and said, "Hi, Santa! Are you building your house?" And Santa Claus House was born in 1952. North Pole, AK, was incorporated a year later.

The streetlights are red candy canes, and the Christmas theme spills over onto the street names. Even the local welding shop has a pair of twin candy canes as posts over the driveway.

Still in the Miller family, the cheerful, candy-striped Santa Claus House is an invitation to any age, and the king-sized likeness of Santa attracts photographers. Mail your letters from here for that impressive North Pole cancellation. Inside the gift shop is a kiddie toyland. You can buy Christmas ornaments and order up a personalized Christmas letter for your favorite little ones. Santa makes regular appearances (with Monday and Tuesday off!) and greets children in his throne room. To order a Christmas letter by snail mail, send $9.95 along with the child's address to Santa Claus House, 101 St. Nicholas Dr., North Pole, AK 99705. Call 907-488-2200. The jolly old man is up-to-date on technology, too. He accepts e-mail. Write him at santa@santaclaushouse.com or browse his website and order the personalized letter online at www.santaclaushouse.com.

Children from all over the world write to Santa Claus at his North Pole, AK, address, and many letters are posted for visitors to enjoy.

Visit Santa's reindeer next door, between Santa Claus House and Santaland RV Park, a park with so many great services, they even offer pet-sitting while you take a tour. Call 907-488-9132 or see www.santalandrv.com.

Several motels and campgrounds are nearby, and other North Pole businesses invite you to drive around town and enjoy all that this city of 2,000 friendly people has to offer. There's free Internet at the library at 301 Snowman Ln. Stop by the Visitor Center Log Cabin at 2550 Mistletoe Dr., or call 907-488-2242. See more about the winter fun you're missing at www.northpolechamber.us. Of course, you're invited back in December. Does it get cold in North Pole? You bet. The record low was measured in 1975, when the thermometer plunged to −67°F (−55°C). No whining now—you're here in the summer, and the summer's record high is 95°F (35°C) in 1983. Enjoy the midnight sun while you may.

LODGING

Beaver Lake Resort Motel
2555 Mission Rd., corner of Mission Rd. and Richardson Hwy.
907-488-9600
www.beaverlakeresort.net
Rooms with cable, free Wi-Fi, laundry, Corporate suites available. Quiet setting on a lake; close to Santa Claus House.

Hotel North Pole
449 N. Santa Claus Ln.
877-488-4801 or 907-488-4800
www.hotelnorthpole.com
71 units, including guest rooms and suites. Continental breakfast, cable and flat-screen TV, free Wi-Fi, business center, adjacent to restaurants and shopping.

North Pole Cabins
907-490-6400
www.northpolecabins.com
Log cabins with continental breakfast. Close to restaurants, shopping, Santa Claus House. Massages by appointment. Open year-round.

CAMPGROUNDS

Chena Lake Recreation Area
Operated by Fairbanks North Star Borough Parks & Recreation
3780 Laurence Rd.
907-488-1655
www.chenalake.com
RV and tent camping in choice of two campgrounds, totaling 80 campsites. Swimming, fishing, boat rentals, picnic area, water, toilets, firepits, tables. No hookups, but a dump station is available.

Riverview RV Park
1316 Badger Rd., between North Pole and Fairbanks
Exit 349 or 357 Richardson Hwy.
888-488-6392 or 907-488-6392
www.riverviewrvpark.net
160 RV sites with hookups, pull-throughs on the Chena River. Tent camping. Showers, laundry, water, dump station. Free car wash, good fishing. Gift shop, groceries, ATM, videos, gas and diesel. Shuttle service to local attractions.

Road's End RV Park
1463 Wescott Garden Ln.
907-488-0295
65 campsites with full hookups and some tent sites. Showers, laundry, dump station.

Santaland RV Park & Campground
125 St. Nicholas Dr.
888-488-9123 or 907-488-9123
www.santalandrv.com
85 RV sites with full hookups and pull-throughs in Christmas-themed park, including 9 tent sites. Free Wi-Fi, showers, laundry, water, dump station. Free camper wash. Tour arrangements.

RESTAURANTS

Benny's Grill
101 Santa Claus Ln.
907-488-5500
www.bennysgrill.com
Corn-fed USDA prime steaks, Alaskan halibut, innovative burgers, salads.

Country Café
235 Santa Claus Ln., #11
907-488-8454
Homestyle American cooking; breakfast all day; children's menu.

The Elf's Den
On Mistletoe Dr., next to visitor center
907-488-3268
Family dining, roasted chicken, Beef Wellington, pizza, lounge.

Little Richard's Family Diner
2698 Hurst Rd.
907-488-2117
Retro American dining, Wi-Fi, take-out. Senior and military discounts.

Pagoda Restaurant
431 Santa Claus Ln.
907-488-3338
www.pagodanorthpole.com
Mandarin, Szechuan, and Cantonese cuisine. Winner of *Fairbanks Daily News-Miner*'s People's Choice for Best Asian Food in 2006, 2007, and 2009.

Thai Cuisine
537A St. Nicholas Dr.
907-488-8260
Authentic Thai cuisine in nonsmoking restaurant. Senior and military discounts.

You'll find the unofficial end-of-the-road milepost next to the Chena River in the heart of Fairbanks. It proclaims the distance between Alaska's second-largest community and the great cities of the world.

Road Notes

It's a quick 12 miles (19 km) from North Pole to Fairbanks, and the Richardson Hwy. is a four-lane route bordered by spruce, aspen, and birch trees as it heads toward town. Then it ends without fanfare, joining the Steese Hwy. near the entry to Fort Wainwright, which lies on the eastern edge of town. An army post today, back during World War II, Fort Wainwright was known as Ladd Airfield. Military spending has often stabilized or boosted the Fairbanks economy during the past 70-plus years.

FAIRBANKS

From Delta Junction, AK: 98 miles (158 km)

From Alaska-Yukon border: 300.5 miles (483.5 km)

From Dawson Creek, BC: 1,488 miles (2,395 km)

Congratulations! You've arrived at Alaska's Golden Heart City, situated at 64.8° north latitude, the unofficial end of the Alaska Hwy. The Arctic Circle is only 66 air miles north.

Fairbanks was incorporated in 1903, two years after a trader named E. T. Barnette landed here by unhappy circumstance. A passenger aboard a stern-wheel riverboat, Barnette had intended to establish a trading post at Tanana Crossing, a location that was more central to the gold miners working in that area. Following the tip of a local Native, he directed the riverboat captain to navigate up the Chena River, which Barnette believed was a shortcut to his destination. The Chena was too shallow, and the summer was quickly coming to an end. In a hurry to return without his argumentative passenger, the captain declared that he'd met the terms of his contract and ordered Barnette and his party, and his trade goods, off the ship. They landed at a spot that's marked today with a modest rock monument next to the Yukon Quest Log Cabin on 1st Ave., near the Cushman St. bridge. (The cairn with a plaque is just steps away from the milepost that marks the unofficial end of the Alaska Hwy.)

An artist and recreational musher, Miriam Cooper relaxes outside the Yukon Quest headquarters log cabin on 1st St., where she chats with visitors and answers questions about sled dogs and racing.

Luck was with Barnette. Within hours, he and his group had their first paying customers in the form of a couple of miners who had spotted the ship's plume of steam. One of the miners was Felix Pedro, an Italian immigrant who struck gold less than a year later. His find ignited a rush to Alaska's Interior, drawing miners from the goldfields of Fortymile country and the Klondike.

The long-term health of this fledgling community was cinched when Barnette struck a deal with federal district judge James Wickersham, who was stationed in Eagle, AK, a gold-mining town northeast of Fairbanks. Wickersham wanted to feed the ego of a political friend by naming a town after him. Charles W. Fairbanks was then a US senator from Indiana; later, he would be vice president under Theodore Roosevelt. In exchange for naming the town after Fairbanks, Wickersham promised Barnette that he would move the judicial seat from Eagle to Fairbanks—which he did, ensuring that the town was firmly rooted (and undercutting Eagle's future).

About 100,000 people live in the Fairbanks area today, roughly 36,000 of them in the city proper. And each year they commemorate Felix Pedro's gold discovery with a weeklong festival called Golden Days. Held in late July, the festival includes sourdough pancake feeds, gold-panning demonstrations and mining lectures, dances, historical exhibits, and an old-fashioned community parade, the biggest in Alaska. The winner of the Pedro look-alike contest leads the parade, and he walks the downtown route with his gold poke full of nuggets. In true rough-and-tumble Alaskan style, The Grizzly Alaskan Contest awards prizes to the bushiest beard, craziest mustache, hairiest chest, hairiest legs, and the ugliest "frontier feet."

A walking bridge crosses the Chena River in downtown Fairbanks.

Gold nuggets are still in the barter system of Fairbanks. Just drop by Oxford Assaying at 29 College Rd. to pick out an Alaska nugget or a finished piece of jewelry (907-456-3967). Long-time Fairbanksans Bill and Rita Bishop of Fishing for Gold create beautiful jewelry originals with nuggets and gems, which can be purchased at retail outlets all over the state (www.fishing forgold.com). Or see Perdue's Jewelers, folks who've been doing business in gold nugget jewelry since Kennedy was president. Their store is inside the Shoppers Forum Mall on 1255 Airport Wy. (907-456-5105). Another resident-recommended favorite is Gold Rush Fine Jewelry at 531 2nd Ave., downtown. And yet another option is to tour the El Dorado Gold Mine, pan for gold, then pick your favorite nugget and have it made into a ring, bracelet, or necklace (907-479-5573). Okay, the likelihood you'll get a big hunk of gold in your pan is rare, but you are guaranteed to come away with a nice sprinkling of fine gold, which they can make into a necklace while you wait. And they do have a showcase of nuggets for sale, and a jewelry designer who can make your custom piece.

Fairbanks has grown from the days of E. T. Barnette into a hub city for all of Alaska's Interior communities. It's also a major jumping-off point for flights into the bush. Overnight tours are available by air and as part of fly/drive packages to Barrow, the Arctic Circle, Nome, Kotzebue, and Anaktuvuk Pass. Another Alaska crossroads city, Fairbanks is the hub for the Elliott, Dalton (via Elliott), Steese, Richardson, and Parks highways. Before you leave town for any of these highway trips, you can call or go online for road conditions, traffic hazards, closures, etc. In Alaska, dial 511 or, if you're calling from out of state, dial 866-282-7577. Also see http://511.alaska.gov.

Get your tour plans organized at the Morris Thompson Cultural and Visitor Center, at 101 Dunkel St., along the Chena River. The information center staff has plenty of literature and insider advice on where to go and what to see in these parts, given your travel schedule. Call 907-456-5774 or 800-327-5774, or browse www.explorefairbanks .com. Also inside this building is the Alaska Public Lands Information Center. Exhibits, a bookstore, films, and lectures are part of what they have to offer, so take advantage of it all. Contact them at 907-459-3730 or 866-869-6887, or visit www.alaskacenters.gov.

Fairbanks loves to play in the summer. Annual events include a summer solstice celebration in late June with a 10K fun run starting and ending in town. Another favorite each year is the late-night baseball game hosted by the Fairbanks semipro baseball team, the Goldpanners. The Midnight Sun Baseball Game begins at 10:30 PM under all-natural light at Growden Park.

Native athletes compete in the World Eskimo-Indian Olympics in late July, where they engage in games that test balance, agility, strength, and stamina—and they're unlike anything you've seen. There's the four-man carry, the knuckle hop, the one-foot kick, the ear pull, and many others that will make you cheer and wince. Held annually since 1961, the celebration also includes a Miss WEIO contest, a baby contest, and a fancy parka–making contest. Call 907-452-6646 or see www.weio.org.

In August, locals flock to the Tanana Valley State Fair, located on College Rd., for agricultural displays, great fair food, rides, and entertainment. Call 907-452-3750 for details or visit www.tananavalleyfair.org.

Each February, mushing fans line the downtown streets for the start or finish of the Yukon Quest International Sled Dog Race, which follows a 1,000-mile route between Whitehorse, YT, and Fairbanks (www.yukonquest.com). You're invited to explore the Fairbanks Community Museum and Dog Mushing Museum, located on the corner of 5th Ave. and Cushman St. in the historic City Hall. Learn about winter life in Fairbanks, the early days of this boom town, the 1960s flood that nearly wiped it out, and its strong ties to dog mushing. You'll find it 410 Cushman, open Monday through Friday, 10 AM to 4 PM, Saturday, 11 AM to 2 PM. Call 907-457-3669. Admission is free.

Also around town, you'll find movie theaters, shopping opportunities, bowling, golf, art galleries, and outdoor adventures.

While you're in Fairbanks, visit some of these other local attractions:

The University of Alaska Museum of the North. This museum is at once an architectural beauty and a rich depository of more than 1.4 million artifacts. Gallery exhibits include dinosaur fossils, ivory carvings, historical photos, totem poles, natural history dioramas, and lots of gold—the largest public display in Alaska. Be sure to visit Babe the Blue Bison, a 36,000-year-old bison mummy that was excavated by a Fairbanks scientist. Videos on the northern lights explain the scientific reason for the phenomenon. The museum store is a shopper's delight, with books, gifts, clothing, and Native art. The Museum of the North is on the University of Alaska Fairbanks campus, at College Rd. and University Ave. Call 907-474-7505 for 24-hour information or see www.uaf.edu/museum.

Creamer's Field Migratory Waterfowl Refuge. What was once the northernmost dairy farm in the country was converted to a waterfowl refuge many years ago, but the old buildings remain at 1300 College Rd., just a mile from downtown. Anna and

Charlie Creamer's farmhouse is now a visitor center, open 10 AM to 5 PM during summer months, and signs along refuge trails describe the migratory birds that feed in great numbers here each spring and fall. Most are Canada geese and sandhill cranes. The Tanana Valley Sandhill Crane Festival is held the last week of August. Call 907-452-5162 or visit www.creamersfield.org.

Golden Heart Park, with its dramatic 18-foot sculpture titled "The Unknown First Family," is a great place to relax and watch the river and other people. Plaques around the statue include names of people who helped build this town during its first century. A few blocks away, still along the river, is Griffin Park, where you'll find a monument to the pilots who ferried planes during WWII's Lend-Lease program, the Russian and American men as well as the Women Airforce Service Pilots.

World Ice Art Championships. Fairbanks in March is such a great place! This time of year, the sun has returned, yet it's still cold enough for clean, crisp snow and nice, clear ice. Sculptors from all over the world converge on Fairbanks to compete with monumental-sized works. You can walk through the Ice Park, which is filled with giant ice statuary, all of it lit with colored lights that sparkle through the nearly clear ice. A play area made of ice is perfect for kids in their slippery snow pants. Call 907-451-8250 or see more at www.icealaska.com.

Pioneer Park. This 44-acre theme park, at Airport Wy. and Peger Rd., was built in 1967 to commemorate the centennial of Alaska's purchase from Russia. The Centennial Exposition grounds, also known as Alaskaland, were divided into themes that echoed Alaska history. In one section, replicas of Native villages were constructed. In another, a gold-rush town was created by relocating some of the oldest cabins and businesses of Fairbanks. The Palace Saloon is still operating as a bar and dance hall. Call the Palace to reserve ticket to its popular "Golden Heart Revue," which shows at 8:15 PM nightly during summer months. Reserve your seat by calling 800-354-7274.

From the Palace, it's just a short walk to the Pioneer Air Museum, where antique aircraft from Alaska's early days, and stories to go with them, are yours to enjoy. In another part of the park, the Alaska Salmon Bake serves delicious northern fare from 5 to 9 PM nightly, and they'll even pick you up at your hotel or RV park. Call 907-452-7274. The Salmon Bake is near the gold-mining "valley," which was created to demonstrate various ways that gold was extracted from the ground. And one of the region's hardworking stern-wheelers, the riverboat *Nenana* (knee-NA-nuh), was dry-docked here after retirement. It has since been beautifully restored. Come aboard for a tour. Pioneer Park admission is free. Visit www.co.fairbanks.ak.us or call 907-459-1087.

Cruise the river on a modern stern-wheeler: the *Tanana Chief* and the riverboat *Discovery* are two favorite tours for panoramic views and a dose of local history. Prime rib dinner and sightseeing cruises are available every evening on the *Tanana Chief*, an authentic stern-wheeler that plies these waters, a replica of a historic vessel. Call 907-452-8687. Browse www.tananachiefak.com for more information. The riverboat *Discovery* is operated by the Binkley family, whose members have been cruising Alaska's rivers for five generations. The *Discovery* offers two tours daily and follows the Chena and Tanana rivers on a narrated cruise that includes stops at a replica of an Athabascan Indian fish site and the sled-dog kennel of late Iditarod champion Susan Butcher. Reservations are a must. Call 907-479-6673 or browse www.riverboatdiscovery.com.

Since 1992, the Fairbanks Shakespeare Theatre productions have continued to gain popularity, so much so that the troupe expanded its offerings and outreach, traveling nationally and internationally. Lucky Fairbanksans get to enjoy their productions year-round. A local favorite each winter is the annual weeklong, nonstop performance of Shakespeare's entire poetry collection in the "Bard-a-thon." Winter shows are held at the historic Empress Theatre, on 2nd Ave. In midsummer, visitors and residents in numbers bring their lawn chairs and blankets to enjoy outdoor performances of Shakespeare on the University of Alaska campus. For tickets and location, call 907-457-7638, e-mail info@fstalaska.org, or visit www.fstalaska.org.

The Fountainhead Antique Auto Museum displays a private collection of vehicles, beautifully restored and exhibited, along with photos of their heyday, at the Wedgewood Resort, 212 Wedgewood Dr. Call 907-456-3642 for details. Your family motorhead will love you for it.

For more information about local attractions and events, day trips, history, fishing, and hunting, contact the Fairbanks Visitor Information Center at 800-327-5774 or 907-456-5774, www.explorefairbanks.com.

LODGING

For B&B accommodations, contact the Fairbanks Association of Bed & Breakfasts at www.ptialaska .net/~fabb.

Alpine Lodge
1221 Gilmore Trail
907-455-4413
www.akalpinelodge.com
Luxury lodge with suites and kitchenettes, cable TV, Wi-Fi, business center, exercise facility, laundry. Near airport, shuttle service, continental breakfast. Full-service restaurant and lounge.

Bear Lodge
212 Wedgewood Dr.
800-528-4916 or 907-456-3642
www.fountainheadhotels.com
Well-appointed lobby and spacious rooms, free Wi-Fi. Adjacent to Creamer's Field Migratory Waterfowl Refuge.

Bridgewater Hotel
723 1st Ave.
800-528-4916 or 907-452-6661
www.fountainheadhotels.com
94 units, dining, cocktails. Free Wi-Fi, computer kiosk in lobby. Downtown location. Airport/train shuttle.

Comfort Inn–Fairbanks
1908 Chena Landing Loop
800-4CHOICE or 907-479-8080
www.comfortinnfairbanks.com
74 spacious guest rooms, cable TV, guest laundry. Indoor pool and spa, free continental breakfast. Pet friendly.

Fairbanks Princess Riverside Lodge
4477 Pikes Landing Rd.
800-426-0500 or 907-455-5024
www.princesslodges.com
200 deluxe units on the Chena River. Gift shop, Wi-Fi, health club, restaurant, lounge. Airport/train shuttle. Tour tickets.

Golden North Motel of Fairbanks
4888 Old Airport Wy.
800-447-1910 or 907-479-6201
www.goldennorthmotel.com
62 units, free continental breakfast. Cable, Internet, free Wi-Fi. Pets allowed. Shuttle service.

Pike's Waterfront Lodge
1850 Hoselton Rd., off Airport Wy.
877-774-2400 or 907-456-4500
www.pikeslodge.com
Guest rooms and deluxe cabins along the Chena River, restaurant, saloon. Free Wi-Fi and cable TV. Shuttle service, sauna, exercise room .

Ranch Motel
2223 S. Cushman
907-452-4783
Clean rooms at reasonable prices, cable TV, full bath and shower. Staff are year-round residents who can answer your questions. Restaurant on-site.

Regency Fairbanks Hotel
95 10th Ave.
800-478-1340 or 907-459-2700
www.regencyfairbankshotel.com
Rooms with kitchens and free Wi-Fi. Suites. Business center, exercise room, lounge, shuttle, laundry. Full-service restaurant.

River's Edge Resort
4200 Boat St.
800-770-3343 or 907-474-0286
www.riversedge.net
Private cottages, each with two queen beds, along the Chena River in the heart of town. Restaurant, tours, shuttle.

Sophie Station Hotel
1717 University Ave.
800-528-4916 or 907-479-3650
www.fountainheadhotels.com
147 suites, kitchens, laundry. Dining, cocktails. Airport/train shuttle. Close to shopping.

SpringHill Suites by Marriott
575 1st Ave.
877-729-0197 or 907-451-6552
www.springhillsuites.com
Spacious studio accommodations with wireless and high-speed Internet, microwave, fridge, coffeemaker. Business center, continental breakfast. Pool, workout room.

Super 8 Motel
1909 Airport Wy.
800-800-8000 or 907-451-8888
www.super8.com
77 units, laundry, pets allowed. Free Wi-Fi, continental breakfast, pet friendly. Walking distance to shopping.

Wedgewood Resort
212 Wedgewood Dr.
800-528-4916 or 907-452-1442
www.fountainheadhotels.com
Elegant suites and guest rooms on beautifully landscaped grounds.

Westmark Hotel & Conference Center
813 Noble St.
800-544-0970 or 907-456-7722
www.westmarkhotels.com
244 well-appointed rooms, free wireless, laundry. Restaurant, cocktails, coffee bar, gift shop. Airport/train shuttle.

CAMPGROUNDS

Chena River Wayside RV Park Campground
221 University Ave.
907-452-7275
Roomy RV sites among the trees. Full hookups, restrooms, dump station. Picnic sites.

Ice Park and RV Campground
1925 Chena Landing Loop Rd.
907-451-8250 or 907-388-6388
ww.icealaska.com
52 campsites; 15 with full hookups. Tent sites. Dump station and freshwater, Internet, free Wi-Fi, laundry, showers, restroom. Walk to Pioneer Park.

River's Edge RV Park & Campground
4140 Boat St.
800-770-3343 or 907-474-0286
www.riversedge.net
190 sites with hookups and pull-throughs, tent camping. Showers, water, laundry, dump station. Free shuttle to attractions. Close to shopping. Assistance with tours.

Tanana Valley RV Park & Campground
1800 College Rd., on Tanana Valley State Fairgrounds
907-456-7956
www.tananavalleyfair.org
32 RV units with hookups and pull-throughs, tent camping. Showers, laundry, firepits/grills, dump station. On-site hosts.

RESTAURANTS

Alaska Salmon Bake
3175 College Rd., in Pioneer Park's Mining Valley
800-354-7274 or 907-452-7274
www.akvisit.com
Salmon over an open fire, deep-fried halibut, roasted prime rib.

The Bakery Restaurant
69 College Rd.
907-456-8600
Pastries and other baked goods fill out breakfast anytime, lunch, and dinner menus.

Co-op Diner
535 2nd Ave.
907-474-3463
Fifties-style diner fare in historic Fairbanks building that once housed the Empress Theatre.

Cookie Jar Restaurant
1006 Cadillac Ct.
907-479-8319
Breakfast, lunch, dinner, baked goods.

Gambardella's Pasta Bella
706 2nd Ave.
907-456-3417
www.gambardellas.com
Italian cuisine for lunch, dinner. Outdoor seating available.

Geraldo's Italian Restaurant
701 College Rd.
907-452-2299
American and Italian specialties, steaks, seafood. Hand-tossed pizza.

Home Town Restaurant
2223 S. Cushman
907-455-9113
Family-style restaurant, three meals a day.

Ivory Jack's
Mile 1.5 Goldstream Rd.
907-455-6666
Alaska dinner specialties: king crab, Nome reindeer. Lunch or dinner and drinks with the locals.

Lavelle's Bistro
575 1st Ave.
907-450-0555
www.lavellesbistro.com
Fine dining; recipient of Wine Spectator Award.

Lemongrass Thai Cuisine
388 Old Chena Pump Rd.
907-456-2200
Authentic Thai food.

Los Amigos
636 28th Ave.
907-452-3684
Authentic Mexican and Tex-Mex dishes.

Myong's Teriyaki
402 5th Ave., downtown
907-452-5560
Japanese specialties. Homemade salad dressing and teriyaki sauces.

Pike's Landing Restaurant & Lounge
4438 Airport Wy.
907-479-7113
Brunch, lunch, dinner along the Chena River. Outdoor seating available.

The Pump House Restaurant and Saloon
796 Chena Pump Rd.
907-479-8452
www.pumphouse.com
Alaskan specialties, steak, seafood. Historic site with outdoor seating along Chena River.

Red Lantern Steak & Spirits
813 Noble St., in Westmark Fairbanks
800-544-0970 or 907-456-7722
Pacific Rim cuisine, seafood specialties; open for breakfast, lunch, dinner.

Sourdough Sam's
3702 Cameron St.
907-479-0523
Popular diner among the locals, especially for breakfast. Indoor and outdoor seating.

Souvlaki
Pioneer Park, Cabin #25
907-452-3672
Souvlaki and other goodies; eat on the boardwalk.

The Turtle Club
10 Mile Old Steese Hwy., in Fox
907-457-3883
Prime rib, prawns, lobster, ribs. Reservations recommended.

The Vallata
2190 Goldstream Rd.
907-455-6600
Italian-American cuisine; open for dinner. Reservations recommended.

Wasabi Bay
1448 S. Cushman St.
907-452-0521
Japanese, sushi.

Wolf Run Restaurant
3360 Wolf Run
907-458-0636
Fresh ingredients in soups and sandwiches, special desserts; in log restaurant.

Zach's Restaurant
1717 University Ave.
907-479-3650
Fine dining in a warm atmosphere.

Takhini Hot Springs can be found off the Klondike Hwy., just a few miles from its junction with the Alaska Hwy. The local name is Mayo Rd.

CHAPTER 7

WESTERN CANADA'S NORTHBOUND BYWAYS

In western Canada, you have plenty of options for exploring even more backcountry than where the Alaska Hwy. roams. From the well-developed, high-speed trans-Canada route to the narrow gravel byways that reach into the Yukon's northernmost regions, choose which route suits your sense of adventure. Spur roads and loops lead through pastureland or tundra, across mountains, or down to the sea. Along them lie ghost towns, industrious small towns, farms, and glittering cities. Use this chapter to discover what lies along the bends of western Canada's beautiful byways.

NORTH KLONDIKE HIGHWAY

Part of the Klondike Loop

From junction with Alaska Hwy. 9 miles (14 km) north of Whitehorse to Dawson City: 323.5 miles (521 km)

24-hour road conditions: Call 511 inside the Yukon, or see www.511yukon.ca for an interactive map.

The Alaska Hwy. skirts along the southern reaches of the Yukon Territory, from Watson Lake to Whitehorse to Haines Junction, then crosses the international border and moves on to Tok, AK. But there's another way to reach Tok—a way that gives you more time in the Yukon.

From Whitehorse, you can drive north to Dawson City (via the North Klondike Hwy.), west to cross the Alaska border (via the Top of the World Hwy.), and then back south to Tok (via the Taylor Hwy.). Together, these three northerly highways are called the Klondike Loop.

If you have the yearning to see some of the Yukon Territory's most scenic vistas and experience even more gold-rush charm, take the Klondike Loop. Better yet, on the way to Alaska, take the Klondike Loop, and on the way back, take the Alaska Hwy. You'll get the best of both.

Travelers will find the beginning of the Klondike Loop 9 miles (14 km) northwest of Whitehorse, where the Alaska Hwy. (Hwy. 1) continues west and the North Klondike Hwy. (Hwy. 2) heads north. Hwy. 2 is paved for all of its 323.5 miles (521 km) to Dawson.

About 3 miles (5 km) north of the highway junction, watch for the left turn to Takhini Hot Springs, which is about 4 miles (6 km) west on a spur road. There you can bask in a naturally heated outdoor pool, winter or summer. Hiking and trail rides are other summertime options. Unlike most hot springs, Takhini's water does not contain sulfur, so it doesn't have that lingering, unpleasant odor. Meals and overnight accommodations are available. Trail rides, a 32-foot climbing wall, and a zip line round out the opportunities for big fun. See more at www.takhinihotsprings.com.

Continuing north on Hwy. 2, you'll soon spot Lake Laberge, made famous in "The Cremation of Sam McGee," by famed Yukon poet Robert Service. The lake is among the bodies of water, big and small, that make up the headwaters of the Yukon River. On the west, the road soon begins paralleling long, narrow Fox Lake, its pristine waters sparkling in the midnight sun. While it appears to be an autonomous body, the lake is connected to Lake Laberge by Fox Creek. Watch for signs that indicate where you can go fishing or find a campsite in one of the Yukon's government-operated campgrounds. They are clean and modestly priced.

The entire North Klondike Hwy. is a pleasure to drive, but one of the greatest pleasures may be found at Mile 55 (Km 88.5) in the kitchen of the Braeburn Lodge: their
world-famous giant cinnamon rolls. These folks even named their landing strip after
the dinner plate–size delicacy: Cinnamon Bun Airstrip. And then there's the annual
Cinnamon Bun Dog Sled Race, a 200-mile event held the first weekend in February.
There are other items on the menu, believe it or not, and the lodge also offers necessities
such as fuel, souvenirs, and tips on local fishing holes. Canoe rentals and campsites are
available here, too. Braeburn Lodge is open year-round; its most famous winter guests
are the mushers and the doggie athletes competing in the 1,000-mile (1,609-km) Yukon
Quest International Sled Dog Race.

The remains of the historic Montague House, one of the earliest roadhouse stops
on the old stagecoach line between Whitehorse and Dawson City, lie along this route,
about 80 miles (128.5 km) north of the Alaska Hwy. junction. You'll cross the Yukon
River about a hundred miles from the junction and enter the community of Carmacks,
a historic stop for steamboats that needed to restock their wood supplies, and later, coal.
There was once a telegraph line through here, and it was a stopping place on the Overland Stage route between Whitehorse and Dawson City. The restored Carmacks Roadhouse, a rambling log lodge with a sod roof, is one of several historic buildings that have
been rescued. For fans of the Yukon Quest International Sled Dog Race, Carmacks is a
well-known place-name, as the town hosts throngs of mushers and their dog teams that
stop at this checkpoint along the trail. Each year, the race starts or finishes in Whitehorse, alternating with Fairbanks on the other end of the route. Fuel, groceries, and
campsites are available in Carmacks, home to 450 people. See more at www.carmacks.
ca or call 867-863-6271. Fifteen miles (24 km) north of Carmacks is an interpretive sign
and viewing area for Five Finger Rapids—among the most treacherous places for stampeders to pass during the gold rush of 1898. There's a pullout here to get a photo of the
killing stretch in the river. The steamboats had to attach to cables and winch themselves
to make safe progress.

The little town of Pelly Crossing lies ahead, about 177 miles (285 km) northwest
of Whitehorse. Home of the Northern Tutchone people, this town of fewer than 300

ON THE SILVER TRAIL

At Stewart Crossing, 45 miles (72.5 km) north of Pelly Crossing, you can begin a side trip along Yukon
Hwy. II to visit the historic silver- and gold-mining towns of Mayo, Elsa, and Keno City on the Silver
Trail. In the early 20th century, Mayo was a major settlement and river port, and is now home to fewer
than 500 people. You will also pass through the traditional territory of the Na-Cho Nyak Dun people.

The Silver Trail is partially paved and leads to areas for swimming, camping, and hiking, as well
as stunning views of glaciated mountains. Government campgrounds, as well as privately owned
motels, are available in Mayo and in Keno, 69 miles (111 km) east of Stewart Crossing. Stop at Mayo's
visitor information center, Binet House, in summer from 10 AM to 6 PM. Take a walking tour of Mayo's
historic sites, and later, down the road, visit the Keno Mining Museum, which documents an era
through artifacts, photographs, and written histories. Call 867-995-3103. There's camping at the
Keno Campground, next to Lightning Creek in town, and recreational gold panning is permitted
nearby, but don't wander too far or you may trespass on a private claim. The town's recreation hall has
public showers and laundry facility. For more, see www.kenocity.info. Call 867-995-2792.

people had its most significant growth spurt when workers were building the Klondike Hwy. Like Carmacks, Pelly Crossing is an important stop on the Yukon Quest and gains international media attention every year. Both communities also feature a First Nations interpretive center, where you can learn more about the area's archaeology and cultural history.

Pelly Crossing marks the halfway point of the North Klondike Hwy.—about equal in distance from Whitehorse and Dawson City. Before the highway was completed in 1950, this was the site of a ferry to cross the river. Basic services for your vehicle, as well as its occupants (bank, groceries, overnight accommodations), are all available here, and you are welcome to take a self-guided tour beginning at the Selkirk Heritage Centre, next to the Selkirk Gas Bar.

In the final 158 miles (254 km) to Dawson City, the road parallels or intersects numerous creeks and rivers, such as Crooked Creek, Moose River, McQuesten River, and Clear Creek. The streams of this gold-mining region continue to pique the interest of placer miners for their proximity to the great discovery by George Carmacks. His 1896 find on Bonanza Creek, just outside of Dawson City, incited the Klondike gold rush.

Apart from Stewart Crossing, you will find few settlements along the remainder of the road. A handful of businesses offer accommodations, sundries, and fuel. Rest areas and pullouts provide the basics of a level surface and a garbage can.

DAWSON CITY

From Alaska Hwy. junction: 323.5 miles (521 km)

From Alaska-Yukon border: 66 miles (106 km)

In 1897, when news of a great gold discovery in the Klondike reached the outside world, more than 100,000 people resolved to pack up and head north, the mayor of Seattle among them. Only about 40,000 actually made it to the Klondike, and of those, a mere fraction made it rich, but the get-rich-quick compulsion was too great to ignore (not unlike the impulse of lottery-ticket buyers when a growing jackpot makes the news). Tens of thousands made uninformed decisions, not realizing that the way was hazardous, the cold could break a person's body and spirit, and the work was murderously difficult. Some men literally worked themselves to death, never enjoying the fruits of their labor. What remained was the romance— stories of men drinking champagne from ladies' slippers while gold nuggets spilled from their pockets. Most of it was bunk.

The discovery of gold in Rabbit Creek, later renamed Bonanza Creek, triggered the famous Klondike gold rush in the late 1890s.

The gold rush still lingers in Dawson City, along with the refurbished and modernized historic buildings that are so attractive. But in little niches off the main streets are the derelict structures that have seen human dramas we can only imagine. Dawson was

Viewed from the top of Midnight Dome, Dawson City is locked in for the winter, except for travel by air or snow machine. The Yukon and Klondike rivers are frozen up, and the highways that lead to Dawson are not plowed in winter months.

nearly falling down several decades ago when, in a drive to save historic buildings, city leaders began fund-raising in earnest. Today, Dawson is an imaginative slice out of time. Begin your visit with a stop at the Dawson City Visitor Information Centre, along the Yukon River at Front and King streets, housed in a replica of the 1897 Alaska Commercial Co. store. If you want a preview of what's happening in Dawson, check in with the Klondike Visitors Association at www.dawsoncity.ca or phone 867-993-5577.

One of Dawson's favorite sons, Pierre Berton, is a trusted storyteller and historian who uses books and videos to share the true story of Dawson's riotous beginning, its years of quiet retirement, and its rebirth as a major visitor attraction. Berton's books and videos are available in gift stores throughout town, including the Dawson City Museum gift shop (or through your favorite online source).

About 2,000 people live here year-round, with an influx of seasonal residents during the summer months, plus another 60,000 visitors. Gold is still king, and you can pan for some yourself. Or buy a hunk of the yellow metal at one of several jewelry stores. You can have your nuggets made into a special piece. The Klondike Nugget and Ivory Shop at Front and Queen streets has been in business since 1904. Gold samples from more than 50 creeks are on display.

Unlike refined gold, nuggets are slightly dull, dimpled, and irregular. They possess a compressed, raw beauty that still strikes a note of discovery in your chest. The metal and its shape remind you of the powerful forces that made it millennia ago under this very ground.

From the vantage point of Midnight Dome above the city, you can look out over this countryside that miners have tried to strip of its gold. Across the confluence of the

Yukon and Klondike rivers, the land below looks as if giant earthworms had burrowed beneath the surface. These peculiar marks are telltale signs of gold dredges, which operated like mechanical soil-eaters. These multistory gold-processing ships floated on small ponds and worked efficiently. Using a conveyor belt of steel buckets, a dredge would eat at the earth in front of it, sort out the gold from the useless rock and soil, then dump these tailings out the back. The dredges slowly moved forward, opening up the pond in front and filling it in behind the dredge. The machines followed the veins of gold, operating until the early 1960s and leaving behind these unique signs that are still visible today. Visit Gold Dredge No. 4 on Bonanza Creek for a Parks Canada interpretive tour of the largest wood-hull dredge in the world, built in 1912. Call 867-993-7200.

Mining remains the most important industry in the Yukon Territory, and tourists are invited to try their hand at gold panning, or digging with a shovel and pickax, at Gold Claim No. 6, above Discovery Claim on Bonanza Creek. This venture is operated by the Klondike Visitors Association, and there is no charge. Bring your own gold pan or rent one in town. From Dawson Creek, take the North Klondike Hwy. (Hwy. 2) east to Bonanza Rd. for 12 miles (18 km). You'll drive past Dredge No. 4 and Discovery Claim. Signs will lead the way from there.

Other gold-panning adventures are offered in the area, possibly at your campground. Ask the folks at the visitor center for details.

Dawson attractions include:

George Black Ferry. This ferry across the Yukon River is a free service offered by the Yukon government, at work 24 hours a day, except between 5 and 7 on Wednesday mornings, when the vessel is serviced. Commercial businesses hold special passes for priority boarding, so make sure you enter the correct lane for boarding your vehicle. Rush hours for tourists are as predictable as those for a big-city workforce. Between 7 and 11 AM, most drivers are outbound tourists. Peak times for those headed into Dawson are between 2 and 8 PM. Work around those rush hours and you'll have a shorter wait. Call 867-993-5441 for information.

Dawson City Museum. The features of this museum on 5th Ave. in the old Territorial Administration Building include goldfield exhibits, a First Nations Collection, films, a Klondike history library, and steam locomotives. Ask about a brochure for the Walking Tour of Dawson City Cemeteries. A gift shop and coffee shop are on-site. Open Victoria Day to Labour Day. Call 867-993-5291 or see www.dawsonmuseum.ca.

Robert Service Cabin. One block south of Mission St. and 8th Ave. is the site of the two-room

The home of the Dawson City Museum was originally the Territorial Administration Building, designed by Thomas W. Fuller, Dawson's resident architect, in 1899. Major renovation and restoration took place in the 1980s, and today the 1901 building is a National Historic Site of Canada.

Robert Service Cabin, a National Historic Site, still standing on a hillside, its roof covered with sod. It was here that Service wrote such classics as *The Trail of Ninety-Eight* and his third and final book of verse, *Rhymes of a Rolling Stone*. He lived here from November 1909 to June 1912. Twice-daily recitals of Service's works are presented on the front lawn. Afterward, interpretive guides invite visitors to peek inside the windows, but the cabin's condition cannot tolerate more than that. Just across the street is the boyhood home of a more contemporary Canadian author, Pierre Berton, which has been renovated and serves as a writers' retreat site.

Just one block south of the Robert Service Cabin, you'll find the Jack London Interpretive Museum. The former Dawson City bank teller who became a famous author (*White Fang* and *Call of the Wild*, among 50 novels) lived in a cabin on the North Fork of Henderson Creek in 1897, when he first made his way to the Yukon. He abandoned mining and the cabin, and it stood empty for decades until it was recovered in 1965 by Yukon author Dick North, who organized the dismantling and transport of the cabin from the backcountry. Portions of it were sent to Dawson City to re-create this replica; other logs went to London's hometown of Oakland, CA. London's original cache stands nearby. Like other visitor offerings in Dawson, the museum is open from late spring to early fall. Call 867-993-5575.

Palace Grand Theatre. Another Klondike National Historic Site, the Palace Grand Theatre at King St. and 3rd Ave. is steeped in stories. The theater opened in July 1899, built by Arizona Charlie Meadows, a showman from the Wild West who was not above performing shooting tricks if the party atmosphere needed a boost. It has been restored to its original splendor by Parks Canada, which offers tours of Dawson's historical buildings. Call 867-993-7200.

Dänojà Zho Cultural Centre. Located on Front and York streets on the waterfront, the center informs visitors about the First Nations people who were so drastically affected by the gold rush. See exhibits on life at a traditional fish camp and enjoy contemporary dance, storytelling, and other special events. Call 867-993-6768 or see www.trondekheritage.com.

Diamond Tooth Gerties Casino. This nonprofit, town-run gambling "parlor" is named for the famous Gertie Lovejoy, an enterprising dance hall queen, who pressed a diamond between her front teeth and found riches by mining the miners instead of the diggings. The casino at 4th Ave. and Queen St. offers three different shows every night. A cover charge gets you in the door for cancan entertainment and gambling from 7 PM until 2 AM, Sunday through Wednesday; 2 PM to 2 AM, Friday and Saturday. Open May through September; 19 and older only. Call 867-993-5525.

Top of the World Golf Resort. This is Canada's northernmost golf course, with grass greens, nine holes, a driving range, and a pro shop. Take the Top of the World Hwy. for 5 miles (8 km) out of Dawson City and follow the signs. Scheduled tee times are not required. Shuttle service from Dawson City is available; golfers arriving by RV are permitted to dry camp overnight. Call 867-993-5888 during the summer months.

Take a cruise. The newest attraction in Dawson is the paddlewheeler *Klondike Spirit*, which was launched in Eagle, AK, in July 2006 to make her maiden voyage of 109 miles (175 km) to Dawson City. Cruises on the Yukon River are filled with insider knowledge as local people are there to interpret the area's natural and human history. Food and beverage service is available, too. Tickets are available at the Triple J Hotel, 5th Ave. and Queen St. Call 867-993-5323 or see www.klondikespirit.com.

miles later is Fort McPherson, home to fewer than 1,000 people, set on a hill overlooking the Peel River. Here, and at the end of the road in Inuvik, a community of about 3,500 people, you realize how far you've come, so don't be in a hurry to leave. Soak in the wonder of these extreme-north places. Inuvik has camping, hotels, and lots of midnight sun. Stop in at the Western Arctic Regional Visitor Centre on Mackenzie Rd. (867-777-7237) and get your frameable certificate verifying that you've crossed the Arctic Circle. See more at www.inuvik.ca/tourism.

For other area travel information, you can also contact Northwest Territories Tourism at www.spectacularnwt.com or call 800-661-0788, toll-free in North America.

CAMPBELL HIGHWAY

Watson Lake to North Klondike Hwy. (near Carmacks): 362 miles (583 km)

Motorists on their way to Dawson City can shorten their drive by taking the alternate route around Whitehorse: the Campbell Hwy. (Hwy. 4). The road heads northwest from Watson Lake and nearly 400 miles later connects with the North Klondike Hwy. (Hwy. 2) just north of Carmacks. About half of the route is paved.

You accomplish three things by taking this route to Dawson City: you save 20 miles on your odometer; you miss out on all the fun that's waiting in Whitehorse; and you eat a lot of dust. On the other hand, you also see some beautiful land as you follow the route of early-day fur traders who worked for the Hudson's Bay Company. Robert Campbell himself was sent here in the 1840s to explore on behalf of the company.

Completed in 1968, this road less traveled wends through the communities of Ross River and Faro, where you can buy gas, food, and groceries, as well as find a place to stay with or without an RV. Faro has a beautiful log visitor center, too: the Campbell Region Interpretive Centre, which is open daily from 10 AM to 6 PM through the summer. It's rich with local information and historical displays. Call 867-994-2728 or see www.faroyukon.ca.

YELLOWHEAD-CASSIAR HIGHWAYS

Prince George to Alaska Hwy. (near Watson Lake): 748 miles (1,204 km)

Alaskabound travelers can shave some 100 miles (161 km) off the drive between Prince George and Watson Lake by taking westbound Yellowhead Hwy. 16 and then northbound Cassiar Hwy. 37. Some motorists are less concerned about time but still take the Yellowhead-Cassiar route for a change of scenery through British Columbia's outstanding Skeena Mountains. Most portions of this route are paved, but drivers should stay alert for sections of washboard in gravel stretches, as well as maintenance crews resurfacing sections.

In the summer of 2010, forest fires at the north end of the Cassiar closed the road for days, and traffic was rerouted onto the Alaska Hwy. Here's a perfect example of how checking ahead for a road report can help you determine which route to take. In British Columbia, check www.drivebc.ca.

Yellowhead Hwy. 16 is a trans-Canada route that extends from southern Manitoba and trends westward and north across Saskatchewan, Alberta, and British

The Yellowhead Hwy. offers access to Mt. Robson Provincial Park, BC's second-oldest park, near Valemont. At 12,972.5 feet (3,954 m), the peak is the highest in the Canadian Rockies.

Columbia. In western Canada, it is a primary east–west route linking Edmonton with Prince George. Through mountain passes, along glacial lakes, and into canyons, the Yellowhead promises stunning vistas and plenty of wildlife-watching.

The Yellowhead continues west to the coastal city of Prince Rupert, BC. From there, travelers may connect with the British Columbia ferry system and the Alaska Marine Highway System. (See Chapter 9, Alaska Marine Highway System.)

The junction of the Yellowhead and Cassiar hwys. is 298 miles (480 km) west of Prince George near the village of Kitwanga. From here, the Cassiar trends north for 450 miles (724 km) to its junction with the Alaska Hwy. 13 miles (21 km) west of Watson Lake.

From the Cassiar Hwy., motorists can access the coastal communities of Stewart, BC, and Hyder, AK. The westbound turnoff to these towns is at Mile 96 (Km 155) on the Cassiar Hwy., at Meziadin Junction. Stewart and Hyder straddle the international border 41 miles (66 km) west of the junction.

The Yellowhead Hwy. got its name from the story of an Iroquois Caucasian trapper who was called *Tête Jaune*, or Yellowhead, for the blond cast to his hair. He led fur traders through the Rocky Mountains and opened the way for a trade route across western Canada.

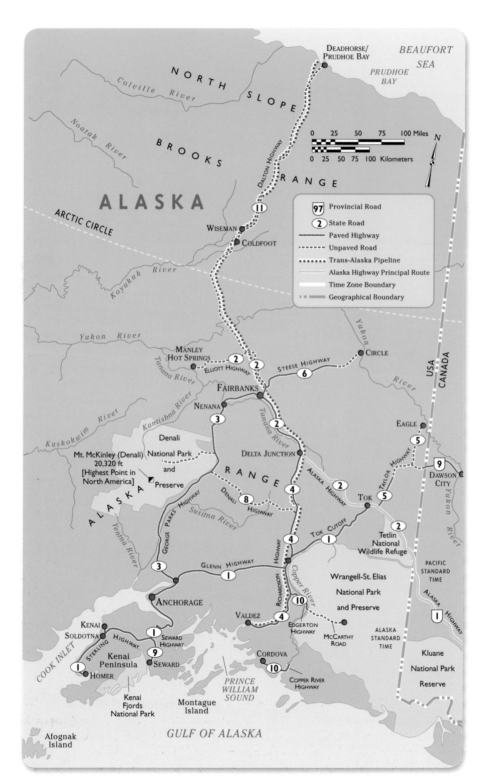

CHAPTER 8

ALASKA'S STATE HIGHWAYS

If you're from "Outside," the term Alaskans use for anywhere that's not Alaska, you may be accustomed to choosing from a vast menu of roads to get where you're going. You read maps and follow your chosen route, watching for your exit to another super-highway. If you ask for directions, you commonly refer to route numbers. Now you're in Alaska, and when you ask, "Where is the exit for Route 9?" the puzzled Alaskan will answer with another question, "Where do you want to go?" Choices are so few that decision making is made easy. Name your destination and there's usually only one way to get there.

You may discover that the locals will answer in terms of time, rather than miles: Portage Lake is about 45 minutes south of Anchorage. Santa Claus House is about 15 minutes southwest of Fairbanks. Denali Park? A couple hours south of Fairbanks; about five hours north of Anchorage. Maps are optional when you drive in the country's biggest state, with fewer roads per square mile than Rhode Island.

A separate issue entirely is the Alaskan preference of calling highways by name, not route number: the Steese, the Parks, the Seward. You'll hear the names regularly, the route numbers rarely. Most of the highways dead-end at small towns along a major body of water. Consequently, the term *end of the road* applies to several communities around the state: Deadhorse, Circle City, Eagle, McCarthy, Skagway, Haines, and Homer, among them.

If you want to drive northwest, west, or southwest from this narrow, north–south cluster of blacktop, you can forget it. Most of Alaska remains accessible only by air or, along Alaska's Panhandle (Southeast Alaska), by marine highway (see Chapter 9, Alaska Marine Highway System).

In 1942, when the Alaska Hwy. was built and attached to the existing Richardson Hwy. at Delta Junction, there were even fewer roads. Alaska's busiest highway between Anchorage and Fairbanks, the Parks, didn't even exist. Travelers had to use the longer, roundabout way via the Richardson and Glenn hwys. The pipeline was still 30 years in the future, so the Dalton Hwy. (also known as the Haul Rd. for pipeline construction) hadn't been conceived. Nor had the Sterling Hwy., which wends down the Kenai Peninsula. If you wanted to go to Homer, you took a ferry.

What are now considered major transportation routes (by Alaska standards) weren't much more than improved trails that had been used by early settlers, traders, and miners. A century ago and more, the pioneering Europeans simply traveled along the ancient trading routes of Alaska's first people, who were familiar with the passes through the mountains, and who graciously showed the newcomers the way.

Today, although Alaska's roads are called highways, a few remain rustic and unpaved. During the snowy months, basically from October to May, the following routes are not maintained, so they are impassable and closed to vehicles: Copper River Hwy., Denali Hwy., Denali Park Rd., Taylor Hwy., and the McCarthy Rd. (Snowmobilers, on the other hand, love these winter highways.) (See the section on Driving in Winter in Chapter 1, Planning and Packing.) Even if a road is regularly plowed, before setting out, wise winter travelers will study the current driving conditions. That's a good plan even in summer, when construction, weather conditions, or other road hazards may cause a delay.

Alaska's Highways

Highway Name	Length	Number	Route Description
Copper River Highway	48 miles 77 km	10	Disconnected from highway system. Connects Cordova, on Prince William Sound, with the derelict Million Dollar Bridge to nowhere; mostly unpaved.
Dalton Highway	415 miles 668 km	11	Splits northbound from Elliott Hwy. (north of Fox) to Deadhorse, where it dead-ends at the Arctic Ocean; mostly unpaved; almost no services.
Denali Highway	134 miles 216 km	8	Road between Richardson Hwy. and Parks Hwy.; connects Paxson and Cantwell; unpaved; few services.
Edgerton Highway	33 miles 3 km	10	Connects Richardson Hwy. (south of Glennallen) to Chitina, 33 miles (53 km) east on paved road; from there, unpaved McCarthy Rd. travels east for 60 miles (96.5 km) almost to McCarthy; few services; not maintained in winter.
Elliott Highway	152 miles 245 km	2	From Fox (north of Fairbanks) to Manley Hot Springs, where it dead-ends at the Tanana River; partially paved; few services.
Glenn Highway	328 miles 528 km	1	Connects Anchorage with Glennallen and the Richardson Hwy. and connects Gakona Junction with Tok via the Tok Cutoff; paved, sections often under repair; services at regular intervals.

A helpful public service by the Alaska Department of Transportation and Public Facilities allows motorists to use any phone or the Internet to obtain the latest information about road conditions, traffic delays, closures, and roadwork by dialing 511 or by visiting http://511.alaska.gov. If you're calling from out of state, dial toll-free, 866-282-7577.

Generally speaking, most of Alaska's major roads are in great shape. The paved roads are well-marked two-lane routes (sometimes even four lanes) with ample shoulders. Unpaved sections are graded regularly, and sometimes serve better than the broken-down parts of paved roads. Small towns, gas stations, and other services appear at regular intervals, and restaurants and lodging aren't hard to find, either. That can't be said for all of Alaska's "highways," though, so read up on your route before you embark.

Road maintenance workers have a particular challenge in Alaska, considering what they have for a subsurface. In many parts of the state, they contend with an underground enemy called permafrost: permanently frozen sections of soil that are riddled with ice. When the insulating overgrowth is scraped away to create a road, the ground begins to melt and sink. Adding a layer of weighty, heat-conductive blacktop creates

Haines Highway	152 miles 245 km	7	Connects Alaska Hwy. at Haines Junction, YT, with Haines, AK, where it dead-ends on Lynn Canal; paved. (Via Yukon Hwy. 3 and BC Hwy. 4)
Klondike Highway	15 miles 24 km	98	Alaska-Canada border to Skagway, where it dead-ends on Lynn Canal. Canadian segment, Klondike Hwy. 2, connects to Alaska Hwy. just south of Whitehorse. (Via Yukon's Klondike Hwy. 2)
Parks Highway	363 miles 584 km	3	Connects Anchorage with Fairbanks via the Glenn Hwy. Completely paved; services at regular intervals.
Richardson Highway	366 miles 589 km	4 & 2	Connects Valdez with Fairbanks. Paved; services at regular intervals.
Seward Highway	127 miles 204 km	1 & 9	Connects Anchorage with Seward, where it dead-ends on Resurrection Bay off the Gulf of Alaska; paved; services at regular intervals.
Steese Highway	161 miles 259 km	6	Connects Fairbanks with Circle City, where it dead-ends on the Yukon River; mostly unpaved; few services.
Sterling Highway	143 miles 230 km	1	Branches off Seward Hwy. for southbound travelers to Homer, where it dead-ends on Cook Inlet; paved; services at regular intervals.
Taylor Highway	160 miles 257 km	5	Connects Alaska Hwy. at Tetlin Junction (southeast of Tok) with Eagle, where it dead-ends on the Yukon River; unpaved; few services. Not maintained in winter.

more subsurface problems. With the freeze and thaw of seasonal change, some roadbeds suffer, and an army of maintenance workers sets out to make repairs each year in the short summer construction season. As a motorist, plan for one or two delays, because flaggers, pilot cars, dust, and lumbering trucks are virtual guarantees. Please be patient. If they weren't out there doing their jobs, you wouldn't be willing (or able) to set out on these passageways into some of America's most magnificent places.

Of course, one must include gawking time in any Alaska road trip. When the evening light turns the sky pink-orange above a mountain range, the view can be distracting. Glacier-fed rivers merge and divide across a broad floodplain, and low clouds drag across the vivid, white mountain peaks. Wild animals step out onto the pavement ahead, or pause to feed along the shoulder, and your camera is at the ready. In the midst of such beauty, making good time loses its appeal.

Since 1993, the Alaska Department of Transportation and Public Facilities has named all or part of a dozen transportation corridors as Alaska Scenic Byways. To qualify for the state designation, a byway must possess some or all of these intrinsic qualities:

scenic or natural beauty, cultural importance, recreational value, or archaeological or historical significance. Not all are paved roadways, however—the Alaska Railroad and the Alaska Marine Highway System are among the names on the beauty list. The Glenn Hwy. was elevated to National Scenic Byway, plus the Glenn and Seward hwys. reached national status with the designation of All-American Road. Others in the state list are the Dalton Hwy., Haines Hwy., Parks Hwy., Richardson Hwy., Steese Hwy., Sterling Hwy. (from Wye to Skilak, and Anchor Point to Homer), the Taylor Hwy., and the Top of the World Hwy. For more information and photos of Alaska's Scenic Byways, visit www.alaska.gov/scenic.

This chapter features Alaska's highways, in alphabetical order, and includes the cities, services, access, recreational opportunities, and attractions that you'll find along this exceptionally scenic road system.

COPPER RIVER HIGHWAY

Cordova to Million Dollar Bridge: 48 miles

Travel Opportunities: Scenic fishing village; flightseeing over Wrangell-St. Elias National Park; Prince William Sound cruises; rafting on the Copper River; chartered fishing for salmon or halibut; Childs Glacier; Million Dollar Bridge; bird-watching.

Among Alaska's unique roads, the Copper River Hwy. is a standout—a mere fragment of a highway that's disconnected from the rest of the highway system, but still official enough to merit a route number: Alaska Hwy. 10. To drive this road, you'll need to fly in and rent a car at Cordova, on Prince William Sound. Or bring your vehicle along on the Alaska Marine Highway System and disembark at Cordova (see Chapter 9, Alaska Marine Highway System). Pay heed to the return schedule if you choose to cruise, or you may stay longer than you had planned.

For centuries, Native Alaskans have lived in this region, moving with the seasons to fish and hunt as they draw life from the land. The ways of the early Native people are not just in museum displays today. In this area, you'll find many Athabascan, Eyak, and Alutiiq people who still follow the cultural practices of their ancestors in dance, song, and art, as well as through a subsistence lifestyle of hunting and fishing for food. Throughout the small Native villages of Southcentral Alaska, people live in log or wood-frame houses, drive cars, go to work, and follow the same TV reality shows as anybody else in the country. Some of them, however, have great-grandmas who remember the moment they saw a white person for the first time.

Explorers, gold seekers, and traders brought the stamp of the Western world to the Copper River Delta, especially during the 19th century. In 1902, geologists made the first major oil discovery in Alaska—at Katalla, southwest of Cordova. In 1907, entrepreneur Michael J. Heney began building the Copper River & Northwestern Railway to transport the ore mined from the Kennecott Copper Mine to the north. The mine and railroad flourished for more than 20 years, closing in the late 1930s.

In the mid-1940s, builders of the Copper River Hwy. chose to follow the railway's bed and planned to join Cordova with Chitina and the Richardson Hwy. In 1964, a natural disaster thwarted the project, and the work stalled out. That year, the Good Friday Earthquake devastated Cordova and many Southcentral coastal communities. The earthquake originally was measured at a magnitude of 8.6 and later was upgraded to an unbelievable 9.2. One section of the Million Dollar Bridge over the Copper River collapsed in the 1964 earthquake, and for the next 40 years it remained in disrepair. It was added to the National Register of Historic Places in 2000. Finally, in 2005, after a year of work to repair it, the Million Dollar Bridge reopened, once more allowing motorists from Cordova to cross the Copper River. Cordova remains disconnected from Chitina by road, however.

The first 12 miles (19 km) of the Copper River Hwy. are paved, followed by a gravel surface that threads for another 36 miles (58 km) through awesome beauty to the historic bridge. There are several USFS trailheads and recreational opportunities along this route.

Near the bridge, you'll get a panoramic view of Childs Glacier. Plan a picnic here amid unforgettable surroundings. A limited number of sites are available for RVers and tent campers who want to spend the night at Childs Glacier Recreation Area. A crude road extends another 10 miles (16 km) beyond the bridge, but only four-wheel-drive vehicles should give it a go.

In the course of its 48.5 miles (78 km), the highway crosses a number of glacially fed streams and the multifingered Copper River Delta. Magnificent glaciers are visible on the north side of the road as you drive east. And all around you, for miles and miles, is Chugach (CHOO-gash) National Forest, close to 6 million acres of it. On this drive, you'll find viewpoint turnouts with informational plaques, numerous trailheads, and two developed recreation areas. Fishing, wildlife-watching, hiking, biking, and camping are popular activities around here, and the Copper River is famed for its annual runs of salmon. Freshwater and saltwater fishing take place in an angler's paradise. Learn about local regulations and closures when you obtain your fishing license at any number of retail outlets in Cordova.

Cordova is a photogenic town with a population of about 2,100 people. Because its economy is largely based on fishing, commercial fishing vessels outnumber pleasure boats in the harbor, and a US Coast Guard vessel is moored just outside the small-boat harbor. It's fun to walk the docks and read the names of the vessels and to watch the fishermen gear up for or down from a trip. The catch may be salmon, halibut, or herring, depending on season. In town, nearly everything you need lies within walking distance. North of Cordova, the Alaska Marine Highway ferry terminal offers scheduled service aboard the M/V *Aurora* or the fast ferry, the M/V *Chenega*, which connects travelers with Valdez and Whittier (see Chapter 9, Alaska Marine Highway System).

The region is a stopover on the largest shorebird migration in the world. Located on a major flyway for 2 million waterfowl and 5 million shorebirds, Cordova hosts the Copper River Delta Shorebird Festival in early May each year. Birders come from all over the world to view the millions of birds that nest and feed in the delta. So vital to the birds' survival, this portion of the Chugach National Forest gained added protection in 1978 when it was named a Critical Habitat Area.

The favorite party of the winter season is the Cordova Iceworm Festival, set each year on the first weekend of February. Events include a parade (featuring a 100-foot iceworm), entertainment, an arts and crafts show, skiing events, a survival-suit race, a best-beard contest, and selection of a king and queen. Call 907-424-5756 for more information. In summer, enjoy the Wild Copper River Salmon Festival, set in mid-July, with music, a half marathon, fun run, and food.

The Cordova Historical Museum and the Cordova Public Library on 1st St. offer exhibits on the rich Native cultures of this region, as well as its exploration in 1778 by

Capt. James Cook, the gold rush, and more recent copper-mining history. Also inside are art displays, a fishing diorama, gift shop, and a modest bookstore. The library also has free Internet access. Call 907-424-6655; visit www.cordovamuseum.org or www.cordovalibrary.org.

At the US Forest Service office, in the original 1925 federal building at 612 2nd St., you can learn about the Chugach National Forest and local natural history. Call 907-424-7661. The USFS offers 19 cabins in the area, available for a fee and by reservation, which you can also handle online at www.reserveusa.com.

Other Cordova options include rafting the Copper River, a fly-in fishing trip, a cruise on Prince William Sound, or a flightseeing excursion above the fabulous Wrangell-St. Elias Range. For more information on what to see and do in Cordova, contact the chamber of commerce at 907-424-7260, or visit www.cordovachamber.com.

LODGING

Alaskan Hotel & Bar
600 1st St.
907-424-3299
Shared and private rooms, downtown location. Meet the locals in the bar.

Cordova Lighthouse Inn
212 Nicholoff Wy.
907-424-7080
www.cordovalighthouseinn.com
Comfortable guest rooms, suites housed in the old Cordova ferry terminal, right on the water. Cable TV, Wi-Fi, private phones. Kitchen and lounging areas.

Cordova Rose Lodge
1315 Whitshed Rd.
907-424-7673
www.cordovarose.com
Historic setting of landlocked barge offers rooms with a view. Tour arrangements. Breakfast and dinner.

The Northern Nights Inn
PO Box 1564
907-424-5356
www.northernnightsinn.com
Rooms with period antique decor, a view of the inlet. Kitchens, cable TV, private telephone, laundry, freezer for your fish. Walking distance to attractions.

Orca Adventure Lodge
2 miles north of Cordova
907-424-7249
www.orcaadventurelodge.com
1880s cannery town rebuilt for adventure clientele. Tours, hikes, kayaking, etc.

Prince William Motel
2nd and Council streets
888-796-6835 or 907-424-3201
16 rooms and kitchenettes. TV, microwave, refrigerator, laundry, store.

Reluctant Fisherman Inn
407 Railroad Ave.
907-424-3272
www.reluctantfisherman.com
Nonsmoking rooms with cable TV, some with harbor views. Free local calls, data ports, wireless. Laundry, free continental breakfast. Bar and grill on-site.

CAMPGROUNDS

Alaska River Expeditions
13 miles outside of town
800-776-1864
www.alaskarafters.com
12 campsites, restrooms, garbage pickup. Water, power, pit toilets. No dump station. Raft adventures, tours.

Odiak Camper Park
Whitshed Rd. off Copper River Hwy.
907-424-7282
24 sites, tenting area, power, water, showers, dump station. Operated by the city.

US Forest Service
877-444-6777 or 907-424-7661
www.reserveusa.com
19 cabins available in this district; most accessible only by boat or plane. Three are on the trail system.

RESTAURANTS

Ambrosia Restaurant
410 1st St.
907-424-7175
Italian.

Cordova Rose Lodge
1315 Whitshed Rd.
907-424-7673
www.cordovarose.com
Sourdough pancakes, seafood specialties.

Killer Whale Café
507 1st St.
907-424-7733
Breakfast and lunch, espresso, baked goods.

OK Restaurant
PO Box 670
907-424-3433
Family-style dining.

Picnic Basket
PO Box 2183
907-424-4337
Pizza, sandwiches.

Powder House Bar and Restaurant
Mile 2 Copper River Hwy.
907-424-3529
Soups, sandwiches, seafood. Eat in or take out.

Reluctant Fisherman Inn
407 Railroad Ave.
907-424-3272
www.reluctantfisherman.com
Bar and grill on deck overlooking Orca Inlet.

A cow moose crosses the lonely Dalton Hwy., where few services mean few noncommercial motorists on Alaska's newest highway.

DALTON HIGHWAY (HAUL RD.)

From Elliott Hwy. to Deadhorse: 414 miles (666 km)

Travel Opportunities: *Trans-Alaska Pipeline views; Yukon River; Coldfoot Camp; Wiseman gold-mining village; Brooks Range continental divide; Arctic Circle crossing; guided tours to Prudhoe Bay oil operations.*

The Dalton Hwy. originally was called the Haul Rd. because it was built for one purpose: to haul goods and supplies for the building of the Trans-Alaska Pipeline. The road was named for James William Dalton, a principal player in North Slope oil development. Although experimental ice roads, seasonal at best, had been built in the Arctic, the Dalton was the first planned and engineered roadway into the farthest north reaches of the state. Even though the Dalton was finished in 1974, its entire length wasn't opened to the public until 1994.

You will share the road mostly with truckers headed to or from Deadhorse and Prudhoe Bay at the top of the state, a small number of hardy souls like yourself, and a handful of tourism operations. As far as services go, this route remains largely undeveloped. With a few exceptions—such as businesses at the Yukon River crossing, Coldfoot, Wiseman, Deadhorse, and a couple of wayside stops—you'll encounter long stretches of no towns, no gas stations, few outhouses, and few other travelers. The only ATMs are at

Deadhorse. Emergency medical services are not available. Officials suggest calling the Alaska State Troopers at 911 or by CB on channel 19. Cell phone coverage ends about 35 miles (56 km) north of Fairbanks, but you'll be able to use your cell phone again once you get to Deadhorse.

As you head north, the terrain changes in degrees of beauty: from sparsely treed rolling hills to lofty mountains to limitless undulating tundra. Your most constant companion is the nearby pipeline, visible only in the stretches where the permafrost in the soil was so bad that builders put the pipeline up on supports and ran it above ground. The 48-inch-diameter pipeline was built between 1974 and 1977. Its 800-mile (1,287.5-km) length stretches from Mile 0 at Prudhoe Bay to its terminus at Valdez, on Prince William Sound. South of Fairbanks, most of the pipeline route parallels the Richardson Hwy.

A mostly unpaved wilderness road, the Dalton extends from Mile 73 of the Elliott Hwy., north of Fox, all the way to Deadhorse and the working oil fields of Prudhoe Bay. Don't expect to waltz in anywhere at will. Security precautions keep many places off-limits to the average traveler. In Deadhorse you'll find an airport, general store, filling station, and a handful of modest hotels, which are the best places to line up a guided tour of the area. With a guide, you may dip your toes in the frigid Arctic Ocean, view Mile 0 of the pipeline, and learn about how the vast oil reservoir beneath Alaska's North Slope was discovered and developed.

Most car rental companies prohibit taking their vehicles on the Dalton, and we don't recommend driving farther north than Coldfoot with your own vehicle, as there are no repair services between Coldfoot and Deadhorse. Consider the following option for less wear and tear on your vehicle and your sensibilities: take a fly-drive combo tour with a number of tour operators. I did this once and found the trip very worthwhile. For travel businesses that specialize in the Far North, contact the Fairbanks Convention and Visitors Bureau at 800-327-5774 or 907-456-5774 to talk to a travel expert. You can also visit their website at www.explorefairbanks.com. Also, the Bureau of Land Management annually updates its travel guide to the Dalton Hwy., available through the Alaska Geographic Association at www.alaskageographic.org as a free download. For other questions, call the BLM's Arctic Field Office in Fairbanks at 800-437-7021 or www.blm.gov/ak/dalton.

On a guided trip to the North Slope, you begin the trip with strangers but make fast friends within hours. Pack an overnight bag, and a shuttle bus will pick you up from your Fairbanks campground or hotel. You'll be well fed throughout the trip.

After a 45-minute flight from Fairbanks to Deadhorse, we boarded an 18-passenger van and cruised around the oil fields, with permitted access to places where we would not have been allowed as independent visitors. Naturally, this is a high-security area, and tourism is still under development. The population of Deadhorse is officially 25—plus 3,500 to 5,000 transient workers. Many work a fluctuating schedule of two weeks on, two weeks off, or something similar. You won't see many people, actually. Most work indoors.

Around the low buildings and ground-level maze of pipes, the road meanders among the oil-company installations and enclosed drilling rigs. We saw numerous caribou, waterfowl, and wildflowers in what I considered unexpected places. In one spot, we saw a group of caribou resting under a raised part of the pipeline. Without trees to block the view, they were easy to spot. At the Arctic Ocean, I handed off my camera to a fellow traveler and asked him to take my picture standing ankle deep in the water. (I threw my arms in the air and said "Hurry!" through a clenched smile. The water was piercing cold in August.)

Our driver had packed lots of good food in coolers, and we had plenty of water, coffee, and soft drinks. Driving south that day, he told us all about the unique forces of nature here, the climate, the geology, and the wildlife. We learned how to pronounce Sagavanirktok River and understood instantly why everybody calls it the Sag.

Farther south we spied a hunter who had bagged a caribou with bow and arrow, and some of us tried walking out to him over the tundra. It was like trying to walk on and between underinflated basketballs that are covered with mossy, leafy growth.

We stopped again to share our drinking water with a British couple on a bicycle journey from Fairbanks to Prudhoe Bay, then visited the century-old mining town of Wiseman. A woman behind the counter in the general store told us that in the last couple of days, a local miner had uncovered a record-size gold nugget: flat and big enough to eclipse a saucer.

After an overnight at Coldfoot, in buildings that once housed pipeline construction workers, we continued our southbound trip and later came upon the only structure around for a hundred miles: the tour company's private, off-road outhouse, placed there just for our comfort. Next stop was the Arctic Circle, marked by a sturdy sign showing its place on the globe. Our driver asked us to wait a moment, then literally rolled out a red carpet and shook our hands, welcoming us across the invisible line. That evening, we pulled in to Fairbanks, tired but thrilled to have seen such rare sights.

My advice is to go with a tour guide if you want the best experience and the least worry. It was a privilege to have someone drive, especially when a good-size piece of gravel damaged the tour van's windshield (and not mine).

Places of note along the Dalton Hwy., from south to north:

Yukon River Bridge. The highway crosses the bridge at Mile 56 (Km 90), where many travelers are happy to find the services of Yukon River Camp for lodging, food, and tours. Here at the crossing, you may launch your boat on the Yukon River, and there are good views of the pipeline. In summer months, the BLM staffs the Yukon Crossing Visitor Contact Station, a rest stop with outhouses, information, and viewing platform. Just a few miles ahead, the BLM maintains the Five Mile site for RV dumping and water fill-ups. Nearby, another popular business, the Hot Spot, offers food and lodging.

This area lies within the Yukon Flats National Wildlife Refuge, which supports moose, caribou, bears, millions of migrating birds, and small furbearers such as lynx, snowshoe hares, foxes, and beavers.

Arctic Circle. At Mile 115 (Km 185), an expansive wayside with viewing platform, outhouses, and great signs is worth a stop to record your momentous crossing of the Arctic Circle—that invisible boundary that encircles the globe at the southernmost latitude, where the sun never sets on the day of the summer solstice (June 21 or 22). Likewise, at this latitude the sun does not rise on the day of the winter solstice (December 21 or 22). Nearby, at Mile 115, the BLM offers undeveloped camping with tables, grills, and outhouses. No potable water is available.

Coldfoot. This former pipeline construction camp was given this name for obvious reasons. Winter temperatures plunge well below zero all along the Dalton Hwy. The farther north you go, the deeper the plunge. I once visited Coldfoot with a television crew in January, and I still remember the heartbreaking sound of an expensive and important part of the camera going *crraack!* in the −50°F air. In summer, Coldfoot is pleasantly warm, but be advised that mosquitoes and other biting insects are a nuisance. There is no town here, but rather a welcome stop in the road at Mile 175 (Km 282), where truckers and tourists refresh and refill at Coldfoot Camp. Here, too, adventurers headed into the Brooks Range often launch from base camp. You can book a float trip or flightseeing adventure here. A post office, 24-hour fuel, tire repair, restaurant, and overnight accommodations can be found in this former pipeline camp facility. RV camping, tent sites, and showers also are available. Call 866-474-3400 or 907-474-3500; visit www.coldfootcamp.com.

A popular attraction at Coldfoot is the Arctic Interagency Visitor Center, open daily noon to 10 PM from late May to early September. Three government agencies jointly operate the visitor center with an Alaska Geographic bookstore, plus exhibits and details on local history, natural history, and recreation. Admission is free. The partnership includes the BLM, the US Fish and Wildlife Service, and the National Park Service. For more information, call 907-678-5209.

In 2005, the BLM opened a developed campground at Mile 180. The Marion Creek Campground, five miles north of Coldfoot, has 27 sites, some for RVs, pit toilet, potable water, and trash containers. You can hike upstream to a 20-foot waterfall. This campground is wheelchair accessible.

Wiseman. Gold miners gather where there's gold to be found. Towns are created by the people who follow: the scores who offer services and supplies for those miners. That's how Wiseman came to be, nearly a century ago here in the Koyukuk Mining District. Disconnected from the rest of the world as it was, the town nearly died out before the Haul Rd. was built. Now located about 3 miles (5 km) off the Dalton Hwy. (at Mile 188) and populated by a scant 18 people, it has managed to cling to life as gold and tourism now feed the town. Pay mind to private property as you walk among the log homes—it's easy to imagine this as a Disney set, but people do live and work here! Visit the Wiseman Historical Museum to learn more about local and regional mining history. It's located in the historic Carl Frank cabin in north Wiseman. On the south end of town, cross the river to reach two log cabin-and-breakfast businesses: Arctic Getaway (907-678-4456) and Boreal Lodging (907-678-4566). Ask permission and directions to the old cemetery on a beautiful hillside above town, where many area pioneers (and their pets) have gone to rest.

Continental Divide. Drive through the majestic Brooks Range and cross the northernmost Continental Divide in the United States, at Mile 245. Atigun Pass, at 4,739 feet (1,444 m), is the highest point on the 800-mile north–south route of the pipeline.

The North Slope. To oil company workers, this name—or its abbreviated version, the Slope—is synonymous with Prudhoe Bay. It is derived from a geographical feature. On the north side of the Brooks Range, this country takes its time returning to sea level. It is that slow, almost unrecognizable slope toward the Arctic Ocean that is referred to in *North Slope.*

Deadhorse/Prudhoe Bay. End of the line. Time to buy some souvenirs. One of the earliest T-shirts for sale at the Prudhoe Bay General Store was designed by Clara King. It read: "If you think Hell never freezes over, you've never been to Prudhoe Bay!"

The General Store and US Post Office can be found at the Colville minimall on Old Spine Rd. Send a postcard from the top of the world, buy hand-crafted Native art, pick up some T-shirts bragging that you survived the Dalton Hwy., or sweatshirts, outdoor gear, hats, and more. Those who had visited the old general store won't recognize its modern look in this new location, yet it remains a gathering place for locals. Call 907-659-2412. Accommodations, meals, and fuel can be found in town.

LODGING/MEALS

At or near Yukon River Bridge:
The Hot Spot Café
Mile 60 Dalton Hwy.
907-451-7543
Rooms, burgers, pies, barbecue.

Yukon River Camp
Mile 56 Dalton Hwy.
907-474-3557
www.yukonrivercamp.com
Clean rooms with men's/women's restrooms and showers. Salmon, halibut, burgers, homemade desserts.

Coldfoot:
Coldfoot Camp
Mile 175 Dalton Hwy.
907-474-3500
www.coldfootcamp.com
80 rooms, plus service station, post office, gift shop. RV hookups for water and electric, and dump station. Tent sites available. Buffet-style dining at breakfast and dinner; some deli items, box lunches for the road.

Wiseman:
Arctic Getaway Cabin and Breakfast
Mile 189 Dalton Hwy.
907-678-4456
www.arcticgetaway.com
Located in a historic building: Pioneer Hall, Igloo #8.

Boreal Lodging
South end of Wiseman
907-678-4566
www.boreallodge.com
Cabins, rooms, showers, phone, TV. Aurora-viewing, sled-dog rides in winter.

Deadhorse/Prudhoe Bay:
Arctic Caribou Inn
Near the airport
877-659-2368 or 907-659-2368
75 rooms with private or shared baths. Near restaurant, gift shop, airport. Authorized tours available: oil field, Mile 0 of the pipeline, Arctic Ocean walk.

Arctic Oilfield Hotel
Corner of Sag River Rd. and Spine Rd.
907-659-2614
Rooms, showers, laundry, buffet-style meals. Tire repair, towing, welding.

Deadhorse Camp
Mile 413.6 Dalton Hwy.
877-474-3565
www.deadhorsecamp.com
Rooms, shared bath facilities for Dalton Hwy. travelers in industrial-style lodgings common to Prudhoe Bay. Dining, snacks. Gift shop, tour reservations.

Prudhoe Bay Hotel
Near the Deadhorse Airport
907-659-2449
www.prudhoebayhotel.com
Rooms, showers, laundry, restaurant, gift shop, ATM, Internet, car rental.

CAMPGROUNDS

Coldfoot:
Coldfoot Camp
Mile 175 Dalton Hwy.
907-474-3500
www.coldfootcamp.com
RV hookups and dump station. Service station, post office, gift shop, café, and saloon. Check in at the café desk.

Deadhorse:
Arctic Caribou Inn
Near the airport
877-659-2368 or 907-659-2368
RV parking is available adjacent to this hotel.

Arctic Oilfield Hotel
Corner of Sag River Rd. and Spine Rd.
907-659-2614
RV parking, showers, laundry, buffet-style meals. Tire repair, towing, welding.

BLM oversees four camping areas along the Dalton Hwy. For more information, contact the Northern Field Office in Fairbanks at 800-437-7021 or visit the bureau's website at www.blm.gov/ak/dalton. The camping areas are:

Five Mile
Mile 60 Dalton Hwy.
Undeveloped 5 acres with dump station, potable water, outhouse, 4 miles (6.5 km) north of the Yukon River. No fee.

Arctic Circle Site
Mile 115 Dalton Hwy.
Undeveloped 5 acres above wayside, outhouse, trash. No water. No fee.

Marion Creek Campground
Mile 180 Dalton Hwy.
Developed 1.5 acres with 27 campsites, some for RVs, firepits, potable water, toilets, campground hosts; 2-mile hike upstream to 20-foot waterfall. Fee area.

Galbraith Lake Site
Mile 275 Dalton Hwy.
Undeveloped 5 acres, outhouse, trash. No water. No fee.

A trio of campers found solitude and a perfect view off the Denali Hwy.

DENALI HIGHWAY

From Richardson Hwy. to Parks Hwy.: 136 miles (219 km)

Travel Opportunities: *No towns, just fabulous mountain vistas; hiking, biking, berry picking; fishing at lakes and stream crossings; wildlife- and bird-watching.*

The Denali Hwy. first opened in 1957 as the only road access to what was then called Mount McKinley National Park. The George Parks Hwy., finished in 1972, made the park even more accessible. Using a grand scale, visualize the Richardson Hwy. and George Parks Hwy. as parallel uprights in the letter *H*. Then the Denali Hwy. is the crossbar that joins them. Connecting Paxson on the Richardson Hwy. to Cantwell on the Parks Hwy., this mostly unpaved wilderness road is a 136-mile shortcut through an awesome landscape...or a destination unto itself.

Three major peaks dominate the skyline in this section of the Alaska Range: Mt. Deborah, at 12,339 feet; Mt. Hess, at 11,940 feet; and Mt. Hayes, at 13,892 feet.

In 1980, the national park's name was changed to reflect local use of the name for the highest peak in the continent: Denali. In the Athabascan language, the word means "the

The grayling were rising in the Tangle Lakes area of the Denali Hwy.

high one." The park became Denali National Park and Preserve, though the official name for the peak remains Mt. McKinley.

The park attracts thousands of visitors, who most often arrive via the Alaska Railroad or with major tour operators, such as Gray Line of Alaska and Princess Tours. But the road travelers are many as well. From June through mid-August, RV and tent campers often fill up every available spot in the park's camping areas. (See the section on the Parks Highway, in this chapter, for tips on securing a campsite reservation.)

The Tangle Lakes, Tangle River, and a dozen other lakes and streams along the Denali Hwy. are popular destinations for anglers. Typical in these waters are grayling, whitefish, burbot, and lake trout. Make friends and ask around in Paxson, campgrounds and lodges along the Denali Hwy., or at Cantwell for licensing and tips on what is biting. Consider hiring a guide for a more fulfilling experience.

The Denali Hwy. is a wonderful drive, particularly during sunny days that offer boundless views of the Alaska Range. RV travelers take heed that while the road out of Paxson is paved and broad, after 20 miles (32 km) it is a gravel road that gradually narrows as it journeys west. The maximum recommended speed, even when no one is around, is 30 mph.

There are few services along its length, but plenty at each end. Milepost addresses are measured from Paxson, on the Richardson Hwy. And, of course, keep your eye out for moose and caribou. This is their kind of country, and just the way the other highways used to look.

LODGING/MEALS

Denali Highway Cabins
.2 Denali Hwy. (at Paxson)
907-822-5972
www.denalihwy.com
Logs cabins with queen beds, baths, and decks near the Gulkana River. Wi-Fi, breakfast. Wildlife-watching, tours.

Maclaren River Lodge
Mile 42 Denali Hwy.
907-822-5444
www.maclarenlodge.com
Cabins, campsites, full-service restaurant. Tire repair, gas, tours and guided fishing.

Tangle River Inn
Mile 20 Denali Hwy.
907-822-3970 (summer); 907-892-4022 (winter)
www.tangleriverinn.com
Rooms, cabins, liquor store, bar, restaurant overlooking Tangle Lakes. Canoe rentals.

CAMPGROUNDS

Dry camping at pullouts along the Denali Hwy. is permitted.

BLM oversees two campgrounds:
Tangle Lakes Campground
Mile 21.5 Denali Hwy. (from Paxson)
20 campsites on 60 acres for RV or tent campers. Hand-pumped potable water, wheelchair-accessible toilets, boat launch, fishing.

Brushkana Campground
Mile 104.5 Denali Hwy. (from Paxson)
12 sites for RV or tent campsites with potable water, toilets, picnic shelter.

The derelict Kennecott Copper Mine saw its heyday in the early 20th century and continues to be restored as a visitor attraction near McCarthy. In 1907, railroad builder Michael J. Heney began construction of the 196-mile Copper River Northwestern Railway. The road to McCarthy was built over a portion of the defunct rail bed.

EDGERTON HIGHWAY

From Richardson Hwy. to Chitina: 33 miles (53 km)

From Chitina to McCarthy (on McCarthy Rd.): 60 miles (97 km)

Travel Opportunities: *Athabascan Indian culture in Tonsina and Chitina; fishing or rafting the Copper River; salmon dipnetting in the Chitina River; historic copper-mining town of McCarthy; derelict Kennecott Copper Mine.*

Named for a former member of the Alaska Territorial Road Commission, US Army major Glenn Edgerton, the Edgerton Hwy. is an eastbound spur road off the Richardson Hwy. at a point 32 miles (51.5 km) south of Glennallen, or 83 miles (133.5 km) north of Valdez. You're on pavement for 33 miles (53 km)—to the village of Chitina (CHIT-na)—and there the Edgerton officially ends.

This village lies at the edge of Wrangell-St. Elias National Park and Preserve, 13.2 million acres of some of the most beautiful glaciated mountain wilderness you've ever seen from ground level. From a plane, its mountain peaks and hanging valleys are even more incredible.

This region is the traditional homeland of the Athabascan Indians, and along the Edgerton Hwy. or in Chitina, take advantage of opportunities to purchase locally made Native art, as well as to visit with descendants of the first Alaskans. Roam around Chitina to view evidence of a boomtown grown old. A few buildings have been restored and placed on the National Register of Historic Places.

In the early part of the 20th century, when the Kennecott Copper Mine was in its heyday, Chitina was a busy center of commerce, with hotels, restaurants, saloons, and even a movie theater. Today's Chitina, population 122, is no longer essential to the defunct copper mine, but neither is it a ghost town. As the gateway to Wrangell-St. Elias National Park, the village sees hundreds of visitors annually.

In summer, the tiny population really swells when the salmon are running in the Copper River and the Alaska Department of Fish and Game declares a "subsistence opener." This is a great time to come and watch the fishing action. Monitoring fish numbers throughout each run, the state opens the river to Alaska residents who depend on fish to feed themselves and their families. They hold a special permit for subsistence fishing. Dipnetting is the fast and preferred method of harvesting the fish. It's a partylike atmosphere as men and women don waders and walk into the river with billowy nets attached to a frame with a long handle. The fishing is as simple as dipping into the water and walking back to shore with the fish.

A flightseeing trip out of McCarthy allows some of the best views of the remote regions, including this shot of Russell Glacier, in Wrangell-St. Elias National Park and Preserve.

It's that easy, or hard. These are weighty fish, ranging from 15 to 35 pounds or better.

You may see places along the river where local Athabascan Indians have set up a fish wheel to capture fish using the river current to turn the net-covered arms of the contraption. Beneath the surface, a fish is swept up and out of the water by the net and, as the wheel turns, the fish then drops into a holding box.

Stop at the Wrangell-St. Elias National Park and Preserve ranger station, housed in the historic Ed S. Orr Stage Company cabin, dating from 1910. Volunteers there share their knowledge of Chitina's colorful history and people, with publications, videos, and other resources for travelers. The office is also a good place to ask about weather and road conditions in the park, as well as questions on land ownership, as much of the land is privately owned. Call 907-823-2205.

From Chitina, the unpaved, 60-mile (96.5-km) McCarthy Rd. leads to the village of McCarthy, within the park. At the end of the spur road, you'll park on one side of the Copper River, cross on a footbridge, and take a van or bus ride to visit the old Kennicott town site and the remains of a once-great copper operation: the Kennecott Mine. (The spelling of both place-names is correct. The mine and town names don't match due to a century-old spelling error!)

The McCarthy Rd. is rugged, however, and big-rig RVs would be advised to think twice about making this adventure drive. Even family-car drivers have to stay under 25 mph to keep their hubcaps on, and flat tires are not unusual. Because the road follows the stripped rail bed of the defunct Copper River & Northwestern Railway, drivers should watch out for old railroad spikes, along with potholes, washboard, or slippery sections in the rain. This isn't to say don't go—just know that it will be slow going.

So think about letting someone else do the driving. The Kennicott Shuttle (907-822-5292, www.kennicottshuttle.com) offers scheduled one-way or round-trip van service between Glennallen and McCarthy, and on to Kennicott. Or you can arrange a fly-in day trip between Chitina and Kennicott with Wrangell Mountain Air, based in McCarthy (800-478-1160, www.wrangellmountainair.com). Other charter air services may be arranged out of Gulkana, Glennallen, or Valdez.

The payoff for putting up with the McCarthy Rd. is getting to the village of McCarthy, population 50, in a striking, mountain-rimmed setting. But bear in mind that you can't just drive into the town itself. The McCarthy Rd. ends in a parking area on the west side of the Kennicott River. Overnight parking is permitted for RV travelers. To reach McCarthy, you still must cross the river via footbridge and travel another mile on land (shuttle service is available). The footbridge here is still a fairly new development, dating from 1997. For some, it's a most welcome replacement for the hand-operated cable tram that once spanned the river. Others believe that losing the tram was a blow to what makes McCarthy so charming. Pieces of the tram lie near the bridge. You decide.

This little village was founded in 1910, at the height of the copper rush. Several historic buildings are still standing and still doing business. In summer, the little community buzzes with activity as wilderness guides, bush pilots, anglers, photographers, mountain climbers, and tourists drift in and out of town.

Arrange for a rafting excursion on the Kennicott River; call Wrangell Mountain Air for a flightseeing expedition; book a shuttle ride to the ghost town of Kennicott and wander amid the ruins of a once-great copper mine. All businesses are within walking distance, and the locals will have answers to your questions.

LODGING/CAMPGROUNDS/MEALS

Kenny Lake:
Kenny Lake RV & Mercantile
Mile 7 Edgerton Hwy.
907-822-3313
Rooms with shared baths. Store, fuel, fishing licenses, RV parking for dry or partial hookups. Tent sites, dump station, self-service laundry, showers, pay phone, café.

Liberty Falls State Recreation Site
Mile 23.5 Edgerton Hwy.
Operated by private concession, Taral Enterprises, 907-823-2223
10 sites, picturesque camping near the falls, but the road is not recommended for large RVs. Toilets, no water.

Wrangell View RV Park
Mile 28.7 Edgerton Hwy.
907-823-2255
Full hookups, dump station, store with groceries, fishing licenses.

Chitina:
Gilpatrick's Hotel Chitina
In the heart of Chitina
907-823-2244 (summer)
www.hotelchitina.com
Restored 1914 building features queen beds in rooms with private baths, restaurant, saloon.

McCarthy:
Currant Ridge Cabins
Mile 56.7 McCarthy Rd.
907-554-4424
www.currantridgecabins.com
Modern log cabins, nicely appointed, family owned.

McCarthy Lodge & Ma Johnson's Historic Hotel
Downtown McCarthy
907-554-4402
www.mccarthylodge.com
All-Alaskan decor in 1916 hotel with modern fixtures, lodge, saloon, fine dining.

Kennicott:
Kennicott Glacier Lodge
Kennicott's main street
800-582-5128
www.kennicottlodge.com
A newer facility in the midst of a ghost town with 25 rooms in main lodge; another 10 in new wing. Dining room, spacious porch, overlooking Kennicott Glacier and Chugach Mountains.

Actual gold miners Yukon Yonda and Dexter Clark demonstrate panning at the El Dorado Gold Mine, off the Elliott Hwy. Afterward, visitors are handed a gold poke, or sack, and a gold pan to try their hand at it.

ELLIOTT HIGHWAY

Fox to Manley Hot Springs: 152 miles (245 km)

Travel Opportunities: *Gold panning at El Dorado Gold Mine; viewing the pipeline; views of Minto Flats; hiking BLM trails; fishing the Tolovana River; wildlife-watching; soaking in Manley Hot Springs.*

The Elliott Hwy. begins a short 11 miles (17.5 km) north of Fairbanks, at the town of Fox. At the only intersection in Fox, continue driving straight ahead and you'll be on the Elliott. Travelers who want to stay on the Steese Hwy. and head toward Chatanika, Central, or Circle have to take a hard right. About half of the Elliott is paved, and in these early miles, the surface is lumpy-bumpy from the damaging work of freeze-thaw action.

Just a mile from the intersection, on the left, is one of the most popular attractions in the Fairbanks area: the El Dorado Gold Mine. Featured on several national broadcasts, the two-hour El Dorado tour begins and ends with a ride on a narrow-gauge railroad, on tracks that were recycled from a railway that once operated among the gold-rich fields of this area. The train's engineer is also a fiddler, and his entertainment and narration make for an enjoyable ride as you pass an old sourdough's cabin, enter a permafrost tunnel, and watch antique mining equipment at work once again. Round a bend to an expansive old-time cookshack, where you are greeted by Yukon Yonda and Dexter Clark, a mining team that has been extracting gold from Interior streams and valleys for more than 35 years. Through their demonstration and banter, you learn about modern mining practices. Next, everybody gets to pan, then have their gold weighed in the cookshack/gift shop (866-479-6673 or 907-479-6673; www.eldoradogoldmine.com).

Mile 5.5 is a must-stop if pie is one of your major food groups. The Hilltop Truckstop feeds the truckers and fills the rigs that are coming or going to the North Slope, and visitors are welcome to dine and fuel up as well. There's an ATM, ice, groceries, propane, and showers, as well as a menu of hearty selections. The cream and fruit pies come to the table in slabs, not slices. Try the Fat Man pie.

For Fairbanks-area hikers, the 20-mile trail up Wickersham Dome is a favorite. The trailhead is at Mile 28, providing access to Summit Trail and Wickersham Creek Trail, both in the White Mountains National Recreation Area. Rated easy to moderate, the elevation change is 1,150 feet (350.5 m).

At Mile 71 (Km 113.5), the turnoff leads to the old mining camp known as Livengood. Although you may want to read that as "livin' GOOD," this place-name is actually pronounced "LIE-ven-good" for Jay Livengood, who, with Nathanel R. Hudson, discovered gold near here in 1914. The settlement boomed and gold mining drove the economy for many decades, until it waned. The post office that opened in 1915 finally closed in 1957, when the town was too small to justify it. Livengood was hopping again in 1969–70, with the construction of the 56-mile Livengood Rd., from here to the Yukon River. Within a few years, the road was incorporated into the pipeline's Haul Rd., now the Dalton Hwy. And during the construction of the Trans-Alaska Pipeline, Livengood was one of 29 camps along the 800-mile (1,287.5-km) route. While the old town hints at the millions in gold that was taken out of the Livengood-Tolovana Mining District, large-scale gold-mining operations have ceased; however, there are still active mining claims in this area, so no trespassing, please. Livengood's population is now about 25 people, and there are no visitor services.

The Elliott Hwy. parallels the Trans-Alaska Pipeline for part of its path through the paper birch and spruce forests. You'll catch views of the aboveground stretches of the pipeline flashing silver through the trees. At Mile 73 (Km 117.5), watch for the fork in the road. Here is Mile 0 of the Dalton Hwy., which trends north while the Elliott veers west, toward the Tanana River.

The Elliott's unpaved sections rise above tree line and allow views of grand valleys on either side of this ridge. Beyond them lie the White Mountains. At Mile 110 (Km 177), a spur road leads to the Athabascan Indian village of Minto. Here you can refuel your car and buy something to eat. This village is centrally located in Minto Flats, through which flows the Tolovana River. The area is exceptionally rich in fish, waterfowl, big game, and small furbearers. It is only natural that Alaska Natives would choose this location for its abundant resources. Residents of Minto, like their ancestors for generations before, are dependent upon hunting and fishing to feed their families. However, contemporary Native Alaskans also shop for groceries at the local store or in Fairbanks as well. Here in Minto, you may be able to buy locally made Athabascan crafts, such as a birch-bark basket or finely beaded moosehide slippers.

Even though the Elliott is unpaved and dusty up and down, the exceptional views and the prize at the end of the road make it all worthwhile. The highway dead-ends at Manley Hot Springs, a modest miniresort town that has offered comfort to miners and travelers for more than a century. It's even more historically significant if you consider that the Athabascans of the Interior knew and loved these springs long before the first non-Natives showed up on the scene.

Manley Hot Springs calls to visitors and Fairbanks residents, winter and summer. A quiet town along the Tanana River, Manley's commercial buildings include a trading post and a roadhouse dating from the early 1900s. Follow the road past the old Northern Commercial Co. store to reach the Tanana River and salmon fishing throughout the summer. Today there is no formal hot springs resort, however the Darts, owners of the greenhouse that's fed by the springs, allow visitors to soak for up to an hour in one of three concrete baths for a fee. At Mile 151, turn uphill, park on the road, and walk up the boardwalk to the greenhouse, where posted instructions advise about reservations.

In another mile, at the road's end, you'll find the Manley Roadhouse, circa 1903, which offers rooms, cabins, dining, and a saloon (907-672-3161). Their displays of Alaskan art and artifacts, as well as some great stories, are intriguing.

Winter travelers to Manley are rewarded with exceptional views of the northern lights, dogsled tours, and the opportunity to converse with local mining and dog-mushing folks. Gas and groceries are available at the Manley Trading Post. Roads are spare in town, so it's easy to find your way around. Dry camping is available at the town park, across from the roadhouse, where you can shower and pay your camp fee.

LODGING/MEALS

Manley Hot Springs:
Manley Roadhouse
152 Elliott Hwy.
907-672-3161
Rooms, cabins, dining room, bar. The roadhouse is a historic gem dating from 1903, with historical artifacts on display. Call for reservations.

CAMPGROUNDS

RV travelers are permitted to dry camp in gravel pullouts along the Elliott Hwy.

Olnes Pond Campground
Mile 10.5 Elliott Hwy.
Campsites, toilets, picnic areas, boat ramp, fishing. In the Lower Chatanika State Recreation Area, not maintained.

Whitefish Campground
Mile 11 Elliott Hwy.
Campsites, toilets, picnic areas, boat ramp, fishing. Also in the Lower Chatanika State Recreation Area, not maintained.

Manley Hot Springs:
Manley Roadhouse
152 Elliott Hwy.
Camping available near the bridge over Manley Slough.
Park with campground, playground, picnic area. Operated by Manley Hot Springs Park Association. Pay at the roadhouse, where showers also are available for a fee.

GLENN HIGHWAY (INCLUDING THE TOK CUTOFF)

Tok to Anchorage: 328 miles (528 km)

Travel Opportunities: *Glennallen; Matanuska Glacier and River; Musk Ox Farm; Independence Mine; Palmer Visitor Center and Garden; Reindeer Farm; Eklutna; Anchorage-area attractions.*

The Glenn Hwy. is a well-traveled route because it connects the Anchorage area (where nearly half the state population lives) to the towns and wilderness areas along the Glenn and Richardson hwys. Further, this is the way to Tok, the Alaska Hwy., and the most-used route to the Lower 48. Likewise, if you're headed into Alaska from Canada and Anchorage is your destination, the Glenn is your highway. The Glenn is the single most important east–west road in the state highway grid.

The Glenn's official start is at Tok, at Mile 1314 (Km 2114.5) Alaska Hwy., where the Glenn branches south and west toward Anchorage, 328 miles (528 km) away. The first 125 miles (200 km) of the Glenn are widely known as the Tok Cutoff—a shortcut between the Alaska Hwy. and the Richardson Hwy. In fact, it may come as a surprise to many Alaskans that this section actually is a part of the Glenn.

After leaving Tok, don't expect to find much development or services along this subtly beautiful stretch of road. An exception is the area of the Eagle Trail State Recreation Site, about 16 miles (26 km) from Tok, which offers a campground with 35 sites, picnic shelter, water, toilets, interpretive signs, and trailhead access. A handful of B&Bs, lodges, and gas stations are tucked into the woods, so watch for their signs.

The Glenn Hwy. connects east-central Alaska with the state's biggest city: Anchorage.

The road crosses Mentasta Summit (2,434 ft/742 m) about 45 miles (72 km) from Tok. From here, most of the Tok Cutoff follows the boundary of Wrangell-St. Elias National Park and Preserve. These northern lowlands of the park are inhabited by caribou, moose, black and brown bears, coyotes, and numerous other creatures.

The cutoff connects with the Richardson Hwy. near the village of Gulkana, about 15 miles (24 km) north of Glennallen. The most traveled portion of the Glenn begins at Glennallen, 139 miles (223.5 km) from Tok at the busy junction of the east–west Glenn Hwy. and the north–south Richardson Hwy. For decades, a gas station on this corner has called itself, in large letters, The Hub of Alaska. It's an active intersection with more than just fuel and snacks for travelers on either road. A spacious visitor center next door is staffed with informative people, along with the usual brochures and newsletters. For more information on local history, businesses, and attractions, call 907-822-5558.

Glennallen is the unofficial capital of this region, situated on the western edge of Wrangell-St. Elias Park and 189 miles (304 km) from Anchorage. This region is the traditional homeland of the Athabascan Indians, who have lived in the Copper River basin for centuries. When a US military party of explorers came through here in 1885, they were amazed at the accuracy of the hand-drawn maps they received from Native Alaskans who assisted them. (Glennallen is named for two of those explorers: Capt. Edwin F. Glenn and Lt. Henry T. Allen.)

Several viewpoint pullouts feature fantastic views of the Matanuska Glacier.

Athabascans continue to fish and hunt for food (as do many other groups who have arrived in the last 120 years). Some people trap for furs; others work at local businesses. Sales of locally made craft items such as birch-bark baskets and beaded combs, slippers, and earrings help support a small cottage industry. Watch for parking-lot craft fairs, where you can learn more about local culture as well as pick up some wonderful gifts.

The Copper River basin is especially popular for winter recreation, such as snowmobiling, skiing, and snowshoeing. Flightseeing, mountaineering, hiking, biking, fishing, and rafting are favorite summertime activities. Numerous creeks and lakes are suitable for a fine day of fishing. For fishing regulations and openers, check with the Alaska Department of Fish and Game office in Glennallen, downtown at Mile 186 (Km 299) Glenn Hwy. Call 907-822-3309. Licenses are available at most retail outlets or online. See www.admin.adfg.state.ak.us/license. You'll need access to a printer to print out proof of your licensing.

From Glennallen, the westward way begins flat and fairly straight, while to the east, the peaks of the Wrangell Mountains are standouts on clear days. On either side of the road, you'll see occasional boggy lowlands and sad, spindly-looking spruce trees that tell a story about survival against the odds. These used pipe cleaners are black spruce trees, tenaciously growing in poorly drained soil where permafrost is present. Their root systems are so shallow that they sometimes tip over into each other, hence the name Drunken Forest. Because of the seasonal freeze and thaw of permafrost, this road can be wavy or sunken in places. Watch for flagged signs that warn Dip in Road. They really mean it.

The state maintains small recreation sites in the stretch between Glennallen and Palmer, with camping, water, and toilets. They include Little Nelchina, at Mile 137.5 (Km 221); Matanuska Glacier, at Mile 101 (Km 162.5); Long Lake, at Mile 85 (Km 136.5); and King Mountain, at Mile 76 (Km 126.5). All distances are from Anchorage.

The land changes as you travel west through dry, treeless uplands and farther still into dazzling mountainous beauty. The road bends, rises, and falls as you follow the Matanuska River valley, which flows between rocky mountains that turn purple in a certain light. This silty, braided river is a head-turner. You'll see it from various angles and elevations along the way, and its beauty is enhanced by the changes in light and weather.

Views of Matanuska Glacier only get better and better. Stop at the marked waysides that offer photo opportunities, or you'll always regret that you didn't. In broad daylight, the glacier is brilliant white with hints of blue, but overcast days are best, when the blue of the glacier seems to glow from within. The Matanuska River, which flows from beneath the glacier, is a milky gray color due to the ground rock flour that is suspended in its water. Float trips or white-water adventures can be arranged at sites along the highway (watch for signs) or in Palmer, 42 miles (67.5 km) north of Anchorage.

About 74 miles from Anchorage, watch for a distinctive rock formation called Lion Head that at first looks like it's blocking the road. This striking feature is a glacial erratic, a minimountain shaped by the Matanuska Glacier as it retreated from the area.

Between Glennallen and Palmer, you can stop at remote, family-operated roadhouses, campgrounds, and restaurants—such as Tolsona Lake Resort (Mile 170.5 from Anchorage), Sheep Mountain Lodge (Mile 113.5), or Long Rifle Lodge (Mile 102)—to bring even more color to your trip.

As you approach Palmer from the east, you'll see signs and a right turnoff at Mile 50 for the Musk Ox Farm, a don't-miss attraction with tour guides to explain the animals' natural history. A herd of musk oxen here are descended from animals transported to Alaska from Greenland in the 1930s. Musk oxen had roamed Alaska since prehistory, until about 1885, when the last of their kind was hunted. The Greenland emigrants were an experiment that flourished in Alaska. Wild herds have been restored, and two domesticated herds exist here and at the University of Alaska Fairbanks. Also, because of the animals, a cottage industry developed among Alaska Native women who knit

Many buildings on the grounds of the historic Gakona Lodge & Trading Post, at Mile 2 Tok Cutoff, have been around since the early days of Alaska's first roads, which followed ancient trails of local Native people. The lodge is on the National Register of Historic Places.

garments from the spun underwool, called qiviut (KIV-ee-oot). A gift shop here and in Anchorage features their handiwork. Tours introduce you to these unique animals and the wonderfully warm and soft garments made from their qiviut. For information, call 907-745-4151 or see www.muskoxfarm.org or www.qiviut.com.

Palmer is 42 miles (67.5 km) northeast of Anchorage, or 147 miles (236.5 km) west of Glennallen. During the Great Depression of the 1930s, the federal government offered Midwest farmers the opportunity to move to this valley for a fresh start in a new land, in a program known as the Matanuska-Susitna Colony Project. Whole families arrived to find that their free land first needed clearing of trees and rocks, and many spent their first cruel winter in a canvas tent with wood floors and a hungry woodstove. Through their hard work and perseverance, the community took root and thrived.

The colony project was the settlement seed for what is now the community of Palmer, with a population of about 5,500. Many descendants of those settlers still live in the Matanuska-Susitna (or Mat-Su) Valley. As you drive along the Glenn Hwy., you'll see farmhouses and barns built in a style reminiscent of the Midwest. Wheat, hay, potatoes, lettuce, tomatoes, carrots, cabbages—the land keeps providing, and the abundance of grain and produce continues to support valley farmers.

Palmer is the seat of the Alaska State Fair, where the stiffest agricultural competition is seen in the giant-vegetables category. Under a blessed 22 hours of summer sunlight, Palmer farmers grow cabbages that balloon to between 40 and 60 pounds. Squash, carrots, and other vegetables thrive in the cool soil and long doses of sunlight. If you're in Alaska in late August and early September, stop by the Palmer fairgrounds to see the giants for yourself, and enjoy the midway rides, food booths, and equestrian competitions. Although it's an Alaska state fair, it feels as cozy as a Kansas county fair, until you lift your eyes and take in the peaks of the Chugach Range, which seems to be just a field away.

Streams and lakes in this valley yield world-class fishing in picturesque settings. Anglers routinely land prized king salmon weighing an average of 20 to 30 pounds, but these fish can reach 70 pounds. Other salmon runs include reds, chums, pinks, and

DAY-TRIPPING IN THE MOUNTAINS

Incredible beauty and gold-mining history combine to make this side trip a memorable drive for the day or even an overnight, but it's not recommended for the big rigs, as a portion of the gravel segment is narrow, steep, and includes switchbacks. If you're still game, turn north off the Glenn Hwy. at Mile 49 (Km 79) and follow Hatcher Pass Rd. This 49-mile road is paved for the first 17 miles and the last 10 miles, where it descends and meets the Parks Hwy. From the Palmer side, the route follows the course of a boulder-strewn, fast-moving stream. Watch for pullouts to let faster drivers pass by, or stop for a picnic and stick your toes in these chilly waters.

From the Palmer side, Independence Mine Historical Park is just over 17 miles (27.5 km) up the road, at Hatcher Pass (elevation 3,886 feet). Getting there is slow driving at times. Where it isn't paved, it's dusty gravel with potholes and washboard that slow you down in a hurry. But it's still worth the effort, and there are gravel pullouts along the way. Walking trails lead throughout this extensive mine site, which includes restored buildings as well as others still in progress. The visitor center is a museum itself, the 1939-era home of the mine manager for the Alaska Pacific Consolidated Mine Co. Nearby, overnight accommodations and meals are available at Hatcher Pass Lodge. Call 907-745-5897 or visit the lodge's website, www.hatcherpasslodge.com.

silvers. Trout, Dolly Varden, northern pike, arctic grayling, and other species also are found in local waters. Pick up your required license at any number of retail outlets, from grocery stores to sporting goods stores.

In Palmer, turn east off the Glenn Hwy. and drive four blocks to the railroad tracks. Across the tracks from the old railroad depot, you'll see the Palmer Museum & Visitor Center, at 723 S. Valley Wy., a log building where a history of the colony can be found in photos and artifacts, and a gift shop stocked with Alaska souvenirs. Ask about a walking tour of Palmer's historic buildings. Call 907-745-8878 or see www.palmermuseum.org.

Next door to the visitor center is the Matanuska Valley Agricultural Showcase, where local gardeners have done a magnificent job of showing what happens when skilled hands sow seed under the midnight sun. Walk around the garden paths for a peaceful break from traveling.

If you thought reindeer could only be found at North Pole, AK, think again. The Reindeer Farm at Mile 11.5 Old Glenn Hwy. invites visitors to step inside and pet their friendly reindeer. Tour guides inform about reindeer biology and the difference between reindeer and wild caribou. They also house moose, elk, and bison here. Stop by the gift shop for a unique souvenir. See www.reindeerfarm.com or call 907-745-4000.

Just a few miles south of Palmer, the Glenn Hwy. is joined by the Parks Hwy., south-bound from Fairbanks, in a recently constructed series of exits and on-ramps that are easy to negotiate and (happily for Alaskans) eliminated a time-consuming, three-way intersection. The Glenn is in excellent shape from here all the way to Anchorage, with four lanes of traffic and a legal speed of 65 mph. The lay of the land changes as you follow the Glenn around this side of the Chugach Range. The divided highway passes through a broad expanse of wild grasses dotted with tall trees that look like they died a long time ago—which they did. This is the Palmer Hay Flats State Game Refuge, which supports a diversity of wildlife, from big game to eagles to waterfowl and more. This entire region dropped several feet during the 1964 Good Friday Earthquake, which damaged so much of the Anchorage coastline. Seawater flooded in, killing mature trees and creating wetlands where once there had been hayfields.

Up ahead, two four-lane bridges cross the Knik (kuh-NIK) River, a popular staging area for waterfowl hunters. Because Cook Inlet experiences such extreme tides (up to 30 feet), the tidal zone of the Knik River likewise fluctuates dramatically. Consequently, it's not a great place for recreational boating.

Twenty-four miles (38.5 km) from Anchorage, an exit leads to Eklutna Historical Park, which includes St. Nicholas Russian Orthodox Church, the Heritage Museum, and nearby graveyard. Developed by the Athabascan residents of Eklutna village (around 400 people), the park offers tours and cultural interpretation. A fee is charged. The tradition of placing brightly colored spirit houses over the graves is neither com-pletely Orthodox nor completely Athabascan. As in other areas of the state, Western religions have been integrated into the Native culture, and some practices reflect a unique third culture. Although the residents of Eklutna live close to Alaska's biggest city, many continue in a largely subsistence-based life, hunting and fishing for much of their diet. Grocery stores supply the rest. For information on the historical park, call St. Nicholas Russian Orthodox Church at 907-688-6026.

Inside the city limits of Anchorage, the Glenn Hwy. peters out, unmarked, some-where along the small-plane airport called Merrill Field. Stay on the same road and it becomes 5th Ave., which leads you into the downtown core.

Anchorage

Born of necessity, as many Alaska towns were, Anchorage was once a tent city along the muddy banks of Ship Creek. The people who gathered here in 1915 were builders of the Alaska Railroad, their families, hoteliers, restaurateurs, laundry operators, freight haulers, and others who supplied services.

When conditions at the tent city became dangerously overcrowded, threatening disease, officials took charge and cleared building lots on the bluff overlooking the creek.

Each weekend, the Anchorage Market and Festival at 3rd and E streets attracts crowds to shop and graze among many vendor stalls. This playful businessman was selling reindeer sausage on a bun.

In July 1915, town-site lots were auctioned off, and building began immediately. Today, few original homes or businesses exist, mainly because they were wooden and therefore fairly expendable as the town matured. Notable survivors include two side-by-side buildings on the 5th Ave. and E St. corner of Town Square.

Anchorage is Alaska's biggest city, with close to 300,000 people, nearly half of the state's population. It is an international crossroads in passenger and air cargo, as well as headquarters for the biggest names in the oil industry. This modern community is bordered on the north by military installations, on the east by the Chugach Range, on the south by Chugach National Forest, and on the west by Cook Inlet. Options for city sprawl are limited. Its proximity to wilderness means that moose often wander into the streets, making the Anchorage bowl a unique urban habitat. Car-moose encounters are causing city officials to ponder what to do as moose numbers continue to multiply. Seasonally, bear sightings in urban areas keep residents on alert, and they're especially careful about storing their garbage.

The Log Cabin Visitor Information Center, on the corner of 4th Ave. and F St., is operated by the Anchorage Convention and Visitors Bureau. Staffers can answer questions about local tours, restaurants, and best views, as well as direct you to a self-guided historical walking tour. Call 907-276-4118 or see www.anchorage.net. Downtown, it's also fun to watch (or participate) in the Ship Creek fishery. Where else on the planet can a tourist walk a few blocks from a major downtown hotel, slip on a pair of waders, and fish for wild Pacific salmon? Check at your hotel's front desk for guidance, or contact the Anchorage Convention and Visitors Bureau.

The outline of Mt. Susitna, or the Sleeping Lady, is well known and loved by Anchorage residents. The name recalls an Athabascan legend of a giant woman who is reclining, waiting for the return of her man.

In summer, Anchorage is a tourism hub. For Alaskans from all over the state, it's a shopping mecca year-round. Its downtown streets are filled with color and the contagious enthusiasm of people. Gift shops, restaurants, street vendors, and musicians lend a partylike atmosphere to every summer day. Dining experiences can range from a stop at a fast-food outlet, hot dog stand, grocery-store deli, or burger joint to elegant dining above Cook Inlet. I suggest you steer away from eating at a chain restaurant and experience a locally owned establishment. If you get the chance, taste reindeer sausage, which is offered on many breakfast menus or at street-cart purveyors.

As Alaska's biggest city and hub of two major highways, this is an ideal spot to consider renting an RV if you didn't arrive in one. You may contact any number of local businesses for daily or weekly rentals (for a list, see the Traveling by RV section in Chapter 1, Planning and Packing). If you are traveling in your own RV, this is a good place to take care of any mechanical or windshield repairs or have your oil changed.

Walking 4th and 5th aves. on foot, you can stop in and book a glacier day cruise on Prince William Sound or on Resurrection Bay, south of Anchorage. Tour operators usually offer rail or shuttle transportation to harbor cities. Down the street, you can book a flightseeing trip to fly over Mt. McKinley and even land on a glacier to walk a bit. Large coaches provide day trips around town, north to the Matanuska-Susitna Valley, south to Portage Glacier, and beyond. Many adventure travelers book fly-in fishing or visits to remote luxury lodges, which include gourmet cooking along with guided trips.

If shopping for Alaska Native–made art is part of your plan—or a pure impulse—learn to read labels. A label with a silver hand indicates a guarantee that the item was made by an Alaska Native artisan. A label with a mom-and-baby-bear silhouette is an official Made in Alaska indicator, but the maker may be an Alaskan company or a state resident, not necessarily an Alaska Native.

Soak up local color as you stroll around downtown. Especially popular is 4th Ave., where in summer every lamppost bears two huge flower baskets of lobelia and marigold, representing Alaska's state colors, blue and gold. In Anchorage's mild temperatures and prolonged light, the flowers are extraordinarily bright and fresh, here and in gardens throughout the city. Due to the low angle of the sun, there is little midday heat to wilt them. Each year, Anchorage recognizes its exceptional gardeners via the city's designation as City of Flowers. If you can't get your fill of flowers, visit the Alaska Botanical Garden for a self-guided tour through their spectacular gardens. Call 907-770-3692 or see www.alaskabg.org for more information.

All winter long, as dusk comes earlier and daybreak comes later, the Anchorage Chamber of Commerce calls for everybody to lighten up with the seasonal theme "City of Lights." Millions of tiny white lights decorate trees, homes, and businesses, further illuminating the snow and creating a sparkling winter wonderland.

Follow the crowds to the outdoor market in Anchorage, where about 400 vendors gather every weekend in the summer, from late May to early September. This minifair includes entertainment, food booths, crafts, and sales of Mat-Su Valley vegetables. On Saturday and Sunday, explore the Anchorage Market and Festival at the 3rd Ave. and E St. parking lot downtown (907-272-5634; www.anchoragemarkets.com).

Other attractions of the Anchorage area include:

Anchorage Fur Rendezvous. This is the country's biggest winter carnival, celebrated in Anchorage at the end of February. Events include snowshoe softball and a waiter/waitress competition in which contestants run an obstacle course while carrying a tray of drinks. Craft fairs, Native art sales, a fur auction, carnival rides, snow sculpture competitions, and an Eskimo blanket toss are other highlights. Don't miss the Outhouse Race, or the Frostbite Footrace. The mainstay of this annual winter carnival is the World Championship Sled Dog Races, with dogs and drivers lining up to start the race on 4th Ave. See www.furrondy.net.

Wild Ride Sled Dog Show. Iditarod Trail Sled Dog Race champion Mitch Seavey, along with other mushers, offer this family-oriented show that's all about the dogs. There are amazing stories from the trail, demonstrations of sled-dog athleticism, and photo ops with Flapjack, a beautiful malamute that starred in the Disney film *Eight Below*. Free shuttle service to the Ship Creek site is available from many downtown locations. Call 907-561-MUSH or check the showtimes, fees, and shuttle schedules on www.iditarodexperience.com.

Iditarod Trail Sled Dog Race. Winter visitors can witness the excitement of the Iditarod starting line, set on 4th St. in downtown Anchorage, on the first Saturday in March. Each year the men, women, and dogs of the 1,049-mile (1,688-km) race are the stars as thousands jam the sidewalks to watch them set out for Nome. (The actual mileage is closer to 1,150. Early organizers called it a 1,000-mile race; the 49 was added as a nod to Alaska as the 49th state.) The Iditarod headquarters and museum is in Wasilla, north of Anchorage off the Parks Hwy. Call 907-376-5155 or visit www.iditarod.com.

The 4th Avenue Marketplace, at 333 W. 4th Ave., is home to the *Alaska Experience Theatre*, where showings of incredible 3-D movies make it possible for you to fly over Alaska, sense the 1964 earthquake's destructive power, and virtually sit under the northern lights. The market also features a permanent art exhibit of a favorite son, the late Fred Machetanz, who lived on 4th Ave. when Anchorage was a newborn town. In the summer, Alaska Native dancers perform three times a week in full regalia, and visitors can enjoy the Alaska Salmon Bake nightly at the Alaska Experience Theatre. Call 907-272-9076 for reservations or get your tickets online at www.alaskaexperiencetheatre.com.

Alaska Railroad. Daily north–south rail service between Anchorage and Fairbanks, with stops in Wasilla, Talkeetna, and Denali National Park and Preserve. Travel in first-class luxury with GoldStar service in a double-decked domed railcar with clear views on both sides of the train, or reserve a seat in a standard railcar, which still affords beautiful views of the wilderness route. Southbound passengers travel between Anchorage and Whittier or Anchorage and Seward. Dining cars and bar service are still part of the package for America's northernmost rail line. See the Alaska Railroad website for the full menu of travel choices, including rail/cruise, rail/bus, and rail/tour packages. Make your reservation at least 24 in advance. Call 907-265-2494 or toll-free at 800-544-0552. Online, see www.alaskarailroad.com. Also offering specialty railcar tours: Gray Line of Alaska (800-452-1737; www.graylinealaska.com) and Princess Tours Rail Operations (800-426-0500; www.princesslodges.com) can advise on special tour packages and travel in their privately owned, luxury-service domed railcars. The Anchorage Depot is located at 411 W. 1st Ave. (below the bluff) and includes a gift shop.

Chugach State Park. Serving as a spectacular backdrop for Alaska's biggest city, the Chugach Range lies along the eastern edge of Anchorage. Here, too, is Chugach State Park, nearly a half million acres, an extremely popular getaway for hikers, bikers, picnickers, or those who simply want to drive uphill and get a great view of the city and the twin bodies of water around it, Knik Arm and Turnagain Arm.

A hike up the sawed-off mountain known as Flattop is invigorating, yet suitable for a family outing. Groomed trails lead the way from the Glenn Alps parking area. On clear days, you can see Mt. McKinley from here. Park headquarters is in the Potter Section House, just south of Anchorage on the Seward Hwy., but the park is accessible from Anchorage's Hillside area as well as from Eagle River. For directions and information, call park headquarters at 907-345-5014. See www.anchorage.net/hike for details on accessing Flattop and other hikes.

Alaska Wild Berry Park. Meet a reindeer, pose by a giant rock man, and watch the experts make the candy you'll want to take home with you. This place has something for everybody, including the chocoholic in the family who will want to dive into the 20-foot chocolate waterfall. Hourly showings on widescreen theater of *Alaska: The Land Beyond* and *Alaska Spirit of the Wild.* Bring the family to 5225 Juneau St. Call 800-280-2927 or 907-562-8858. See www.alaskawildberryproducts.com.

Alaska Native Heritage Center. One of Anchorage's most popular attractions focuses on the wonders and diversity of Alaska's Native cultures. It's a gorgeous place, located near the intersection of Glenn Hwy. and Muldoon Rd. The Heritage Center features art, music, photography, films, and a variety of exhibits. The spacious Welcome House at the center offers programs of dancing and singing in the theater, photography and artifact exhibits, and a chance to watch an artist at work. In fact, all summer long, from 9 AM to 5 PM daily, you can observe a carver at work. From the Welcome House, paths lead to five village settings that show traditional home-building methods and tools. Interpreters from each culture are on-site too. Free shuttle service from several downtown locations, or book a package through the Alaska Railroad and arrive by train. Call 907-330-8000 or browse www.alaskanative.net.

Anchorage Museum at Rasmuson Center. The museum, at 121 W. 7th Ave., is an architectural beauty. Recently expanded, the facility holds permanent and rotating exhibits of art, history, and science treasures. The Alaska Gallery includes exquisite displays from Alaska's Native, Russian, and US history, along with small-scale and full-size dioramas of early Native Alaska life. Other features include a children's gallery, gift shop, café, and special programs in a theater that entertains visitors and residents year-round. The new Thomas Planetarium features three shows daily. For more information, call 907-343-4326 or browse www.anchoragemuseum.org.

Other popular museums include the fantastic Alaska Aviation Heritage Museum, near the airport (907-248-5325; www.alaskaairmuseum.org), the Alaska Law Enforcement Museum, downtown at 245 W. 5th Ave. (907-279-5050; www.alaskatroopermuseum.com), and the Alaska Heritage Museum, housed in the Wells Fargo Building, 301 W. Northern Lights Blvd. (907-265-2834). Open daily from noon to 4 PM, the collection includes Alaska Native artifacts, Alaska fine art, and a 2,600-volume Alaska reference book library.

Town Square Park. A small army of city gardeners takes exquisite care of this floral showcase. Split by curving paths, with a simple fountain at the center, Town Square Park is frequented by businesspeople, travelers, walkers, and people-watchers. In places, inscribed sidewalk bricks pay homage to people and businesses that have helped make Anchorage great. The adjoining Alaska Center for the Performing Arts is a venue for national and international talent, further evidence that Anchorage has come a long way since its days as a tent city.

LODGING

The Mat-Su Bed & Breakfast Association has information on rooms, apartments, and cabins from Glennallen to Anchorage to Denali. Visit the association's website, www.alaskabnbhosts.com.

Tok: See listings in the section on Tok in Chapter 6, The Alaska Highway.

Glennallen:
Caribou Hotel
Mile 187 Glenn Hwy.
907-822-3302
www.caribouhotel.com
55 rooms, suites, kitchenettes, wheelchair access. Satellite TV, whirlpool. Caribou Café family restaurant, gift shop, fuel, propane, tires.

Gakona Lodge & Trading Post
Mile 2 Tok Cutoff (Glenn Hwy.)
907-822-3482
www.gakonalodge.com
Rooms and cabins at confluence of Gakona and Copper rivers in collection of old and newer buildings. Historic 1904 roadhouse from the Valdez–Fairbanks Trail still stands, but travelers stay in comfortable, modern accommodations. Restaurant, saloon, guided fishing and other tours.

Lake Louise Lodge
Mile 160 Glenn Hwy. turnoff to Mile 16 Lake Louise Rd.
877-878-3311 or 907-822-3311
www.lakelouiselodge.com
Log lodge with rooms and cabins, free breakfast and use of canoe. RV parking with electric. Fuel, propane, oil. Full-service restaurant. Swimming, fishing, boating. Open year-round.

The Point Lodge
Mile 160 Glenn Hwy. turnoff to Mile 17 Lake Louise Rd.
800-808-2018 or 907-822-5566
www.thepointlodge.com
13 comfortable rooms in a Lake Louise lodge with water on three sides. Hearty meals, plenty of recreational activities.

Sutton:
Matanuska Lodge
34301 W. Glenn Hwy.
907-746-0378
www.matanuskalodge.com
Private rooms and baths in lodge setting. Breakfast, dinner, hot tub. Lake access.

Palmer:
Alaska Choice Inn Motel
Mile 41 Glenn Hwy., across from Alaska State Fairgrounds
907-745-1505
www.alaskachoiceinnmotel.com
30 rooms and suites, fridge, microwave, free Wi-Fi, plenty of parking, satellite television, free local calls. Pets on approval.

Colony Inn
325 Elmwood St.
907-745-3330
Charming rooms decorated with antiques; located in former teachers' dorm from the 1935 Mat-Su Colony. In the heart of town; walk to shopping and attractions.

Fox Run Lodge & RV Campground
Mile 36 Glenn Hwy., on Matanuska Lake
877-745-6120 or 907-745-6120
www.foxrun.freeservers.com
Rooms and efficiencies overlooking Matanuska
Lake. Camping area. Boat rental, tackle.

Gold Miner's Hotel
918 S. Colony Wy.
800-7ALASKA or 907-745-6160
Large rooms, all with fridge and microwave.
Restaurant, lounge. Downtown location. Pets upon
approval.

Pioneer Motel
124 W. Arctic Ave.
907-745-3425
www.thepioneermotel.com
28 units with cable TV. Daily or weekly rentals.
Dogs on approval. Veterans and senior discounts.

Valley Hotel
606 S. Alaska St.
800-478-7666 or 907-745-3330
Rooms with private bath, cable TV. 24-hour coffee
shop. Lounge, liquor store.

Anchorage:
*For B&B accommodations, call the Anchorage
Alaska Bed & Breakfast Association at 888-
584-5147 or 907-272-5909, or browse www
.anchorage-bnb.com.*

America's Best Value Inn Executive Suite Hotel
4360 Spenard Rd.
907-243-6366
www.executivesuitehotel.com
35 rooms, near airport. Free continental breakfast,
shuttle. Close to dining and attractions.

Anchorage Grand Hotel
505 W. 2nd Ave.
888-800-0640 or 907-929-8888
www.anchoragegrandhotel.com
31 luxury suites, kitchen, cable TV, Internet, free
continental breakfast. Downtown location.

Anchorage Marriott Downtown
820 W. 7th Ave.
800-228-9290 or 907-279-8000
www.marriott.com
392 rooms in full-service hotel. Pool,
exercise facility.

Best Western Golden Lion Hotel
1000 E. 36th Ave.
907-564-2464
www.bestwesterngoldenlion.com
83 large rooms with microwave, fridges,
exercise room, restaurant.

Clarion Suites
325 W. 8th Ave.
888-389-6575 or 907-274-1000
www.clarionhotel.com
Suites with fridge, microwave, phone, two TVs.
Free continental breakfast. Pool, spa. Free 24-hour
airport and train shuttle.

Coast International Inn
3450 Aviation Ave.
800-544-0986 or 907-243-2233
www.intlinnanchorage.com
141 rooms with coffeemakers, hair dryers. Sauna,
fitness center, restaurant, lounge. Free airport
shuttle.

Comfort Inn
111 W. Ship Creek
800-4CHOICE or 907-277-6887
100 rooms and suites, free continental breakfast.
Indoor pool, spa. Along Ship Creek, downtown.
Airport shuttle.

Courtyard by Marriott
4901 Spenard Rd.
907-349-6478
www.marriott.com
Spacious luxury guest rooms, fitness center, pool,
restaurant, lounge.

Creekwood Inn
2150 Gambell St.
800-478-6008 or 907-258-6006
www.creekwoodinn-alaska.com
Rooms and cabins with private bath, kitchenettes.
Coffee, cable TV, data ports, bicycle rentals.
Blackout curtains against the midnight sun.

Crowne Plaza Anchorage–Midtown
109 W. International Airport Rd.
877-348-2424 or 907-433-4100
www.crowneplaza.com/anchorageak
165 guest rooms in midtown location, free Wi-Fi,
fitness center, saline pool and spa. Meetings room,
business center.

Days Inn Downtown
321 E. 5th Ave.
800-DAYSINN or 907-276-7226
www.daysinnalaska.com
130 rooms, Internet, near shopping
and restaurants.

Dimond Center Hotel
700 E. Dimond Blvd.
866-770-5002 or 907-770-5000
www.dimondcenterhotel.com
Boutique hotel next to major shopping mall. Free
breakfast, wireless, free shuttle.

Embassy Suites Anchorage
600 E. Benson Blvd.
907-332-7000
www.anchorage.embassysuites.com
All luxury, full-service suites. Pool, fitness center, business center, parking, local shuttle, free cooked-to-order breakfast buffet.

Fairfield Inns & Suites Anchorage Midtown
5060 A St.
888-236-2427 or 907-222-9000
www.fairfieldinnanchorage.com
Spacious units in full-service facility. Midtown location.

Hampton Inn
4301 Credit Union Dr.
800-HAMPTON or 907-550-7000
www.hamptoninn.com
Rooms with deluxe breakfast. Indoor pool, fitness facility. Midtown location. Free shuttle.

Hawthorn Suites by Wyndham
1110 W. 8th Ave.
888-469-6575 or 907-222-5005
www.hawthorn.com
Comfortable suites with fridge and microwave. Free breakfast buffet, parking, wireless, pool, shuttle. Downtown location.

Hilton Anchorage
500 W. 3rd Ave.
800-245-2527 or 907-272-7411
www.hiltonanchorage.com
Deluxe accommodations, fitness room, gift shops, three restaurants. Walking distance to downtown attractions.

Hilton Garden Inn Anchorage
4555 Union Square Dr.
800-HILTONS or 907-729-7000
www.hiltongardeninn.hilton.com
Rooms include free Internet. Pool, fitness facility. Free shuttle.

Historic Anchorage Hotel
330 E St.
800-544-0988 or 907-272-4553
www.historicanchoragehotel.com
Boutique hotel in central downtown location. Free breakfast, newspaper, Internet. On National Register of Historic Places.

Holiday Inn Express–Anchorage Airport
4411 Spenard Rd.
800-HOLIDAY or 907-248-8848
www.hieanchorage.come
Rooms with pool, spa, fitness facility, free continental breakfast, shuttle. Near airport.

Homewood Suites by Hilton Anchorage
101 W. 48th
800-225-5466 or 907-762-7000
www.anchorage.homewoodsuites.com
Studios, 1- and 2-bedroom suites in midtown, fully equipped kitchens. Premium cable channels, clock radio with MP3 connection, complimentary hot breakfast.

Hotel Captain Cook
4th Ave. and K St.
800-843-1950 or 907-276-6000
www.captaincook.com
Rooms and suites, health club, travel agency, gift stores, café, lounge. Penthouse-level restaurant with view. Central downtown location.

Howard Johnson Plaza Hotel
239 W. 4th Ave.
800-446-4656 or 907-793-5500
www.hjplazaanchorage.com
Downtown location, close to attractions, shopping, dining. Indoor pool.

Inlet Tower Hotel & Suites
1200 L St.
800-544-0786 or 907-276-0110
www.inlettower.com
Boutique hotels offers free parking, free airport shuttle. Restaurant.

Lake Hood Inn
4702 Spenard Rd.
866-663-9322 or 907-258-9321
www.lakehoodinn.com/acvb
Rooms with private decks overlooking floatplane lake. Near airport. Free continental breakfast, airport shuttle.

Lakeshore Motor Inn
3009 Lakeshore Dr.
800-770-3000 or 907-248-3485
www.lakeshoremotorinn.com
45 rooms and suites close to airport and Lake Hood.

Long House Alaskan Hotel Anchorage
4335 Wisconsin St.
888-243-2133 or 907-243-2133
www.longhousehotel.com
54 rooms, free continental breakfast. Close to airport; shuttle service.

Microtel Inn & Suites Anchorage–Airport
5205 Northwood Dr.
888-771-7171 or 907-245-5002
www.microtelanchorage.com
Rooms, suites, free continental breakfast, laundry facility. Close to airport; shuttle service.

Millennium Alaskan Hotel Anchorage
4800 Spenard Rd.
800-544-0553 or 907-243-2300
www.millenniumhotels.com/anchorage
248 deluxe guest rooms, some lakeside rooms with views of floatplanes. Wildlife displays, historical photos decorate lobby. Gift shop, restaurant, lounge.

Motel 6 Anchorage–Midtown
5000 A St.
800-4MOTEL6 or 907-249-2503
www.motel6anchorage.com
Midtown location, shuttle service, near restaurants.

Ramada Anchorage Downtown
115 E. 3rd Ave.
866-RAMADA-7 or 907-272-7561
www.alaskaramada.com
Full-service hotel with business center. Microwave, fridge, safe in each room. Downtown location.

Red Roof Inn
1104 E. 5th Ave.
800-733-7663 or 907-274-1650
www.redroof.com
Budget rooms and suites close to downtown. Free Internet.

Rodeway Inn–Voyager
501 K St.
800-424-6423 or 907-277-9501
www.rodewayinn.com
40 well-appointed rooms in downtown location. Close to shopping, dining, entertainment.

Sheraton Anchorage Hotel
401 E. 6th Ave.
800-478-8700 or 907-276-8700
www.sheraton.com/anchorage
Well-appointed rooms and suites, cable TV, room and laundry service, fitness room. Gift store, lounge, penthouse restaurant with view.

Sourdough Visitors Lodge
801 Erickson St.
800-777-3716 or 907-279-4148
www.alaskasourdoughlodge.com
32 suites with kitchens. Close to dining, recreation.

SpringHill Suites by Marriott
3401 A St.
877-729-0197 or 907-562-3247
www.springhillsuites.com
Spacious suites near shopping, entertainment in midtown. Free continental breakfast, wireless.

Super 8 Motel of Anchorage
3501 Minnesota Dr.
800-800-8000 or 907-276-8884
www.super8.com
Comfortable rooms with cable TV, 24-hour shuttle.

Westmark Anchorage Hotel
720 W. 5th Ave.
800-544-0970 or 907-276-7676
www.westmarkhotels.com
Deluxe accommodations in one of Anchorage's few high-rise buildings. Views, restaurant, fitness center.

CAMPGROUNDS

Tok: See listings in the section on Tok in Chapter 6, The Alaska Highway.

Glennallen:
Lake Louise Lodge
Mile 160 Glenn Hwy. turnoff to Mile 16 Lake Louise Rd.
877-878-3311 or 907-822-3311
www.lakelouiselodge.com
RV parking with electric, satellite television. Fuel, propane, oil. Full-service restaurant. Swimming, fishing, boating. Open year-round.

Tolsona Wilderness Campground
Mile 173 Glenn Hwy.
907-822-3865
80 creekside campsites with full or partial hook-ups, tenting, creekside location. Showers, laundry, dump station, Internet, store.

Moose Horn RV Park
Mile 187.5 Glenn Hwy.
907-822-3956
12 RV sites, some full hookups, wireless, dump station, potable water hose.

Northern Nights Campground & RV Park
Mile 189 Glenn Hwy.
907-822-3199
Campsites with partial hookups, pull-throughs, tent sites. Restrooms, hot showers, phone, wooded setting, close to visitor center and shopping. Open May–September.

Midway, Glennallen to Palmer:
Grand View RV Park & Lodge
Mile 110 Glenn Hwy.
907-746-4480
24 sites including pull-throughs; some with full hookups; 10 for slide-outs. Café, espresso, views of glacier and mountains.

Palmer:
Fox Run RV Park & Campground
Mile 36 Glenn Hwy., on Matanuska Lake
877-745-6120 or 907-745-6120
www.foxrun.freeservers.com
Full hookups, restrooms, showers, tables, play-ground, e-mail access. Tenting area, boat rental, tackle.

The Homestead RV Park

Mile 36 Glenn Hwy., .5 mile east of Glenn and Parks junction
800-478-3570 or 907-745-6005
www.homesteadrvpark.com
71 campsites with a glorious view. Partial hookups, tent sites, dump station, showers, laundry, walking trails, wireless. Area tours available.

Mountain View RV Park

Off Old Glenn Hwy. on Smith Rd.
800-264-4582 or 907-745-5747
www.mtviewrvpark.com
83 sites with full hookups, most pull-throughs, laundry, restrooms, pay phone.

Town & Country RV Park

Mile 39.5 Glenn Hwy.
907-746-6642
Full hookups, pull-throughs, laundry, showers, dump station. Close to golf, stocked lakes, fairgrounds, Musk Ox Farm.

Anchorage:
Anchorage Ship Creek Landings RV Park

Ingra St. north to E. 1st Ave.
800-778-7700
Full hookups, pull-throughs, dry sites. Showers, wireless, laundry, gift shop. Handicap access. Blocks from downtown.

Centennial Campground

8300 Glenn Hwy., off Muldoon
907-343-6986 (May 21–Sept 12); 907-343-6992 (off-season)
100 campsites on a first-come, first-served basis. Includes 6 pull-throughs, tent camping, 2 group sites, showers, toilets. Firewood for sale. Dump is free for guests; fee for others. Open in summer months only.

Creekwood Inn

2150 Seward Hwy.
800-478-6008 or 907-258-6006
www.creekwoodinn-alaska.com
RV hookups, cabin rentals with fridge, coffeemaker, hair dryer, cable TV. Walking distance to restaurants, shopping.

Golden Nugget RV Park

4100 Debarr Rd.
800-449-2012 or 907-333-2012
www.goldennuggetrvpark.com
Full and partial RV hookups, tables, weekly barbecues, nightly entertainment. Walking trails nearby.

RESTAURANTS

Tok: See listings in the section on Tok in Chapter 6, The Alaska Highway.

Glennallen:
Caribou Café Family Restaurant

Downtown Glennallen
907-822-3656
Open daily; homemade soups, pies, baked goods.

Lake Louise Lodge

Mile 160 Glenn Hwy. turnoff to Mile 16 Lake Louise Rd.
877-878-3311 or 907-822-3311
www.lakelouiselodge.com
Full-service restaurant specializing in steaks and seafood.

Omni Park's Place

Mile 187.5 Glenn Hwy.
907-822-3334
Grocery deli serving hot foods, espresso, sandwiches.

Palmer:
Butte Café

3655 N. Old Glenn Hwy.
907-746-3688
Breakfast, burgers, northern hospitality.

Colony Kitchen/Noisy Good Café

Mile 40.5 Glenn Hwy.
Across from fairgrounds
907-746-4600
Breakfast all day; steaks, burgers, salad, pie.

Gold Miner's Restaurant

918 S. Colony Wy., in Gold Miner's Hotel
800-7ALASKA or 907-745-6160
Steaks, seafood, burgers, sandwiches, salad bar.

The Inn Café

325 Elmwood Ave.
907-746-6118
Fine dining in historic Colony Inn, live entertainment.

La Fiesta Mexican Restaurant

132 W. Evergreen Ave.
907-745-3335
Mexican fare.

Open Café

606 S. Alaska St., in Valley Hotel
907-745-3330
Gourmet pizza, full menu, take-out available. Open 24 hours.

Palmer Bar
828 S. Colony Wy., downtown
907-745-3041
Bar food and special grill-your-own-steak nights.

Peking Garden
775 W. Evergreen Ave.
907-746-5757
Chinese specialties.

Pioneer Pizza
Mile 3.2 Palmer-Wasilla Hwy.
907-745-5400
www.pioneerpizzas.com
Pizza, sandwiches.

Pizzaria Delphi
103 Arctic St., off Old Glenn Hwy.
907-745-2929
Pizza, Italian and Greek specialties. Beer and wine.

Turkey Red Café and Bakery
550 S. Alaska St., in Downtown Palmer Plaza
907-745-5544
www.turkeyredak.com
Breakfast, lunch, and dinner: healthy food, organic ingredients, promoting local agriculture.

Vagabond Blues
642 S. Alaska St., in downtown Palmer
907-745-2233
www.vagblues.com
Homemade soups, wraps, quiche, pastries. Coffee and live music.

Anchorage:
Anchorage's downtown hotels include one or more excellent restaurants, often with outstanding views of Cook Inlet. Be sure to consider those fine-dining establishments as you make your dinner plans.

Alaska Salmon Chowder House
443 W. 4th Ave.
907-278-6901
Casual dining featuring crab, halibut, salmon.

Arctic Roadrunner
5300 Old Seward Hwy.
907-561-4016
All-American burgers, fries, shakes since 1964. Locals love it.

Bombay Deluxe
555 W. Northern Lights
907-277-1200
Indian cuisine in the Far North.

Café Amsterdam
530 E. Benson Blvd.
907-274-0074
www.cafe-amsterdam.com
Popular spot for delicious breakfast and lunch. Get there early.

Club Paris
417 W. 5th Ave.
907-277-6332
Steakhouse and bar serving Anchorage since 1957. Dark wood, secluded feel, great beef.

Country Kitchen
346 E. 5th Ave.
907-677-2122
Family restaurant in downtown core.

Dianne's Restaurant
550 W. 7th Ave., in Atwood Building
907-279-7243
Fresh ingredients in soups, salads, sandwiches, lunch specials.

Downtown Deli & Café
525 W. 4th Ave.
907-276-7116
From sourdough pancakes to reindeer stew, and more. Close to shopping.

Fancy Moose
4800 Spenard Rd., in Millennium Alaskan Hotel
907-226-2249
Light meals, sandwiches; overlooking floatplane lake. Outdoor seating.

Glacier Brewhouse
737 W. 5th Ave.
907-274-2739
www.glacierbrewhouse.com
Spacious, inviting brewpub featuring wood-grilled seafood, pizzas, grilled meats.

Gwennie's Old Alaska Restaurant
4333 Spenard Rd.
907-243-2909
Alaska decor, Alaska-size meals. Popular breakfast place.

Humpy's Great Alaskan Alehouse
610 W. 6th Ave.
907-276-2337
50-plus brews on tap, live music nightly. Downtown.

Jens' Restaurant
701 W. 36th Ave.
907-561-5367
Fine dining, featuring pepper steak, seafood, lamb, veal.

1961. Call 907-983-2420 or see www.yukoninfo.com/skagway/info/museum.htm.

The saloons, restaurants, gift shops, and soda fountains of Skagway are all wrapped in historical storefronts. A horse-and-buggy tour operator is dressed in the garb of old. The storefront windows along Main St. are trimmed with the hats, gloves, and doodads that would have pleased your grandma. The big difference between then and now, besides the plumbing and telephone lines, lies in the harbor: enormous cruise ships bring their passengers to Skagway to soak up a little atmosphere of the "Days of '98."

A century ago, outlaw Soapy Smith reigned here, along with his gang of con artists and thugs who took advantage of the weak, the innocent, and even the dead. One story tells of the terrible avalanche that killed dozens of men on the Chilkoot Trail. Soapy set up a "morgue" near the site, and he and his men dug up bodies, took them into his morgue, and stripped them of their valuables before the real authorities arrived. His reign ended when he was confronted by a man named Frank Reid, who shot Soapy several times and was mortally wounded himself.

The graves of both men, in the Gold Rush Cemetery, are visited by thousands of people every year. To get to the cemetery, go north on State St., then follow the signs. Reid's grave bears these words: He gave his life for the honor of Skagway. Every July 4, the city remembers those days with an event called Soapy Smith's Wake.

Speaking of Soapy, must-see entertainment is the "Days of '98 Show," performed four times a day at the Eagles Hall, 6th Ave. and Broadway. It's an hour-long musical drama with Soapy Smith as the classic bad guy. Great fun. Call 907-983-2545.

LODGING

At the White House
8th and Main streets, near downtown
907-983-9000
www.atthewhitehouse.com
Rooms with private baths in 1902 family-run inn. Cable TV, Wi-Fi, phones. Complimentary breakfast buffet. Walking distance to town.

Chilkoot Trail Outpost
Dyea Valley
907-983-3799
www.chilkoottrailoutpost.com
Modern luxury log cabins nestled in the woods, Wi-Fi, group campsite, free breakfast. Bicycles, cooking gazebo.

Morning Wood Hotel
444 4th St., above the Pizza Station
907-983-2200
10 rooms, some with bath.

Sgt. Preston's Lodge
6th Ave. and State St.
866-983-2521 or 907-983-2521
http://sgtprestons.eskagway.com
30 new or newly renovated rooms on street level. Cable TV, private baths, phones. Internet access. Courtesy van. Close to bank and post office.

Skagway Bungalows
Mile 1 Dyea Rd.
907-983-3986
Log cabins in forest, furnished with microwave, fridge, king- or queen-sized bed.

Skagway Inn
7th Ave. and Broadway St.
800-752-4929 or 907-983-2289
12 rooms decorated with antiques, in historic district. Wi-Fi, Internet. Breakfast, van service. Reservations for White Pass & Yukon Route, shows, tours. Restaurant.

Westmark Inn Skagway
3rd Ave. and Spring St.
800-544-0970 or 907-983-6000
www.westmarkhotels.com
151 deluxe rooms, nonsmoking available. Cable TV, Wi-Fi, two restaurants, lounge. Free cribs; children under 18 are free. Close to shopping and entertainment.

CAMPGROUNDS

Garden City RV Park
State St., between 15th and 17th aves.
866-983-2378 or 907-983-2378
Level sites with full and partial hookups, pull-throughs, Wi-Fi. Laundry, restrooms, coin-op showers.

National Park Service Ranger Station & Dyea Campground
6 miles from Skagway in Dyea
907-983-2921
22 tenting campsites. Bring your own water. Vault toilets, picnic tables, bear-proof food storage containers, fire rings. Self-registration.

Pullen Creek RV Park
2nd Ave., next to Alaska State Ferry dock
800-936-3731
www.pullencreekrv.com
Partial hookups. Showers, dump station. Walking distance to shopping and attractions.

Skagway Mountain View RV Park
12th Ave. and Broadway St.
888-778-7700
Wooded sites with partial hookups, pull-throughs, cable TV access. Picnic tables, firewood. Showers, laundry, restrooms, dump station. RV wash facilities. Tour reservations. Near downtown historic district.

RESTAURANTS

Alaska Garden Gourmet
5th Ave. between Broadway and State St.
907-983-2289
Home cooking with local seafood and produce.

Bonanza Bar & Grill
On Broadway, between 3rd and 4th aves., at the Westmark Hotel
907-983-6214
Salads, burgers, ribs, seafood, pizza, drink specials, entertainment.

Chilkoot Dining Room
242 3rd Ave., at the Westmark Hotel
907-983-6000
Meat, pasta, salads, crab legs.

The Corner Café
4th Ave. and State St.
907-983-2155
Three meals a day. Hamburgers, salads, soups.

Excelsior Café
270 2nd Ave.
907-983-2908
Espresso, bakery, deli.

Gold Rush Brewery & Restaurant
Mile 2.2 Klondike Hwy.
907-983-3175
www.klondikegolddredge.com
Barbecue, smoked meats, designer brews; gift shops, brewery tour, pan for gold.

Northern Lights Pizza
380A 3rd Ave.
907-983-2225
Greek, Italian, Mexican, American.

Olivia's Restaurant
7th and Broadway, in Skagway Inn
907-983-2289
Alaskan tapas menu, with full bar and select wine list. Wild salmon, organic kitchen garden.

Poppies Restaurant
Mile 1.5 Klondike Hwy., inside Jewell Gardens & Glassworks
907-983-2111
Luncheon or tea service in conservatory or sunroom. Fine dining in evenings.

The Red Onion Saloon
2nd Ave. & Broadway St.
907-983-2222
Food and libations in 1898 saloon, entertainment, brothel museum.

Skagway Brewing Company
700 Broadway
907-983-BREW
Salads, fish and chips, desserts, brews.

Skagway Fish Company
201 Congress Wy.
907-983-FISH
Seafood chowder, fish and chips.

Skagway Pizza Station
444 4th Ave.
907-983-2200
Dine in, take out, or delivery.

Starfire
4th Ave. between Broadway and Spring
907-983-3663
Gourmet cooking, Thai food.

Stowaway Café
205 Congress Wy.
907-983-DINE
Thai, French, Cajun, with fresh Alaskan ingredients.

Sweet Tooth Café
315 Broadway St.
907-983-2405
Breakfast, lunch, dinner. Homemade donuts, soups, bread, fries. Take-out available.

The Parks Hwy. wends through the Alaska Range.

PARKS HIGHWAY

Anchorage to Fairbanks: 358 miles (576 km)

Travel Opportunities: *Iditarod Trail Sled Dog Race Headquarters, Wasilla; Independence Mine; Talkeetna;
Denali State Park; Denali National Park and Preserve; Fairbanks.*

The (George) Parks Hwy. connects the state's two largest cities, Anchorage and Fairbanks, in a 358-mile south-to-north trek from the Southcentral coast into Alaska's great Interior. It is among the newest of the highways (completed in 1972) and sees heavy summer use, often by motorists on their way to Denali National Park and Preserve.

To reach the Parks Hwy. from Anchorage, take the Glenn Hwy. north for 35 miles (56 km). At a major interchange near Wasilla, the Glenn continues east, while the northbound Parks is marked with clear roadside signs directing drivers toward Denali Park and Fairbanks. Even though this place is the official start of the Parks Hwy., roadside mileposts will reflect total mileage from Anchorage. (For details on Anchorage-area attractions, lodging, campgrounds, and restaurants, see the section on the Glenn Highway, in this chapter.)

Just north of the Glenn Hwy. and Parks Hwy. junction is Wasilla. Once a sleepy little stop along a two-lane road, Wasilla has experienced a population boom in the past two decades; every lane of the four-lane Parks Hwy. is busy as the road passes through town. It has also attracted national attention as the home of former Alaska governor Sarah Palin and her news-making family. Wasilla is a good last-chance full-service shopping stop before you begin your lengthy road trip north. Although many small, family-operated stores and service stations lie ahead, Wasilla offers a variety of goods, services, fast-food restaurants, grocery stores, and so forth. Most of the shopping district lies at roadside.

To learn more about local history, visit the Dorothy Page Museum & Historic Town Site, 323 N. Main St., in Wasilla. Permanent exhibits focus on the development of the Iditarod Trail Sled Dog Race, area homesteading, and settlement in the Mat-Su Valley. Admission is charged. For information, call 907-373-9071.

At the Knik-Goose Bay Rd. traffic light in Wasilla, you can turn west and follow the road for a little more than 2 miles (3 km) to the impressive log building that is Iditarod Trail Sled Dog Race Headquarters. Inside are the administrative offices of the famous 1,150-mile race across Alaska, as well as a free museum, video theater, and gift shop. Admission is free. Here at Iditarod headquarters, you can take a summer dogsled ride in a wheeled cart. At a replica of a checkpoint cabin, learn more about this phenomenal distance race. Call 907-376-5155 or visit the Iditarod website, www.iditarod.com.

Transportation buffs will enjoy a visit to a special museum north of Wasilla off the Parks Hwy. at Mile 47 (Km 75.5). Follow the signs for another mile to the Museum of Alaska Transportation & Industry, at 3800 Museum Dr. Here you'll see early snowmobiles, vehicles, airplanes, trains, historic buildings, and more. Open seasonally, May through September. Call 907-376-1211 or see www.museumofalaska.org.

As you drive north on the Parks Hwy., you'll occasionally pass through little enclaves where people choose to live far away from big cities. Willow is such a town. It has its own post office, library, convenience store, gas station, café, lodge, and dozens of little homes sprinkled throughout the surrounding forests and around lakes. Roadside fishing opportunities exist all along this stretch of the Parks Hwy. Even if you don't fish, it's fun to pull over and watch the anglers.

A popular attraction for campers and fishers is Nancy Lake State Recreation Area, at Mile 67.5 (Km 107) Parks Hwy., developed with two separate campgrounds, both with water and toilets. The Nancy Lake State Recreation Site, on the northeast shore, has 30 campsites, water, toilets, a trail, and a boat launch. The South Rolly Lake Campground has 99 sites and is accessed at the end of Nancy Lake Pkwy. To contact the Nancy Lake Ranger Station, call 907-495-6273.

Just past Willow at Mile 71 (Km 114.5) is the westbound turn for Willow Creek State Recreation Area, located at the end of the Willow Creek Pkwy., about 5 miles (8 km) off the highway. The area is nicely developed with 140 campsites, no restrictions on RV size, water, outhouses, tent camping, trails, and river access.

Just north of the entrance to Willow Creek Pkwy. is the eastbound turnoff for Hatcher Pass Rd. and access to Independence Mine. (See details in the section on the Glenn Highway, in this chapter.)

Take a side trip to Talkeetna for a taste of old Alaska. Almost 99 miles (159 km) north of Anchorage, make the right turn onto the spur road that leads to Talkeetna. This is an excellent drive along a paved 14-mile (22.5-km) road that dead-ends in a historic gold-mining town. On clear days, views of Mt. McKinley practically fill up the windshield. And at certain times of the year, Talkeetna is overrun with mountain climbers who have journeyed here from all over the world. Local bush pilots fly the climbers and their gear to the base camp of Mt. McKinley for ascents up North America's tallest peak. And tourists flock here to sign on for a flightseeing trip over the mountain, sometimes landing for a walk on a glacier. Or another favorite: a jet-boat tour with Mahay's Jetboat Adventure (800-736-2210; www.mahaysjetboat.com). They can take you touring or arrange a ride for a day of fishing.

Several of Talkeetna's buildings are on the National Register of Historic Places. Although it's small, the town features museums, two roadhouses, a modern National Park Service ranger station, a post office, motels, a country store, restaurants, and several gift shops. Tent camping can be found right in town at the end of Main St. RVers can check in at Talkeetna Camper Park, Mile 13.9 on the Spur Rd. (907-733-2693; www .talkeetnacamper.com), or dry camp at Talkeetna RV (907-733-2604), near the Swiss Alaska Inn.

GOOD BOY

Of all the famous dogs in Far North lore, real and fictional, few match the true story of a historic lead dog named Togo, an Alaskan husky who consistently won Nome's All-Alaska Sweepstakes Races during the early 20th century. Togo and his kennelmate, Balto, belonged to winning musher Leonhard Seppala.

In January 1925, Alaska's mushers and sled dogs were called upon to transport lifesaving diphtheria serum from the railway at Nenana across the wilderness to Nome, where the epidemic threatened the townspeople. Twenty teams worked together in the relay, traveling day and night, passing along the serum package like a baton and ensuring that it wouldn't freeze in below-zero temperatures. Seppala chose Togo has his leader and loaned out Balto to his dog handler for leading another team. Newspapers across the country covered the progress of all the mushers, Native and non-Native, and readers eagerly absorbed each new update. The race to Nome was successful, and the serum staved off the epidemic.

In the end, Balto garnered national attention because he and his driver brought the serum into Nome through the killing cold, but it was Togo, with Seppala, who traveled the farthest distance: an extraordinary 260 miles in brutal conditions. In addition, Balto was 3 years old; Togo was 12. Seppala ended up giving Balto to the driver and was himself miffed that Balto, not his Togo, was the darling of the country. Fans even installed a statue of Balto in New York's Central Park. "The newspaper dog,"

Seppala huffed. Still, both dogs enjoyed celebrity status to the ends of their lives, although Balto's new owner later sold him to a vaudeville sideshow, where he lived in poor conditions until his rescue by a group of concerned Cleveland citizens. As for Togo, most of his senior years were spent with his companion, Seppala, and he died at age 16 on December 5, 1929.

The remains of Balto are now part of the collection at the Cleveland Museum of Natural History. But Togo's mount can be found at a mushing museum inside the headquarters of the Iditarod Trail Sled Dog Race, just 2 miles outside Wasilla on Knik-Goose Bay Rd. Here is a genuine piece of history. Togo was a testament to the athletic ability of Alaska sled dogs, an unforgettable hero, and a good boy.

Togo was a national star in the 1920s. His mount is on display at the Iditarod Trail Sled Dog Race headquarters museum, just outside Wasilla.
Photo by Bill Hess

The Alaska Railroad offers flag-stop service between Talkeetna and Hurricane, Thursday through Sunday in the summer. The ride is good fun, and you get to meet some interesting locals who prefer to live off the road system. Ask about the schedule at the depot, call 907-265-2494, or buy your ticket on board.

Each winter, Talkeetna hosts a bachelor auction and the Wilderness Woman competition, where women can prove their mettle by chopping wood and hauling water while packing a baby doll in a carrier on their backs. In summer, it's the infamous Moose Dropping Festival on the second weekend of July. Come for the parade, the food, the entertainment, and games with moose droppings. (Yes, droppings, as in scat.)

Here you can arrange a jet-boating adventure, a flightseeing trip, a float trip, or a day or more on the water fishing for big salmon. In Talkeetna, you'll find a number of outfitters, some of them with storefronts along Main St. Ask for directions at the visitor information cabin by the sign that says Welcome to Beautiful

Nenana is home port for a couple of barge operations that ply the Tanana and Yukon rivers, moving freight to dozens of remote villages off the road and rail system, but along the big rivers.

Downtown Talkeetna. The Talkeetna Chamber of Commerce can be reached at 907-733-2330 or browse www.talkeetnachamber.org.

On clear days, a crowd gathers at the Mile 135 (Km 237) wayside on the Parks Hwy. From here, you'll gain the best roadside view of 20,320-foot Mt. McKinley and the lesser surrounding mountains, which would receive more notice were they not flanking McKinley. Neighboring peaks include Mt. Foraker, rising to 13,395 feet (4,082 m); Mt. Hunter, at 14,580 feet (4,444 m); and Mt. Silverthrone, at 13,220 feet (4,029 m); plus three others with summits that exceed 12,000 feet (3,658 m). Interpretive signs name the mountains and offer more about this terrain. Other stops along the highway are at Mile 174, 158, and 162. There's no way to make the mountain visible when the clouds are out, though, so be prepared. You may never see it, even though it's right in front of you.

The southern boundary of Denali State Park lies about 135 miles (217 km) north of Anchorage. This park straddles the highway and offers 325,240 acres filled with recreational opportunities: fishing, hiking, biking, camping, canoeing, floating. Three state-operated campgrounds are in the park: Byers Lake, Lower Troublesome Creek, and Denali View North. Thirty-seven miles (59 km) of developed trails thread above and below tree line in a panoramic landscape. Its road address is Mile 135–164 Parks Hwy. For more information, call the Alaska State Parks office in Wasilla at 907-745-3975, or visit www.dnr.state.ak.us/parks.

A popular landmark at Mile 188.5 (Km 303) is a private business that has long been a curiosity as well as a milepost: a three-story igloo. The giant geodesic structure originally was built as a hotel but never served that purpose. The igloo marks roughly the halfway point between Anchorage and Fairbanks.

At Mile 210 (Km 338), near Cantwell, an eastbound turnoff leads to the Denali Hwy., which connects the Parks Hwy. with the Richardson Hwy. (See the section on the Denali Highway, in this chapter.)

The crown jewel of North America, Mt. McKinley rises within the 6-million-acre Denali National Park and Preserve. And while views of The Mountain tease motorists during their northbound drive, the park entrance doesn't arrive until Mile 237 Parks Hwy. (Km 382), about 4.5 hours north of Anchorage.

Dropping in for a day or an afternoon, motorists can drive to the Denali Visitor Center, a newer complex with great interpretive displays and a theater. Ranger-guided walks start here, and they have information on shuttle bus schedules. Nearby, you'll find a bookstore, cafeteria, and bathrooms. And a few steps away is the beautiful Murie Science and Learning Center, open year-round.

There are six campgrounds in the park, with various levels of creature comforts and accessibility. Three are set up for RVs; all can accept tent campers. An overnight visit to Denali National Park takes some advance planning, because most of the time reservations are necessary for campsites, hotel rooms, and seats on the shuttle buses that travel on the only road that penetrates the park. Private vehicles may not go farther than Savage River Bridge, a little more than 13 miles into the park.

To figure it all out, drop in to the Wilderness Access Center, about .5 mile from the park entrance, on the right. They dispense information and make reservations for camping in the park. They'll also arrange your bus ride to the end of the 90-mile (145-km) park road. For advance arrangements, just call the nationwide reservation number at 800-622-7275; in Anchorage, call 907-272-7275. See www .reservedenali.com. Bus drivers don't sell tickets, so you either buy them on the spot, or order by phone or online and pick them up inside the Wilderness Access Center, then catch the bus outside.

Most visitors to the park stay in RV parks or hotels along the Parks Hwy. just a few miles farther north, where development of restaurants, gas stations, hotels, gift shops, and tour operators has clustered outside the park's boundaries.

For the best chance to see wildlife, you have to take the shuttle bus. Wildlife-watching (and mountain-watching) remain the top draw. Chances are you might see a bear, caribou, moose, ptarmigan, fox, Dall sheep, or snowshoe hare.

Rafting the Nenana is a popular pastime for visitors to Denali National Park and Preserve.

In downtown Fairbanks, the centerpiece of Golden Heart Park is a statue known as "The Unknown First Family."

The Alaska Railroad depot lies within the park, too, and shuttle buses transport passengers to their waiting hotels. The place is abuzz with activity—and the scenery, close and far away, is awesome. Out on the Parks Hwy., the Nenana River races below the road's edge. Look for white-water rafters down there any time of day. Overhead, small airplanes and helicopters engage in viewing Denali from the top down. Sign up for some of the same fun. Ask about it at the visitor center in the park.

About a half hour farther north on the Parks Hwy., the coal-mining town of Healy lies in the northern foothills of the Alaska Range. This is the next place along the road to find a meal, accommodations, and fuel. A small community, Healy is growing as more visitors to Denali National Park want to leave the crowds behind when they find a hotel room.

From here, the Parks Hwy. continues north through the boreal forests of Alaska's Interior. Set between the Alaska Range and the Brooks Range, this vast region charts the coldest colds and the hottest hots in the state. From Healy to Nenana, you'll find occasional services, gift shops, and gas stations, but little other development.

The section of the Parks between Nenana and Fairbanks wends through the Tanana uplands, round-topped tall hills (they would be called mountains elsewhere) that border the Tanana Valley. As you cross these hills, passing lanes are available for faster traffic. Be sure to stay to the right if your vehicle pulls hills slowly. Every few miles, pullouts offer clear views, from the top down, of the braided Tanana River and its tributaries. Local forests are mostly spruce and birch and aspen.

About 5 miles (8 km) before entering Fairbanks on the Parks Hwy., you'll note signs that lead west to Ester, once a vibrant gold-mining town, but now a snug little hamlet of historic buildings and creative people. Jewelry designer Judie Gumm has her studio there, as does popular Alaskan cartoonist Jamie Smith. The old Malemute Saloon drew crowds for decades until recently; locals and tourists who loved it are keeping an eye out to see if it will reopen soon.

For information on Fairbanks history, attractions, events, lodging, campgrounds, and restaurants, see the section on Fairbanks in Chapter 6, The Alaska Highway.

LODGING

The Mat-Su Bed & Breakfast Association has information on rooms, apartments, and cabins. Visit the association's website at www.alaska bnbhosts.com.

Wasilla:
Agate Inn
4725 Begich Cir.
907-373-2290
Country-style inn located just north of Anchorage. Open year-round.

Alaska Kozey Cabins
351 E. Spruce
907-376-3190
www.alaskakozeycabins.com
Cabin rentals throughout the Mat-Su Valley.

Alaskan View Motel
2650 E. Parks Hwy.
907-376-6787
www.alaskanviewmotel.com
26 rooms, Alaska decor in log building. Cable TV, mountain and inlet views. Senior and military discounts. Guided fishing.

Best Western Lake Lucille Inn
1300 W. Lake Lucille Dr.
907-373-1776
www.bestwesternlakelucilleinn.com
54 deluxe rooms, suites, Internet. Athletic facility, whirlpool, gift shop. Floatplane and boat docks, boat rentals. Complimentary breakfast. Handicap accessible.

Grand View Inn & Suites
2900 E. Parks Hwy.
907-357-7666
www.grandviewak.com
79 rooms in newer facility; views of Chugach Mountains and Cook Inlet. Fishing and shopping nearby.

Trout's Place and the Windbreak Café
2201 E. Parks Hwy.
907-376-4484
www.windbreakalaska.com
Rooms, plus café serving breakfast, lunch, dinner. Lounge.

Denali Park:
Denali Backcountry Lodge
Kantishna, end of 95-mile Park Rd.
800-841-0692 or 907-783-1342
www.denalilodge.com
30 units, dining, cocktails. Inside the park. Private wildlife-viewing bus. Train shuttle service.

Denali Bluffs Hotel
Mile 238.5 Parks Hwy.
866-683-8500 or 907-683-7000
www.denalialaska.com/denali-bluffs-hotel
112 rooms with views, private bath, coffee service, fridge, phone. Restaurant, tour desk, gift shop. Shuttle service.

Denali Cedars Lodge
Mile 231 Parks Hwy.
800-208-0200
www.denalirivercabins.com/cedars_lodge.htm
48 hotel-style rooms in two-story cedar buildings. Deck, sauna, courtesy shuttle, activities desk. Free deluxe continental breakfast. Borders the Nenana River.

Denali River Cabins
Mile 231 Parks Hwy.
800-230-7275
www.denalirivercabins.com
43 cedar cabins with private baths. Hot tubs, dining. South of park entrance, train shuttle service.

Denali Crow's Nest Log Cabins
Mile 238.5 Parks Hwy.
888-917-8130 or 907-683-2723
www.denalicrowsnest.com
39 deluxe cabins with private baths, close to park entrance. Views, hot tub, tour desk, shuttle. Bar and grill.

Denali Grizzly Bear Resort
Mile 231 Parks Hwy.
907-683-2696
54-room cedar hotel with private decks on the Nenana River; kitchenette units, laundry. Pets allowed. Campsites.

Denali Princess Wilderness Lodge
Mile 238.5 Parks Hwy.
800-426-0500
www.princesslodges.com
Deluxe accommodations, outdoor hot tubs, tour
desk, shuttle service. Free train transfers from the
depot. Pizza pub, espresso, full-service restaurant.
Health and tanning spa.

Grande Denali Lodge
Mile 238 Parks Hwy.
866-683-8500 or 907-683-8500
www.denaliparkresorts.com
159 roomy guest rooms, deluxe cabins, amenities
in the wilderness. Lounge, gift shop, tour desk,
laundry, courtesy shuttle. Alpenglow Restaurant.

McKinley Chalet Resort
Mile 238.5 Parks Hwy.
800-276-7234 or 907-279-2653
www.denaliparkresorts.com
Beautifully appointed lobby, café, gift shop. 345
units, restaurant, cocktails. Train shuttle service.
Wildly popular theatrical production *Alaska Cabin
Nite Dinner Theater.*

McKinley Princess Wilderness Lodge
Mile 133 Parks Hwy., in Denali State Park on
Chulitna River
800-426-0500
www.princesslodges.com
Luxury accommodations with views of the mountain. TV, phone, hot tub, tour desk, theater, gift
shop. Restaurants, lounges. Shuttle service.

McKinley Village Lodge
Mile 231 Parks Hwy.
800-276-7234 or 907-276-7234
www.denaliparkresorts.com
150 luxury units, dining, cocktails. Rafting
adventures. Overlooks Nenana River. Train
shuttle service.

McKinley Creekside Cabins & Café
Mile 224 Parks Hwy.
888-5DENALI or 907-683-2277
www.mckinleycabins.com
Lodge, cabins, café on Carlo Creek near the park.

Healy:
Denali Park Hotel
Mile 247 Parks Hwy.
866-683-1800 or 907-683-1800
www.denaliparkhotel.com
Lobby is refurbished Alaska Railroad train car. King
or two full beds. Satellite TV, phone. Located in
Healy, 10 miles from the park entrance.

Motel Nord Haven
15 minutes north of park entrance on Parks Hwy.
800-683-4501
www.motelnordhaven.com
28 rooms with queen beds, RVs, phone, private
bath.

Park's Edge
Off Mile 247 Parks Hwy. on Hilltop Rd.
907-683-4343
www.parks-edge.com
Standard and deluxe log cabins in quiet,
convenient location. Adjacent to golf course
and restaurant.

Totem Inn
Mile 249 Parks Hwy.
907-683-6500
www.thetoteminn.com
50 clean and comfortable rooms, fridge, RVs, free
Wi-Fi, plus laundry, café, lounge, fitness center.

Fairbanks: See listings in the section on Fairbanks
in Chapter 6, The Alaska Highway.

CAMPGROUNDS

Wasilla:
Alaska R & R Laundry & RV Park
Mile 49.5 Parks Hwy.
907-373-7286
16 RV sites with full hookups, 4 pull-throughs.
Dump station, restrooms, laundry.

Big Bear RV Park & Cabins
Mile 37 Parks Hwy.
907-745-7445
43 full and partial hookup campsites with pull-
throughs available. Laundry, dump, propane.
Cabin rentals.

Iceworm RV Park
8620 W. Parks Hwy.
907-892-8200
Sites with full hookups, pull-through, fire rings,
showers, laundry, dump station. Horseshoe pit,
Wi-Fi, propane sales. Open year-round.

Lake Lucille Park (operated by City of Wasilla)
Follow signs from Mile 2.5 Knik-Goose Bay Rd.
907-745-9010
www.cityofwasilla.com
57 campsites in treed area, some pull-throughs.
No electric or dump station. Covered picnic area,
firewood, restrooms. Walking distance to lake and
fishing. On-site host.

Denali Park:
Denali Grizzly Bear Resort
Mile 231 Parks Hwy.
866-583-2696 or 907-683-2696 (summer); 907-374-8796 (winter)
www.denaligrizzlybear.com
40 RV sites with full hookups and pull-throughs, tent sites. Showers, laundry, water, dump station.

Denali Rainbow Village RV Park
1 mile north of Denali Park entrance
907-683-7777
www.denalirv.com
77 sites with full or partial hookups, satellite TV, close to park and activities.

Denali Riverside RV Park
Mile 240 Parks Hwy.
907-388-1748
www.denaliriversiderv.com
Sites with hookups, satellite TV, dump station, drinking water, showers, toilets, laundry, store. Tent camping. Tour desk. Pets allowed.

Healy:
McKinley RV and Campground
Mile 248.5 Parks Hwy.
800-478-2562 or 907-683-2379
www.mckinleyrv.com
77 RV sites with full hookups and pull-throughs, tent sites. Fireplace/grills. Showers, water, dump station.

Waugaman Village RV Park
Mile 3.8 Healy Spur Rd., off Mile 249 Parks Hwy.
907-683-2737
Full hookups in quiet wooded area. Can accommodate up to 60-foot parking. Laundry, dump, free showers. Tenting area. Pets welcome.

Fairbanks: See listings in the section on Fairbanks in Chapter 6, The Alaska Highway.

RESTAURANTS

Wasilla:
Evangelo's Trattoria
2530 E. Parks Hwy.
907-376-1212
Italian food at its best, pizza, pasta, beer, and wine.

Jalapeno's Mexican Restaurant
431 W. Parks Hwy.
907-373-2929
Authentic Mexican fare.

Mat-Su Resort
1850 Bogard Rd.
907-376-3228
www.matsuresortak.com
Elegant dining experience. American cuisine, seafood, steaks. Weekend breakfasts. Reservations suggested.

Tailgaters Sports Bar & Grill
161 W. Parks Hwy.
907-376-1314
Family dining in sports venue.

The Windbreak Café and Trout's Place
2201 E. Parks Hwy., in the Windbreak Hotel
907-376-4484
www.windbreakalaska.com
Breakfast, lunch, dinner. Fishing stories.

Denali Park:
Coffee shops, pizza places, salmon bakes, and fine-dining establishments can be found on both sides of the Parks Hwy. just outside of Denali National Park and Preserve.

Check the Denali Park lodging listings, above. Nearly every hotel has one or more restaurants for every level of dining experience, from sandwiches to fine dining.

Fairbanks: See listings in the section on Fairbanks in Chapter 6, The Alaska Highway.

RICHARDSON HIGHWAY

Valdez to Fairbanks: 364 miles (587 km)

Travel Opportunities: Valdez; glacier cruises, pipeline terminus on Prince William Sound; Thompson Pass; Worthington Glacier; pipeline pump stations; Delta Junction; North Park; Fairbanks.

The original name for this historic route was the Valdez–Fairbanks Trail, Alaska's first highway and the only inland trail connecting the Interior to the coast. Work on the road began in 1903, after the Tanana Valley gold strike near Fairbanks. In 1904, the government pushed development along by requiring every man along the length of the road to work two days per year on the project or pay a tax of $8.

You are forgiven if you pronounce Valdez as val-DEZ, because everywhere else in the world, that's how you'd say it. But in Alaska, a mispronunciation has stuck and it's called val-DEEZ. The massive 1964 earthquake and tsunami virtually destroyed the original

townsite, killing 30 people on the dock and 3 more onboard the steamer *Chena*. Three years later, the townsite was declared unstable, and a new location was chosen four miles east. Some 52 buildings were moved, and a new city arose. A 1:20 scale replica of the former townsite, called "Remembering Old Valdez," is on display at 436 S. Hazlet St. It's fascinating not only to those who remember the old days. If you take a few minutes to visit the old site, you'll find gravel

Grayling have a distinctive dorsal fin that's almost as wide as their body.

roadbeds, remnants of pilings, and a few pieces of scrap metal—a very sobering sight.

This is an ice-free, deepwater port on an arm of Prince William Sound in an area that's also known as Alaska's Little Switzerland, as it is surrounded by the Chugach Mountains, the tallest coastal range in North America. Here, too, is the terminus of the 800-mile Trans-Alaska Pipeline. From town, you can see the terminal and massive tanker ships coming and going.

With a population of about 4,100, Valdez lies along the Alaska Marine Highway System, with the ferry terminal located near Hazelet Ave. and Harbor Dr. Valdez is the place for outdoor adventures. You can arrange for a fishing charter, rent a kayak, book a glacier-viewing cruise, go whale-watching, or sign up for a white-water rafting trip. There's hiking, tours of the salmon hatchery, gold panning, or taking in all the history that's wrapped around this place. The Valdez Convention & Visitors Bureau can help with ideas and charter details at 907-835-4636 or www.valdezalaska.org.

This little city gets more snow than any other in Alaska. The average annual snowfall is 325.6 inches. In the winter of 1989–90, a record 560.7 inches of snow accumulated, paralyzing the town. That's almost 47 feet of snow—enough to bury a house, or at least cave in its roof during many months when there is rare chance of any snow melting. Snow, and what to do with it, is the reason Valdez is laid out as it is. Side streets end in cul-de-sacs with rights-of-way for snowplows to push snow out of the streets and into dump areas behind the homes (which, by summer, are park strips). Note that most roofs are metal and angled so that snow slides off into yards, not onto walkways or driveways.

You'll find lots of opportunity to view wildlife in and around Valdez, so keep your telephoto lens or field glasses handy. Make noise while hiking or biking so you don't surprise the bears. It's common to see eagles, sea otters, harbor seals, humpback whales, and orcas. Shorebirds and waterfowl move through seasonally.

The Maxine & Jesse Whitney Museum, at 303 Lowe St., houses an amazing collection of Alaska Native artifacts and art from pioneers who, as far back as 1947, began purchasing pieces directly from the artists for resale in their shops. Mrs. Whitney also acquired another extensive collection of Native art in the mid-1980s, and in the late

1990s donated it all to Prince William Community College, which carefully stored the rare pieces until this museum opened in 2008. It's a gem.

The Valdez Museum & Historical Archive is another must-see for history lovers. Centrally located in the heart of Valdez, at 217 Egan, it has terrific exhibits and photos on town history, the gold rush, cultural history, and the *Exxon Valdez* oil spill that tainted Prince William Sound in 1989. Call 907-835-2764 or see www.valdezmuseum.org.

Each year, Prince William Sound Community College hosts The Last Frontier Theater Conference, which attracts top writers and actors, debuts new works by developing play-wrights, and continues to gain in national prominence. Summertime visitors will want to catch a show. Call 907-834-1614 for information.

Traveling north from Valdez, from Miles 14 through 17 on the Richardson Hwy., you'll pass through Keystone Canyon, an awe-inspiring place that echoes with the sounds of cascading waterfalls such as Horsetail Falls and Bridal Veil Falls (where there's a turnout for motorists). A shoot-out took place here in the days when powerful men were trying to secure right-of-way for a railway, as gold and copper interests stood to make a fortune.

Almost 29 miles north of Valdez, the looming Worthington Glacier is a National Natural Landmark and an Alaska State Parks Recreation Site. A visitor information wayside at Thompson Pass, elevation 2,678 feet (816 m), provides information about the nearby glacier. The deepest snowfall in a single day made history at Thompson Pass on December 5, 1955, when 62 inches fell. Visitors learn that the place where they stand was once beneath 4,000 feet of ice—about 20,000 years ago, that is. The route to Thompson Pass remains a daunting climb, even in modern vehicles, but a century ago and more, the trail included numerous switchbacks to make it easier for the horse-drawn double-ender sleighs that traveled in winter and the wagons that crossed the pass in summer. For your comfort today, at the recreation site, you'll find a picnic area, shelter, toilets, and trails.

Sea kayakers near Valdez work together to move their kayaks above tide line.

Record snowfall on the pass in the winter of 1952–53 measured 974.5 inches. And yet Thompson Pass is not the highest on the Richardson Hwy. That honor goes to Isabel Pass, at 3,000 feet. It was named for the wife of Fairbanks founder E. T. Barnette, who traveled with his wife, Isabelle (yes, it's spelled differently than the pass), over this route several times, summer and winter, in a horse-drawn sleigh or stage.

Eighty-three miles (134 km) north of Valdez, the Edgerton Hwy. splits off to the east, leading to Chitina (CHIT-na). From Chitina, the McCarthy Rd. continues to the town of McCarthy, and access to the former mining town of Kennicott. (See the section on the Edgerton Highway, in this chapter.)

Watch for views of the Trans-Alaska Pipeline along the Richardson Hwy. and pull-outs for pump stations with signs that explain the operation of these sites.

Plan to stop farther north, about 106 miles (170 km) north of Valdez, where the National Park Service staff at Wrangell-St. Elias National Park Visitor Center in Copper Center can answer questions, direct you to nearby campgrounds and attractions, and name the mountains you've been admiring. A theater, 3-D interactive map, displays, walking trails, restrooms, and a gift shop can be found here, too. The next big community, Glennallen, is just a few miles away.

Some 115 miles (185 km) from Valdez, Glennallen marks the junction of the Richardson and Glenn hwys. (See the section on the Glenn Highway, in this chapter.) For 14 miles, the Richardson and Glenn hwys. now share the same route—until Mile 129 (Km 207.5) on the Richardson, at Gakona Junction, where the Glenn veers northeast toward Tok. This section of the Glenn is widely referred to as the Tok Cutoff.

From Gulkana to Paxson, you'll be driving on the Richardson toward the Alaska Range and great picture-taking possibilities. The Gulkana River near Sourdough, Mile 147.5 (Km 237), is popular with anglers, canoeists, and river rafters. Gulkana River paddlers usually put in at Paxson, almost 30 road-miles ahead, and then float the 50 river-miles down to Sourdough Creek for takeout. Managed by the BLM, the Gulkana was designated a Wild and Scenic River in 1980. A BLM campground at Sourdough Creek offers 60 campsites near the boat launch.

Farther north, at Paxson, is the turn onto the Denali Hwy., which travels west to meet the Parks Hwy. near Denali National Park (see the section on the Denali Highway, in this chapter). Here in the foothills of the Alaska Range, the views are broad and mountainous and plenty of camping opportunities exist, either in developed campgrounds or simply along a broad road wayside, where it is permissible to dry camp overnight. Paxson is home to about 40 people. Services include lodging, meals, fuel, and fishing guides.

At Delta Junction—266 miles (428 km) north of Valdez and 98 miles (157 km) south of Fairbanks—the Alaska Hwy. joins the Richardson Hwy. at the community that marks the official end of the Alaska Hwy. The Richardson gets the credit for finishing the ride into Fairbanks, passing through the community of North Pole on the way. For details on attractions, lodging, and restaurants in Delta Junction, North Pole, and Fairbanks, see the last portion of Chapter 6, The Alaska Highway.

LODGING

Valdez:

Numerous bed-and-breakfasts operate in Valdez. For more information, browse the Valdez Convention & Visitors Bureau website at www.valdezalaska.org/ visitorServices/bedBreakfasts.html.

Best Western Valdez Harbor Inn
100 Harbor Dr.
888-222-3440 or 907-835-3434
www.valdezharborinn.com
88 rooms with pillowtop beds, flat-screen TVs, free Wi-Fi, microwave, fridge, DVD player. Situated on the harbor with views of the water on three sides. Barbershop, airport and ferry shuttle.

Downtown B&B Inn
113 Galena Dr.
800-478-2791 or 907-835-2791
31 rooms with private or shared baths, free continental breakfast. Near Valdez small boat harbor and free Wi-Fi. Airport and ferry pick-up.

Glacier Sound Inn
210 Egan Dr.
888-835-4485 or 907-835-4485
www.glaciersoundinnvaldez.com
40 rooms, microwave, fridge, coffeemaker. Restaurant, lounge, free continental breakfast. Close to ferry.

Keystone Hotel
401 W. Egan Dr.
888-835-0665 or 907-835-3851
www.keystonehotel.com
107 rooms with free continental breakfast. Close to ferry.

Mountain Sky Hotel & Suites
100 Meals Ave.
800-478-4445 or 907-835-4445
103 rooms and spa suites, family suites. Indoor pool, spa, cable, fridge, microwave, iron and board. Free continental breakfast.

Pipeline Inn/Club
112 Egan Dr.
907-835-4444
15 rooms, cable TV, restaurant, lounge.

Robe Lake Lodge
Mile 6 Richardson Hwy.
907-835-9118
www.robelakelodge.com
New log lodge on Robe Lake. Rent a room or the entire lodge. Tour booking available.

Totem Inn
144 E. Egan Dr.
888-808-4431 or 907-835-4443
www.toteminn.com
70 units including suites, standard rooms, cottages. Restaurant, gift shop. Central location.

Copper Center:
Copper River Princess Wilderness Lodge
1 Brenwick Craig Rd.
907-822-4000
www.princesslodges.com/copper_river_lodge.cfm
4 miles from Wrangell-St. Elias National Park Visitor Center
85 rooms and suites on 200 acres at the junction of the Klutina and Copper rivers. Situated on a bluff with mountain or forest views from every window. Restaurant, café, espresso, lounge, gift shop.

Glennallen, Delta Junction, North Pole, and Fairbanks: See listings under the respective town names in Chapter 6, The Alaska Highway.

CAMPGROUNDS

Valdez:
Bayside RV Park
230 Richardson Hwy.
888-835-4425 or 907-835-4425
www.baysiderv.com
95 RV sites with full and partial hookups, cable TV, Wi-Fi available. Showers, laundry, propane. Bookings for cruises and charter fishing trips.

Bear Creek Cabins & RV Park
3181 Richardson Hwy., at Mile 2
907-835-2723
www.bearcreekcabinsrvpark.com
RV camping and cabin rentals. Bathhouse, restroom.

Bear Paw RV Park
101 N. Harbor Dr.
907-835-2530
www.bearpawRVpark.com
150 sites with full or partial hookups. Cable TV, Internet, showers, laundry, dump station. Separate RV and tent areas for adults. Fishing charter office on-site.

Eagle's Rest RV Park & Cabins
131 E. Pioneer Dr.
800-553-7275 or 907-835-2373
www.eaglesrestrv.com
Campsites with full or partial hookups, pull-throughs, tent camping. Showers, laundry, dump station. Freezer space and fish-cleaning table. Tickets for local tours. Private cabins available.

Valdez Glacier Campground
Just 5 miles from town
907-873-4058
94 standard campsites, 14 pull-throughs, tables, firepits, grills, showers, and toilets. Picnic shelter. Nesting bald eagles on-site.

Glennallen, Delta Junction, North Pole, and Fairbanks: See listings under the respective town names in Chapter 6, The Alaska Highway.

RESTAURANTS

Valdez:
Alaska Halibut House
208 Meals Ave.
907-835-2788
Seafood, burgers, salad bar. Lunch and dinner. Senior discount.

Ernesto's Taqueria
328 Egan Dr.
907-835-2519
Authentic Mexican food; serving breakfast, lunch, and dinner.

Fu Kung Chinese Restaurant
207 Kobuk St.
907-835-5255
Mandarin, Szechuan, Thai, and Chinese cuisine. Fresh sushi and local seafood Chinese-style. Lunch and dinner.

The Harbor Café
255 N. Harbor Dr.
907-835-4776
Breakfast, lunch, dinner with a view of the harbor. Located across from the Harbor Master.

Mai Thai
310 Pioneer St.
907-835-4505
Traditional Thai made with locally caught salmon, shrimp, and halibut.

Mike's Palace
201 N. Harbor Dr.
907-835-2365
Greek, Italian, Mexican, and American. Seafood and pizza. Beer and wine.

Old Town Burgers
Eagle's Rest RV Park, E. Pioneer Rd.
907-831-1434
Handmade patties for good burgers; salmon or halibut sandwiches.

Pipeline Inn/Club
112 Egan Dr.
907-835-4444
Steaks, Alaska seafood. Lounge, entertainment.

A Rogue's Garden
354 Fairbanks Dr.
907-835-5880
www.roguesgarden.com
Fresh and organic lunches and pastries, gift shop.

Totem Inn Restaurant
144 E. Egan Dr.
907-835-4443
Family dining. Hearty breakfast, lunch, and dinner, Alaskan seafood, steaks.

Glennallen, Delta Junction, North Pole, and Fairbanks: See listings under the respective town names in Chapter 6, The Alaska Highway.

SEWARD HIGHWAY

Anchorage to Seward: 127 miles (204 km)

Travel Opportunities: Potter Marsh; Turnagain Arm; Alyeska Ski Resort at Girdwood; Portage Glacier and Exit Glacier; Seward and Resurrection Bay.

The Seward Hwy. was named for former secretary of state William H. Seward, a key figure in the purchase of Alaska from Russia in 1867. Looking at a map of Alaska, you'll see that the Seward name gets around. The Seward Hwy. is on the Kenai Peninsula; the Seward Peninsula is in northwest Alaska; and then there's Fort Seward in Southeast Alaska.

The views along this highway are so stunning that the road has been designated a National Scenic Byway. From Anchorage heading south, it cuts into the foot of the mountains along the edge of Cook Inlet's Turnagain Arm. Wending between the mountains and the water, motorists may see Dall sheep, eagles, and running salmon. Rest stops and recreation areas are plentiful. Most of what you're driving through is public

A spur road off Seward Hwy. leads to Portage Lake and views of the glacier in the distance that feeds icebergs into the water.

land, either Chugach State Park or Chugach National Forest. Only a handful of small communities existed before development of the parks.

Just south of Anchorage, the road borders Potter Marsh, a portion of the Anchorage Coastal Wildlife Refuge. A boardwalk trail winds above the wetlands, with interpretive signs. Here, and in other places along the Seward Hwy., you'll see some unusual areas of sunken land where the ground dropped by several feet during the huge 1964 earthquake. In these coastal areas, still-standing dead trees were killed when the land dropped and their roots were flooded with salt water from Turnagain Arm.

Continuing south on the Seward, Turnagain Arm flanks the right side of the road. The water is not the cerulean blue that one might imagine at oceanside, but rather a flat gray from the many tons of glacial silt that are carried in streams pouring from the mountains. Over the centuries, the silt buildup has created a mudflat all around Anchorage's coastal areas, and the extreme tide at this point (sometimes surpassing 30 feet) means that for part of every day, the view is of gray mudflats. At other times, it's a vision—especially when the returning water creates a bore tide, sometimes a foot high or more, which floods the twin arms of Cook Inlet on either side of Anchorage. In Turnagain Arm, sightings of the bore tide often cause motorists to pull over and watch in awe. In a bore tide, the volume of returning water is so great that a low wall of water forms the leading edge of the incoming tide. Signs warn about the dangers of walking on the mudflats. Even though the surface looks firm, it's possible to become trapped in the silty mud—a perilous spot when the tide is about to turn.

Turnagain Arm was given its name by Capt. James Cook. In his search for the Northwest Passage, Cook ventured down this body of water, mistakenly believing it was a river. When Cook saw the retreating tide taking the water out from beneath his ship, he realized his error and advised his men to hurriedly "turn again." Take your time and stop at the waysides for photos.

Most drivers slow down at bridges to check on the progress of salmon fishermen or hooligan dipnetters. Keep your eye out for Indian Creek, Bird Creek, and Twentymile Creek. Hiking trails are well marked, too, with parking at trailheads.

Thirty-seven miles (59.5 km) south of Anchorage, turn left at the spur road into Girdwood for world-class skiing at Alyeska Ski Resort. This picturesque little town beneath 3,939-foot (1,200.5-m) Mt. Alyeska has been on the map since a minor gold rush in the early part of the 20th century. It was only in the last half of the century that Girdwood discovered its economic potential as a ski resort.

Although known internationally, Girdwood and Alyeska Resort retain a small-town feel. Among the area's amenities is luxurious Alyeska Prince Resort, as well as

an enclosed tram that travels up the mountain to the Seven Glaciers Restaurant. The views are spectacular, summer or winter. At ground level, take Crow Creek Rd. to Crow Creek Mine, where you can pan for gold (they'll show you how) or enjoy a picnic among the old buildings and artifacts. Crow Creek Mine is a national historic site in the Chugach National Forest. Dry camping is available here. See www.crowcreekgoldmine.com.

Farther down the Seward Hwy., view the remains of Portage, a small town that was ravaged in the 1964 earthquake. You can still see remnants of homes and business structures in the abundant fireweed along the road. Dead trees in this area are a testament to that terrible event, too.

Near Portage, 50 miles (80 km) south of Anchorage, the Portage Glacier Hwy. links the Seward Hwy. with Whittier, a port on Prince William Sound, via the Anton Anderson Memorial Tunnel, North America's longest railroad-highway tunnel. A toll is charged to pass through the 2.5-mile-long tunnel for eastbound travelers; there is no fee for westbound drivers. The travel direction in the tunnel alternates every 15 minutes, as it is a one-lane road and not open to bicycles or foot traffic. There are vehicle size restrictions, too. If you want to make a ferry connection at Whittier, make sure the

Pullouts along the road allow a safe means to rest, watch the movement in Cook Inlet's Turnagain Arm, or search for Dall sheep in the mountains behind you.

tunnel schedule doesn't ruin your plans. Check ahead at www.tunnel.alaska.gov. For recorded information, call 877-611-2586. The Alaska Railroad also offers passage from Portage to Whittier.

Whittier is a port on the Alaska Marine Highway System, connected with the towns of Valdez and Cordova by ferry. Whittier was originally a military post, valued for its ice-free, deepwater location on Prince William Sound. Today the harbor is home port for dozens of pleasure vessels and several cruise operations, including day trips for seeing glaciers and marine life. If you book your cruise in Anchorage, operators often make the arrangements for travel by bus to Whittier for a Prince William Sound cruise, or to Seward for cruises on Resurrection Bay.

Travelers wishing to see Portage Glacier should veer right on the Portage Glacier Hwy. when the road forks, leading to Portage Lake, within Chugach National Forest. At lakeside you'll find cafeteria-style food and Alaskan gifts at the family-owned Portage Glacier Lodge. Nearby is the Begich, Boggs Visitor Center, where hands-on displays, historical photos, film, and lots of other natural history information make it a great stop for families. Kids will have fun touching fur samples and bones from various animals and learning more about them. Photos tell the story of a gold rush that boomed here a century ago.

Because Portage Glacier has been in retreat for decades, it's difficult to see it from the visitor center. But you can travel near the face of the glacier on a one-hour cruise aboard the M/V *Ptarmigan*, operated by Gray Line of Alaska. It's good bang for your buck. Call 888-452-1737 or visit www.graylinealaska.com.

Back on the Seward Hwy., at Mile 79, look for the Alaska Wildlife Conservation Center, where you can view bison, elk, eagles, moose, caribou, and musk oxen in a natural setting. All of the wild residents in this nonprofit operation are orphaned or displaced animals. This educational drive-through park is open seven days a week. A frontier-style building houses clean restrooms and a well-stocked gift shop. Call 907-783-2025 or see www.alaskawildlife.org.

The Seward Hwy. rounds the end of Turnagain Arm, which is fed here by the Placer River. Sometimes, especially during late winter and early spring, a dozen or more moose may be seen resting here among the sparse trees. It's a rare sight, as moose are usually solitary travelers. They tend to "yard up" if snow is particularly deep in the higher regions, as food is more accessible here down below.

A welcome sign greets drivers at the gateway to the Kenai Peninsula, and the road now rises and falls as it wends its way through the pristine Kenai Mountains above and below tree line. There are no exit ramps on this highway, but there is one fork in the road about 89 miles (143 km) south of Anchorage. To stay on the Seward, all you have to do is drive straight ahead. The town of Seward lies another 38 miles (61 km) away. (A right turn at the fork marks the start of the Sterling Hwy., which leads to Soldotna, Kenai, and Homer. See the section on the Sterling Highway, in this chapter.)

At Mile 3 Seward Hwy., turn on Exit Glacier/Herman Leirer Rd. to access a rare sight: a glacier that's accessible by foot. This is the only walk-up glacier in Kenai Fjords National Park. Just follow the paved road for 8.6 miles to the Exit Glacier Nature Center, where you'll find informational displays and a bookstore. There's also tent camping in a 12-site campground. Well-marked trails lead the way to the glacier, or you can take a ranger-led tour. Be wary—multiple signs warn of the falling-ice dangers.

The oceanside community of Seward waits at the end of the Seward Hwy., 2.5 hours south of Anchorage. As if Mother Nature hasn't already made Valdez overwhelmingly beautiful, the city is covered with delightful murals, making it Mural Capital of Alaska in 2009.

Settled in 1903, Seward was founded as a shipping port and in 1915 became the southernmost terminal on the Alaska Railroad. It's also a major Southcentral port on the Alaska Marine Highway System and a destination for several cruise lines that land their passengers here and take them farther into Alaska by rail or bus.

At the edge of Resurrection Bay, protected waters off the Gulf of Alaska, Seward's fabulous Alaska SeaLife Center is a must-visit. Educational exhibits bring viewers close to seabirds and to marine mammals such as sea lions, seals, and otters. The center also

Flanked by water and mountains, the Seward Hwy. is exceedingly beautiful, earning it the designation of National Scenic Byway.

serves as a research lab and a rehabilitation facility, designed so marine biologists can work as visitors look on. Call 907-224-7908 for ticket information, or visit www.alaska sealife.org.

As the gateway to Kenai Fjords National Park, Seward's small-boat harbor is filled with pleasure craft as well as commercial fishing vessels and tour boats. Just walking the docks and reading the names of the boats is a fun way to spent an hour or more. The Kenai Fjords National Park Visitor Center, at the harbor, has information on the birds and animals that inhabit the park; call 907-224-3175. Cruise operators offer full-day or half-day tours for wildlife-watching or glacier-viewing or both. Usually a meal is served on board or at a stopover like Fox Island. At the harbor, you can also find fishing charters. Seward's Silver Salmon Derby and Jackpot Halibut Tournament are hot competitions sponsored by the local chamber of commerce. The Silver Salmon Derby alone offers more than $150,000 in prizes. Catching a single tagged fish can garner a $50,000 cash prize.

For mushing fans, here's your chance to meet a history-making family of Iditarod mushers named Seavey and tour their 85-dog kennel at Seavey's Ididaride Sled Dog Tours, just minutes outside of town. You can also see Hugo, one of the stars in Disney's *Snow Dogs*, cuddle a puppy, and go on a summertime sled-dog adventure, a 2-mile ride behind a team of huskies. Named one of the top attractions in Alaska, Seavey's Iditarod Sled Dog Tours offers a behind-the-scenes look at how mushers and dogs train in the off-season. Space fills up quickly, so make your reservation early at 907-224-8607. See more at www.ididaride.com.

Seward was among the coastal communities severely damaged in the 1964 earthquake. See the Resurrection Bay Historical Society Museum, at Jefferson St. and 3rd

Ave. The collection includes historical and cultural artifacts, photos from the 1964 earthquake and World War II, and other pieces of local history. The Seward Community Library, at 5th Ave. and Adams St., presents a movie and slide show about the devastating 9.2 earthquake at 2 PM daily, except Sunday, throughout the summer.

Each July 4, scores of runners and walkers assault Mt. Marathon, the 3,022-foot peak just at the town's back. It's a grueling race to the top and back down, and city streets are choked with spectators. The walkers' trailhead is at 1st Ave. and Monroe St. Runners begin their trek at 1st Ave. and Jefferson St.

Check at the Chugach National Forest district office at 334 4th Ave. for information on hiking and biking. Call 907-224-3374.

Seward's visitor information center is at Mile 2 Seward Hwy. Stop by and learn more about how to make the most of your time here. Staffers can also direct you on how to book a fishing charter, show where to park your RV, and offer maps for a walking tour of the town's historic area. Call 907-224-8051 or see www.sewardak.org.

LODGING

Anchorage: See information at the end of the section on the Glenn Highway, in this chapter.

Indian:
Bird Ridge Motel
Mile 101 Seward Hwy.
907-653-0100
www.birdridge.com
Rooms near excellent fishing and hiking trails. RV parking, café, and bakery.

Brown Bear Saloon & Hotel
Mile 103 Seward Hwy.
907-653-7000
Rooms and cabins with private baths, kitchens. Near salmon fishing, hiking, wildlife watching.

Girdwood: You may book Girdwood accommodations through Alyeska/Girdwood Accommodations Association at 907-222-3226 or www.agaa.biz.
Alyeska Prince Resort
1000 Arlberg Ave.
800-880-3880 or 907-754-1111
www.alyeskaresort.com
307 deluxe rooms, suites in AAA 4-Diamond hotel. Fitness center, shops, tour desk, tramway sightseeing. Lounges, casual to gourmet dining.

Moose Pass:
Summit Lake Lodge
Mile 46 Seward Hwy.
907-244-2031
www.summitlakelodge.com
Rooms, plus gift shop, restaurant, lounge in beautiful lakeside setting.

Trail Lake Lodge
Mile 29.5 Seward Hwy.
800-865-0201 or 907-224-5559
www.traillakelodge.com
Rooms with private bath and TV. Fishing and kayaking packages. Just 30 minutes north of Seward.

Seward:
A number of B&Bs, cabins, and cottages are available. For a listing, contact the Seward Chamber of Commerce Conference and Visitors Bureau at www.seward.com.

Alaska's Orca Inn
309 3rd Ave.
866-524-9188
www.orcak.com
Apartment-style suites, full kitchens, cable TV, Wi-Fi, laundry room. Walking distance to attractions.

Best Western Edgewater Hotel
200 5th Ave.
888-793-6800 or 907-224-2700
www.hoteledgewater.com
Well-appointed rooms with cable TV, Wi-Fi, fridge, microwave. Nonsmoking. Cocktail lounge, conference center, overlooks Resurrection Bay in downtown Seward.

Breeze Inn
303 N. Harbor
888-224-5237 or 907-224-5237
86 rooms, nonsmoking available. Gift shop, coffee and espresso bar, restaurant, lounge. At the small-boat harbor.

Glacier Lodge
.25 Mile Exit Glacier/Herman Leirer Rd.
907-224-6040
www.sewardglacierlodge.com
15-room lodge in Resurrection River valley, just
outside Seward. Private bathrooms, cable TV,
Wi-Fi, free video and DVD rentals, free breakfast.
Near Salmon Bake Restaurant and Pub. Freezer
space available for your fish.

Harborview Inn
804 3rd Ave.
888-324-3217 or 907-224-3217
www.sewardhotel.com
Rooms and family suites with view of the bay.
Cable TV, Wi-Fi. Walking distance to tours, train,
downtown. RV/truck parking. Handicap access.

Holiday Inn Express Seward Harbor
1412 4th Ave.
800-HOLIDAY or 907-224-2550
www.hiexpress.com
82 rooms on the harbor with bay or mountain
views, Internet, swimming pool, free hot breakfast.
Walk to attractions.

Hotel Seward
221 5th Ave.
800-655-8785 or 907-224-8001
www.hotelsewardalaska.com
Rooms and executive suites, nonsmoking available, cable TV, movies. Half block to Alaska
SeaLife Center.

Marina Motel
Near train station
907-224-5518
www.sewardmotel.com
Two double beds, private bath, fridge, coffeemaker, cable TV, free movies.

Miller's Landing
On Resurrection Bay
866-541-5739 or 907-224-5739
Oceanfront cabins and camping on 1950s homestead beyond the town of Seward. Laundry, showers, toilets, Wi-Fi. Tours, fishing, kayaking, water
taxi. Country store, fish-cleaning stations.

Murphy's Motel
911 4th Ave.
800-686-8191 or 907-224-8090
www.murphysmotel.com
Rooms with a view, cable TV, free Wi-Fi, fridge,
microwave.

Saltwater Safari Company
At the small-boat harbor
800-382-1564 or 907-224-5232
Fishing lodge on the boardwalk in the boat harbor.
Nine waterfront suites with luxurious appointments
and private baths. Company-owned 53-foot ves-
sels for access to fishing and hunting. Views of
Resurrection Bay and marine life.

Seward Military Resort
2305 Dimond Blvd.
800-770-1858 or 907-224-5559
www.sewardresort.com
Motel rooms, cabins, RV sites. Fishing charters.
Exclusive use by current and retired military per-
sonnel, their guests and families, as well as federal
employees, their guests and families.

Seward Windsong Lodge
31772 Exit Glacier/Herman Leirer Rd.
888-959-9590 or 907-224-7116
www.sewardwindsong.com
Comfortable, newer rooms with cable TV, VCR,
phone. Forested setting. Dining, lounge. Info on
local tours and attractions.

A Swan Nest Inn
504 Adams St.
866-224-7461 or 907-224-3080
www.aswannestinn.com
Elegant rooms in 1918-era building once housed
the International Order of Odd Fellows. Log furniture, original art, tour booking service.

Taroka Motel
235 3rd Ave.
907-224-8975
www.alaskaone.com/taroka
Rooms and kitchenettes, cable TV, Wi-Fi. Close to
downtown, Alaska SeaLife Center. Pet friendly.

The Van Gilder Hotel
308 Adams St.
800-204-6835 or 907-224-3079
www.vangilderhotel.com
Antique furnishings and modern amenities in this
1916-era hotel, on the National Register of Historic
Places since 1980. Free Wi-Fi, cable TV, private
bath. Downtown location.

CAMPGROUNDS

Anchorage: See information at the end of the section on the Glenn Highway, in this chapter.

Bird Creek:
Bird Creek Campground
26 miles (42 km) south of Anchorage, Chugach
State Park
28 campsites, picnic tables, water, toilets. Close to
salmon fishing, bike trails.

Girdwood:
Crow Creek Mine
3 miles (5 km) up Crow Creek Rd.
907-278-8060
Historic gold mine offers sites for dry camping
and tenting.

Portage:
Portage Valley Cabins & RV Park
Mile 1.7 Portage Glacier Rd.
907-783-3111
www.portagevalleyrvpark.com
Cabins, RV park, campground. Hiking trails,
stocked fishing ponds.

Williwaw Creek Campground
Mile 4 Portage Glacier Rd.
877-444-6777 for reservations
60 campsites, picnic tables, water, toilets. Deck for
viewing spawning salmon late July–mid-September.
Nature trails. Campground managed by US Forest
Service. To reserve a campsite online, visit www.
reserveamerica.com at least 5 days in advance.

Seward:
Bear Creek RV Park
6.5 miles (10.5 km) north of Seward on Bear Lake
Rd.
907-224-5724
www.bearcreekrv.com
Full and partial hookups. Showers, laundry, restrooms, dump station, store. Fishing and glacier
tours, courtesy van.

Miller's Landing
On Resurrection Bay
866-541-5739 or 907-224-5739
Oceanfront cabins, RV and tent camping on 1950s
homestead beyond the town of Seward. Laundry,
showers, toilets, Wi-Fi. Tours, fishing, kayaking,
water taxi. Country store, fish-cleaning stations.

Seward Waterfront Park
Runs the length of Ballaine Rd. along the water
907-224-4055 (may leave message)
www.cityofseward.net/parksRec/campgrounds.htm
99 sites with utilities; others without. No pull-
throughs.

Stoney Creek RV Park
From Mile 6.3 Seward Hwy., off Stoney Creek Ave.
907-224-6465
www.stoneycreekrvpark.com
81 creekside campsites, full and partial hookup,
some pull-throughs. Satellite TV, showers, laundry.

The municipality operates five campgrounds within
the park on a first-come, first-served basis, except
for caravans, which can reserve. Coin-op showers, free dump. Self-registration. Some sites are
for tents or smaller RVs; must fit on the pad. For
information on two other municipal campgrounds,

see website. An informational campground brochure can be mailed upon request. Write to City
of Seward–SPRD, Parks & Campgrounds, PO Box
167, Seward, AK 99664-0167.

RESTAURANTS

Anchorage: See information at the end of the sec-
tion on the Glenn Highway, in this chapter.
Turnagain House
Mile 103 Seward Hwy.
907-653-7500
Steaks, Alaskan seafood specialties, with views of
Turnagain Arm.

Girdwood:
Alyeska Prince Resort
1000 Arlberg Ave.
800-880-3880 or 907-754-1111
www.alyeskaresort.com
Choose from several restaurants for the dining experience of your choice: Aurora Bar & Grill, the Pond
Café, Sakura Sushi Bar, and Tramway Café. Casual
to fine dining (see Seven Glaciers Restaurant).

The Bake Shop
At Alyeska Ski Resort
907-783-2831
www.thebakeshop.com
Homemade soups, sourdough pancakes,
breads, pizza.

Chair 5 Restaurant
5 Linblad Ave., off Hightower Rd.
907-783-2500
www.chairfive.com
Seafood, pizza, microbrews, pool table.

Double Musky Inn
On Crow Creek Rd.
907-783-2822
www.doublemuskyinn.com
Cajun specialties, Alaska seafood. Funky Alaska
decor, since 1962.

Jack Sprat Restaurant
165 Olympic Mountain Loop
907-754-5225
www.jacksprat.net
Dinner nightly; Saturday and Sunday brunch.
Innovative menu; beer and wine from around
the world.

Seven Glaciers Restaurant
1000 Arlberg Ave., at Alyeska Prince Resort
907-754-2237
www.alyeskaresort.com
AAA 4-diamond dining in a mountaintop restaurant. Take the tram up to sample signature Alaskan
entrées, award-winning wines, and full bar. Call
for reservations or go online. Tram ride is free with
advance dinner reservations.

Portage:
Portage Glacier Lodge
Across from Begich, Boggs Visitor Center
907-783-3117
Soups, sandwiches, cafeteria-style. Eat in or
take out.

Moose Pass:
Summit Lake Lodge
Mile 46 Seward Hwy.
907-244-2031
www.summitlakelodge.com
Burgers, halibut, prime rib. Lakeside lodge, lounge,
gift shop.

Seward:
Apollo Restaurant
229 4th Ave.
907-224-3092
www.apollorestaurantak.com
Mediterranean, Italian.

Breeze Inn
1306 Seward Hwy.
888-224-5237 or 907-224-5237
www.breezeinn.com
Family-friendly dining with a view; seafood specialties. At small-boat harbor, adjacent to motel.

Chinooks Waterfront Restaurant
1404 4th Ave.
907-224-2207
www.chinookswaterfront.com
Seafood, steaks, pasta; serving lunch and dinner.
At small-boat harbor; views of Resurrection Bay.

Exit Glacier Salmon Bake
.25 Exit Glacier/Herman Leirer Rd.
907-224-2204
www.sewardalaskacabins.com
Full-service restaurant. Salmon, halibut, steaks,
burgers.

Lombardo's Eatery
308 N. Harbor St.
907-224-5055
Pizza, grinders, hamburgers, salads.

Peking Restaurant
338 4th Ave.
907-224-5444
Chinese cuisine.

Ray's Waterfront
1316 4th Ave.
907-224-5606
Seafood specialties. Overlooking Seward Boat
Harbor.

Resurrection Roadhouse Restaurant
Mile .7, Exit Glacier/Herman Leirer Rd.
800-208-0200 or 907-224-7116
www.sewardwindsong.com
Good food, casual atmosphere with a view,
microbrews.

Yoly's Bistro
220 4th Ave.
907-224-3295
www.yolysbistro.com
Calamari, king crab, shrimp, halibut, Angus beef.

STEESE HIGHWAY

Fairbanks to Circle City: 162 miles (261 km)

Travel Opportunities: Chena Hot Springs; Gold Dredge No. 8; Fox; Chatanika; Eagle Summit;
Central, Circle Hot Springs, and Circle City.

If the Steese Hwy. were ever renamed, it should be the Gold Road, for this is the his-
toric transportation corridor between some of the state's richest goldfields in the Circle
Mining District and Fairbanks, the boomtown that was built on the discovery of gold.
In fact, the road edges Pedro Creek, near the very place where Italian immigrant Felix
Pedro discovered gold in 1902, launching yet another gold rush. By 1910, nearly $2 mil-
lion in gold had moved through Fairbanks.

The Steese Hwy. begins at the intersection of Airport Wy. and Gaffney Blvd. in
Fairbanks. Quickly, it splits into the Old Steese and, a block away, the New Steese. The
older road has been absorbed into a district of malls, gas stations, and businesses. But
the New Steese is a four-lane highway that skirts Fairbanks then heads north. Drive
carefully on this section, as the pavement rocks and rolls for several miles on your way

A day-old domesticated reindeer and his mother are part of a small, private herd off the Steese Hwy. Whenever the herder gets an invitation for a school visit, the female simply steps into the open back of a minivan for the drive into town.

to the community of Fox. Insidious permafrost works against the road builders' best efforts. These early miles of the Steese are heavily used by Fairbanks residents who live in the surrounding hills.

Just a few miles out of town is the turnoff to Chena Hot Springs Rd. Take this 56.5-mile (91-km) paved spur road east to its dead end and you'll land at Chena Hot Springs Resort, a good pick for a delicious day trip. Winter or summer, you can soak in 100°F pools of mineral water that seem to suck the tension out of every pore. The resort offers nicely appointed rooms or rustic cabins, a restaurant, and an RV park with electricity and a dump station. Swim in an enclosed pool area, or soak in outdoor hot tubs. You can go horseback riding, hike, pick blueberries, and, in winter, view the aurora. The country's first ice hotel was built here in 2004. Visit the Aurora Ice Museum, which is refrigerated year-round, and have your drink served in a piece of ice that's ground into a glass as you watch. Call 907-451-8104 or visit www.chenahotsprings.com.

Back on the Steese Hwy., continue on past Chena Hot Springs Rd. to experience some of the area's best tourist sights, as well as unparalleled views of the Tanana Valley and beyond.

Ahead on the Steese, portions of the Trans-Alaska Pipeline will be visible on your right. At Mile 8.5 (Km 13.5), a spacious parking area with interpretive signs allows visitors to roam around and walk up to the pipeline. A visitor information center there is usually staffed, and free brochures are available. A sign cautions, Please do not climb on the pipeline. Near here, the Steese Hwy. reduces from four lanes to two, but remains paved for many more miles.

A mile later, turn left onto Goldstream Rd. and follow the signs to the Old Steese Hwy. to access Gold Dredge No. 8, a piece of mining history that has been restored for visitors. The attraction includes tours aboard this floating gold-processing ship and in these historic buildings. You can pan for gold yourself and learn more about the operations of the old Fairbanks Exploration Company. Call ahead to arrange a tour at 907-457-6058 or learn more at www.golddredgeno8.com.

If you plan to continue traveling on the Steese, the upcoming intersection, at Mile 11 (Km 18), may be confusing. The Old Steese joins New Steese here, so a right turn is necessary to stay on this particular highway. If you go straight, you'll be on the Elliott Hwy. and bound for the Brooks Range. The Fox General Store and gas station on this intersection is the last place to fuel up, buy propane, or stock up on snacks for many miles, so top off here if you haven't done so in Fairbanks.

One other option is well worth your time, particularly if you're hungry or thirsty. Turn left onto the Old Steese, and you'll be driving through the main street of "downtown" Fox, where few people live, but

The Trans-Alaska Pipeline is at roadside on this northbound road out of Fairbanks. It's a regular stop for large touring coaches as well as independent travelers.

many come to eat and drink. Notable businesses include The Howling Dog Saloon, your classic funky Alaska bar (which also claims it's world famous). Pizza and other bar grub are available, as well as a full bar selection of beverages. There's live music on the fare, too. Across the road is the Silver Gulch Brewing & Bottling Co., home of the historic Fox Roadhouse. This is America's most northern brewery and offers lunch and dinner, with locally produced beers on tap. Tours are available, too. A few miles farther down the road, The Turtle Club is a Fairbanks-area favorite for prime rib and king crab. Dinner reservations are suggested.

Back on the Steese Hwy., 20 miles (32 km) from Fairbanks at the Cleary Summit Scenic Viewpoint, outstanding valley views were marred by wildfires in summer 2004. Regrowth is visible today.

At about Mile 28 (Km 45), watch for the turnoff to the old Fairbanks Exploration Gold Camp, which is on the National Register of Historic Places. The company's bunkhouse, built between 1922 and 1925, is part of a complex that includes original miners' cabins and the old Chatanika Schoolhouse. The FE Gold Camp is now a restaurant and lodge, open March through September. Chatanika was the site of an old gold-mining town. Miners here pulled about $70 million in gold out of the ground between 1926 and 1957. During those years, more than 10,000 people lived here, making it larger than Fairbanks.

Drive a half mile down the road for a peek at another remnant of Chatanika's boom days, Gold Dredge No. 3, which operated until 1962. Although the old dredge may be barely visible from the road, it lies on private property and trespassing is not permitted. You can learn more about it and the boomtown and enjoy a homestyle meal and a cold one across the highway from the dredge at the Chatanika Lodge, where you may have to step over a sleeping dog to get to the bar. This place is authentic Alaska, and there's stuff to look at in every nook and cranny: big-game mounts, photos, tanned furs for sale, even a reclining nude over the bar. Friendly folks. Worth the drive from Fairbanks.

Just a few miles ahead is the entrance to Poker Flat Research Range, a 5,132-acre site where the University of Alaska Fairbanks Geophysical Institute, in conjunction with the National Aeronautics and Atmospheric Administration, has conducted studies on the aurora borealis, the arctic atmosphere, and the ionosphere since 1979. For more on the university's work in space science, see www.pfrr.alaska.edu.

Up ahead, a series of summits and interesting switchbacks make driving the Steese an on-your-toes proposition. For one, you run out of pavement. However, the gravel surface is well graded in summer, and the snowy surface is plowed often in winter. Views of the river valleys from above are panoramic, and as you drive over the mountain range, above tree line, with few guardrails along the road, you can experience something like vertigo.

The road wends over Cleary Summit to Twelve-Mile Summit at Mile 85.5, where hikers can access the 27-mile (44-km) Pinnell Mountain National Recreation Trail, managed by the BLM. The ridgetop trail above timberline promises spectacular views in every direction. In case of a storm, emergency shelters can be found along the way. For maps of this trail and others in the area, contact the BLM's Fairbanks District office at 800-437-7021 or visit www.ak.blm.gov.

Shirley Franklin offers a warm welcome at the Chatanika Lodge, where hearty food and cold drinks, as well as rousing conversation, have made it a local favorite. Drop-ins may end up rubbing elbows with a gold miner or two.

At Mile 107.5 (Km 173), you'll cross Eagle Summit, the tallest of them all at 3,652 feet (1,113 m) above sea level. For those accustomed to trees and roadside businesses, the trek up and over Eagle Summit will come as a surprise in its nakedness. The road threads over rolling mountains and above tree line with nothing between you and the distant valley floor except fresh air. At the top, the view is nearly dizzying—just undulating country on all sides. Here, dozens of people gather on either June 20 or 21, summer solstice, to observe and photograph an unobstructed view of the midnight sun. Their photographs, taken over several hours with timed exposures, will show an orange orb gently touching down to the horizon line before beginning its slow ascent.

In the village of Central, 127 miles (203 km) northeast of Fairbanks, most of the residents are gold miners or have been miners or are related to a miner. Members and friends of the Circle Mining District hold their annual picnic here each summer, plus a big-game potluck in the fall. This tiny town of log cabins includes a school, a small grocery and gift shop, a couple of cafés, and some roadside lodging, including the Steese Roadhouse, a checkpoint on the route of the Yukon Quest International Sled Dog Race. Stop in for fuel, food, laundry, showers, or fresh water at 10 cents a gallon. The roadhouse has rooms, or you can camp. Call 907-520-5800. The people of Central raised money to open the town's mining museum, which is open noon to 5 PM during summer months. The indoor and outdoor collection of mining materials, and history of this place, is well worth a nice, long browse. E-mail museum@steesehighway.org for information.

From Central, an 8-mile, unpaved spur road leads southeast to Circle Hot Springs, and a three-story wooden building that served as a resort for nearly a century. The business is currently closed. The natural springs drew Athabascan Indians long before gold miners discovered the natural wonder in the late 1800s. A century ago, pioneers Frank and Emma Leach ran the hotel, worked this ground, and watered their superb gardens with hot-springs water. Their graves are on a nearby hill, and it is said that they still haunt the place. The resort may be closed, but camping and cabin rentals are available here at Nugget Gulch, operated by Jim Crabb. Call ahead, 907-520-5322.

Beyond Central, the Steese Hwy. consists of nearly 34 unpaved miles (54 km) of winding road through the boreal forest. At the end of the road, you'll find Circle City and a sign welcoming you to the banks of the Yukon River, a braided stream in this section and one of only three places in Alaska where motorists can drive to the river. (The other two are the village of Eagle on the Taylor Hwy., and the Yukon River bridge on the Dalton Hwy., aka the Haul Rd.) The Yukon is a 2,000-mile waterway that flows westward from its headwaters in Canada to Alaska's Bering Sea.

Several boomtowns seemed to have claimed the title "Paris of the North" during the gold rushes of the late 1800s. Such was true for Dawson City, YT, but Circle City came up with it even earlier. Founded in 1893 and misnamed by early miners who thought they were on the Arctic Circle (they were 50 miles off), the city was home to more than 1,000 at its peak, attracting the usual rabble, along with others who brought with them the cultural refinements of home, including theater productions, teas, readings, and book exchanges.

Looking at this little community of about 100 people today, it's hard to believe what once stood here. A smattering of cabins makes up the town. The H. C. Company Store, at the end of the road, serves the community year-round with groceries and gas. If you're interested, ask here for directions to the Pioneer Cemetery, but be careful to skirt private property as you walk. Camping is available near the river, as boaters frequently access the river here.

JACK MCQUESTEN'S SOURDOUGH THERMOMETER

Arthur Harper, Alfred Mayo, and Leroy N. "Jack" McQuesten were three traders and prospectors who made their way overland to the Yukon River basin from British Columbia. They traded for furs and developed ties with Native people. Rumors of gold in the Yukon River basin persisted among prospectors, and American veterans of the gold rushes in California and British Columbia started to arrive.

Perry Davis's "vegetable elixir" was patented in 1845 and reportedly was the first advertised remedy for general pain. Ingredients were all natural: opiates and ethyl alcohol.

For over two decades, these three American traders supplied prospectors in the Yukon River basin. Their trading posts, operated for the Alaska Commercial Company as well as their own stores, were long lasting.

In 1874, Jack McQuesten established Fort Reliance, a trading post about 6 miles below present-day city of Dawson...In 1879 the Hudson's Bay Company employed him to run their trading post, and later he did the same for the Alaska Commercial Company. He used Fort Reliance as his trading post for about a dozen years. While at the Fort he made the first weather record of the Yukon—that was in 1880–81. It was during the same period that Jack became widely known as the inventor of the "Sourdough Thermometer."

The thermometer consisted of a row of four bottles, each containing either mercury, coal oil, Jamaica ginger, or Perry Davis' Painkiller. The bottles were set outside where they could be seen from a window. If the mercury froze, it was –40°F (–40°C). The coal oil froze at –49°F (–45°C). If the Jamaica ginger froze, it was –59.8°F (–51°C). The ultimate measuring device of Jack's Sourdough Thermometer was the fourth bottle: Perry Davis' Painkiller. The patent medicine would turn white at –59.8°F (–51°C), crystallize at –70.6° F (–57°C), and freeze solid at –76°F (–60°C). Jack's thermometer was very popular outside roadhouses between Whitehorse and Dawson. Most stayed home when the mercury froze, but when the painkiller froze, it was considered unsafe to travel very far from a fire. It has been said the invention saved many lives in that harsh climate.

In 1893, Jack McQuesten established Circle City, Alaska, as a trading center twelve miles upstream from its present location. The three partners and their families also constructed a log trading post at Fortymile, which became the first [non-Native] town on the Yukon River. By 1895, Fortymile had two trading posts, two saloons, an opera house, an Anglican mission, and a contingent of Northwest Mounted Police. Following the gold strikes on Birch Creek in 1894, the McQuestens started an Alaska Commercial Company store at Circle City. After word of the Klondike discovery reached Circle, the city emptied as miners moved to Dawson. Fearing the dismal conditions in the boomtown of Dawson and a pending food shortage, Jack, at the well-worn age of 58, retired and moved his family to Berkeley, California.

—Cecil Munsey, PhD, excerpted with author's permission from
"Yukon Jack," published in *Bottles and Extras*, Summer 2004

LODGING/CAMPGROUNDS/MEALS

Fox:
Howling Dog Saloon, Motel & Café
Mile 11 Old Steese Hwy.
907-456-HOWL
http://howlingdogsaloon.alaskansavvy.com

Silver Gulch Brewing & Bottling Co.
2195 Old Steese Hwy.
907-452-2739

The Turtle Club
Old Steese Hwy.
907-457-3883
Prime rib, seafood, salad bar, lounge. A local favorite.

Chatanika to Central:
FE Gold Camp
Mile 27.5 Steese Hwy.
907-389-2414
Bunkhouse accommodations and mess-hall restaurant. Open during summer months only.

Chatanika Lodge
Mile 28.5 Steese Hwy.
907-389-2164
10 rooms with sink and TV, shared bath facilities. Bar and restaurant, and real Alaskan character.

Upper Chatanika State Recreation Area
Mile 39 Steese Hwy.
Concessionaire Kenneth Faust: 907-456-1104 or 907-460-1218
39 campsites, no RV length limit. Toilets, water, picnic sites, boat launch.

Long Creek Trading Post
Mile 45.5 Steese Hwy.
907-389-5287
Rooms and cabin rentals; dry camping for RVs, tent sites. Showers, laundry, sani-dump. Gold panning, canoe rentals.

Cripple Creek Campground (managed by BLM)
Mile 60 Steese Hwy.
12 campsites with tables; short trail along Cripple Creek. Hand-pump water, pit toilets, trash cans. No dump station.

Central:
Nugget Gulch
Mile 8 Circle Hot Springs Rd.
907-520-5322
Cabin rentals and campsites.

Steese Roadhouse
Mile 128 Steese Hwy.
907-520-5800
www.steeseroadhouse.com
Motel rooms, showers, laundry. Café, bar, store, gas, propane.

Circle City:
H.C. Company Store
End of the Steese Hwy.
907-773-1222
Gas, diesel, AV gas, groceries, snacks, phone, tire repair. Free camping near the river.

STERLING HIGHWAY

From Seward Hwy. to Homer: 143 miles (230 km)

Travel Opportunities: *Kenai Lake at Cooper Landing; fishing the Kenai and Russian rivers; clamming at Clam Gulch; deep-sea charter fishing at Anchor Point or Homer; day trips to Seldovia and Halibut Cove.*

The Sterling Hwy. leaves the Seward Hwy. at a fork 90 miles (145 km) south of Anchorage. It wends west and south through a sparsely populated wilderness area and passes through a handful of small towns on the way to its dead end in another small town, Homer. Lofty mountains shoulder the two paved lanes, and nearby lakes and streams run clean and cold. Most of the land is included in the 1.9-million-acre Kenai National Wildlife Refuge. Moose and bear numbers are strong, and you might see Dall sheep, caribou, loons, eagles, and trumpeter swans. Offshore, watch for sea otters, seals, puffins, and numerous birds.

Flightseeing operations offer bird's-eye views of unbelievable beauty. Hiking, canoeing, and rafting are other recreation offerings on the Kenai Peninsula. Nature photography ranks high on the list as well. Beautifully adorned subjects lie all around you. Distant glaciers flow from the Harding Icefield, and along the road the gem green Kenai Lake flows into a magnificent river of the same color and name.

One in every 65 Alaskans holds a license to fly a small plane. Here, an Anchorage resident has landed his floatplane on Skilak Lake for a day of fishing.

The biggest towns along the Sterling Hwy. are Cooper Landing, Mile 12 (Km 19), 102 miles (164 km) south of Anchorage; Sterling, at Mile 44.5 (Km 71.5); Soldotna, at Mile 58.5 (Km 94); and the end of the road, at Homer, Mile 143 (Km 230). In each town, you'll find gas, food, campgrounds, services, fishing licenses, hotels, and opportunities to line up a guide or gather some local knowledge.

What the Kenai Peninsula may be best known for worldwide is its prime fishing. Sportfishers travel great distances to fish the Kenai River, to wade into turquoise-colored waters in the hope of wrestling with a king, the salmon that can grow into the size and weight of a seven-year-old child. (The world-record king salmon of 97.4 pounds was taken from the Kenai River in 1985.) Equally attractive is another world-class roadside sportfishing stream, the Russian River. On this river, the prized fish is the red salmon.

Every day of every summer, campgrounds near these rivers are jammed with RVs and cars as anglers head for the water. This is a camping experience like no other. Don't expect peace and solitude when the salmon are running. Anglers stand shoulder to shoulder and work in cooperation to flip out their lines to drift with the current without tangling with those of their neighbors. The cry "Fish on!" is the signal to reel in your line and get out of the way until a lucky angler nets his or her fish.

Charter fishing operations at Anchor Point, Deep Creek, Ninilchik, and Homer lead clients to unforgettable deep-sea halibut fishing. Getting a 100-pound lunker off the bottom and over the side of the boat takes more than finesse. It's just sheer muscle-fishing. The biggest halibut caught in Cook Inlet weighed about 465 pounds.

I caught a halibut off Anchor Point myself that weighed 211 pounds, and we weren't in a tour boat, so I didn't have the advantage of a fighting chair, or any chair for that matter. It was an open set-net skiff. Thankfully, my captain friend was an experienced angler who had a gaff and the muscle to use it. I brought the fish to the boat, but he got it over the side. (Yes, we ate halibut for a long time.)

Six peninsula towns offer prizes for the biggest salmon or halibut in annual fishing derbies (combined, the prizes equal about $100,000). The Soldotna Visitor Information Center is across the bridge in Soldotna, at 44790 Sterling Hwy., and offers information on wildlife viewing, fishing, and other outdoor recreation. Here also you'll find the mount of that 97.4-pound world-record king salmon. The mount hangs on the wall; the mouths of visitors simply hang open. Call 907-262-9814 or visit www.soldotnachamber.com.

Fishing in a new region always carries with it a hefty learning curve, so consider whether you want to devote the time necessary to learning how these fish behave. Hiring a guide is often the best option. They know the best holes, the best time of day, and the regulations. It's likely, too, that a guide will haul you away from the crowds in a boat or floatplane. Most places can arrange to have your fish smoked or frozen and shipped home when you're ready to receive it. Check with any of the visitor centers on the peninsula for referrals to reliable guides.

The biggest town on the Kenai Peninsula lies on the shores of Cook Inlet and shares the same name as the peninsula: Kenai. Located on the Kenai Spur Hwy., westbound from Soldotna, the city is home to fishing and oil industry workers, tourism operators, and other people in support services.

On the docks in Homer, a boater heads out with supplies for a few days on the water.

Watch the tide tables to determine the best time to access the beach at Clam Gulch. Four-wheel-drive vehicles can access the full length of the beach; others must park and walk in with their clamming gear.

In Kenai, you'll find the visitor information log cabin at the corner of Main St. and the Kenai Spur Hwy. Pick up a walking map for Old Town Kenai, and learn about its early Kenaitze Indian and Russian residents. The Holy Assumption of the Virgin Mary Russian Orthodox Church has stood here since 1894. The Dena'ina Athabascans have lived and hunted in this region for thousands of years. Get information about the area at 907-283-1991 or see www.visitkenai.com, where you can order a visitor guide by mail, or just download it.

From Kenai and the neighboring village of Nikiski, the view across Cook Inlet is panoramic: Mt. Spurr, Mt. Redoubt, and Mt. Iliamna are the cone-shaped volcanoes on the horizon—and they are not dormant. There have been several eruptions in the last 20 years, as Mt. Kiska, Mt. Redoubt, and Mt. Spurr each rumbled to life, spewing fine ash that rained down on Southcentral Alaska for hundreds of miles. Most recently, Mt. Redoubt began a series of eruptions on March 22, 2009, and continued to erupt sporadically, causing interruptions in air traffic for months. For updates and photos of Redoubt in action, see the Alaska Volcano Observatory website at www.avo.alaska.edu/activity/Redoubt.php.

Private campgrounds may be found near or in the towns that dot the length of the Sterling Hwy. and the Kenai Spur Hwy. The state maintains several recreation areas and sites along these roads, too, and campsites are plentiful at Clam Gulch, Deep Creek, Ninilchik, Kenai, Nikiski, and Johnson Lake, and in Homer at Kachemak Bay State Park. Another dozen less-developed grounds also offer campsites, restrooms, and water. For full details, call the Division of Parks and Outdoor Recreation's Soldotna office at 907-262-5581.

The Kenai is steeped in the ancient Kenaitze Indian culture and in that of the Russians, whose two centuries of influence are still visible in the blue-domed churches at Kenai and Ninilchik. Native surnames often possess an echo of Russia, as do place-names such as Kalifornsky, Nikiski, Kasilof, and Ninilchik. At the village of Ninilchik, the Russian Orthodox church majestically overlooks Cook Inlet from atop a bluff. Visitors are welcome to photograph the church, but remember that this is a place of worship. The local people ask that you do not enter the cemetery. Throughout the Kenai, shops offer handmade Native crafts and Russian gift items, as well as the more typical Alaska souvenirs.

The Sterling Hwy. ends at the sea at Homer, a town that's a wonderful mix of artist colony, commercial fishing seaport, small-town Alaska, and tourist destination. Homer is a port of call on the Alaska Marine Highway System; for information, call 800-642-0066 or visit www.ferryalaska.com.

The Alaska Islands and Oceans Visitor Center, headquarters for the Alaska Maritime National Wildlife Refuge, is right at the entrance to Homer at 95 Sterling Hwy. The 4.4-million-acre refuge extends along much of the Alaska coastline. Allow lots of time to explore this beautiful building and the free exhibits. Call 907-235-6961. Visit their website at www.islandsandocean.org.

More than 100,000 shorebirds migrate through this part of the state annually. Each May, the city joins forces with the US Fish & Wildlife Service and the National Wildlife Refuge System to host the Kachemak Bay Shorebird Festival, drawing hundreds of birders to witness thousands of sandpipers, turnstones, dowitchers, and dunlins. Eagles are year-round residents. Festival keynote speakers include notable bird biologists, authors, and wildlife managers. The Homer Chamber of Commerce even includes a birding hotline number on its website: "Call 907-235-PEEP (235-7337) to hear what birds are being spotted in Homer right now!" Check the site for news of upcoming festivals, www.homeralaska.org.

The end of the Sterling Hwy. lies at the end of Homer Spit, which reaches out into Kachemak Bay for several miles.

There's more about the natural and cultural history of this area at the Pratt Museum in Homer, 3779 Bartlett St. off Pioneer Ave. Artifacts from prehistory to homesteaders, information on marine mammals, and guided ecology tours are among the offerings. The items for sale at the art gallery and gift shop include Alaska-made crafts and collectibles. Call 907-235-8635 or see www.prattmuseum.org.

Fine art galleries featuring the work of local and guest artists may be found throughout town and on the Homer Spit, a 4.5-mile finger of land that extends into Kachemak Bay. Homer is a creative place, so take a gallery trek. Along the Homer Spit, you can walk along an elevated boardwalk and watch happy anglers posing with the day's catch of halibut. You can book a salmon or halibut charter or arrange a day boat trip across the bay to visit the tiny villages of Seldovia and Halibut Cove. Look into the options at the Homer Chamber of Commerce, 907-235-7740 or www.homeralaska.org.

On the Homer Spit, there are hotel rooms, RV and tent camping, gift shops, art galleries, pleasure boats, and commercial fishing vessels. Have a cold drink at the Salty Dog Saloon; enjoy a meal with an amazing view at Land's End; walk the beach with your kids and examine what high tide has delivered. The Homer Spit, with its festival-like atmosphere, is a gathering place for revving up or winding down. Rest your eyes on the horizon. You've reached the end of the road.

LODGING

Cooper Landing:
Gwin's Lodge
Mile 52 Sterling Hwy.
15.5 miles from junction of Seward and Sterling hwys.
907-595-1266
www.gwinslodge.com
Historic log lodge with cabins, rooms, full RV hookups, restaurant, bar. Tours, charters, outdoor clothing, licenses, souvenirs. Fish processing and shipping drop site. Open since 1952.

Kenai Princess Wilderness Lodge
17245 Frontier Cir., off Sterling Hwy.
800-426-0500
www.princesslodges.com
Expansive, modern log hotel overlooking Kenai River. Adventure tours, luxury accommodations. Dining, elegant or casual.

Sterling:
Naptowne Inn & Café
Mile 84.5 Sterling Hwy.
907-260-2005
15 rooms with queen-sized beds, restaurant serving three meals a day.

Soldotna:
Alicia's Eagle Rock Lodge
286 Arlington Ct.
907-283-1951
www.aliciaseaglerocklodge.com
Single and double rooms, plus suites with full kitchens. All with cable TV, free Wi-Fi, coffee, firepit, barbecue grill. Close to The Pillars and Eagle Rock boat launches.

Aspen Hotel
326 Binkley Cir.
907-260-7736
63 rooms and suites. Pool, spa, exercise room, free deluxe continental breakfast. Open year-round.

Best Western King Salmon Motel, RV Park & Restaurant
35546A Kenai Spur Hwy.
888-262-5857 or 907-262-5857
www.bestwestern.com
Large rooms, kitchenettes, cable TV, Internet, coffee. Restaurant. 39 RV sites, most pull-throughs. Full hookups, restrooms, showers, laundry.

Eagle's Roost Lodge
35555 Kenai Spur Hwy.
907-262-8444
www.eaglesroost.us
Log cabins, RV and tent camping. Sauna, tackle and gift shop, salmon bake, smokehouse. Fishing charters, boat rentals.

Hooligans Lodging & Saloon
44715 Sterling Hwy.
907-262-9951
www.hooliganslodge.com
Lodging, dining, saloon, free Wi-Fi, dance floor.

Kenai River Lodge
393 Riverside Dr.
800-977-4292 or 907-262-4292
www.kenairiverlodge.com
Deluxe rooms with queen beds, cable, full baths, barbecue facilities, boat moorage. Walk to restaurants, shopping.

The Riverside House
44611 Sterling Hwy.
877-262-0500 or 907-262-0500
www.alaska.net/~clc1972
Rooms, RV parking, restaurant, lounge, nightclub.

Soldotna B&B Fishing Lodge
399 Lovers Lane
877-262-4779 or 907-262-4779
www.soldotnalodge.com
16-unit European-style lodge on banks of Kenai River. Mulilingual hosts. Full breakfast, fishing packages, guides, private bank fishing, and other charters.

Soldotna Inn
35041 Kenai Spur Hwy.
907-262-9169
Apartments and single rooms with fridge, microwave, coffee, free Wi-Fi, continental breakfast. Pet
friendly. Dining at Mykel's Restaurant.

Kenai:
Beluga Lookout Lodge & RV Park
929 Mission Ave., in historic Old Town
907-283-5999
www.belugalookout.com
Lodge rooms. 75 full-hookup spaces, pull-
throughs, grills, picnic tables, restrooms, showers,
laundry, Internet. Gift shop, bike rentals.

Kenai Merit Inn
260 S. Willow St.
907-283-6131
Rooms with cable TV, phone, free continental
breakfast. Fishing packages. Downtown location.

Homer:
*To learn more about Homer-area cabins, cottages,
vacation rentals, and bed-and-breakfasts, call 877-
296-1114 or 907-226-1114 or visit www.homerbed
breakfast.com.*

Alaska Windjammer Suites Motel
412 E. Pioneer Ave.
888-730-2770 or 907-235-9761
www.akwindjammersuites.com
Queen beds and full bathrooms, kitchens.
Free Wi-Fi. Walk to downtown. View of bay
and mountains.

Bay View Inn
Overlooking Kachemak Bay
877-235-8485 or 235-8485
www.bayviewalaska.com
Rooms, kitchenettes, and cottages with a view,
TV, free wireless and local calls. Free continental
breakfast.

Best Western Bidarka Inn
575 Sterling Hwy.
866-685-5000 or 907-235-8148
www.bidarkainn.com
Full-service hotel, restaurant, sports bar, charters.
Pet friendly.

Driftwood Inn & Lodge
135 W. Bunnell Ave.
800-478-8019 or 907-235-8019
http://thedriftwoodinn.com
Beachfront rooms and kitchenettes with freezer.
Cable TV, Internet, barbecue grills.

Land's End Resort
4789 Homer Spit Rd.
800-478-0400 or 907-235-0400
www.lands-end-resort.com
Beachfront rooms, mountain and bay vistas,
Wi-Fi, spa, assistance with charters. Chart Room
Restaurant.

Ocean Shores Motel
3500 Crittenden Dr.
800-770-7775 or 907-235-7775
www.oceanshoresalaska.com
Seaside rooms, kitchenettes, laundry, freezer,
private beach, walking distance to town.

CAMPGROUNDS

Cooper Landing:
Kenai Princess RV Park
Mile 47.5 Sterling Hwy.
907-595-1425
35 sites, power, tables. Shower, laundry, water,
dump station. Groceries. Next to Kenai Princess
Lodge. Turn at Mile 47.5 (Km 76.5), then drive 2
miles (3 km) on Bear Creek Rd.

Kenai Riverside Campground & RV Park
Mile 50 Sterling Hwy.
888-536-2478 or 907-595-1406
www.kenairv.com
25 partial hookups, dump station, restrooms, showers. Fishing and licenses on-site.

Kenai-Russian River Access Parking
Mile 55 Sterling Hwy.
Access site operated by concessionaire Alaska
Recreation Management includes 24-hour parking in two gravel areas accommodating about
200 vehicles, depending on length. Spaces fill up
quickly during salmon season and are first come,
first served. Fees vary, depending on vehicle length.
Boat launch, picnic area, and toilets. No tent camping. Site of ferry crossing to opposite bank and
mouth of Russian River; separate fee is charged.

The Forest Service manages the following
campgrounds in the Chugach National Forest
near Cooper Landing. Reserve a site at www
.recreation.gov.

Quartz Creek Recreation Area
Turn off at Mile 45 Sterling Hwy. and follow Quartz
Creek Rd.
45 RV parking and tent sites. Water, toilets, fishing.
Boat launch, dump station. Caution for bears in the
area. Pets on leash.

Cooper Creek South Campground
Mile 50.7 Sterling Hwy.
23 wooded RV parking and tent sites adjacent
to Kenai River and Cooper Creek. Water, toilets.
Reserve at least 5 days in advance. Store all food
in vehicle.

Russian River Campground
Mile 54 Sterling Hwy.
907-522-8368
84 RV parking and tent sites. Water, toilets, dump station. Excellent salmon fishing in season. Fish-cleaning stations. Popular place, so reserve at least 5 days in advance. In consideration of bears in the area, keep food in the vehicle.

The Kenaitze Indian Tribe operates a traditional/cultural campground within the Seward Ranger District of the Chugach National Forest:
K'Beq Footprints
Mile 52.6 Sterling Hwy.
907-335-0669
www.kenaitze.org (click on "For Visitors," then "K'Beq")
Camping, guided cultural tours, traditional plane lore, legends, stories. Gift shop.

Skilak Lake:
The US Fish & Wildlife Service has two fee camp-grounds between Cooper Landing and Sterling: 21 miles (33.5 km) west from the junction of Sterling and Seward hwys. is the first turnoff for Skilak Lake Rd., a loop along which there are two campgrounds: Upper Skilak Lake and Hidden Lake, with a total of 110 RV sites and 10 tent sites. Both have firepits, toilets, water, and boat ramps. Hidden Lake campers enjoy campfire programs on Friday and Saturday evenings in an outdoor the-ater. Campground hosts.

Sterling:
Alaska State Parks manages the following recreation sites and campgrounds near Sterling. All three have water and handicap-accessible toilets. No electric, no dump station. The Kenai Area State Park Office can answer your questions at 907-262-5581.
Bing's Landing, Mile 79 (Km 127), 36 sites.
Izaak Walton, Mile 81 (Km 130), 25 sites.
Morgan's Landing, Mile 85 (Km 136.5), 41 sites.

Alaska Canoes & Campgrounds
Mile 84 Sterling Hwy.
907-262-2331
RV sites, laundry, showers. Canoe and mountain bike rentals. Shuttle service. Fishing licenses and gear.

Cast Away Riverside RV Park
34630 Stephen
800-478-6446 or 907-262-7219
RV park, lodge rooms, and luxury cabins on the Kenai River.

Mike's Moose River Resort & Hot Tub
Overlooking river at Sterling
907-262-9777
www.mooseriverresort.com
Riverfront chalet & RV park, private river access and dock. Freeze, smoke, ship your fish.

Moose River RV Park
Mile 81.5 Sterling Hwy.
907-260-7829
Full hookups; some pull-throughs. Visitor center, restrooms, Internet, satellite TV, showers, laundry. Café. Local fishing.

Real Alaskan Cabins and RV Park
Mile 80 Sterling Hwy., near Bing's Landing
907-262-6077
www.realalaskan.com
33 sites with full hookups, cabins, wooded setting, showers, laundry. Park/fishing packages. Boat rentals.

Soldotna:
Centennial Park Municipal Campground
On Funny River Rd. near Mile 96 Sterling Hwy.
126 campsites, some along river, tables, firepits, firewood, water, dump station. Boat launch and on-site fishing.

Best Western King Salmon Motel, RV Park & Restaurant
Downtown Soldotna
888-262-5857 or 907-262-5857
www.bestwestern.com
39 RV sites, most pull-throughs. Full hookups, rest-rooms, showers, laundry. Restaurant.

Discovery Campground, Captain Cook State Recreation Area
Near intersection of Kenai Spur and Sterling hwys. Operated by park concessionaire Alaska Recreation Management: 907-522-8368.
53 campsites, hiking trail, water, fireside programs.

Edgewater RV Park
44770 Funny River Rd.
907-262-7733
www.sunriseresorts.com/edgewater.jsp
40 full hookups and pull-through sites, 20 partial hookups, showers, clubhouse, laundry. Bank fishing on the river, guide services, fish-cleaning station.

The Riverside House
44611 Sterling Hwy.
877-262-0500 or 907-262-0500
www.alaska.net/~clc1972
RV park, hotel, riverview dining, lounge, nightclub.

Swiftwater Park Municipal Campground
Turn south onto Redoubt at Mile 94 Sterling Hwy. Just past Fred Meyer
40 sites above Kenai River, some pull-throughs. Tables, firepits, water, dump station, firewood, boat launch.

Kenai:
Beluga RV Park
929 Mission Ave., in historic Old Town
907-283-4939
www.belugalookout.com
Lodge rooms. 75 full-hookup spaces, pull-throughs, grills, picnic tables, restrooms, showers, laundry, Internet. Gift shop, bike rentals.

Captain Cook State Recreation Area
Miles 36–29 Kenai Spur Hwy.
Campsites, fishing, hiking, picnic shelter, boating.

Diamond M Ranch RV Park, Cabins & B&B
Mile 6 Kalifornsky Beach Rd.
907-283-9424
www.diamondmranch.com
RV sites, pull-throughs, laundry, shower, fish-cleaning station, wireless. Family-owned working ranch.

Kenai Riverfront Campground & RV Park
Mile 2 Big Eddy Rd.
907-262-1717
www.kenairiverfront.com
10 RV sites with electric, gravel sites, riverfront views. Boat launch, bank fishing. RV rentals, powerboat rentals, guided trips.

Kenai RV Park
507 Upland St.
907-398-3382
18 sites with hookups, tent camping, showers, laundry, restrooms. One block from Kenai visitor center.

Clam Gulch:
Clam Gulch State Recreation Area
Mile 117 Sterling Hwy.
Alaska State Parks Soldotna office: 907-262-5581
120 campsites with 30-foot limit on RV length. Toilets, water, picnic shelter. Fishing.

Anchor River:
Kyllonen's RV Park
Mile 1 Anchor River Beach Rd.
888-848-2589
www.kyllonensrvpark.com
Full and partial hookups, fish-cleaning station, free firewood, showers, restrooms, laundry. Gift shop, espresso bar. Licenses and charters. Close to Cook Inlet and Anchor River.

Homer:
Driftwood Inn & RV Park
135 W. Bunnell Ave.
800-478-8019 or 907-235-8019
http://thedriftwoodinn.com
Full hookups on beachfront sites, showers, free Wi-Fi. Laundry, fish-cleaning station. Open year-round.

Heritage RV Park
3550 Homer Spit Rd., by the Fishing Hole
800-380-7787 or 907-226-4500
www.alaskaheritagervpark.com
Bayview sites with 20-, 30-, or 50-amp power, sewer, water, satellite TV. On-site gift shop, coffee shop, showers, restrooms, laundry. Walking distance to fishing, beach, shopping, restaurants.

Homer Spit Campground
At the end of the road
907-235-8206
Oceanfront camping for RVs, with partial hookups, tent camping, showers, dump station. Gift shop, charter bookings, trailer rentals.

Oceanview RV Park
173 Sterling Hwy.
907-235-3951
www.oceanview-rv.com
Full and partial hookups, pull-throughs, tent camping. Panoramic views. Showers, restrooms, gift shop. Special charter rates.

Alaska State Parks manages the following campgrounds between Ninilchik and Homer; for more information, call the Kenai Area Office at 907-262-5581.

Ninilchik River Campground
North end of Ninilchik
Mile 134.5 Sterling Hwy.
RV parking and tent sites. Water, toilets, dump station. Fishing.

Ninilchik Beach Campground
Beach access road, Mile 135 Sterling Hwy.
35 campsites, toilets, water.

Ninilchik View Campground
Mile 135.7 Sterling Hwy., east side of highway
12 campsites, water, toilets, fishing.

Deep Creek State Recreation Area
Mile 137.3 Sterling Hwy.
164 sites near excellent halibut and king salmon fishing.

Anchor River State Recreation Area
Mile 157.5 turnoff to Anchor River Beach Rd.
5 campgrounds with more than 150 campsites.

RESTAURANTS

Cooper Landing:
Gwin's Lodge
Mile 52 Sterling Hwy.
907-595-1266
www.gwinslodge.com
Restaurant, bar, cabins, rooms, RV hookups.

Soldotna:
Acapulco Mexican Restaurant
44758 Sterling Hwy.
907-260-4999
Authentic Mexican cooking.

Bear's Den Restaurant & Bakery
45015 Kalifornsky Beach Rd.
907-262-6546
Salmon, scallops, chowder. Baked goods.

Buckets Sports Grill
43960 Sterling Hwy.
907-262-7220
www.bucketssportsgrill.com
Burgers, wings, brews.

China Sea Buffet Restaurant
Soldotna Mall, half a mile north of the bridge
907-262-5033
All-you-can-eat buffet, salad bar.

Frosco's
35433 Kenai Spur Hwy.
907-262-5306
Family restaurant featuring Greek, Italian, Mexican.

Golden Dragon Restaurant
36100 Kenai Spur Hwy.
907-262-6366
Chinese cuisine.

Grand Burrito Restaurant
44096 Sterling Hwy.
907-262-2228
Mexican fare.

Jersey Subs
44224 Sterling Hwy.
907-260-3393
Hot and cold submarine sandwiches.

King Salmon Restaurant
35545 Kenai Spur Hwy., Best Western Hotel
907-260-8292
Breakfast, lunch, and dinner; sack lunches for fisherman.

Moose Is Loose
44278 Sterling Hwy., at Soldatna Inn
907-260-3036
Pastries.

Mykel's Restaurant
35041 Kenai Spur Hwy., at Soldatna Inn
907-262-4305
www.mykels.com
Beef, seafood, especially salmon and halibut.

Nikko Garden
36100 Kenai Spur Hwy.
907-262-7122
Japanese cuisine. Sushi.

The Riverside House
44611 Sterling Hwy.
877-262-0500 or 907-262-0500
Riverview dining, lunch and dinner; lounge, nightclub.

Sal's Klondike Diner
Mile 95.5 Sterling Hwy.
907-262-2220
Alaskan and Yukon burgers, breakfast anytime. Sack lunches to go.

St. Elias Brewing Company
434 Sharkathmi Ave., off Sterling Hwy.
907-260-7837
Chicken, pizza, beer.

Wild King Grill Restaurant
Mile 101.5 Sterling Hwy.
907-262-9887
Steaks, halibut, cedar-plank salmon, special desserts.

Kenai:
Burger Bus
912 Highland, next to Kenai RV Park
907-283-9611
Burgers, hot dogs, fries, and more. Call for take-out.

Charlotte's Restaurant
115 S. Willow St.
907-283-2777
Home cooking and baking. Soups, desserts, and more.

Don Jose's
205 Willow St.
907-283-8181
Authentic Mexican food.

Louie's Steak & Seafood
Mile 47 Spur View Dr., adjacent to Uptown Motel
907-283-3660
Fine Alaska seafood.

Paradiso's Restaurant
811 Frontage Rd.
907-283-2222
Mexican, Greek, Italian.

Veronica's Coffee House
604 Peterson Wy.
907-283-2725
Breakfast, lunch, dinner. Live music on weekends, in historic building in Old Town.

Homer:

Boardwalk Fish & Chips
4287 Homer Spit Rd.
907-235-7749
Chowder, fresh halibut, and the works.

Captain Patties Fish House
4241 Homer Spit Rd.
907-235-5135
Lunch and dinner; sack lunches for anglers.

Caribou Family Restaurant
672 East End Rd.
907-235-5148
www.cariboufamilyrestaurant.com
Fine dining with a view.

Crabbies Seafood & Steak House
639 E. Pioneer Rd.
907-235-7300
Steaks, seafood, specials.

Fresh Sourdough Express Bakery & Café
1316 Ocean Dr.
907-235-7571
www.freshsourdoughexpress.com
Breakfast, lunch, dinner; box lunches, desserts, espresso, bakery.

Hole in the Wall BBQ & Rib Shack
Homer Spit Rd. boardwalk
907-235-8022
Ribs, sandwiches.

Homestead Restaurant
Mile 8 East End Rd.
907-235-8723
www.homesteadrestaurant.net
Fine dining, lunch and dinner; views of Kachemak Bay.

Maura's Café & Fine Catering
106 W. Bunnell St.
907-235-1555
Soups, sandwiches, baked goods.

TAYLOR HIGHWAY

Part of the Klondike Loop

From Alaska Hwy. to Eagle: 160 miles (257 km)

Travel Opportunities: Town of Chicken; Fortymile gold-mining country; Eagle Historic District; Yukon River; riverboat Yukon Queen II.

In 1951, the new road between Tok Junction on the Alaska Hwy. and Eagle on the Yukon was officially named the Taylor Hwy., to honor Ike P. Taylor, a newly retired chief engineer of the Alaska Road Commission. Simultaneously, the new townsite of Tok was laid out, with 124 lots offered at public auction. A reporter wrote, "It is the first townsite in Alaska, outside of the rail belt, to be planned before settlement took place."

The Taylor is the highway for stouthearted drivers who promise to pay close attention to the road; let your navigator take the pictures for you to enjoy later. Partially paved and narrow, the Taylor climbs and descends, turns and doubles back, changing its mind multiple times in a matter of miles as it wends through and above some of the most spectacular country in east-central Alaska. For those who want a taste of what the Alaska Hwy. used to be like, this compacted gravel route is the road to drive.

The Taylor Hwy. actually takes off northward from Tetlin Junction on the Alaska Hwy., about a dozen miles east of Tok. The Taylor is part of the Klondike Loop, a series of three highways that connects Tok and Whitehorse via Dawson City. (See the sections on the North Klondike Highway and the Top of the World Highway in Chapter 7, Western Canada's Northbound Byways.)

Remember, as you plan your travel route, be sure to check road conditions well in advance. Heavy rains and runoff in the spring and early summer of 2010 created washout conditions that closed this highway from the Alaska-Yukon border to the community of Chicken. To avoid an annoying and time-consuming backtrack, consult

CHAPTER 9

ALASKA MARINE HIGHWAY SYSTEM

The Inside Passage marine route from Washington State to Alaska gained international fame in the late 1890s when Klondike miners and their gold arrived in Seattle and ignited a gold rush. The news spread quickly, and people came to believe that they, too, could get rich quick in the Far North—and that all it took was to jump on a steamer headed up the Inside Passage.

The thrill of traveling by ship on the Inside Passage has taken on a new slant today. Even occasional dreary weather cannot suppress the extraordinary beauty of a trip on these protected waters between mainland and islands. As you travel, you are free to walk the decks, sleep when you're tired, buy a meal when you're hungry, and visit with the people around you. There's nothing else to do but enjoy the incredible vistas as they slowly slide by.

Three ferry systems operate in these waters:

- BC Ferries, an arm of British Columbia's transportation system, owns a fleet of 36 vessels of all sizes, which cruise among the islands and mainland ports, up to 47 of them, in the province. From Victoria to Prince Rupert, with many stops between, BC Ferries connects with the Alaska Marine Highway System at Prince Rupert.
- The Inter-Island Ferry Authority operates in the southernmost part of the Alaska Panhandle, linking the Prince of Wales Island communities with communities of Coffman Cove, South Mitkof with Wrangell, and Hollis with Ketchikan. In both routes, schedules allow for connections with the Alaska Marine Highway. Their website is www.interislandferry.com.
- The 11 Alaska Marine Highway System ferries, affectionately called the "blue canoes," stick to a routine schedule for picking up and dropping off passengers at coastal communities, almost like a vast city bus system. The vessels of the fleet also vary in size and in their specialized routes. In 2005, the MV *Chenega* joined the fleet, a high-speed ferry operating between Cordova, Valdez, and Whittier in the Southcentral region. Two other newer vessels, inaugurated in 2004, include the MV *Fairweather* and the MV *Lituya*.

The southeastern portion of the Alaska system offers scheduled service from Bellingham, WA, on the southern end, to Prince Rupert, BC, then farther northward to the cities of Alaska's Inside Passage, up to Skagway. The MV *Kennicott*, the largest vessel in the fleet, crosses the Gulf of Alaska every couple of weeks from May to September, linking the marine highway with blacktop at Prince Rupert, BC, and Whittier, AK. From Whittier, on the Kenai Peninsula, ferry travelers can connect with the southwestern Alaska ferry route, continuing to skirt the coastline for many hundreds of miles, exploring small towns and island villages off the road system.

The southwestern portion of the Alaska system serves the towns and villages of Chenega Bay, Cordova, Homer, Kodiak, Port Lions, Seldovia, Tatitlek, Whittier, and Valdez. And eight times per summer, the MV *Tustumena* sails among the communities of the Aleutian Islands and the Alaska Peninsula: Akutan, Chignik, Cold Bay, False Pass, King Cove, Sand Point, and Unalaska/Dutch Harbor.

People come aboard the Alaska state ferries on foot, sometimes for a day trip to a nearby town. Or they arrive in campers, ready to drive their rigs into the hold and then head upstairs to a stateroom and a warm bed. Others carry their belongings on their

Bellingham, WA, is the southernmost terminal on Alaska's state ferry system, connecting the 49th state with the Lower 48 states, as well as linking coastal communities within Alaska.

backs. Travelers without a stateroom are welcome to bunk under the stars on the vessel's top deck. This is freedom at its finest—come one, come all—and presents plenty of opportunity to make friends with someone from a local village or someone from the other side of the planet.

Major ports of call in Southeast Alaska are Ketchikan, Wrangell, Petersburg, Sitka, Juneau, Haines, and Skagway. Between them, shorter trips link larger towns with the villages of Kake, Angoon, Tenakee, Hoonah, Metlakatla, Pelican, and Yakutat.

These major Inside Passage ports each claim a unique personality: Petersburg, the fishing town with Norwegian roots; Sitka, the former capital of Russian America, as Alaska was known before its 1867 purchase by the United States; Native villages that welcome visitors eager to know more about Tlingit, Haida, and Tsimshian cultures; Juneau, Alaska's capital—which, like most Southeast Alaska towns, is inaccessible by road. Skagway and Haines, the northernmost ports in Southeast Alaska, are connected to the Alaska Hwy. by spur roads. (See the sections on the Haines Highway and Klondike Highway 2 in Chapter 8, Alaska's State Highways.) Consider a southbound trip on the marine highway as a way to return home after your northbound drive up the Alaska Hwy., or vice versa.

The cost for passage depends on distance between ports, whether a stateroom is reserved, length of your vehicle, and other factors. You can customize your trip so that you can disembark and tour the towns of your choice before continuing on your journey.

Here are some contacts for more information on marine travel in Alaska and along the Inside Passage:

Alaska Marine Highway System
800-642-0066
www.ferryalaska.com

BC Ferries
888-223-3779 from within British Columbia
250-386-3431 from outside the province
www.bcferries.com

Inter-Island Ferry Authority
Southern Southeast Alaska
866-308-4848 or 907-755-4848
www.interislandferry.com

FURTHER READING

Canada

Acorn, John. *Deep Alberta: Fossil Facts and Dinosaur Digs*. Edmonton: Univ. of Alberta Press, 2007.

Berton, Pierre. *The Klondike Fever*. New York: Carroll & Graf, 1985.

———. *The Klondike Quest: A Photographic Essay 1897–1899*. North York, ON: Stoddart Publishing, 1997.

Davies, Gordon. *Fishing BC Rivers: Big Fish and Accessible Waterways*. Surrey, BC: Hancock House, 2004.

Dixon, Joan, and Tracy Read. *Celebrating the Calgary Exhibition & Stampede: The Story of the Greatest Outdoor Show on Earth*. Calgary, AB: Altitude Publishing Canada, 2005.

Coull, Cheryl. *A Traveller's Guide to Aboriginal BC*. Vancouver, BC: Whitecap Books, 1996.

Duff, Wilson. *The Indian History of British Columbia: The Impact of the White Man*. Victoria, BC: Royal British Columbia Museum, 1997.

Finch, David. *Hell's Half Acre: Early Days in the Great Alberta Oil Patch*. Victoria, BC: Heritage House, 2005.

Haigh, Jane. *The Alaska Highway: A Historic Photographic Journey*. Whitehorse, YT: Wolf Creek Books, 2001.

Hildebrand, John. *Reading the River: A Voyage Down the Yukon*. Madison: Univ. of Wisconsin Press, 1997.

Hughes, Nancy, et. al. *Birds of the Yukon Territory*. Seattle: Univ. of Washington Press, 2003.

Matthews, Bill, and Jim Monger. *Roadside Geology of Southern British Columbia*. Victoria, BC: Heritage House, 2010.

North, Dick. *The Lost Patrol: The Mounties' Yukon Tragedy*. Guilford, CT.: The Lyons Press, 2004.

Russell, Chester L. *Tales of a Catskinner: A Personal Account of Building the Alcan Highway, the Winter Trail, and Canol Pipeline Road in 1942–43*. Published by the author, Coos Bay, OR, 1999.

Shewchuk, Murphy. *Cariboo Trips and Trails: A Guide to British Columbia's Cariboo Gold Rush Country*. Markham, ON: Fitzhenry & Whiteside Publishing, 2008.

Trelawny, John G. *Wildflowers of the Yukon, Alaska, and Northwestern Canada*, 3rd ed. Madeira Park, BC: Harbour Publishing, 2009.

Wolf Creek. *The Klondike Gold Rush: Photographs from 1896–1899*. Whitehorse, YT: Wolf Creek Books, 1997.

Zuehlke, Mark. *The BC Fact Book*. Vancouver, BC: Whitecap Books, 1995.

———. *The Yukon Fact Book*. Vancouver, BC: Whitecap Books, 1998.

Alaska

Brown, Tricia. *Silent Storytellers of Totem Bight State Historical Park*. Anchorage: Alaska Geographic Association, 2009.

Gates, Nancy, ed. *The Alaska Almanac: Facts about Alaska*, 30th ed. Portland, OR: Alaska Northwest Books, 2008.

Griggs, William E. *The World War II Black Regiment That Built the Alaska Military Highway: A Photographic History*. Jackson: Univ. Press of Mississippi, 2002.

Hunt, William R. *North of 53°: The Wild Days of the Alaska-Yukon Mining Frontier, 1870–1914*. New York: Macmillan, 1974.

Jettmar, Karen. *The Alaska River Guide: Canoeing, Kayaking, and Rafting in the Last Frontier*, 3rd ed. Birmingham, AL: Menasha Ridge Press, 2008.

Kavanagh, James, and Raymond Leung. *The Nature of Alaska: An Introduction to Familiar Plants, Animals & Outstanding Natural Attractions*, 2nd ed. Phoenix, AZ: Waterford Press, 2006.

Limeres, Rene, and Gunnar Pedersen. *Alaska Fishing: The Ultimate Angler's Guide*, 3rd ed. Roseville, CA: Publishers Design Group, 2007.

Littlepage, Dean. *Hiking Alaska*, 2nd ed. Helena, MT: Falcon, 2006.

McPhee, John. *Coming into the Country*. New York: Farrar, Straus and Giroux, 1991.

Morgan, Lael. *Good Time Girls of the Alaska-Yukon Gold Rush*. Seattle: Epicenter Press, 1998.

Murie, Margaret E. *Two in the Far North*, 2nd ed. Seattle: Alaska Northwest Books, 1997.

Naske, Claus-M., and Herman Slotnick. *Alaska: A History of the 49th State*. Norman: Univ. of Oklahoma Press, 1994.

Piper, Ernie. *Alaska Sportfishing*. Anchorage: Alaska Geographic Guides, 1997.

Pratt, Verna. *Field Guide to Alaskan Wildflowers*. Anchorage: Alaskakrafts Publishing, 1990.

Purdy, Anne, and Robert Specht. *Tisha: The Story of a Young Teacher in the Alaska Wilderness*. New York: Bantam, 1984.

Satterfield, Archie. *Chilkoot Pass: A Hiker's Historical Guide*, rev. ed. Seattle: Alaska Northwest Books, 1998.

Smith, Dave. *Backcountry Bear Basics: The Definitive Guide to Avoiding Unpleasant Encounters*. Seattle: The Mountaineers, 2006.

Tremblay, Ray. *On Patrol: Adventures of an Alaskan Game Warden*. Portland, OR: Alaska Northwest Books, 2004.

Woolcock, Iris. *The Road North: One Woman's Adventure Driving the Alaska Highway, 1947–1948*. Anchorage: Greatland Graphics, 1990.

ALASKA HIGHWAY DISTANCE CHARTS

Distances in Western Canada and the United States

In **Miles** and Kilometers

	Cache Creek, BC	Calgary, AB	Dawson City, YT	Dawson Creek, BC	Edmonton, AB	Fairbanks, AK	Fort Nelson, BC	Great Falls, MT	Prince George, BC	Seattle, WA	Watson Lake, YT	Whitehorse, YT
Anchorage AK,	**2135**	**2125**	**506**	**1608**	**1975**	**363**	**1328**	**2473**	**1855**	**2435**	**993**	**724**
	3416	3420	814	2573	3160	584	2137	3960	2985	3896	1598	1158
Cache Creek, BC		**436**	**1701**	**527**	**545**	**2013**	**802**	**753**	**272**	**300**	**1132**	**1411**
		702	2738	843	872	3221	1291	1205	438	483	1822	2258
Calgary, AB			**1752**	**550**	**180**	**2037**	**835**	**315**	**614**	**738**	**1165**	**1436**
			2820	885	290	3259	1345	504	988	1181	1875	2298
Dawson City, YT				**1204**	**1562**	**393**	**937**	**2078**	**1449**	**2022**	**608**	**33**
				1937	2499	632	1508	3325	2332	3235	978	536
Dawson Creek, BC					**368**	**1488**	**285**	**867**	**245**	**827**	**615**	**886**
					592	2395	451	1387	394	1331	990	1418
Edmonton, AB						**1855**	**53**	**500**	**434**	**923**	**983**	**1253**
						2968	1050	800	698	1485	1582	2005
Fairbanks, AK							**1203**	**2353**	**1740**	**2313**	**873**	**699**
							1936	3765	2800	3701	1405	964
Fort Nelson, BC								**1353**	**530**	**1102**	**330**	**604**
								2177	853	1773	531	966
Great Falls, MT									**934**	**681**	**1442**	**1751**
									1503	1090	2321	2818
Prince George, BC										**572**	**860**	**1131**
										921	1384	1820
Seattle, WA											**1442**	**1707**
											2321	2781
Watson Lake, YT												**275**
												442
Whitehorse, YT												

To read, choose a place-name at the bottom of a column and scan upward to meet the corresponding horizontal line.

Distances within Alaska

In **Miles** and Kilometers

Anchorage	520	340	501	363	187	775	226	847	127	823	328	304
	832	547	802	584	299	1240	362	1355	204	1324	525	486
Circle	257	541	162	409	809	746	1972	646	872	368	526	
	414	866	261	658	1302	1194	3155	1034	1395	589	842	
Delta Junction	280	98	151	550	566	587	467	503	108	266		
	450	157	242	885	911	945	735	811	174	426		
Eagle	379	311	620	727	868	627	579	173	427			
	606	501	992	1163	1389	1003	926	277	683			
Fairbanks	250	648	584	489	484	710	206	364				
	402	1043	934	783	779	1136	330	582				
Glennallen	581	415	739	314	535	139	115					
	935	668	1189	505	861	224	185					
Haines	1001	1142	901	359	447	701						
	1602	1827	1442	574	715	1122						
Homer	1073	173	1058	554	530							
	1717	277	1693	886	848							
Prudhoe Bay	973	1199	695	853								
	1557	1918	1112	1365								
Seward	958	455	430									
	1533	726	688									
Skagway	504	758										
	806	1213										
Tok	254											
	406											
Valdez												

To read, choose a place-name at the bottom of a column and scan upward to meet the corresponding horizontal line.

INDEX

ABOUT THE AUTHOR

A former writer and editor for the *Fairbanks Daily News-Miner*, the *Anchorage Daily News*, and *Alaska* magazine, Tricia Brown has spent more than 30 years traveling nearly every inch of Alaska's road system and flying into the bush to write about the state and its people. She has published numerous books on Alaska for adults and for children, including the critically acclaimed *Children of the Midnight Sun*, *Wild Alaska*, and *Fairbanks: Alaska's Heart of Gold*. She and her husband, Perry, make their home in Oregon, when not exploring the 49th state.